Refugees, Forced Migrants, and Human Tragedies

Refugees, Forced Migrants, and Human Tragedies

An Interdisciplinary Critical Perspective

Edited by
Fonkem Achankeng

LEXINGTON BOOKS
Lanham • Boulder • New York • London

Published by Lexington Books
An imprint of The Rowman & Littlefield Publishing Group, Inc.
4501 Forbes Boulevard, Suite 200, Lanham, Maryland 20706
www.rowman.com

86-90 Paul Street, London EC2A 4NE

British Library Cataloguing in Publication Information Available

Library of Congress Cataloging-in-Publication Data Available

ISBN 978-1-7936-2165-8 (cloth)
ISBN 978-1-7936-2166-5 (electronic)

Dedication

To Ewokolo Ngalia Fonkem

Contents

Preface

Refugees, forced migrants, and internally displaced persons are big themes, but this is not a book about an even bigger theme: how the three themes intersect and interact. That they do seems obvious enough. Events in our imperial world system causing the forced displacements of people are legendary and what increasingly gets worrisome are the human tragedies associated with the forced migrations of persons brought into our homes daily by the evening news. Refugees, migrants, and internally displaced persons are all connected, especially that the persons involved are all "forced" to move and are also often very exposed to what we may characterize as tragic endings to many. What this book does is that it continues to explore the connections in refugee, migrant, and internally displaced persons themes in the social science literature.

In a very modest way, the goal of this book is to sketch out some ways of thinking about refugees, migrants, and internally displaced persons. Indeed, I hope to demonstrate through the different chapters in the book that by understanding the different themes on forced migration issues, we can incorporate them in our empirical and theoretical canvases.

Acknowledgments

In writing my acknowledgments, I need to begin with my family. Without all members of my family, this book and my continuous research work would not have occurred. Over the years, I have found a great deal of support from each and every one of them. I have learned that family is supreme. I thank you all. Special thanks go to my spouse, Dr. Patience E. Fonkem, who inspired me deeply to return to school to complete my degrees much later in life when I had lost all hope, having missed the opportunity offered to me by the University of Benin, Benin City, in 1984 for lack of a passport.

I am also indebted to Goodnews Osah and Chinedu Eti, at the Department of Political Science, Babcock University, for the several hours they put into the editorial work and technical assistance in putting together this manuscript. These supportive colleagues and friends will remain close to my heart after I leave Babcock University at the end of my sabbatical year there.

I have often said that without my friendship with Shane Boeder, my former Department Chair at Marian University in Fond du Lac, Wisconsin, I never would have returned to this manuscript. Shane Boeder was my first true colleague. She put in several weeks and months of checking the details in this manuscript at a time when I did not have a minute to spare. Her support has always been a valued part of my immigrant life and academic career.

Finally, this book would not have been possible without the active contributions of the different scholars who contributed to the different essays that make up chapters in the book. Each chapter in the book brings to the reader different perspectives on refugees, forced migration, and internally displaced persons. These different perspectives are all important as we try to understand the plight of this population, who remain victims in a not-so-very-kind world.

Introduction

Fonkem Achankeng

In a twenty-first-century global existence, which remains much like the twentieth century in terms of violent conflicts, inequality, and scathing poverty in many parts of the world, problems of injustices and intolerance, human displacement, and attendant tragedy remain recurrent and a subject of many conversations across the world as the number of refugees, forced migrants, and Internally Displaced Persons (IDPS) continues to increase. This volume focuses on a sustained analysis of the nature of forced displacement with an emphasis on the attendant human tragedies that come with the forced displacement of people. The book is therefore an open invitation to continue the conversation and further advance inquiry into the theory, experiences, and politics of refugees and forced migrants across disciplines.

International, regional, and civil conflicts create several forms of human misery and displacement that lead to the protracted flow of refugees, asylum seekers, and IDPs. A complex interplay of geopolitical, economic, and social factors has, over the decades, dictated where people are displaced from and where they run to for asylum and refuge where they will eventually be resettled, in what numbers, and from where.

This publication provides scholars, administrators, and other practitioners with an enhanced understanding of theories, models, research, best practices, and issues related to the protracted global crisis of refugees, asylum seekers, and IDPS. To equal the gravity of the crisis, this volume raises important questions on the global discussion on the issues of refugees, asylum seekers, and IDPS in different geographical theaters. It also highlights initiatives to address specific refugee situations. These questions and solutions are contextualized and embedded in the case studies presented in the volume.

The publication also aims to answer the following questions: (a) What discourses are created around refugees, asylum seekers, and IDPs from different parts of the world? (b) What is the relationship between those discourses and foreign policies and national politics in the North and South? As scholars from different parts of the world experiencing the refugee and forced migrant crises, we need to examine the different situations to which this population is exposed as a contribution to understanding thc refugee and forced migration crises in terms of the causes, ramifications, and lived experiences. Therefore, the overall purpose of the volume is to provide an interdisciplinary critical perspective on this protracted global crisis

In the situation of refugees and forced migrants considered as a colossal humanitarian catastrophe of our times, this book aims at a rigorous understanding of the contexts within which policies on refugees and displaced groups and peoples are pursued. It sheds important light on the motivations for policy changes. Such an approach may also be useful in identifying opportunities to promote more solutions-oriented approaches and/or identify the factors that need to be addressed if such approaches are to be encouraged. Ultimately, the case studies illustrate how "refugee and forced migrant-relevant" research can play an important role in contributing to the protection of refugees and forced migrants as we try to find a solution to their plight.

The chapters in this volume focus on a substantive area of the forced migration of refugees, asylum seekers, and IDPs. Such chapters are case studies of migration of refugees, asylum seekers, and IDPs, the causes, ramifications, and lived experiences; articles that offer a critical conceptual and theoretical perspective on refugees, asylum seekers, and IDPs; essays that offer multiple stakeholder perspectives on the asylum, rehabilitation and resettlement of refugees, asylum seekers and IDPS; skeptical perspectives that challenge any aspect of the politics and/or economics causing the conflicts that force the migrations of refugees, asylum seekers, and IDPs; and studies, reflections, and testimonies of life as a refugee, asylum-seeker, IDP, or similar case studies by a researcher or a humanitarian worker who witnessed the day-to-day life of refugees, asylum seekers, or IDPs.

In this connection, this book refocuses on the discourse on refugees and forced migrants at a time when some administrations in Washington D.C. and in some states in the United States appeared to ignore the basic nature of the United States as "a nation of immigrants." As the manuscript was being put together, The *New York Times* published a story titled, "Justice Dept. Establishes Office to Denaturalize Immigrants" to bring justice to terrorists, war criminals, sex offenders, and other fraudsters. Many feared this move would enhance a crackdown on new Americans by an American Right which remained very apprehensive of immigrants.

In chapter 1, Eric Kraemer presents an examination of the disturbing increase in forced displacement and migration that have propelled the issues of migration and immigration to the forefront of the world's current moral problems. From a philosophical standpoint, the author focuses on four basic concerns relating migration to multicultural and pluralistic democracies in terms of the philosophical foundations of citizenship in multicultural pluralistic democracies and the corresponding treatment that migrants and immigrants should receive, the *border status* of multicultural pluralistic democracies, *responsibilities* that migrants and receiving states have, and questions of numbers of migrants that should be admitted into a host society.

In chapter 2, Tatah Mentan focuses on the connection between imperialism and refugees, forced migration and the forced displacement of peoples in conflicts across the world, and the management of a massive reserve army of labor. This contributor clarifies what imperialism is and what it is not, how it functions worldwide currently, and how it impacts vulnerable states with vital natural resources that industries in the West direly need. Imperialism, the author clarifies, is not just a policy option available to the governments of rich capitalist countries should they choose to use it, though such policy options play an important role in imperialism and in the anti-imperialist struggle. Imperialism is not just a set of conspiracies against poorer countries, hatched in the capitals of the wealthy capitalist ones, though such conspiracies also play a role in shaping imperialism. Tatah Mentan indicts the specific policies and conspiracies that guide imperialist ventures, where they are going, and how they affect workers not only in poor countries but in rich countries like the United States as well. He links the military interventions in other countries and the vast number of military bases all over the world as part of imperialism and argues that the official response to this humanitarian crisis—which is after all the product of "humanitarian interventions"—has nothing to do with whether or not the West can cope with a "swarm of people" aiming to exploit the "host" countries. An important consideration for the author is what we should be doing to combat the evil of imperialism and the humanitarian crisis the evil causes for humankind.

In chapter 3 "Citizenship as Commodity," Philip Sutherland makes the case that citizenship is analogous to other forms of property. From a discussion of the history of birthright citizenship and its different forms, he places birthright citizenship in the context of Cheryl I. Harris' (1993) article "Whiteness as Property" in which she argued that historically and legally whiteness has acquired many of the characteristics of intangible property even though its similarity to traditional forms of property is often overlooked. He also argues that citizenship shares many of these same properties, especially as a valuable property that can be traded in a market; he uses Shachar's (2009) framework to discuss why we should resist this commodification of citizenship. Considering citizenship as a good whose value is not reducible to the price it can get on the market, Sutherland concludes by suggesting that a framework of citizenship based upon active political participation can aid in resisting commodification by transforming citizenship from unearned property to an earned privilege.

Chapter 4 links refugee and migrant crises to European colonialism and the nature of the decolonization process. Fonkem Achankeng argues that the legacies of colonialism produced the conditions and the tensions in the postcolonial states' origins of the refugees and forced migrants. With the example of the 2015 refugee crisis and why the individuals embarked on the hazardous journeys to Europe and other destinations, the chapter qualitatively analyzed the narratives of fifteen survivors collected purposively from media accounts on the refugee and migrant crisis. The author also examined the crisis from historical accounts and theoretical perspectives of colonialism and forced migration. Drawing from the scholarship on colonialism with Nicholas Dirks (1992), Nicholas Thomas (1994), Bernard Cohn (1996), and Susanne Mueller (2014) who predominantly focus on the colonial past, but also recognize the present implications colonialism continues to exert for colonized people, he makes the claim in agreement with Nicholas Dirks (1992, p. 23) that "colonialism lives on in ways that perhaps we have only begun to recognize." From a colonial standpoint, Fonkem also claims that the global community, and above all many in the former imperial states, turn a blind eye to the refugees and the many disasters (Muscat, 2015) because the refugees and forced migrants remain for some in Europe mere "objects conceived primarily as incomplete or imperfect rather than as peoples of a comprehensibly distinct kind" (Thomas, 1994, p. 71). The chapter concludes that the outcome of the colonial experience persisting in many postcolonial settings contributed to the biggest refugee crisis in Europe since World War II.

In chapter 5 "Refugees and Immigrants: The Tragedy of Arab Politics in the Early Twenty-First Century," Ali R. Abootelabi argues that the Arab World since the end of the Cold War has experienced accelerated political decay and a crisis of governance, which generated thousands of refugees from the region. The so-called Arab Spring since 2011, he argued was derailed with detrimental results for Arab Politics. The United States and its allies' disastrous policy of intervention and regime change in the Middle East and North Africa since 2001 also produced damaging results. The consequence of this was the collapse of the old regime with widespread devastation and millions displaced or the consolidation of authoritarian rule that hastened further political decay. For Abootelabi, the movement of Syrian and other refugees into Europe since 2011 was only the most recent manifestation of both the crisis of governance and Western intervention. To remedy the situation, he argues, the leading NATO (European Union) members, along with the United States, must share the burden of responsibility for the refugee stream into Europe, with all its real, legal, and ethical responsibilities attached.

In chapter 6 by Osita Adah, "Beyond Resettlement of Internally Displaced Persons in Bakassi: Challenges and Vistas," the author examines the socio-political and economic effects of resettlement of the displaced population of Bakassi long disputed by Nigeria and Cameroon. The chapter argues that it was a lack of commitment on the part of the Nigerian government to make institutional arrangements including funding that militated against the provision of the welfare needs of the IDPs. The author makes the claim that the Nigerian government should allocate sufficient funds and take legislative and administrative measures to provide a comprehensive legal framework on IDPS and establish designated institutions to manage the affairs of the IDPs, address the lack of social amenities in Bakassi and the right of the IDPs to vote, and participate in public affairs and in economic activities.

In chapter 7 "Refugees with or without Papers: Stories of Persecution, Flight, and Resettlement in the United States," Donald F. Hones, Mayra Pasayes, and Txerthoj Vang share immigrant stories of persecution and flight to the United States. Txerthoj Vang is a refugee from Laos who supported the United States as part of the Hmong secret army during the Vietnam era. Mayra Pasayes is an immigrant from El Salvador who fled that country's civil war during the 1980s. Though they each faced a high level of violence in their home country, Txerthoj was granted official refugee status. Mayra was not, and only later obtained residency. The granting, or denial, of asylum to each would have major impacts on their lives and their perspectives. They each continue to support refugees with or without papers in their work as educators in public schools. Their individual stories mirror those of hundreds of thousands of others who fled Laos and El Salvador during the 1970s and 1980s, running from crisis and war, taking arduous journeys, and resettling, with or without official status, in the United States.

Patience E. Fonkem in chapter 8, "Rudolphs Searching for Sleighs: Parallels, Paradoxes, and the Emotional Challenges of Standing Out without a Stage," uses personal case narratives of immigrants to understand firsthand the emotional challenges immigrants experience because of the mistrust and misinterpretations of their intentions mostly motivated by racism and xenophobia, especially in contexts where immigrants are considered as misfits, rapists, drug dealers, thieves, and criminals. The chapter provides an empowering, emancipatory, and transformative opportunity to explore procedures that rely on the participants' experiences to capture individual consciousness and the diversity of personal experiences of immigration. In the chapter, Patience E. Fonkem argues that appreciating the emotional challenge as well as the conscious and unconscious biases of migrant host communities is beneficial for social activists and other policymakers in the quest for social justice because such appreciation provides the opportunity to re-examine attitudes and behaviors.

Chapter 9, "The Hmong American Experience: The Shifting, Cultivation, Transformation, and Preservation of an Ancient Culture" by Pao Lor, discusses the lives of Hmong Americans as originally a preliterate, semi-nomadic, animistic, and agrarian ethnic hill tribe who, prior to 1975 primarily resided in southern China, Laos, Vietnam, Thailand, and Laos. He shares in broad strokes some key highlights of their quest to reestablish their cultural identity in the United States.

In chapter 10, "Involuntary Migration and Human Security in Africa: Exploring Legal Frameworks and Regional Infrastructure for Refugee Protection," Goodnews Osah, Abiola Abayomi Isikalu, Nwadiuto Franca Nwakanma, and Uzzibi Methuselah Irmiya examine the legal and regional structures aimed at the protection of refugees in Africa in order to determine the extent to which these frameworks and related mechanisms promote the paradigm of human security as relates to persons who are victims of forced displacement. Using a comparative qualitative methodology, this chapter assesses ECOWAS and the SADC with a view to understanding how successful the policies on international migration have been. The chapter finds that due to poor implementation levels of international frameworks for the protection of the human rights of refugees and IDPs, as well as inadequate policy frameworks at subregional levels, there has been a general lack of human security indices within both subregions. The authors recommend that the African Union can serve as the prime candidate for the development and implementation of a migration crisis solution that emphasizes the human security of individual migrants within a regional scope.

Chapter 11, "ESTHER, Refugees, and Immigrants in the Fox Valley Region," explores the living experiences of refugees and forced migrants in the Fox Valley area, the fastest growing region of Wisconsin, consisting of sixty cities, villages, and towns located along the Fox River in the North Eastern part of Wisconsin (Fox Cities Regional Partnership, 2019). The chapter understands the efforts put forth by ESTHER, an interfaith community organization located in the Fox Valley region, whose mission is to empower all people and ensure they are treated fairly and equally. In the chapter, Hannah P. Schmidt also highlights how ESTHER has influenced policy changes to empower people with the aim of achieving the collective responsibility and commitment toward establishing a more empathetic society on the understanding that with resources and support, refugees and forced migrants would become contributing members of their new communities.

In chapter 12 "Migration and African Diasporic Living Conditions," Chibuzor Ayodele Nwaodike, Goodnews Osah, and Uduakobong Edy-Ewoh present explanations of historical antecedence of African diasporic migration from the founding myth of African diaspora in Europe and America to contemporary diaspora when migration is necessitated by poverty, hunger, political instability, and economic degradation in Africa. This chapter focuses on the lived experiences of African emigrants in the United Kingdom, United States, and Canada. Using determinants of living conditions such as access to health care and education, quality housing, clean water, sanitation, social protection, and universal health care for analytical narrative, the chapter concludes that African immigrants contribute immensely to key sectors of the economies of the host countries.

In chapter 13 "Complexities of Boko Haram-Induced Displacement in Nigeria," the authors Michael Ihuoma Ogu and Olajumoke Yacob-Haliso analyze the burden of internal displacement imposed by the protracted Boko Haram insurgency in Nigeria's north-east. Drawing on the human security literature, this chapter demonstrates how the nature of the conflict itself foreshadows and predicts the particular challenges of the displaced in this context. The authors argue that the complexities of poor governance, religious extremism, and the regionalization of the spread of Islamic terrorism created conditions for the neglect of humanitarian principles of protection for the displaced and made durable solutions difficult to attain. Furthermore, as the conflict prolonged, internal displacement was complexified by the coeval presence of other displacement inducing conflicts in the northern region of Nigeria, creating not only previously unseen numbers of the displaced but also a less effective counterinsurgency, which allowed terrorism to thrive and in a vicious cycle perpetuate displacement. The solutions proffered are both humanitarian and political toward restoring human security for all populations in the troubled region.

In chapter 14, "Public Art, Public Voices: Changing the Narrative on Borders and Belonging," Shane Boeder examines how activist art uses found items, unexpected spaces, and the border wall itself as a canvas to counter negative stereotypes of migrants and reveals the grim realities they flee at home and the consequences of exclusionary policies of the United States such as Prevention through Deterrence and border imperialism that drive the very migration they propose to deter. To counter the vitriol and misinformation in prevailing narratives that demonize migrants, artists are using public spaces to re-image them and foster the growth of inclusive communities. In murals, performances, installations, photography, music, and multimedia, the artists interrogate the politics of exclusion, arouse empathy, and act as catalysts for change. Activist art invites participation. Using a variety of media, artists in the United States and abroad create a democratizing people's theater to address power structures and the shared humanity that binds us.

In chapter 15, the final chapter, Jodi Meyer and Donald F. Hones depict the lived experiences of refugees and forced migrants through poetry. Distinguished Teaching Professor at the University of Wisconsin Oshkosh, Alfred Kisubi and Professor Donald Hones spent long months at the United States southern border studying the lives of border crossers. Professor Alfred Kisubi passed away when this book project was in progress.

This book will be of interest to students of governance, refugee studies and migration, international law and relations, history, peace and conflict studies, postcolonial studies, and development studies.

REFERENCES

Harris, C. I. (1993). Whiteness as Property. *Harvard Law Review*, 106(8): 1710–1791.

Shachar, A. (2009). *The Birthright Lottery: Citizenship and Global Inequality*. Cambridge, MA: Harvard University Press.

Chapter 1

Expanding the Social Contract

Responding Ethically to the Immigration Crisis

Eric Kraemer

On the World Health Organization website, we find four disturbing numbers: 258 million international migrants, 763 million internally displaced migrants, 65 million forcibly displaced from their homes, and 86 percent of forced displaced populated housed in developing countries. These numbers underscore the existence of a world crisis regarding migration, in particular, forced migration, and further indicate that the burden of caring for forced migrants is falling disproportionately, hence unfairly, on countries that are not among the richer nations of the world. An additional number to keep in mind is 40 million, the estimated number of Americans who move at least once during a given year.[1] The number of migrants in the United States in 2017 was estimated at 21 million [out of 330 million]. The number of people who achieved permanent resident status in the United States last year is 1.7 million. The number of people who became U.S. citizens last year is 600,000. Further investigation reveals relatively few cities in the United States (NY, LA, Miami, DC, Houston, Chicago, San Francisco, Boston) attracting the vast majority of recent immigrants, again indicating unfair distribution of burdens.[2]

The world migration crisis and especially the disturbing increase in forced displacement and migration have propelled the issues of migration and immigration to the forefront of the world's current moral problems.[3] However, philosophers have been slow to consider the issues related to migration and immigration to multicultural pluralistic democracies.[4] This chapter presents such an examination by focusing on four overarching questions. What is the proper philosophical foundation of citizenship in multicultural pluralistic democracies? Should the borders of multicultural pluralistic democracies be open or closed to migrants? What responsibilities do migrants and receiving states have toward each other? And, how many migrants should be admitted? While there are other kinds of societies—tribes, theocracies, monarchies, oligarchies, and police states—these are not typically concerned with the ethics of migration and immigration. Multicultural pluralistic democracies, on the other hand, because they are committed to affording equal rights to different cultures, embracing both ethnic and religious pluralisms, as well as being democratic in their practices are thereby also committed to seriously taking into account concerns about the ethics of migration.

This chapter is divided into four parts. The first part of the discussion considers which philosophical theory best accounts for migration and successful immigration to multicultural pluralistic democracies and defends the claim that the social contract theory is the best explanation for both native-born and immigrant citizenship in such democracies. Using this account, this section addresses the question of how migrants should be received. The second part of the chapter scrutinizes the debate between those who advocate major restrictions on migration and immigration and those who favor Open Borders. It demonstrates that arguments currently proposed for restricting migration and immigration are mostly unsound and defend a modified version of the Open Borders approach. The third section of the chapter examines which responsibilities migrants and immigrants acquire when migrating to a multicultural pluralistic democracy, and, correspondingly, which responsibilities fall on the welcoming culture. The final section of the chapter considers moral arguments for increasing migration and immigration to pluralistic multicultural democracies and concludes that a strong moral case can be made for significantly increasing migration and immigration to multicultural pluralistic democracies. And, using Affirmative Action as a model, this section presents an additional moral argument for affording some measure of preferential treatment for admitting forced or displaced migrants.

MIGRATION, IMMIGRATION, AND THE SOCIAL CONTRACT

It might seem as though the obvious place to ground a sound philosophical basis for evaluating migration and immigration would be human rights. But, while it is commonplace for citizens of multicultural pluralistic democracies to appeal to human rights, it is not obvious how a rights-based theory would explain which people should be members of which state. Let us instead consider how people become a state. Early organization principles included tribes and monarchies. But, tribes, organized by traditions and family relations, are too limited in terms of size and variety, and traditional justification for monarchies (Divine Right of Kings) is dubious. Appeals to ethnic similarities fail to explain schisms within ethnic groups. To account for membership in the modern state, another approach is needed. We would do better to look at classical and modern accounts to explain what makes a state just.

Ever since Plato's *Republic*, philosophers have been trying to determine what makes a society just. Plato suggests that the just society is to be achieved by intentionally creating a state *de novo* with the right class structure, which is to be achieved by correctly selecting and properly educating the members of each class to perform their proper role. More modern efforts have concentrated on social contracts and recognizing basic rights.[5] John Rawls provides an influential account of how justice is to be achieved by providing a conceptual mechanism (the "Veil of Ignorance") to identify basic social rules that are fair for all. While all these proposals provide insight as to how a more just society might be achieved, it should be emphasized that these accounts are fundamentally static—they do not address the topics of admitting migrants to and accepting them as full-fledged members of the state.[6] But, the current migrant challenge demonstrates that this assumption is unwarranted. Any attempt to explain what makes a society a just society should not be limited solely to concerns about its original inhabitants; it must also consider the claims of those who migrate and immigrate.[7]

Dating back to an earlier Platonic dialogue, *The Crito*, defenders of social contract theory speak of duties and rights deriving from a social contract, in virtue of which an individual agrees to contribute to the state and abide by its requirements in return for security provided by its institutions. In explaining why he needs to abide by the decision of the Athenian government to put him to death, Plato famously has Socrates enunciate the view as follows:

> You, Socrates, [by leaving would be] breaking the covenants and agreements which you made with us at your leisure, not in any haste or under any compulsion or deception, but having had seventy years to think of them, during which time you were at liberty to leave the city.[8]

While Socrates' agreement with Athens can be termed as tacit, immigrants' agreement with their new state is instead explicit. Those who immigrate take explicit advantage of institutions that make migration and immigration from one country to another possible. The very acts of migrating and then agreeing to be processed as an immigrant may be interpreted as explicitly agreeing to abide by the requirements of those institutions. And, of course, agreement in this case entails promising to behave in potentially new ways dictated by institutions of the new state, which will likely be significantly different from the immigrant's native customs.

Defenders of social contract theory maintain one has responsibilities toward the state because one has agreed, not only to abide by the laws of the state but also to act as a responsible member of the state. Those born into a given state may be said to "sign on" when they apply for identification cards [social security], register to vote, obtain property deeds, serve as a juror, etc. All these activities involve adhering oneself to existing social mechanisms. Immigrants, of course, are keenly aware that their immigrant status is tied directly to explicitly promising to be a responsible member of their new state. This promise binds them to contributing positively to the institutions of their new state in return for the benefits they receive. It should also be noted that the social contract theory explains the organizational principles and structures that characterize modern multicultural pluralistic democracies. Given that in such a democracy where there is no single religious or ethnic set of traditions to provide rules for daily living, principles that will be acceptable to a wide variety of groups and embrace diversity will naturally be adopted. This situation leads us directly to consider how migrants and immigrants should be treated in multicultural pluralistic democracies compared to their citizens.

The Treatment Problem

How should migrants and immigrants be treated? Since immigrants and migrants (as potential immigrants) are also included in the social contract, there is a straightforward and ethically defensible answer: fairly, without bias, and hospitably, that is, in a friendly and openhearted manner, and with the respect due all persons. Migrants should be treated kindly; they should not be discriminated based upon morally irrelevant factors such as ethnicity, religion, and country of origin. Treatment of both migrants and immigrants should be addressed both at the level of the nation-state and locally. The nation-state sets basic rules that everyone must follow and does so following general standards for what fair treatment consists in, standards which, encouragingly in most multicultural countries that claim to be ethical, seem to improve over time—at least with respect to providing equal treatment across social classes, religions, ethnicities, sexes, ages, ability levels, and sexual orientations. Similar things should be said about the treatment of migrants at the metropolitan level. Both internal migrants from other parts of a given nation-state and external migrants from other cultures may expect to face prejudicial treatment in a variety of situations ranging from finding housing, employment, ease of interaction with both local officials and residents based upon cultural, ethnic, religious, and other factors. Yet, if such treatment is unethical and should be punished, where suitable, with legal sanctions based on laws prohibiting overt discrimination or deserving of criticism by other community members, this would be more effective.

What is interesting to consider are those cases in which there are significant treatment differences between national and local levels. National policies that support fair treatment can conflict with *de facto* local policies of discrimination. So, it is appropriate for the nation-state, through the mechanisms of its legislature, judiciary, and administration, to ensure that fair treatment is afforded to immigrants. The other kind of treatment divergence occurs when the nation-state engages in unfair treatment toward specific populations of immigrants, and this unfairness is recognized by individual municipalities that contain significant representation from these migrant populations. In this case, it is appropriate for those within municipalities, either private citizens with connections to the affected populations or public officials with the explicit consent of the municipality, to attempt to influence the nation-state's legislature, judiciary, or administration to improve awareness of the situation and to encourage fair treatment for concerned populations. But migration also raises serious problems.

THE QUESTION OF BORDERS: OPEN OR CLOSED?

The major concern currently facing multicultural pluralistic democratic societies involves setting limits on migration and immigration, and also to worry about how to do so ethically, especially in light of current forced displacement. Again, it is common for discussions of setting limits on migration to begin with appeals to basic human rights. Ever since 1948, it has been internationally recognized in the United Nations Charter on Human Rights that everyone has certain basic rights that relate to migration and immigration, namely, the right to Freedom of Movement (Article 13), the right to seek Asylum from Persecution (Article 14), and the right to Nationality (Article 15). It is important to emphasize what is critically missing from this list. First, while there is a right to migrate, there is no corresponding right to immigrate. Second, as many have noted, while there is a right to migrate, this is not the same as the right to migrate to a specific country. And, third, while there is a right to a nationality, this is not the same as the right to acquire a specific nationality.

This leads us to a major dispute in political philosophy regarding migration. This is the conflict between Open Borders Defenders, who reject placing any significant restrictions on immigration and "Restrictionists," who claim that nation-states are justified in imposing significant restrictions for any variety of reasons. Let us first consider a recent, influential case for Restrictionism.

In his recent important book, *Strangers in Our Midst*, David Miller defends a version of Restrictionism. Miller rejects the adequacy of the following arguments that have been made in favor of the Open Borders View: (1) appeal to common ownership of the earth, (2) appeal to global equality of opportunity, and (3) arguments postulating a human right to immigrate.[9] He claims that while the first argument supports the right to make use of the earth's resources, it does not generate a general right to cross territorial boarders. He rejects the second argument for not providing a means to measure equality of opportunity and not demonstrating a link between migration and global equality of opportunity.[10] And, he rejects the third argument for not being justifiable, either as a basic or instrumental right.[11]

Suppose for the sake of argument that we grant that these three common arguments for Open Borders, they are less than compelling. They nevertheless indicate important moral barriers to purely arbitrary versions of Restrictionism, such as those claiming that a country should be free to follow any policy on migration and immigration it wants without having to provide any sort of justification. Consider the case of forced migrants deprived of both their original land and property and to access to traditional instruction schooling, networking, and community instruction. Consider also that there are individuals who have not been accepted as refugees by any country proximate to their country of origin; if housed, they are in make-shift UNHCR camps and their lives are in danger from marauders, lack of food, and disease. Even lacking a universally accepted metric to measure opportunity, such cases, while not pointing to a right to immigrate, put serious moral pressure on countries able to accommodate forced refugees with relative ease to provide aide in such extreme cases of forced displacement.

In addition, one should note that even if the three standard arguments in support of open boarders fail, it does not follow we should reject the open boarder position in all of its versions. To see why let us also look at arguments proposed to defend Restrictionism. Miller explicitly endorses three arguments for restricting borders: (1) Self-Determination, (2) National Heritage, and (3) Resources Concerns. Of these, only the third should be taken seriously.

Consider concerns regarding self-determination and national heritage. Countries can decide what specific language, education, culture, and moral customs they wish to impose. And, this can be achieved by means of requiring both migrants and immigrants to modify their behaviors in public spaces and in the raising of their children. What this approach should not do is restrict individuals on the basis of features over which they have no control (e.g., genetic features). States should not restrict immigration based upon religion or ethnic tradition, though practices causing unnecessary harm and suffering deserve scrutiny and may require modification. By enforcing educational requirements, both self-determination and national heritage can be preserved, even with relatively Open Borders. Let us now turn to the vexed topic of resources.

Basic Social Protections Argument and Its Consequences

What makes immigration and migration to multicultural pluralistic democracies with substantial safety nets valuable is that these countries both allow great personal freedoms and provide significant support to meet basic needs. They are able to do so due to the existence of adequately funded mechanisms to provide such support, not only to their native-born but also to those who immigrate. It is these mechanisms that are of significant value in these cultures. Therefore, to ensure their continued existence to promote good outcomes for all, they need to be protected. If a proposed migration or immigration policy threatens the continued well-functioning of these mechanisms, a strong moral case needs to be made to reject the policy in light of its negative consequences. But, while some Restrictionists urge that the current forced migration crisis is such a situation, this claim seems unjustified.

The upshot of these remarks is that the presumption should be in favor of an Open Borders policy in a multicultural pluralistic democracy up to the point where additional migration and immigration truly would threaten the mechanisms that make the multicultural pluralistic democracy a decent place to live for its all inhabitants. This, in turn, places the burden of proof firmly on those who would restrict immigration to demonstrate that taking in additional immigrants would seriously threaten existing social structures. In opposition to Restrictionists, I favor instead an open-boarders policy tied to a sustainable number of migrants and immigrants that a given society could accommodate. It seems helpful to refer to the operative notion here as the *carrying capacity* of a given social structure.[17] Different multicultural pluralistic democracies should be expected, because of resource and institutional differences, to have different carrying capacities. Some will be able to accommodate many more migrants than others. But, as I shall argue later, it seems reasonable to suppose that all multicultural pluralistic democracies could accept many more migrants as immigrants than is currently the case. Furthermore, increased access should be combined with a hefty commitment to support migrant and immigrant responsibilities to the new receiving society. Fulfillment of migrant and immigrant responsibilities will in turn produce behaviors that will cohere with existing social structures. And, this coherence will support the existing social institutions which nurture both migrant and nonmigrant alike.

MIGRATION AND IMMIGRATION RESPONSIBILITIES

Let us now consider the question of migrant and immigrant responsibilities, as well as the related question of state and citizen responsibilities to migrants and immigrants. First a point of clarification: it is important to distinguish several different kinds of people. In order of less to more serious commitment with respect to going to or just through another culture, we may distinguish (1) travelers, (2) political refugees, (3) migrants intending to stay for an extended period but not intending to become citizens, and (4) those immigrants intending to become full-fledged citizens. There are differences in responsibilities for these various groups.

With respect to migrant responsibilities, we can enumerate five different categories: being law-abiding, demonstrating appropriate respect, comporting oneself *as* a member of a local community in certain essential matters, acting as if one were a citizen and acting as a citizen. Let us consider each of these elements in turn.

Law-Abiding: The most commonly cited responsibility for migrants and immigrants is to follow the laws and regulations of the locality and country. Presumably, where it would not be expected to be obvious to all what the laws and regulations are, they would be made known to all by appropriate means.[13] An example of this would be speed limits. It is expected that all of the four groups listed above would have this minimal responsibility. To see that this does not constitute the whole of migrant and immigrant responsibilities, note that this requirement holds for travelers passing through, who are not expected to understand local customs and regulations. What other responsibilities would more permanent members have?

Respect: It seems reasonable to require that migrants and immigrants demonstrate respect for the local community and respect for the host country. While the term "respect" is widely accepted as a suitable moral term, it turns out to be difficult to give an exact noncircular account. Respect involves an appropriate form of deference. In particular, it seems to involve both an awareness of and a minimal observance or at least nondisturbance of certain local customs. Which local customs?[14] Customs exhibited in the "Public Square?"[15] What does respect mean to migrants and immigrants? Here, are some suggestions.

1. Awareness of the customs of others, their rationale, and their meaning
2. Awareness of what the local signs of respect are
3. Attempts to integrate these signs into one's new daily public routine
4. Awareness that the public/private distinction may need to be re-drawn
5. Awareness of how one's public behaviors are interpreted using local customs
6. Attempts at integration: engage in at least minimal efforts to integrate into local life
7. Effecting small not large changes: engage in behaviors that do not overly change the nature of public places.

Again, it seems all four categories of migrants would have the responsibility of respect, though with varying degrees of depth depending upon the nature of an individual's commitment.

Who has the responsibility to do the most adapting? The migrant and immigrant. Though, as David Miller recently grants, nonimmigrant citizens also have adaptation responsibilities. In pluralistic, multicultural democracies, a basic principle is awareness and acceptance of cultural differences. But it may be asked: How is one to know the "unwritten covenants" by which most natives live? Here, it is reasonable to claim that the state has the responsibility, through its institutions, to provide relevant education to migrants and immigrants.[16] This is especially the case if the receiving state expects new members of society to acquire specific linguistic skills (such as being able to speak a particular national language).

Comporting oneself as a member of a local community in essential matters. One cannot directly participate in the activities of an entire country but must do so by being a member of a local community. For migrants and immigrants, it is expected to have a learning curve in figuring out exactly how to comport oneself in the new country. However, if one is taking advantage of the institutions of the local community to further one's own personal interests, then in order to protect these institutions and also one's own personal interests, one needs to figure out how to be a meaningful part of that community. This does not necessarily mean simply copying the behaviors of local paradigm members, although this might be a very good start, trying to figure out what practices are required for the well-running of the local community.[17]

An example here is how one deals with the environment. If one comes from a culture in which there are no specific rules for dealing with the environment, and people are in the habit of doing whatever they want with the environment, then on migrating to a culture which more carefully controls the environment one has the responsibility to figure out how to modify one's environment habits. One reason is that previously the environment habits, if widely practiced, would have significant adverse reactions on the migrant and immigrant's new community. If migrants and immigrants do not follow cultural environmental treatment rules, this can put the migrant in a morally deficient position of being a "Free Rider," one who attempts to avoid doing something that everyone else does, which is clearly unfair.[18] When migrants come to be perceived as free riders, negative pressures are put on mechanisms that made migration initially possible, thereby threatening further migration and immigration.

Acting as if one were a citizen. If one already is a citizen, then clearly one has the duty not only to act as a citizen but also to be a citizen. This entails acting in accordance with values and rituals deemed key to the state. But what if one is not a citizen but intends either to apply for citizenship in the future or to continue living and working in the state? In these cases, as well, one has an obligation to act as if one were a citizen.[19] Why so? Let us assume that those who find themselves in this situation have freely chosen to be in the new situation indefinitely and not short-term political refugees who are trying either to return to their home countries when things settle down or to move on to another environment. If so, then the immigrants being allowed to continue to stay in their new situation depends upon them not being perceived to be a threat to the major supporting institutions of the new culture. Those who reject or work to overthrow—as opposed to reform—those institutions, are, in fact, attacking the same institutions of immigration and migration that support and protect immigrants and migrants in their new situation.

What does acting as if one were a citizen entail for the noncitizen? First, it entails being engaged in the political process, even if one cannot directly participate by voting. This requires being informed about the policy options being considered by those currently in power and in contributing one's special expertise to the discussion, namely, the migrant and immigrant perspective, by conversing with local representatives about the situation of migrants and immigrants. This category of responsibilities holds not only for those who are actively in the process of becoming citizens but also those who wish to do so, those who are unclear about whether they want to do so (they have not yet ruled this option out), and those who have resided for a long period of time in a new country, profiting from the protections afforded to them. In so doing, they are strengthening immigration and migration institutions by demonstrating how the process works to benefit the country.

Acting as a citizen. This category entails the full panoply of what is expected of citizens: voting, engaging in local group activities, helping maintain "order" according to local standards, etc. These responsibilities are relatively well spelled out but need to be accompanied by an appropriate commitment to become, to some significant degree, bi-cultural. It seems reasonable not only for those who were citizens but also for those who are going through the immigration process to engage (to the extent legally permitted) in these activities. One reason is that it is advisable to start working on changing one's cultural identity from mono- to bi-cultural as soon as one is reasonably involved in the process which will bring it about. Those who acquire citizenship but never act as citizens, preferring instead to act as members of another culture, negatively affect the institutions of immigration and migration in addition to not fulfilling the obligations they incurred by becoming citizens.

Implementing Mutual Responsibilities

The task of implementing responsibilities should be addressed through the three areas of mutual adaptation, knowledge acquisition, and cultural training to establish and enforce guidelines for mutual responsibilities, both for migrants and immigrants and also for citizens. That there should be uniformity throughout the nation-state is clearly most desirable for both parties, as this would make it possible for both to be aware of what the expectations of each were and would help both figure out how to behave appropriately in a wide variety of situations. And, if both maintain a firm commitment to mutual respect, in all of its ramifications, then the interactions between the two groups should be smoothed and tensions minimized.

On the part of citizens, respect for migrants and immigrants involves not only treating them using the same norms they employ in everyday life with other citizens but also factoring into their interactions an understanding that some local mores may not well understood by migrants and immigrants and that appropriate reactions should not involve censure but rather tolerance and education.

On the part of migrants, however, the responsibilities are also significant in terms of basic language acquisition, learning differences between both local laws and customs, and attempting to adjust one's behaviors to act in ways that would promote harmony. Again, it would be appropriate for the nation-state to help improve interactions in some municipalities, and also for enlightened municipalities to help the nation-state improve its standards in cases when it is obvious that current national governmental activities are inconsistent with moral and legal precedents that have been widely supported.[20]

A Special Complication for the Social Contract Theory

One concern for appealing to the social contract theory to explain migration and immigration into multicultural pluralistic democracies that need to be addressed is that some of these same democracies contain peoples for whom it is difficult to make the theory fit. In particular, with respect to the United States and Canada, there are both populations of descendants of African slaves and populations of First Nations People who are not neatly accommodated by the social contract model. The ancestors of the former did not choose to inhabit their current country but were forcibly brought there as noncitizens and forced to endure the hardships of slavery. The latter groups witnessed the takeover of their habitat by groups that formed the current multicultural society and then marginalized and restricted their own way of life.

The relation of slave descendants to their current governments is further complicated by concerns about less than full citizen status treatment in a variety of respects that continues to the present day. The policy of Affirmative Action has been employed to try to mitigate past injustices, and some expect that an ever-increasing number of members of the African American community will include themselves to the social contract. But, the current situation (2019) is not as optimistic as was previously hoped.

The situation with First Nation Peoples is more complicated as there seems to be significant variation across these populations. Some First Nation People argue that no one can possess territory, but it must be shared with all. Other

First Nation People reject this view, regarding those who created multicultural pluralistic democracies to be colonist intruders without a legitimate claim to land over which First Nation Peoples alone are sovereign. And, there are, to be sure, yet other views. In any event, it is by no means clear how to include First Nation Peoples within a social contract organized by a colonial government. It is not enough simply to think of First Nation Peoples as one culture among many others. With regard to both special populations, multicultural pluralistic democracies must admit that there is much more that needs to be done to make the social contract model truly inclusive. Let us now consider the case for increasing migration and immigration to multicultural pluralistic democracies.[21]

ON INCREASING MIGRATION AND IMMIGRATION TO MULTICULTURAL PLURALISTIC DEMOCRACIES

Should multicultural pluralistic democracies accept more migrants, perhaps a *lot* more immigrants than are currently admitted and allowed to become immigrants? As we have seen in the previous two sections of this chapter, two of the most common arguments against doing so, the self-determination and national heritage arguments fail, and the third common worry, the resources argument, can be counter-balanced so long as migrant and immigrant admissions are directly tied to the receiving society's carrying capacity. Clearly, there is an important perceived benefit in terms of an improved form of life that those who migrate to multicultural pluralistic democracies are seeking. What other positive reasons support increasing migrant and immigrant admissions?

There are four strong moral reasons in favor of doing so. Consider, first, the virtue of kindness to the stranger. This has long been recognized as morally significant.[22] Second, philosophical defenders of utilitarianism will point to enormous positive moral value that results from the beneficence of providing a secure haven to those in need. This is also tied to the further value that increased diversity brings to multicultural pluralistic democracies.[23] Third, those who take the guidance of the Golden Rule seriously will note that by helping migrants we are doing "unto others what we would have them do unto us." Fourth, we may also note that by supporting increased migration and immigration, we are repaying the debt of gratitude that we all owe to those who envisioned the multicultural pluralistic society in which we currently enjoy our lives and also to those who gave their lives to preserve the institutions that support such a society. This last moral feature deserves special consideration.

Gratitude is owed to those institutions who served all of us in the past by incorporating either us or our distant ancestors into a new society. It is important to emphasize that no one who is a citizen of a multicultural pluralistic democracy can plausibly assert original entitlement rights that would justify not extending membership to others. All members of such democracies owe their membership either to a pure accident of birth or to being recipients of a successful immigration process. Those who were born into such a democracy can all cite ancestors, perhaps distant, who were recipients of such a process. And, even those who claim that all of their ancestors were part of some original process of forming such a democracy must acknowledge that the original society into which their distant ancestors were born has radically changed since its inception, typically from relatively nonmulticultural and nonpluralistic to being much more inclusive at present. So, the very different structure in which they happen, by accident, now to find themselves is very different, and that their current membership is in fact due, as was Socrates, to their own actions. Whether or not one's ancestors were citizens of a given state does not guarantee a similar status to their descendants. This follows directly from accepting the social contract theory. A person's ancestors cannot accept the social contract for anyone else, including their descendants. This solely depends on each individual to whom the opportunity of citizenship is offered; each person either accepts the social contract or not by how they choose to live their lives.[24]

But there are other ethical worries to be considered in connection with the concern regarding *immigrant carrying capacity*. Addressing this topic is challenging because the wealthiest multicultural pluralistic democracies currently refuse to address seriously disturbing issues of their current social norms such as (1) over-population, (2) environmental sustainability, (3) pressures on existing infrastructure, and (4) how to sustain a decent quality of life for descendants. When another complicating factor, (5) immigrant and total population carrying capacity, is being added to the mix, attempts to determine overall carrying capacity for a given society are rendered difficult indeed. Some pessimists may even claim that it is impossible to determine. But, as with concerns about other complex matters such as global warming and climate change, inclusive models need to be constructed and empirically tested. Responding ethically to migration challenges crucially requires having good empirical data, functionally adequate models, and strong moral principles.

The Special Problem Posed by Forced Migration

Still, the super-hard problem is Forced Displacement and Migration. How can we respond with sensitivity so that forced migrants might receive minimally decent lives? There is no single solution for all forced migration cases. For some displaced migrants, the solution lies in figuring out how to enable their peaceful return. In this case, increased support for temporary living accommodations seems to be a good first step. For other forced migrants, peaceful return is not an option. This puts those in a position to grant refuge in a morally demanding situation. Granting refuge is clearly a good thing, something all of us would desire for ourselves and our families, if we were in the forced migrants' position.

So, what could be done to help forced migrants? One reasonable first step is to employ the concept of Affirmative Action to cases of forced migration. Affirmative Action in multicultural pluralistic democracies is a policy that is designed to correct past injustices in hiring and in school admissions to members of groups that have previously been prevented from getting due consideration based on discriminatory policies. In its less controversial form, the policy advocated minimal preferences of otherwise qualified candidates for various social positions. The moral justification provided for Affirmative Action is based on the ideas of reparation, attempting to correct past injustices, and social improvement by providing visibility for members of marginalized groups to succeed in areas in which they had not been allowed to compete. Applying Affirmative Action to the case of forced migrants would entail that, other things relatively or approximately equal, forced migrants would be given preferential treatment with respect to migration and immigration over the non-forced. How might such a policy be defended, other than by appealing to the obvious fact that forced migrants are basically in much more dire circumstances than non-forced migrants, and thus it follows that a greater good is achieved, other things roughly equal, by favoring forced over non-forced migrants?

It can be pointed out that certain multicultural pluralistic democracies have a history of being powerfully influenced by the acceptance of forced migrants, and it can be argued that increased migration can be directly tied to the economic success of a number of multicultural pluralistic democracies. Thus, some of the very success of these states can be linked to the accessibility of immigration for forced migration. Thus, some will claim that there is a special moral obligation of these states to accommodate the requests of other forced migrants.

There is a further argument to consider. Much of the forced displacement that is now occurring around the world is due at least in part to activities of the governments of certain multicultural pluralistic democracies to interfere in the political stability of countries which are currently experiencing forced displacement. There is another suggestion that some of the forced displacement is due to the repressive activities of drug cartels in countries which currently supply a significant amount of the illegal drugs that are currently being consumed in certain multicultural pluralistic democracies. There are also suggestions that forced displacement is related in some cases to climate change which, some claim, is exacerbated by the reckless energy consumption habits of people in certain multicultural pluralistic democracies. If these suggestions, and others in a similar vein, are correct, then there seems to be a significant moral responsibility that incurs to these multicultural pluralistic democracies to correct the wrongs of their past and current behaviors by increasing the migration opportunities of those forcibly displaced from the affected countries.

So, can multicultural pluralistic democracies do more? Surely, there are strong moral reasons to support the claim that if we are able to do more without disrupting existing mechanisms of support for current citizens, then we should. Nations and cities, could, for instance, adopt a policy of adding 1 percent of the world's forced migrants to their population each year for the next ten years. While the various common objections that have already been discussed earlier can be expected to be raised against this proposal (such as fear of cultural destruction), all cultures could easily afford to accommodate some more migrants, and some could accommodate even a lot more migrants, and could manage their cultures perfectly well if many more became successful immigrants.

Some may object that the 1 percent increase proposed above is insufficient and that it should be much higher. And, that may in fact be correct. But until we develop adequate models, we are not in a position either to judge or to convince others. Attempting a 1 percent increase in migrants accepted over previous highs is a good start.

So, let us conclude. Citizens of multicultural pluralistic democracies, who contract to be part of a nation or municipality for the purpose of creating social mechanisms that in turn will support them must come to accept that they cannot and do not create these social structures on their own; they depend on others to join with them and to work with them, and also to replace them when they are no longer alive to benefit. Citizens of multicultural pluralistic democracies need to grant that their citizenship status is not based upon merit but because a remarkable accident of birth bestowed a great privilege upon them. With great privilege, of course, comes great responsibility. These citizens owe gratitude for what they have received from others who made their being citizens possible; they owe gratitude to those who defended our liberties, even to the death, to make it possible for them still to be here living in great luxury and privilege when things might have turned out very differently. They are thereby morally required to figure out how to pay forward the enormous opportunity they have received, not only to their loved ones but to all who deserve their moral consideration.[25]

NOTES

1. https://www.usatoday.com/story/money/economy/2018/07/05/cities-americans-growing-population-migration/35801343/

2. https://www.abodo.com/blog/the-8-u-s-cities-most-attractive-to-immigrants/
3. See Appendix.
4. One prominent exception is the work of James Hudson.
5. See Thomas Hobbes' *Leviathan* and John Locke's *Second Treatise of Government*.
6. This point is forcefully made by David Miller, 2016, chapter 2.
7. Cosmopolitans, such as Appiah, equally skirt the migration issue by only considering a future world government in which the problem does not exist.
8. Plato, *Crito*, Final argument, Jowett translation.
9. Miller, p. 39.
10. Miller, p. 48.
11. Miller, chapter 2.
12. See Barry Common's influential discussion of "The Tragedy of the Commons."
13. Some cultures are what E. T. Hall calls "low context" (do not assume that most adults are well informed, such as the USA or Germany) and other cultures are high context (do assume that adults both should and do understand the basic rules that govern society, such as France and Japan.) Problems arise when migrants from low context cultures migrate to high context cultures.
14. The distinction between Public and Private Spheres of Action holds in most social contexts. Only for those societies in which there is no private sphere would the distinction not apply.
15. Customs that one follows in the intimate privacy of one's own personal space are another matter.
16. Perhaps those most capable of answering would include recent migrant and immigrants.
17. This responsibility applies to the second, third, and fourth categories of migrant mentioned above.
18. See Rawls.
19. This category of responsibility falls on the third and fourth groups.
20. As I write this chapter, there is a significant disconnect between policies and procedures that have long been in place and the activities of the current administration of the U.S. government directly concerning matters of migration and immigration. The current administration has engaged in discriminatory policies that seem inconsistent with the current basic values of the country.
21. There are, to be sure, arguments that can be made for increasing migration to other kinds of states. With respect to theocracies, for example, one can use religious arguments to accept co-religionists. With respect to mono-cultural ethnic states, one can use ethnic arguments to accept those of the same ethnicity. That the vast majority of current displacement migrants are currently located in countries with similar religion and/or ethnicity is testimonial to the power of these latter arguments.
22. See the Parable of the Good Samaritan.
23. See Kraemer 2016.
24. For discussion of an objection to applying the Social Contract to the United States and Canada with respect to the special populations whose ancestors were not part of the social contract, namely First Nation Peoples and descendants of slaves.

25. Versions of parts of this chapter have been presented at the European Studies Conference, University of Nebraska–Omaha, October 2019, the Wisconsin Institute for Peace and Conflict Studies Conference, St. Norbert's College, April 2019, The Ethical City Conference, Viterbo University, April 2019, as well as several informal audiences at the University of Wisconsin–La Crosse. I am grateful to comments from those who participated in earlier presentations, and I especially want to thank Francine Klein, Sarah Kraemer, and Paul Wattez for their insights and help.

REFERENCES

Appiah, Kwame, 2006, *Cosmopolitanism*, New York: W.W. Norton.

Commoner, Barry, 1971, *The Closing Circle: Nature, Man, and Technology*, New York: Knopf.

Etzioni, Amitai, 2006, "The Rights and Responsibilities of Immigrants," *Quadrant*, June, Vol. 50, no. 6, pp. 9–13.

Hall, E. T., 1976, *Beyond Culture*, New York: Random House.

Hobbes, Thomas, 1651, *Leviathan.*

Hudson, James, 1984, "The Ethics of Immigration Restriction," *Social Theory and Practice*, Vol. 10, pp. 201–239.

Kraemer, Eric, 2016, "Utilitarianism, Religious Diversity, and Progressive Pluralism," in Luis Cardiero-Rodriguez and Marko Simendec (eds.), *Philosophies of Multiculturalism*, London: Routledge, pp. 115–130.

Locke, John, 1689, *Two Treatises of Government.*

Mill, John Stuart, 1863, *Utilitarianism.*

Miller, David, 2016, *Strangers in Our Midst*, London: Oxford University Press.

Plato, 360 B.C.E., *Crito.*

Plato, 381 B.C.E., *The Republic.*

Rawls, John, 1971, *Theory of Justice*, Boston, MA: Harvard University Press.

Ross, W.D., 1930, *The Right and the Good*, Oxford: Oxford University Press.

The Book of Luke, 63, Book 10: 25–37, "Parable of the Good Samaritan."

United Nations Charter on Human Rights, 1948, https://www.un.org/en/sections/issues-depth/human-rights/.

Wattez, Paul, forthcoming, *Iyiyuu iithun ou le savoir-faire iyiyiw: Reconfigurations épistémologiques, politiques et ontologiques dans la stratégie d'auto-patrimonialisation de la culture des Iiiyuyuch*, University of Montreal.

World Health Organization website, https://www.who.int/.

Chapter 2

Global Refugee Crisis

A Product of Imperialist Accumulation by Dispossession

Tatah Mentan

INTRODUCTORY BACKGROUND

After the catastrophic attacks of September 11, 2001, monumental sorrow and a feeling of desperate and understandable anger began to permeate the American psyche. A few people at that time attempted to promote a balanced perspective by pointing out that the United States had also been responsible for causing those same feelings in people in other nations, but they produced hardly a ripple. Although Americans understand in the abstract the wisdom of people around the world empathizing with the suffering of one another, such a reminder of wrongs committed by America got little hearing and was soon overshadowed by an accelerated "war on terrorism."

The widely circulated photo of Aylan Kurdi, a three-year-old Syrian boy whose body was found on a beach in Turkey and whose family was "making a final, desperate attempt to flee to relatives in Canada even though their asylum application had been rejected"[1] by the Harper government, has caused widespread outrage and forced Western leaders to acknowledge that there is a "refugee crisis."[2] The real tragedy is the refusal of Western leaders to acknowledge the cause of the refugee crisis—Western imperialism's genocidal and never-ending wars on the people of the Middle East, Central Asia, and Africa. There are now more refugees than at any time since World War II, and the number of refugees has increased markedly since the start of the "Global War on Terror."[3]

Wherever the United States and its imperialist allies have intervened, whether through direct military action or indirect proxy wars, economic sabotage, and coups, in the name of "democracy," the "War on Terror," or the "responsibility to protect," death and despair have been forced upon millions of innocent people, who have been left no other choice than to abandon their native lands to embark on a dangerous future of desperate struggle. In Afghanistan, Iraq, Libya, Syria, Yemen, Pakistan, Somalia, Mali, Korea, Vietnam, East Timor, Sudan, Ukraine, and elsewhere the livelihoods of millions have been destroyed by the forces of U.S. and Western imperialism.

In the 1980s, Afghanistan had a "genuinely popular government," according to John Ryan, a retired professor from the University of Winnipeg, that was implementing widespread reforms.[4] Labor unions were legalized, a minimum wage was established, hundreds of thousands of Afghans were enrolled in educational facilities, and women were freed from age-old tribal bondage and able to earn an independent income. U.S. and Western imperialism, fearful of that kind of equitable distribution of wealth, supported the feudal landlords and fundamentalist mullahs to sow chaos across the country, bringing rise to elements that later formed al-Qaeda and the Taliban. The Afghan people were once more dealt a severe punishment by the forces of Western imperialism following 9/11, despite a lack of conclusive evidence linking either the Taliban or al-Qaeda to the attacks. Thirty years of U.S. intervention in Afghanistan have left the people impoverished, traumatized, and desperate. The conflicts in Libya and Syria are eerily similar to the Western destabilization of Afghanistan. In 2011, when the Arab Spring protests swept across the Middle East and North Africa, Western imperialism hijacked legitimate grievances of the masses as a pretext for intervention in the name of the "responsibility to protect" and "democracy promotion."

Prior to the 2011 U.S./NATO intervention, Libya was among the wealthiest and most stable countries in Africa, with the continent's highest standard of living. Housing was enshrined as a human right, education and healthcare services were free for all citizens, and the country was pushing to establish an African currency linked to gold to help end the vicious cycle of debt and impoverishment of the African masses by Western imperialism.[5] Under the cloak of the United Nations, Western imperialism, using the pretext of protecting the people of Libya from Gaddafi's murderous rule, launched airstrikes on Libya and allied themselves with al-Qaeda in the Islamic Maghreb and other Libyan extremists.[6] NATO airstrikes killed hundreds of civilians and forced Libya back into the Stone Age; Gaddafi was mercilessly tortured and murdered by the rebels. Thousands have been killed as rival tribal and extremist factions, some now allied with ISIS, battle for control of the country.

The conflict in Syria is frequently referred to as "Libya 2.0." U.S. imperialism with the support of Israel, Turkey, and the Persian Gulf States, trained and financed "moderate" rebels to overthrow the secular and popularly supported government of Bashar al-Assad. The "Free Syrian Army," that is, the "moderate" rebels, was virtually eliminated in the conflict despite millions

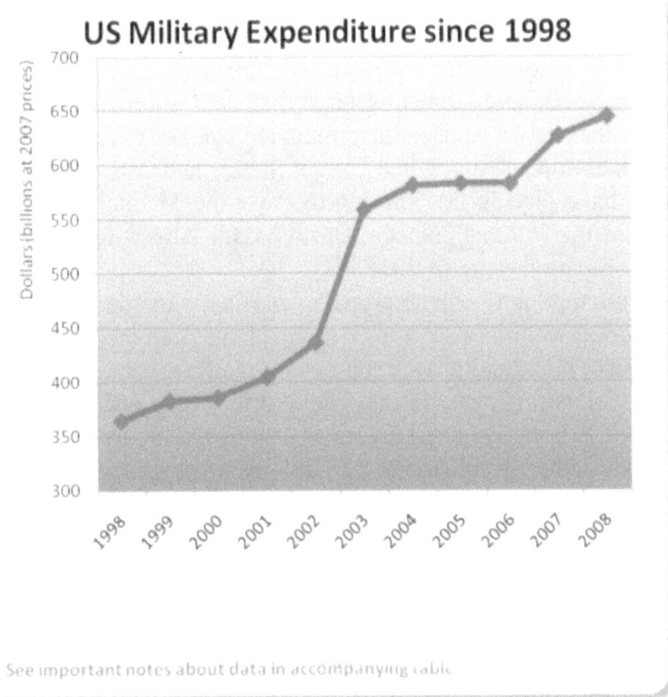

Figure 2.1 U.S. Military Expenditures since 1998. *Source*: http://www.globalissues.org/Geopolitics/ArmsTrade/Spending.asp.

of dollars in aid from the United States and its regional allies.[7] FSA fighters have deserted to the ranks of ISIS *en masse*, itself a product of the illegal U.S. occupation of Iraq that killed 1 million Iraqis.[8] There is overwhelming evidence that the United States and its allies have been actively training and supporting ISIS elements since the start of the proxy war in Syria.[9]

It was not until ISIS invaded Iraq with its new Toyota technicals, courtesy of U.S. imperialism, that ISIS was declared a threat to the world. Western imperialism changed its tactic from supporting ISIS to airstrikes on Iraq and Syria, with the support of other Western imperialist states, Turkey, which is also conveniently bombing anti-ISIS Kurdish fighters,[10] Saudi Arabia, and the Persian Gulf States, but without consultation with the Syrian government, Iran, or Hezbollah that have been fighting ISIS and al-Qaeda elements since the start of the conflict. Hundreds of thousands have died in the West's proxy war against the Syrian government.

From Libya to Afghanistan, the Democratic Republic of the Congo, Pakistan, and Somalia, United States and Western imperialist interventions, coups, and sanctions have displaced and killed millions of people. Physicians for Social Responsibility estimated that in Afghanistan, Iraq, and Pakistan alone, Western imperialist interventions have caused the deaths of 1.3 million people.[11] It is no wonder then that hundreds of thousands seek asylum elsewhere; however, after traveling huge distances overland and on water, refugees find themselves abused, discriminated against, held in detention, or rejected from Europe, Canada, the United States, and Australia. More than 2,500 might have died in 2015 trying to cross the Mediterranean Sea into Europe, while the International Organization for Migration estimates that 30,000 could die by the end of 2015.[12]

Refugees attempting to enter Europe, even if they are granted asylum in a mainland European country such as Germany, have been met with police violence in Greece, Italy, and other countries on the Mediterranean that are the first landing points for boats sailing from North Africa and Turkey. During Greek riot, police brutally beat refugees protesting the failure of local governments to process their applications. Conditions are so poor for refugees that while waiting for processing, newborn babies have died in Greece.[13]

On the Macedonia–Greece border, where more than a thousand refugees are crossing daily, refugees that broke through the barbed wire fences were shot at with stun grenades, and the Macedonian police have treated refugees as rioters, according to Amnesty International.[14]

Italian police forcibly removed African refugees camping out at the French border after France refused to grant them asylum.[15] Hungary is building a fortified wall, similar to the barbaric wall that divides the U.S.–Mexico border, to stop refugees from crossing the border.[16] The thousands of refugees that seek asylum in Australia are detained in detention facilities in Papua New Guinea and the small island nation of Nauru dubbed the "Guantanamo Bay of the Pacific."[17] Refugees can be detained for several years in these facilities, where social workers have observed "profound damage" to those detained through "prolonged deprivation of freedom, abuse of power, confinement in an extremely harsh environment, and uncertainty of future, disempowerment, loss of privacy and autonomy and inadequate health and protection services."[18]

An Australian Senate investigation received reports of guards raping women on tape and sexually exploiting children as young as two years old.[19] Just as Britain refuses to assist drowning refugees in the Mediterranean out of fear that it will encourage more migrants to seek asylum, the unannounced policy of Australian authorities is to make refugees suffer abuse and inhumane living conditions to deter them from seeking asylum[20] in Australia, as if Australian imperialism hasn't inflicted enough suffering on the people of the Middle East, South, and Southeast Asia.

U.S. and Western imperialism is the root cause of the "refugee crisis." Everyday men, women, and children are killed by U.S. drone strikes in

Pakistan, U.S.- and Western-backed militias in Afghanistan, Syria, and Somalia, European and North American mining and oil conglomerates in Central and Western Africa or are starved to death in Yemen by the U.S.-backed Arab blockade of the country. Until the genocidal aims of U.S. imperialism, with the support of Canada, Australia, the European Union, and regional allies, are defeated, the "War on Terror" will continue to make life too unbearable for working people in Asia, Africa, and the Middle East to remain in their home countries.

The re-deployment of U.S. troops and military bases could best be understood through the nature of U.S. interventionism in different regions of the world. This militarization process characterized by armed aggression and warfare, as well as interventions, is referred to as "cooperation agreements." The latter reaffirmed America's economic design in the areas of trade and investment practices. Economic development is ensured through the miniaturization or the control of governments and organizations. Vast resources are thereby expended and wasted in order to allow such control to be effective, particularly in regions which have a strategic potential in terms of wealth and resources and which are being used to consolidate the Empire's structures and functions. This chapter unravels: (a) the re-launching of imperialist policies of violent global domination in search of cheap and flexible labor of refugees, as well as natural resources from the South; (b) the growing asymmetries among and within countries and regions; (c) the increase and intensification of social inequalities; (d) the configuration of a gigantic global reserve army of labor associated with the emergence of severe forms of labor prevarication and exploitation; and (e) the predominance of forced migration as the primary mode of human mobility under conditions of extreme vulnerability.

From this perspective, the migration and labor questions of millions of refugees are two sides of the same coin, whose currency translates into unbearable conditions of systematic oppression and mindless exploitation of the working class. To combat this, there must be, among other things, a unity of social organizations and movements in alliance with progressive Trotsky-style intellectuals in order to foster a process of social transformation.

ACCUMULATION BY CONTAMINATION AND DISPOSSESSION: THEORETICAL SITUATEDNESS

The conviction that capitalist production requires laborers who are not only dispossessed of autonomous means of reproduction but are also legally free to offer their capacity to labor on the market has been central to Marxist analyses of capitalism. Any endeavor to confront this thesis with the actual history of capitalism not only runs counter to the dominant content of traditional

Marxist analysis but also to the fundamentally optimistic Marxist philosophy of history. Notwithstanding exploitation, pauperization, injustice, and all the other evils of this historical epoch, Marx, Engels, and Marxists also conceive of capitalism as one step further in the development of humanity.

Much like the proponents of capitalism, Marx and Marxists explained that while direct violence against producers was constantly threatened and often applied in pre-capitalist forms of production, violence is no longer required for capitalist forms of exploitation. It is, indeed, even contrary to the successful production of surplus value, and hence profit. Capitalism, then, is conceived of as a marker of human progress in comparison to pre-capitalist forms of production, not only because of its surpassing of direct violence but also because it brings about the social, technological, and ideological conditions which make socialism possible.

Nonetheless, while Marx, Engels, and Marxists concur with proponents of capitalism in their conception of this political-economic system as a progressive stage in the history of mankind, they are neither in agreement with the latter's conception of capitalism as the final stage of history nor with their explanation of its historical origin. This difference is spelled out at the end of the first volume of *Capital* in Marx's explication of "primitive accumulation," conceived of as historical prerequisite to the accumulation that becomes dominant in capitalism.

After having made fun of Adam Smith's anecdotal narrative of the origin of capitalism, Marx explains that primitive accumulation of capital was "dripping from head to foot, from every pore, with blood and dirt" (Marx-Engels, Werke (*MEW*), Vol.23:788). The seven paragraphs of the chapter on "so-called primitive accumulation" contain extensive historical descriptions. However, they do not represent historical analysis as such. Instead, Marx highlights strategies and processes which resulted in the dispossession of laborers from autonomous means of reproduction and in the accumulation of capital. While the latter was achieved through "colonialism, national debt, taxation, protectionism, trade wars, etc." (*MEW*, Vol.23, Ibid: 785) the former was brought about through forceful appropriation and expropriation. All of these strategies were ripe with violence, and all of them made use of state power.

That these practices are considered to be conducive of the establishment of capitalist production, but not of its continuous reproduction, is made clear by the famous statement about violence being the midwife of any old society which is pregnant with a new one. We might smile about Marx's choice of word, since instead of using the word "*Hebamme*" (midwife), he entrusts historical progress to a male, designating him as "*Geburtshelfer*" (obstetrician). Let us leave that aside. Let us also leave aside the extensive debate on revolution in the course of which this sentence has, again and again, been cited (Etienne Balibar, 2009: 99–125). But this statement is not only relevant for debates on revolution; it also concerns the analysis of capitalism. Having helped a woman in labor to give birth to new life, the mission of a midwife is fulfilled. Assuming that Marx chose his terms conscientiously, this also applies to the role of violence in history. And, indeed, it is in the same chapter that we are told that extra-economic violence, though exceptionally still made use of in capitalism, has been replaced by the "natural laws of production" (MEW 23, 792). In other words, the open violence of former times has been replaced by the silent force of market conditions.

Of course, neither Marx nor Marxists have conceived of capitalism as being devoid of violence. Instead, they have remarked, the site of violence has changed. It is no longer in the open, executed through the state, or—in places where the monopoly of legitimate physical violence has not yet been appropriated by the state—by open private violence. Once material conditions have forced men, women, and even children to offer their capacity to labor on the market, direct violence is no longer necessary to establish exploitation, because this result is achieved by the impersonal functioning of competition on the labor market. And it is this impersonal power which ensures the acceptance of dominance that is inherent in every capitalist labor relation. This capitalist form of violence, no longer in the open and no longer sporadic, has become the central element of the everyday life of capitalism. Its analysis forms the center of the Marxist analysis of capitalist labor, and rightly so. Nevertheless, by focusing exclusively on the violence inherent in the everyday command over the application of one's capacity to labor, and hence over the bodies and the intellectual capacities of wage-laborers themselves, one only grasps specific historical developments of capitalist labor, albeit important ones.

This situation helps in explaining why the concept of accumulation by contamination emerged to study the dynamics of social metabolism (Martinez-Alier, 2002) and capitalism (Harvey, 2003) through a lens of environmental conflicts (Armiero, 2008). The multidimensional crisis that our societies are facing highlights the instability and the crisis tendencies of capitalism. The crisis also offers the possibility to revitalize the Marxist theory of over-accumulation. This theory views the economic crisis as due to a lack of capital for profitable investment opportunities. Potential solutions to the crisis can be found in the search for lower input costs (i.e., land, raw materials, labor, etc.) and in the expansion of markets (i.e., trade with noncapitalist social formations). Capitalist development needs something "outside of itself," and for this reason continuously aims to open up "territories" (Harvey, 2003). The issues at stake are how this process interacts with social metabolism and the social and environmental consequences.

In addressing these issues, there are gaps in the existing literature. The concept of ecological distribution conflicts (Martinez-Alier, 2002) fails to deeply investigate the driving forces of social metabolism today in the era of neoliberalism. In this regard, it is useful to link two lines of thought, namely, ecological economics and political ecology, to show how capitalism appropriates nature and the labor force to expand domination through dispossession (expropriation of rights) and contamination (cost-shifting). In this sense, the neoliberal project is about the release of assets (both inputs and outputs of the social metabolism) at a very low cost.

Capitalism is understood here as a relation of social production in which laborers have no control over the means of production (e.g., workers in a mine or factory). Accumulation is the process by which the separation between laborers and their means of production is continuously reproduced. Over-accumulation is in contrast a result of the accumulation process generating excessive capacity for capital beyond available opportunities for dispossession (or contamination) (Harvey, 2003).

These concepts are linked to historical Marxist debate over primitive accumulation (De Angelis, 2001). Lenin and others, like Dobb in development studies, have argued that primitive accumulation is a clear-cut historical process that gave birth to the preconditions of a capitalist mode of production (i.e., Historical Primitive Accumulation). On the other hand, Rosa Luxemburg, and writers such as Amin and Wallerstein argued from a World System Theory perspective that primitive accumulation is an ongoing process whereby the extra-economic prerequisite to capitalist production is an inherent and continuous element of modern societies (i.e., Inherent-continuous Primitive Accumulation).

In Marx's theory, primitive or original accumulation of profits and capital by colonial robbery and enclosures would be substituted in due course by the exploitation of labor as the capital/labor ratio in the economy increased and new technologies enhanced labor productivity together with new methods of disciplining wage labor. Harvey's footnote to Marx (the concept of accumulation by dispossession), in line with Rosa Luxemburg, emphasizes that primitive or original accumulation has never been as important as it is today.

Having briefly clarified the terms of the debate, I argue that there are two complementary strategies of capitalism. First, accumulation by dispossession (Harvey, 2003) is the inherent necessity of the capitalist system to separate, through extra-economic means, the laborers from the means of production to perpetuate the capitalistic relation (e.g., bio-prospecting, patent rights, privatization of public utilities, etc.). Second, accumulation by contamination is the process by which the capitalist system endangers, through cost-shifting, the means of existence (and subsistence) of human beings to perpetuate the capitalistic relation (e.g., air pollution, alteration of biogeochemical cycles, etc.).

In the case of dispossession, that which pre-existed outside the capitalist system is brought inside, for example, by the privatization of public assets or commons (Harvey, 2003). Normally, a specific social group is dispossessed by another one to obtain profit (e.g., farmers are dispossessed of their land by violent global land grabbers). In the case of contamination, an appropriation of de-facto property rights takes place resulting in the shifting of costs and risks, that is, exploiting the sinks over their sustainable assimilative capacity (e.g., climate change). The consequences most likely fall upon the most vulnerable social groups (e.g., small-scale farmers in the South), but society as a whole can be affected. Such unequal distribution can be intra-generational and/or inter-generational. Harvey's second key concept, of accumulation by dispossession, begins from the observation that neoliberalism was "redistributive rather than generative" and as such had to find concrete ways in which to "transfer assets and channel wealth and income either from the mass of the population towards the upper classes or from vulnerable to richer countries" by force where necessary (Harvey, 2007: 34).

As one may ask: What is the working class? A relatively simple question, but not one with a simple answer. These days most Marxists would emphasize "relationship to the means of production," defining class in terms of extraction of surplus value and the wage relation. This isn't wrong—surplus value and the wage relation are central to class and class struggle—but this approach tends to telescope the *entirety* of the meaning and making of class and class struggle into the workplace. A closer reading of Marx suggests that a wider, and more relevant, vision can be recovered.

For Marx, capitalism and class began as dispossession. In his debate with orthodox political economy, Marx insisted that the secret of the origins of capitalism, as a class system, lay in an initial accumulation of capital that rested upon "the complete separation of the laborers from all property in the means by which they can realize their labor." The robbery of masses of humanity—be they serfs or sailors, artisans or Aboriginal peoples—of their productive capacities and guarantees of existence was central to class formation. Expropriation was written "in the annals of mankind in letters of blood and fire." The proletariat is not therefore defined by the wage relation itself. It is defined by dispossession—the brutal process by which producers are forced to depend on the wage for survival.

Contemporary capital therefore accumulates, expanding social metabolism and capitalist markets through dispossession and contamination. The result is an unequal distribution of costs and benefits, which lead to socio-environmental conflicts. In response, different actors resist capital accumulation in different ways. The dispossessed complain about the expropriation of (or separation from) their means of production (e.g. land), while victims of contamination complain about the costs shifted to the detriment of their environment and health (e.g., wars such as those for regime change like that in Libya and against terrorism around the globe as well as climate conditions like the Asian Tsunami). The reason is that capitalist production requires laborers who are not only dispossessed of autonomous means of reproduction but are also legally free to offer their capacity to labor on the market has been central to Marxist analyses of capitalism. Any endeavor to confront this thesis with the actual history of capitalism not only runs counter to the dominant content of traditional Marxist analysis but also to the fundamentally optimistic Marxist philosophy of history. Notwithstanding exploitation, pauperization, injustice, and all the other evils of this historical epoch of violent globalization and its attendant chaotic flooding of the world with helpless and hopeless refugees, Marx, Engels, and Marxists have also conceived of capitalism as one step further in the development of humanity.

REFUGEES CRISIS OR "THE NEW SLAVE TRADE AND SLAVERY" IN EUROPE?

According to Peter Koenig in the November 13, 2015 "*Information Clearing House,*" the flood of refugees entering Europe is endless. Nobody knows exactly how many there are and where they go. In 2015, up to November, estimates vary from the low of 750,000 to a high of 2 million. Most of them went to Germany or want to go to Germany. Up to a million, perhaps more might have ended up in Germany by the end of the year. For 2016, predictions were for up to 2 million. They are the direct results of the Washington-NATO-driven wars and conflicts in the Middle East, which keep raging on; creating completely deliberate and manmade chaos.

The German government made a commitment to accept a comparatively extra-large contingent of refugees, to give them shelter, to feed them. But where and with what? Was it guilt, therefore, that struck Madame Merkel and Co. for being complicit in the destruction of their lands, their homes, their families, their economies—in one short word, their lives?

The Global Reserve Army

In order to have a firmer grasp of this issue, it is crucial to look both empirically and theoretically at the global reserve army as it appears in the current historical context—and then bring to bear the entire Marxian critique of imperialism. Without such a comprehensive critique, analyses of such

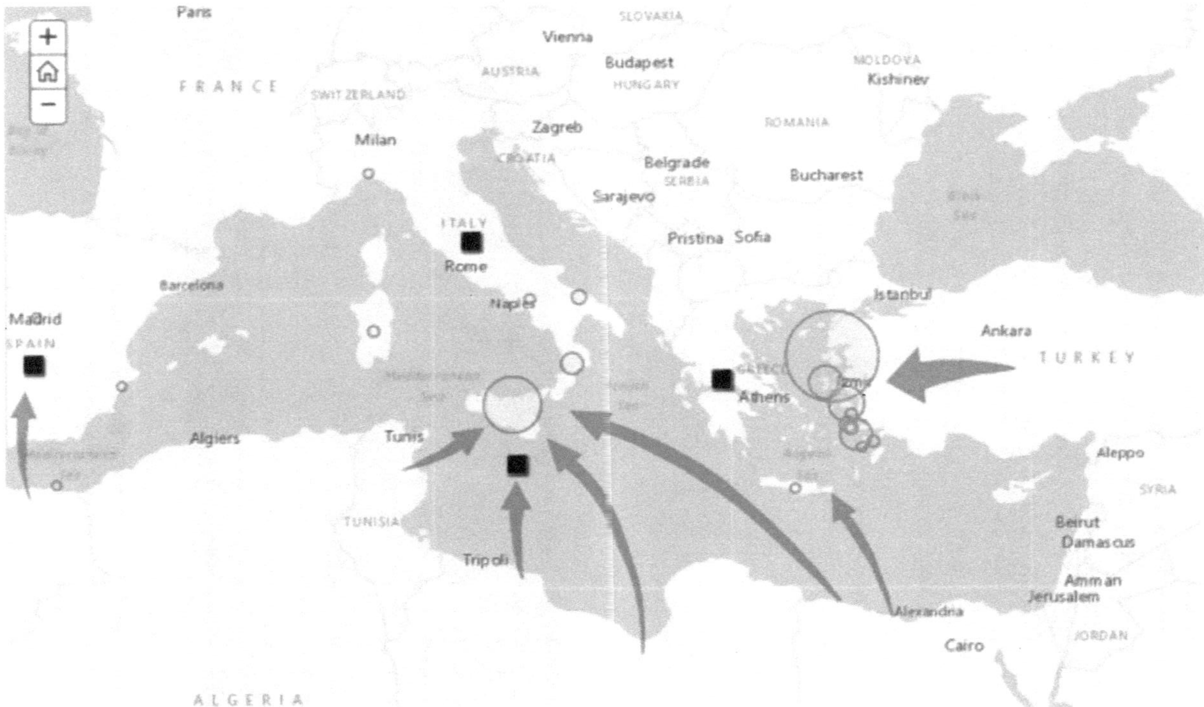

Figure 2.2 A Map That Dramatizes (and Helps Explain) the Refugee Crisis. The image above is a screenshot from a new interactive map produced by our friends at Esri, the Geographic Information Systems (GIS) company that has been one of the partners in American Futures reports.

problems as the global shift in production, the global labor arbitrage, deindustrialization, etc., are mere partial observations suspended in mid air (James Petras and Henry Veltmeyer, 2007: 70).

The data on the global workforce compiled by the ILO conforms closely to Marx's main distinctions with regard to the active labor army and the reserve army of labor. In the ILO picture of the world workforce in 2011, 1.4 billion workers were wage workers—many of whom were precariously employed, and only part-time workers. In contrast, the number of those counted as unemployed worldwide in 2009 consisted of only 218 million workers. It is noteworthy that in order to be classified as unemployed, workers need to have actively pursued job searches in the previous few weeks. The unemployed, in this sense, can be seen as conforming roughly to Marx's "floating" portion of the reserve army.

A further 1.7 billion workers are classified today as "vulnerably employed." This is a residual category of the "economically active population," consisting

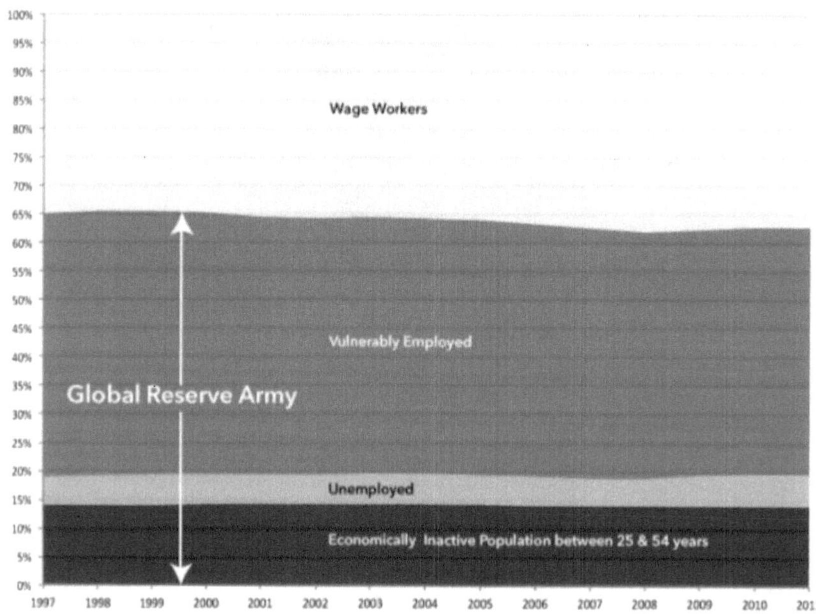

Figure 2.3 The Global Workforce and the Global Reserve Army. Note: The proportion of "vulnerably employed" and "unemployed" was estimated based on percentages from the "Global Employment Trends" reports. The chart includes total world population (15 years and over) excluding the economically inactive population less than 25- and greater than 54-years of age. International Labor Office (ILO), "Economically Active Population Estimates and Projections (5th edition, revision 2009)," LABORSTA Internet (Geneva: International Labour Organization, 2009); ILO "Global Employment Trends," 2009, 2010, and 2011 (Geneva: International Labor Office).

of all those who work but are not wage workers—or part of the active labor army in Marx's terminology. It includes two categories of workers: "own-account workers" and "contributing family workers."

Indeed, the flood of refugees or the reserve army of unemployed, ordered by the Washington Dictator to be retained by Turkey at the tune of 2.5 million—or more—in camps with full infrastructure that have cost some 6 billion dollars to build—not counting their maintenance—and then let lose in huge hordes at the appropriate times, like now, in stormy fall weather, followed by harsh European winters, also by orders of the dictator. He, in turn, is comfortably protected between two oceans, oblivious to the pain of far-away others—creating purposely more confusion, destabilization, and havoc within the EU—which has never really been a union, with or without refugees. The refugees are used as a weapon of destabilization.

And yes, he the Washington strongman can, because the Europeans are his trusted vassals. One by one, these un-solidary union members are pushing and shoving the stream of forced migrants, desperate hungry and sick people—on to the next country. Some build walls, or lock their borders with barbed wire fences, patrolled by armed police, military and vicious dogs. Sea-water or rain-soaked refugees are beaten, families pulled and pushed apart, and dragged in dirt. Police and military hatred and brutality in Serbia, Hungary, the Czech Republic, and others know no limits. Blood is flowing, small children in the arms of their hopeless and hapless parents—crying, not understanding the cruel world they have been born into—and will have to endure. Misery for millions in a world where injustice is ever more becoming the order of the day. And we are blinded to it. Cohabitation with misery and injustice by millions has become the new normal.

Misery, hardship, and submission are part of the dogma of the neoliberal masters we have allowed to take over our Western world in the last thirty years. Our comfort and obscene consumerism have blinded us—and is still blinding us—to the drip-by-drip brainwashing MSM propaganda. The neocons are in the driver's seat and will remain there until *We, The People*— the vast majority of the planet—99.99 percent—show them the way to get lost: lost for good. Yes we can. We really can. But we have to become conscious of what's going on and transpose our conscience to a level of nonacceptance.

Individual faces of those poor souls on the run don't count. Small children, women, old men– thousands and thousands die *en route* to a "more decent life"; they are mere statistics, faceless numbers. They are used as weapons to destabilize, to weaken other nations, to soften them, so to speak, for easier dominance and digestion of the hungry arrogant, outsized beast, appearing in the form of the United States of America, but representing a global, Zionist-led elite, with an intimidating, scary killer army that absorbs more than half of the world's military budget.

Obey or you will be sanctioned. Economically or by forced *regime change*. Either you follow the dictate, or a *false flag* will make you guilty deserving of punishment and annihilation. Europe has been "bought," coerced, and manipulated into this humiliation. The European Union is a sham. The European Commission is a deceit. There is not one non-neoliberal country in the entire twenty-eight member European nonunion. How is this possible? It is a uniform world view whether your label is "right" or "left"—all meaningless.

Universal election fraud is presented on a silver platter like the severed head of democracy, but nobody wants to see it. It's like admiring the emperor's wonderful clothes, not wanting to admit that he is stark naked. We keep talking about democratic elections. Nonsense! There is no democracy anymore as it was crafted 2,500 years ago by the minds of the philosophers of Delphi in ancient Greece. Most of all and everybody in the Western world are buyable. Rare is the politician who isn't. He won't last. Money reigns.

Why can't Europeans admit to the falsehood of things? In their deep conscience, they all know that "something is wrong." Millions of refugees suddenly flooding the European continent—something must be wrong. Does anybody see the systematic destruction of the entire Middle East and North Africa (MENA) region and make the connection to the refugees?

The propaganda lies of the media are ever bolder, more flagrant. The world senses it. But nobody does anything about it. If people were, they would not live in a world of permanent war, conflicts, killing for power, dominance and greed, exploitation–endless egocentricity. Mankind would not believe the barrage of lies it is showered with day-by-day by the corrupt mainstream media. They would not be forced to run from one fire to the next. There would be no refugees, but instead these proud and honest people would be building their countries and cultures and striving to live well—which is the right of every human being.

Back to reality. In some small German villages, the number of refugees is larger than the local population. With all good will, shelters cannot be created fast enough and warm enough (as winter approaches) —and the food supply. Who pays? The nationals feel overwhelmed. The mood among Germans is cheery. Welcome signs everywhere! Yes, welcoming the refugees, with smiles, with hugs, with food, and gifts. The warmness of the German people has been stunning. Europeans and Germans, in particular, are beset by confusion. The EU leaders (sic) are saying one thing but doing another. They are confused at best and lying at worst. Trust has been corrupted by lies after lies after lies. People do not seem to see through the scheme, a multi-faceted Machiavellian plan:

Refugees are becoming the new slaves. Many are highly educated but poor, hungry, and without shelter. They will work for peanuts just to feed their families, pressing on local wages, increasing unemployment—destroying local economies, creating fear, anxieties among locals—anxious people have no energy to stand up for their rights and defend themselves of their sovereignty. They are easy prey. That's what Washington and its associated vassal dictators want.

The exit of millions from Syria, Iraq, Libya—the MENA region as a whole—is a brain drain for the refugees' home countries, creating a "brain-overflow" in Europe, in Germany in particular—competing with locals, demoralizing, fomenting jealousy, dividing communities and entire societies—breaking down livelihoods. These educated refugees are fleeing north, a few to Sweden Denmark, and Norway, but the vast majority to the assumed heaven of well-being—Germany, where cheap labor and low-wage academics may eventually replace locals, increasing unemployment, lowering production costs, boosting profits and widening the gap between rich and poor, rapidly increasing social inequity.

Why is Germany singled out by the overseas masters? Is it still the old Churchill saying, "*keep Americans in, Germans down and Russians out (of Europe)*?" Does Madame Merkel not understand this—the strongest link in Europe has to be weakened on as many fronts as possible, to make it vulnerable for easy takeover by the Washington masters. If you control Germany, you control Europe. That dogma appears not having changed since Churchill. The flood of refugees may also contain large numbers of disguised jihadists, Islamists (some estimates say at least 10 percent, but there is no proof, of course), with the intent of establishing cells in Europe—explosive cells to create unrest when needed by the Big Dictator, *à la* failed *Arab Spring* and the infamous so-called "*Colour Revolutions*" —remember? For which it is known by now infiltrated "sleeper" cells are responsible.

These are Zionist-Washington's well-targeted challenges for Europe. Challenges Europe is unable to cope with. One wonders what these lackeys in Brussels and the newly "elected" neolibs in the so-called EU member-countries were told, when they were given the marching orders—or else. They must have been given some incentives, because any halfwit would understand that this—plus the TTIP yes, the TTIP—will have Europe crumble economically, if not by World War III, and also would crumble their careers and livelihoods. Perhaps they were given the promise of a free ticket to Florida—"The Sunshine State" —or the Bahamas, when the moment comes.

UNHCR carries in its worldwide statistics about 50 million refugees (people at risk), but in reality by now they are more like 60–70 million. Imagine these refugees as hordes of poor homeless, roofless, hapless, hungry, and often sick and desperate people—a pool of cheap labor—called otherwise *SLAVES*. All the system needs to do is direct them to the "right" countries, those on the list of having to be subdued. Germany has Europe's lowest unemployment rate of 4.5 percent. If Germany "falls," Russia becomes considerably more vulnerable. Russia will have to fight for Germany, for Europe's survival, and Vladimir Putin knows it and is already doing it.

There are also the artificial "economic crises" all instigated by the *Washington Consensus*, the Western fraudulent fiat monetary system, managed and directed by the FED, Wall Street, BIS (Bank for International Settlement), and IMF. These crises maintain and accelerate the rate of unemployment in Europe which, according to Eurostat, has been hovering on average between 9 percent and 11 percent over the last twenty years. New work forces, like the slaves made from refugees will increase unemployment, lower production costs, increase corporate profits—create human misery on the one end of the spectrum and capital gains for the elite.

Marx in his *Das Kapital* called unemployment the "cushion" for capital that presses wages down. The cushion needs to become greater in as much as capital grows. Unemployment and underemployment embody the concept of the "*industrial reserve army.*" The larger the cushion, the better for the capitalists, for the investors. Others, like Keynes, have countered that capitalism could survive practically with full employment. That's a nice thought, but unsuitable for today's no-holds-barred capitalism—called neoliberalism.

Capital Accumulation

It was Marx's contention that the production of surplus value is "the absolute law" of the capitalist mode of production, that most of this surplus value is continually reconverted into capital—called capital accumulation—and that the system reproduces the capitalist relation: "on the one side the capitalist, on the other the wage-laborer." Capitalism is inherently an expanding system, for capitalists must constantly accumulate and extend their capital in order to preserve it; they must continually expand in order to remain capitalists, for if they did not, they would be destroyed by competitors; they would be consumers and not capitalists. This expansion eventually occurs on a worldwide basis, for capitalists must push their mode of production into every nook and cranny of the globe. Nevertheless, capitalists also have an urge to enjoy the consumption of their capital. The overcoming of this urge is supposed to be "abstinence," which is a bourgeois justification, according to Marx, for the private appropriation of surplus value.

Marx asserted that the general law of capitalist accumulation is that it creates both wealth and poverty. That is to say, capitalist accumulation has an antagonistic character, in that it produces and contains a unity of opposites. The same causes which develop the expansive power of capital, Marx wrote, develop also the labor power at its disposal, including the reserve army of labor (a relative surplus population), whose misery and pauperism grow in step with wealth at the other pole. Furthermore, Marx continued, capital accumulation transforms the workplace into a despotic, degrading, alienating environment, one which mutilates the laborer into a fragment of a man and destroys "every remnant of charm in his work." Capital accumulation produces an accumulation of wealth at one pole and an accumulation of misery, agony of toil, slavery, ignorance, brutality, mental degradation, at the opposite pole. Poverty and misery are not capitalism's negligence but it is imperative, it is inevitable progenies. This is Marx's principal message about the process of capitalist accumulation.

That message today may sound wild, and indeed, in some respects, Marx can now be seen as having incorrectly extrapolated conditions prevalent in his time. However, before my reader plunges in to judge the message too harshly, he should be aware of its depth. For Marx, wealth could not exist by itself, just as a capitalist class could not exist in isolation. Wealth in capitalism has no other meaning than a concentration of much of society's production (its means and its products) in relatively few hands, and there is no way for that to occur without the simultaneous creation of its opposite—poverty, the material deprivation of the many, at least in relative terms. But poverty and misery, Marx contended, must be understood not only as exploitation but as alienation as well not only materially but also "spiritually."

The Marxian theory of alienation seeks to explain how individuals in capitalist society have lost their understanding and control of the world around them and have, in the process, been stunted and perverted into something less than full human beings. For Marx, the source of all alienation lies in the work process. Alienation means that individuals no longer have an immediate and intimate relationship to the environment; they have been specialized and sorted, made into "the most wretched of commodities," divorced from the products they produce, split into mental workers and manual workers, into town people and rural people, divided into dominant and subordinate classes, thrown into selfish competition with one another. The result of alienation is the loss of personal identity—a transference of an individual's essential powers to others and to "things," even to commodities. Alienation is the negation of productivity, the diminution of one's powers.

Marx saw human beings in capitalistic society as alienated not only from the products they create and from their own labor but also from others and from themselves. That is, workers under capitalism lose control of their products, produce as cogs in a process they do not understand, are separated from and pitted against their fellow workers, and are deprived of their essential powers. They believe that power resides outside of themselves, in the products they have actually fashioned, and they humble, demean, and almost destroy themselves before the commodity world. In the same way, a religious person might fashion a wooden idol with his own hands, kneel before it, transfer his own powers to it, and thus reduce himself to something less than a full human being. In their manifold alienated states, people lose their inner selves and become passive; they allow themselves to be directed by outside powers that they do not control and do not want to control; they subject themselves willingly to manipulation; they have a sense of powerlessness; they cannot act effectively. Marx did not believe that capitalism was the original cause of alienation—for it existed before that—but under capitalism alienation in all of its forms is maximized.

The proletariat shares with the bourgeoisie every aspect of this commodity-dominated world. But, Marx stated, the latter experiences it as "a sign of its own power," while the former "feels destroyed in this alienation." The bourgeoisie, for Marx, sees no need for piercing the surface of phenomena; indeed, it has a special interest in not revealing what is below, and even in deceiving itself on this score. On the other hand, the proletariat, while equally baffled, has a special interest in discovering the true relations and thus in developing a revolutionary consciousness. Productive activity is the catalyst of this transformation.

The capitalist mode of production extracts surplus value from wage labor for the class of capitalists. The surplus value is used to expand capital, a process which is inherent to this social formation and which is reinforced by competition. The accumulation process tends to generate increasing demands for labor to work cooperatively with the expanding means of production. However, accumulation leads to concentration of capital, which places greater magnitudes of capital in fewer hands and at the same time raises the organic composition of capital—the capital intensity of production—thereby moderating the growing demand for labor. Accumulation is also accompanied by the centralization of capital, by the larger capitalists gaining what smaller capitalists lose, by the expropriation of capitalist by capitalist.

The centralization of capital is the dynamic element in the accumulation process. It is furthered by the development of the credit system, which draws together scattered money resources for the use of larger capitalists; by competition, which destroys the weak and bolsters the strong; and by economies of scale (falling average costs), which give increasing cost advantages to the already-large capitals over the smaller ones, enabling the larger capitals to beat the smaller.

If capitalist accumulation is to persist, it requires above all else an ample supply of wage labor that is continually replenished and available for work at wage levels that ensure the further production of surplus value for the class of capitalists. It is for this reason that Marx considered the reserve army of labor to be an essential ingredient of capitalism, a relatively redundant population of laborers that would expand and contract according to the requirements of the system. As soon as the accumulation process diminishes this surplus population to the point of endangering the further production of adequate amounts of surplus value (by raising wages and other advantages of labor), a reaction sets in: accumulation lags, the introduction of labor-saving machinery is quickened, the reserve army is replenished, and the rise in wages is halted. In these ways, Marx maintained the foundations of the capitalist system are protected from the dangers of lessened exploitation. "The law of capitalist accumulation . . . excludes every diminution in the degree of exploitation of labor, and every rise in the price of labor, which could seriously imperil the continual reproduction, on an ever-enlarging scale, of the capitalistic relation." According to Marx, the laborer exists to satisfy the needs of capital; material wealth does not exist to satisfy the need of the laborer to develop into a complete human being.

Consequently, capitalist accumulation demands the replenishment of poverty and misery, through the reserve army, to serve its requirements. But, Marx continued, there are other ways that degradation is created by the process of accumulation. First, accumulation and capitalists' pursuit of ever-larger surplus value add to the geographical concentration of the means of production in industrial urban centers. As Marx and Engels (MEW, Vol. 23) observed, this causes a "heaping together of the laborers, within a given space . . . therefore the swifter capitalistic accumulation, the more miserable are the dwellings of the working people." Second, accumulation of capital tears apart the fabric protecting individual proprietors, craftsmen, and self-sufficient producers, transforming them into a surplus of dependent wage-laborers. Third, it draws wealth and talent from outlying areas into industrial and urban centers, converting the former into backward, stagnant subeconomies or it reduces these outlying areas to specialized suppliers of raw materials for industrial capital, thereby increasing their vulnerability to adverse developments; and it transfers wealth from these areas via the price-market mechanism. Fourth, on an international scale, the capitalist mode has augmented its capital through forceful, market control of weaker areas and has drained surpluses from them into the industrial regions. By these means, wealth and poverty are created together, a unity of conflicting opposites.

The higher the pressure on the labor force, the more instant profit accrues as a critical aspect of capital accumulation. No consideration for tomorrow. No respect for the worker, or the environment. Endless exploitation is required by constant growth, needed for capitalism to survive. Growth and GDP are our Western economic fetishes. They are the gods of our predatory economic system which is not sustainable. In fact, it is suicidal as any logic shows. The Western world today uses natural resources at the rate of about four times what Mother Earth has to offer. And she is very generous. As long as we are hooked to the Western monetary and linear, growth-bound economic system, we are cooked. We are economically powerless and in the hands of the globalized Washington-directed ZAS elite which are marching rapidly toward Full Spectrum Dominance.

Not a conspiracy. There are many internet sites that give you plenty of background information on this and other burning subjects—Global Research, Information Clearing House, *CounterPunch*, VNN, New Eastern Outlook-NEO, to name just a few—for you to form your own ideas and opinion. For example, the FED has just sanctioned Deutsche Bank with 250 million dollars for violating the U.S.-imposed sanction regime, that is, for dealing with such sanctioned countries as Iran, Syria, and Libya. DB is also being probed for "illegal" business with Russia. Earlier, BNP Paribas, France, was fined US$ 8.9 billion and Crédit Agricole US$ 800 million for dealing with "sanctioned" countries. You may say that is peanuts for such banks. That's not the point. The point is: Is it right that they have to follow Washington's dictate?

Why do they not just ignore the fines? Simply because if they don't pay, they would be barred from using the privately owned international transaction clearing system, SWIFT / BIS which is so far the only system for Western monetary transfers. Not paying the fines would put them out of business in the Western world. So, the banks almost immediately acquiesce and pay. That's the extent to which Washington-FED is coercing its fraudulent corrupt system upon the world.

Fortunately, the system is crumbling, as there are alternatives emerging: The Russia–China monetary exchange system, or CIPS (Chinese International Payment System) which is already in use for transactions between Russia and China and also among most BRICS and SCO countries. Hence, it is already accessible for about half the world population, representing about one-third of the globe's economic output. This system is not forced upon any country. Sovereign nations are free to join if and when it suits them.

Remember, the economies of many countries for no fault of theirs still heavily depend on the fraudulent U.S. dollar system. Switching quickly may have damaging consequences, like sanctions, embargos of a country's assets abroad. A slow and gradual transition may be the order of the day.

Nevertheless, it is worth noting that according to the Western international transaction system, *SWIFT*, the Chinese Yuan has become the second largest international trading currency after the U.S. dollar. "Things" are on the move. The prospects for a new and more democratic monetary system are on the horizon.

Refugees or new slaves? Former French President Hollande announced that French labor laws were to be revised. The sacrosanct 35hr/week was being questioned, among other hard-fought-for union gains over the last half a century. This means, future labor contracts could be negotiated directly between workers unions and corporations, without the backing of the government as a regulatory body behind the workers. Hence, deregulating labor laws would be playing directly into the hands of the new arriving labor force in the form of refugees and into the possible future playing field of the TTIP.

Now you compound all these tentacles of destabilization with the nefarious and secretly negotiated TTIP (Transatlantic Trade and Investment Partnership), which all hope would not pass despite Brussels and thanks to the German public which demonstrates ferociously against it. But passing it would imply corporations dictating labor laws, and unemployment in Europe would increase exponentially with good jobs switching to the United States as labor standards are lower there than they are in Europe, with the TTIP-imposed private corporate courts that would have supremacy over national legislation—if that happens, the continent will be further destabilized. Europe ceases to be the way we know it. It may be reduced to just a geographic land mass. Future generations may be enslaved by globalized corporate power not much different from what the wave of refugees will be—if they, the refugees, stay in Europe.

Apropos staying in Europe—Madame Merkel recently negotiated a deal with Turkish President Erdogan, basically telling him, *you keep the refugees locked away in your refugee camps, we will give you 3 billion euros and may reconsider Turkey's membership in the EU.* That situation in itself sounds like a deal made by mafia. Instead of seeking a treaty with untrustworthy terrorists supporting Turkey, Madame Merkel may contemplate talking to Justin Trudeau, Canada's new prime minister. He may want to consider settling the vast, fertile, and unpopulated western Canada with refugees from the Middle East. The 3 billion euros Merkel promised Erdogan could become a joint German–Canada cooperation project to help develop the basic infrastructure to accommodate the new settlers. This could become a huge "win-win" situation: economic development for Canada and well-being for Middle-Eastern migrants chased from their lands by empirical wars.

There may be, after all, a light at the end of the tunnel for Germany and even Europe, for those willing to abandon Washington vassal-hood. And this with regard to the new wave of migration and all its implications, as well as a new approach to national economies, for which the East may offer an alternative.

IMPERIALIST WARS AND INTERVENTIONS FUEL REFUGEE CRISIS IN AFRICA

On March 9, 2017, Thomas Gaist, as quoted in a UNICEF report, said large numbers of persons fleeing war and famine in sub-Saharan Africa are transiting through Libya in a desperate effort to reach Europe. An estimated 80,000 refugees, including 25,000 children, left Libyan ports in an effort to cross the Mediterranean Sea and enter southern Europe last year, with 4,000 of them dying during the crossing.

Another 320 refugees died attempting the crossing during the first two months of 2017 alone, a 300 percent increase from the same period in 2016. Some 16,000 African refugees have crossed from Libya to Italy so far this year, nearly double last year's figure for the same period. Twenty-two refugees from sub-Saharan Africa were killed and 100 wounded during clashes between smugglers along Libya's Mediterranean coastline.

There are 5.5 million Africans currently refugees in other countries, while 11 million Africans are displaced within their home countries, the Internal Displacement Monitoring Center (IDMC) reported in January. The United Nations High Commissioner for Refugees says 18 million people living in sub-Saharan Africa are at risk of becoming refugees in the coming year. The tide of refugees comes predominantly from countries where the United States and its European allies have intervened most heavily. In Africa, just as in the Middle East, decades of imperialist warfare have shattered entire societies and turned large sections of the population into refugees. This is the most important factor underlying the huge exodus of dispossessed people now struggling to reach European shores.

Libya, which was destroyed and plunged into chaos by the 2011 U.S.–NATO war, has become the epicenter of Africa's refugee crisis. Refugee smuggling routes from across sub-Saharan Africa converge on the country, which has a long Mediterranean coastline and virtually no functionary authorities. A growing number of criminal networks and extremist militias specialize in transporting and extracting money from the refugees. While most of Libyan society remains in chaos, a system of detention centers, including for-profit camps run by militia groups, has managed to take hold.

"There are dozens of illegal prisons over which we have no control. There are at least thirteen in Tripoli. They are handled by the powerful armed militias," a Libyan police official told UNICEF, quoted in the organization's report, "A Deadly Journey for Children: The Central Mediterranean Migration Route." In Uganda, 120,000 South Sudanese refugees have crossed the border fleeing war in the past two months (July and August, 2017) alone. Thousands of South Sudanese are fleeing the country every day, the United Nations refugee agency reported this week. The South Sudanese civil war (2013–present), fought out between factions of a regime installed by Washington in 2011, is causing an unprecedented social collapse. The violence is fatally disrupting economic life, causing widespread famine, and has forced 1.5 million to flee the country.

The South Sudanese war is producing "the destruction of all the social fabric in all parts of the country," according to a secret report by the United Nations secretary-general, leaked to the *Washington Post* Monday. The South Sudanese government in Juba is blocking humanitarian aid from reaching areas in need, according to UN humanitarian secretary Stephen O'Brien. January 2017 saw preparations for airstrikes by US F-16 warplanes based in Djibouti, with speculation they could be directed against targets in South Sudan.

The war in northern Nigeria is producing another humanitarian catastrophe that is among the worst in Africa. Five million northern Nigerians are in need of food in the northern provinces of Borno, Gombe, and Adamawa, and 2 million Nigerians may starve in the coming year, UN officials reported Monday. The Nigerian war has involved a steadily growing U.S. role. The Obama administration steadily expanded the U.S. troop presence in neighboring countries. In May 2014, the Obama administration sent 80 U.S. Air Force soldiers to Chad, under the pretext of searching for Nigerian schoolgirls abducted by Boko Haram. In March 2015, a U.S.-backed Chadian army invaded northern Nigeria and seized several towns. In May 2015, the White House authorized direct U.S. military operations in Nigeria. In October 2015, the U.S. Defense Department sent 300 soldiers to Cameroon, along Nigeria's eastern border.

The following November, US AFRICOM General Donald Bolduc told the *New York Times* that the Lake Chad Basin, where Nigeria, Niger, Chad, and Cameroon share borders, is becoming "ground zero for the fight against militant Islam in Africa." Of the 30 million residents of the Lake Chad Basin, 2.6 million are already displaced as a result of military violence, according to the International Organization for Migration.

Although presented as the fault of "radical Islam," Africa's refugee crisis has, in reality, developed out of the crisis of world capitalism and the worldwide eruption of U.S. militarism. The transformation of millions of Africans into homeless refugees, fleeing for their lives, is above all the responsibility of the American ruling class, and the criminal strategic aggressions it has pursued during the past two and a half decades. Prior to the 1990s, the existence of the Soviet Union imposed constraints on U.S. imperialism's efforts to dominate Africa. The end of the USSR removed a political obstacle inhibiting the imperialist powers from pursuing the military conquest of their former colonies. It marked the beginning of a new scramble to re-divide and enslave the countries of Africa, Asia, and Latin America.

For twenty-five years, Washington has sought to violently re-order African society and politics in accordance with the interests of American capitalism. Africa's national elites eagerly adapted to the new situation and have grown rich amidst the spread of war and famine. They have welcomed ever more U.S. and NATO soldiers into Africa and have thrown open their economies for unrestrained exploitation by foreign capital. Today, decades after Africa's "independence" and decolonization, thousands of American troops are permanently stationed in Africa. The United States maintains an elaborate military infrastructure across large areas of the continent, including "forward bases" and "security locations" in Burkina Faso, Cameroon, Central African Republic Chad, Djibouti, Ethiopia, Gabon, Ghana, Kenya, Mali, Niger, Senegal, the Seychelles, Somalia, South Sudan, and Uganda.

"AFRICOM, as a new command, is basically a laboratory for a different kind of warfare and a different way of posturing forces," Oxford Research Group security director Richard Reeve said. "There are a myriad of 'lily pads' or small forward operating bases . . . so you can spread out even a small number of forces over a very large area and concentrate those forces quite quickly when necessary." And, the very week, joint U.S.-African war exercises took place along the Nigerian border, involving thousands of U.S. and Africa soldiers, including forces from Burkina Faso, Tunisia, Cameroon, Mauritania, Morocco, and Chad.

THEORETICAL AND HISTORICAL REPRISE

The purpose of this chapter was to clarify what imperialism is and is not, how it is functioning worldwide currently, and how it impacts vulnerable states with vital natural resources that industries in the West direly need. Imperialism is not just a policy option available to the governments of rich capitalist countries should they choose to use it, though such policy options play an important role in imperialism and in the anti-imperialist struggle. Imperialism is not just a set of conspiracies against poorer countries, hatched in the capitals of the wealthy capitalist ones, though such conspiracies also play a role in shaping imperialism.

Military interventions in other countries, and the vast number of military bases all over the world, are part of imperialism, but only a part. Imperialism is these things but much more. To focus exclusively on specific policies and conspiracies is to run the risk of losing the larger perspective of what imperialism really is, where it is going, how it affects workers not only in poor countries but in rich countries like the United States as well, and most importantly, what we should be doing to combat it.

LENIN'S CHARACTERIZATION OF IMPERIALISM

The best starting point for understanding imperialism is V.I. Lenin's book *Imperialism, the Highest Stage of Capitalism*. Lenin was the most

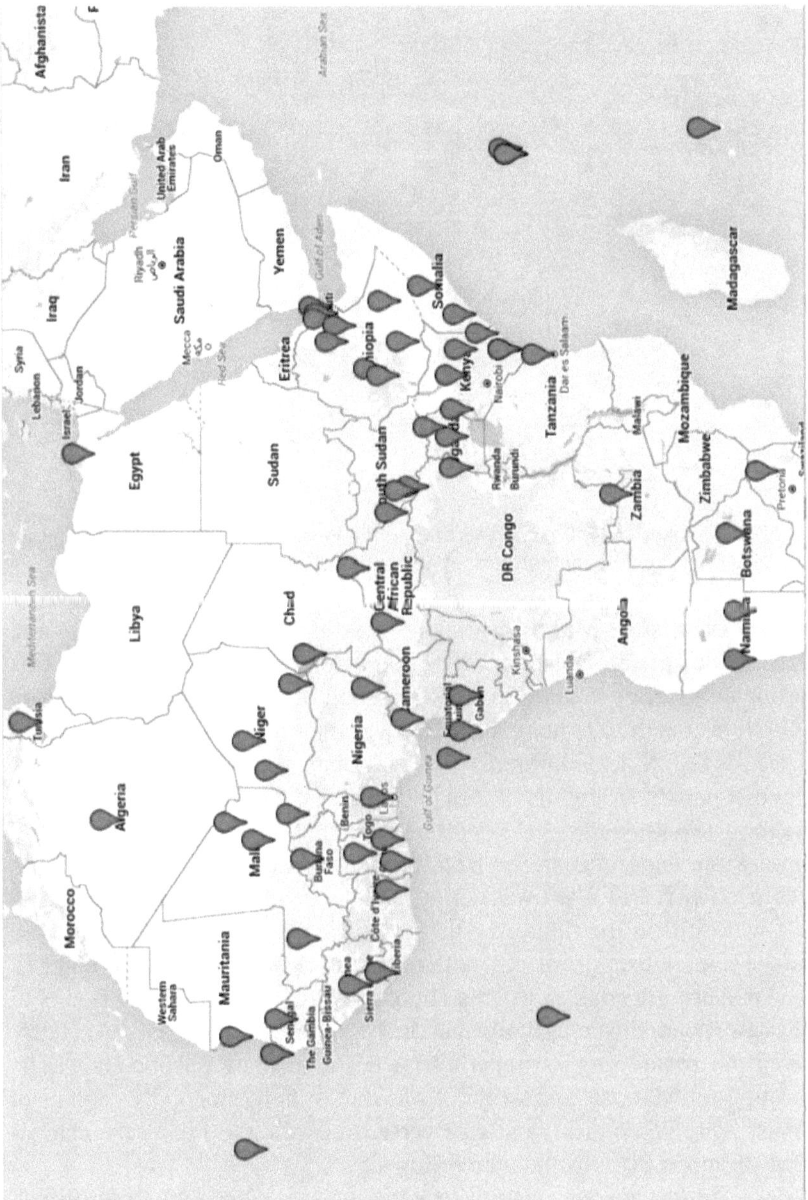

Figure 2.4 U. S. Military Bases in Africa. The Nation Online, November 17, 2015.

Figure 2.5 The American Military Bases around the World (2001–2003). *Source*: http://www.globalpolicy.org/empire/intervention/index.htm.

influential theorist of Marxism after the deaths of Marx and Engels, and also the leader of the Bolshevik Revolution of October 1917. Lenin was the prime minister of revolutionary Russia and then the Soviet Union from 1917 until his death in January 1924. He was instrumental in the creation of the COMINTERN, or Communist International, the coordinating body of communist parties around the world until it was dissolved on the insistence of Stalin in 1943.

Lenin wrote *Imperialism: The Highest Stage of Capitalism* in 1916, while he was in exile. World War I was raging, and the February and October Revolutions were still in the future. Lenin's purpose in writing the book was to locate the imperialism of his day within its historical and economic context. He saw modern imperialism as "the Highest Stage of Capitalism." That is to say, he saw monopolistic capitalism at the beginning of the twentieth century as being the *same thing* as imperialism, not a separate phenomenon. The implication for Marxists and workers was that to fight monopoly capitalism you must fight imperialism, and vice versa. According to Lenin, the characteristics of imperialism include the following:

**"Free trade" among capitalist entities is replaced by world-scale monopolies.*

**Finance capital grows greatly, combines with industrial capital in an increasingly dominant position.*

**There is no longer just the export of goods (e.g., British-made textiles to India) but also the export of capital from the rich capitalist countries to their colonies and to the poorer independent countries (China, Iran, etc.).*

**Transnational monopoly capital based in the rich capitalist countries subordinates the economies of all the poorer countries, not only the predominantly agrarian ones.*

**Imperialism, as the highest stage of capitalism, does not bring about a world of peace and mutual cooperation but rather one of intensified conflict, violence, and war, involving rivalries among major capitalist powers but also (we should add) the violent suppression of resistance in the poorer countries it dominates.*

Imperialism since Lenin

Much of what Lenin wrote in 1916 still holds true today, but there have also been important changes. After the end of World War I, the victorious Entente powers, plus the United States and Japan, continued to increase their domination over the poorer countries of the world. France in Indochina and in North, West, and Central Africa, Britain in South Asia and most of the rest of Africa, Belgium in the Congo, Japan in East Asia, and the United States in the Philippines and much of Latin America, plus the Netherlands in Indonesia promoted the interests of their own monopoly corporations worldwide, creating major economic and social disruptions in every poor country, and resulting in armed rebellions in a number of them.

The October Revolution and the creation of the Union of Soviet Socialist Republics (USSR) and the COMINTERN had a major impact on the dynamics of imperialism and anti-imperialist resistance. Increasingly, the world communist movement became a source not only of ideological inspiration but also of potential material support for colonial and semi-colonial peoples wishing to break out of the stranglehold of imperialism.

The defeat of the Axis in World War II increased the prestige of the USSR and later of the socialist states of Eastern Europe and the People's Republic of China as bulwarks of anti-imperialism. In subsequent years, a number of countries that had been dominated by imperialism, including China, Korea, Cuba, Vietnam, and Laos, were able to embark on a socialist path, in spite of efforts of the imperialist centers to stop them.

As a result of the bankrupting and thus weakening of the European imperialist centers and also Japan by the war, most African, Asian, and Caribbean nations were able, with heroic struggle, to gain political independence in the postwar period. At the same time, the United States stepped into the shoes of the former European colonial powers as the principal state-level bulwark of imperialism.

The end of colonialism by no means meant the end of imperialism. In 1965, Kwame Nkrumah, the president of newly independent Ghana, warned that while the British, French, Dutch, etc. flags no longer flew over the former colonies, the corporations based in the former colonial powers continued to expand their penetration and exploitation in the poorer nations of the world. Nkrumah called this "neo-colonialism," but it was and is simply the continuation of the development of imperialism using other political tools. Since Nkrumah wrote this, it has continued to develop and expand—vastly.

THE COLLAPSE OF EUROPEAN AND SOVIET SOCIALISM AND THE RISE OF NEOLIBERAL IMPERIALISM

We do not have space here to discuss neoliberalism in all its dimensions and its application within rich capitalist countries like our own. Briefly, neoliberalism is the economic theory and practice which stresses so-called free trade (actually domination by transnational monopoly capital), deregulation of the economy (or laissez-faire policies), privatization of public enterprises and services, and austerity. In spite of the use of the word "liberalism," this is a project of the worldwide far right and of monopoly capital. The neoliberal period of imperialism began while the anti-imperialist struggles were going on worldwide and achieving victories in some places. The U.S.-supported military coup d'état in Chile on September 11, 1976, created an opening for U.S. and Chilean neoliberal economic theorists to test out their noxious ideas.

After the collapse of the Soviet Union and the Eastern European socialist states of Poland, Czechoslovakia, Hungary, Romania, Yugoslavia, Bulgaria, Albania, and the German Democratic Republic, a process that began in the late 1980s and was completed by 1991, the neoliberal paradigm of imperial control became by far the dominant one. The ideology of neoliberalism was aggressively pushed by conservative, "liberal," and social democratic parties in power and out of power, and in both wealthy and poor capitalist countries. It even penetrated the thinking of some currents within the communist movement.

In a very short period, poor countries of Africa, Asia, and Latin America, as well as the former European socialist countries found themselves pushed up against the wall. No longer having an alternative source of trade and development aid, they had to rely on trade and economic relationships with the most powerful capitalist states in order to merely survive, let alone to advance to a better future for their people. Those poorer countries that tried to resist the neoliberal pressure found themselves subjected to economic sabotage, destabilization campaigns, and even direct military intervention by the major capitalist powers and their local allies.

As the world developed in a more and more unipolar direction, the United States and other wealthy capitalist countries found their position vis-à-vis the poor countries of Asia, Africa, and Latin America now unchallenged by the socialist bloc. They used various mechanisms to keep those poorer countries dependent and economically subordinate to transnational monopoly capital.

STRUCTURAL ADJUSTMENT PROGRAMS UNDER NEOLIBERAL IMPERIALISM

Among the many mechanisms employed for this purpose were (and are) the "Structural Adjustment" programs which the International Monetary Fund and the World Bank imposed on poor countries that sought their aid in the form of loans and development aid. And of course, the IMF and World Bank were and are entities dominated by the United States and the European Union. As both a class strategy of elite core interests concerned about their falling profits and an imperial strategy to assert additional controls over resources, markets, and capital flows in developing nations, SAP-imposed demands for privatization and deregulation had devastating consequences for numerous countries and their populations.

"Structural adjustment programs," called *the Washington Consensus* in their Western Hemisphere manifestation, involved, in exchange for aid, agreement to policies that basically track the outlines of the overall neoliberal program of "free" trade (meaning allowing transnational monopoly capital to penetrate all aspects of your country's economy), deregulation, privatization, and austerity, as well as monetary policy, sky-high interest rates, and other things.

The reason given for requiring these things in exchange for World Bank and/or IMF support is that they would supposedly encourage the growth of the private sector in the poor country, which the ideology of neoliberalism posits as the requirement for real growth and development. Furthermore, Structural Adjustment is promoted as a method of making sure that poor countries are not locked out of future financial aid, because the budgetary measures promoted are supposed to free up funds to pay off existing debts expeditiously (including by debt restructuring agreements) and thus keeping the poor country's credit-worthiness intact. Socialism having supposedly "failed," this reasoning, which is highly ideological, became dogma, starting before the collapse of the Soviet Union and the Eastern European socialist states and hitting its stride after that process was completed in 1991.

The result for the poorer countries who submitted themselves to "structural adjustment" ranged from unsatisfactory to catastrophic. Far from being able to pull themselves out of poverty, countries that accepted these neoliberal rules found their social safety nets decimated and themselves inundated in unpayable debt. But "structural adjustment" has been a bonanza for transnational capital, especially (but not only) finance capital, whose profits are assured at the expense of some of the poorest people on the planet. In Africa, especially, Structural Adjustment Programs have decimated already rickety health and education systems, leading to the premature deaths of countless children and adults.

Yet, these programs continue to be promoted by the United States and other wealthy capitalist states, whose ruling classes profit mightily from them. By forcing poor countries to concentrate on export of cheap raw materials, or by turning them into low-wage havens for major corporations looking to outsource their production, Structural Adjustment and the neoliberal program overall close off avenues of development that might really be effective in decreasing poverty. Such policies neither create an internal market within the poor country (because they keep the mass of the consuming population too poor) nor do they create the skill sets for more balanced kinds of industrial development (because they starve the educational system of necessary resources). Export of cheap commodities without the development of a manufacturing sector means that the poor country has to pay high prices to import all kinds of finished products, also.

What's not to like? Transnational finance capital is guaranteed high profits from its investments. Monopolistic extractive industries (oil, mining, etc.) are guaranteed access to cheap raw materials with a minimum of environmental and labor regulation by the government of the poor country. U.S. agribusiness profits mightily from being able to sell taxpayer-subsidized grain in Mexico, or rice in Haiti, at prices at which Mexican and Haitian farmers cannot compete and therefore are pushed off the land. All the already wealthy capitalist sectors of the rich countries get wealthier off structural adjustment policies as a central element of neoliberal imperialism.

THE DEBT TRAP

In 2000, as he had on other occasions, then Cuban President Fidel Castro pointed out that the growth of the debt of the poorer countries was so enormous as to be literally unpayable. He called for the cancellation of the entire debt of the poorest countries in the world, its sharp reduction in many other countries, and the abolition of the IMF. Though millions around the world agreed with his assessments and the solutions he proposed, the political conditions did not exist at that time to make headway on those demands. Very few of the leaders of poorer, indebted countries at the time were willing to stand up to pressure from the IMF, the World Bank, the United States, and the other rich capitalist centers and make a decisive break with neoliberalism.

True, various programs have been introduced at the international level to cut or renegotiate these debts since that time. But today, seventeen years later, the unpayable debt problem has only grown greater. And the mere effort to pay it cripples the ability of poor countries to develop their infrastructure, to educate, feed, and provide housing and health care for their people and even maintain a very hardscrabble level of existence for the majority.

Has adherence of poor countries to Structural Adjustment, Washington Consensus neoliberal policies managed to get out of the high levels of debt that these programs were supposed to combat? No, on the contrary in many poor countries, the level of debt has simply increased. Even when in 1995 and on other occasions the International Monetary Fund agreed to major write-offs of existing debt, debt soon piled up to the same or higher levels. In a number of African countries, for example, by 2012, the debt had piled up even higher than before (it is true that rich capitalist countries also pile up debt, but this is offset by the debts owed to them by the poor countries).

The utter failure of the neoliberal/structural adjustment/Washington Consensus approach to deliver anything resembling healthy "development" in the poor countries of Africa, Asia, and Latin America has led to waves of financial and economic crises in many countries. But the rich capitalist countries, the lending institutions, and the ruling classes of the poor countries have returned again and again to the same failed neoliberal formula.

In 1982, Mexico, in the throes of a debt repayment crisis, turned sharply away from its previous import substitution strategy of growth, re-privatized its recently nationalized banks, and began the process of getting on board the neoliberal program full blast. In 1994, shortly following the inception of the neoliberal North American Free Trade Agreement, Mexico underwent another crisis whose impact spread beyond its borders but did not subsequently deviate from neoliberal orthodoxy. Each of these crises had specific characteristics (the one in 1994 involved a run on the Mexican peso because of selectively leaked information about a coming devaluation) but in no case did it cause the Mexican government to move to bolster the social safety net and other protective mechanisms for its most vulnerable citizens. Privatization, austerity, and the opening of the economy to penetration by transnational monopoly capital moved inexorably forward.

There have been too many such crises to enumerate here. There was the "lost decade" Latin America in the 1980s, and then the "lost half-decade" in the second half of the 1990s. Both of these crises had to do with inability to repay debts to international lenders.

As the neoliberal phase of imperialism gained steam from the late 1980s on, all over the world, poor country leaders who had been promoting "socialist" measures found themselves in retreat and knuckling under neoliberal "structural adjustment" policies. Jamaica is just one example. In his first term in power (1972–1980), Prime Minister Michael Manley aligned his country with socialist Cuba, denounced imperialism and tried to build his economy on the basis of nationalizations and the expansion of public education, health care, and other services. Jamaica was promptly subjected to destabilization and sabotage campaigns which had the effect of causing Manley's People's National Party to lose power for a while. Returned to power in 1989, Manley found that he had no choice but to give in to the neoliberal demands of the United States. Manley's second term in power saw Jamaica forced to accept most of the neoliberal package in exchange for foreign investment and aid, which plunged Jamaica deeply into the trap of bottomless debt. This gave transnational monopoly capital and its U.S. government backers unassailable leverage over all the decisions of the Jamaican government. Yet in Jamaica and other poor countries, the level of debt is such that vast proportions of the country's national income are drained off to international finance capital, allowing little to support the needs of the Jamaican people, let alone to finance the balanced development that Jamaica and similar countries so desperately need.

This pattern continued to be repeated in poor country after poor country. And the adoption of neoliberal measures imposed by the IMF, the World Bank, the wealthy capitalist governments, and monopoly capital itself has never pulled any country out of poverty. On the contrary, they sink deeper into debt and poverty. Underdevelopment, seen, I think correctly, by the late Guyanese scholar Walter Rodney as an active process fomented by the wealthy capitalist countries, is intensified, rather than solved, by neoliberal imperialism and the "solutions" it imposes on the poor countries.

There are other dimensions to the trap the poor countries find themselves in. They can fund their people's basic services by selling commodities, or by inviting in foreign investment, or by a combination of both. To rely on the sale of commodities subjects poor countries to fluctuations in the price of those commodities. These can be manipulated by transnational monopoly capital and the rich states whose desire for cheap energy, mining products, and other things is one of the main bases of imperialism. This is the dilemma in which Venezuela finds itself today. Since the election of leftist Hugo Chavez as president in 1998, Venezuela had made great strides in improving the living conditions of its poorest citizens, while maintaining an independent stance toward the United States. But the sudden drop in worldwide oil prices in 2015 has severely damaged these efforts, creating great political instability due to shortages and inflation. The right wing within Venezuela has taken advantage of this situation to make a play for restored power, and the U.S. government has used the situation to try to destabilize Venezuela's "Bolivarian" government by helping the opposition and declaring Venezuela to be a threat to U.S. national security.

The alternative of throwing one's country open to large-scale foreign investment in the hope that this will bring in enough capital to jump start one's economy also has given poor results. This is the strategy that Mexico has followed, accelerated since the beginning of the implementation of the North American Free Trade Agreement (NAFTA) in 1994. Many other countries have adopted this strategy. The trouble with it is that foreign corporations only invest in a poor country on the basis of its government's acceptance of the full neoliberal package of "free" trade, privatization, and austerity. If workers demand wages the foreign corporation does not wish to pay, or if the country's government passes too many regulatory laws, including ones to protect workers' rights and the environment, the foreign corporations decamp to even poorer countries with cheaper labor and weaker environmental regulations.

This state of affairs was the reason why South Africa, immediately after the fall of the apartheid regime and the election of Nelson Mandela as president, could not immediately embark on the planned socialist path and had to make many concessions to neoliberal imperialism. Only already-socialist Cuba was able to resist the massive pressure, but even for Cuba this was extremely difficult.

INSTITUTIONS OF NEOLIBERAL IMPERIALISM

Neoliberal imperialism is maintained through a dense network of national and international institutions which have been created by the wealthier capitalist states and benefit the largest corporations. These include not only the rich capitalist countries' armed forces (and alliances such as NATO) and "security" services (such as the C.I.A. and Britain's MI 6) but also multinational entities involved with economic integration.

In spite of the role of transnational corporations, the role of the state in each rich capitalist country is crucial. International trade entities, including big neoliberal trade pacts, are created and maintained by the participating states, and the more powerful the states involved, the more powerful the impact on the lives of poor countries and their inhabitants.

For example, there is the World Trade Organization (WTO), founded in 1995, which sets the rules for international trade in a way that favors the biggest corporations based in the most powerful capitalist countries. In the 1990s, the United States appealed to the WTO to block the countries of the European Union, and specifically Britain, from favoring Jamaica over U.S.-dominated Central American countries in the purchase of bananas. The United States won this dispute, with the result that Jamaican banana farmers were ruined, because slave-labor-like conditions in Central America's banana plantations, owned by U.S.-based corporations, could produce bananas more cheaply. This horror story is recounted in Stephanie Black's gripping documentary film *Life and Debt.*

Also covered in *Life and Debt* are the roles of the "Bretton Woods" organizations: the International Monetary Fund and the World Bank. These entities, created after World War II for the purpose of stabilizing the world's currencies, have become the source of last resort for poor countries looking for credits and development aid. But such aid is only given if the poor country accepts all or most of the neoliberal package of "free" (meaning monopoly-dominated) trade, austerity, and privatization. To accept these conditions shreds the poor country's social safety net and grows the unpayable national debt.

Recently, an aspect of international trade treaties like NAFTA has been in the spotlight worldwide, namely, the Investor-State Dispute Settlement (ISDS) tribunals. These are corporate-controlled tribunals, established in the context of neoliberal "free" trade treaties, which rule on accusations that governments in treaty nations have enacted laws or policies that infringe on future profits of foreign corporations. The tribunals are not accountable to any laws or courts in the countries affected, and certainly not to the voters. These tribunals serve another mechanism of corporate domination, especially over poorer countries which are in a worse position to pay up, if the tribunals rule against them than the wealthier countries. Since NAFTA came into force on January 1, 1994, numerous cases have been brought against all three countries. Mexico has had to pay out $204 million in such judgments under NAFTA. Canada has had to pay out $160 million and the United States—not a single penny. These may appear to be comparatively trivial amounts, but the real damage is done by inhibiting countries from enacting progressive environmental, public health, labor, and other standards lest they fall afoul of some tribunal's judgment against them. The United States and Canada are wealthy countries and Mexico is a very large one, but smaller and poorer countries can be very seriously affected by these undemocratic infringements on their national sovereignty. In Central America, there are indications that some governments, especially Guatemala, are violently repressing indigenous and environmental activists who are protesting against rapacious Canadian and U.S. mining activities out of fear that concessions to the protestors will cause the governments to be fined under the ISDS mechanisms of the

Dominican Republic-Central America Free Trade Agreement (DR-CAFTA). This dimension of neoliberal imperialism is characterized by savage violence reminiscent of the Opium Wars of the nineteenth century.

Of course, there is U.S. and Western European "foreign aid." But there is little of this, and much of it is channeled through entities in the poor country that promote the whole neoliberal approach. The United States Agency for International Development (USAID), the National Endowment for Democracy, the National Republican Institute, and the National Democratic Institute are credibly accused of this kind of bias. It is clear that poor countries cannot pull themselves out of poverty by means of this kind of "foreign aid."

The U.S. dollar plays an important role as the main reserve currency of the world. This gives the United States a lot of leverage in keeping the poorer countries in line. The hegemony of the dollar has been challenged but it still dominates.

The bond rating agencies—Standard and Poor's, Fitch and Moody's—are not government entities but purely private ones, accountable to nobody but the big financial corporations themselves. Yet they act as gatekeepers for poor countries seeking private credit on the world bond market. To stay on the good side of these entities is very important for poor countries; if they lower the rating of your bonds, your country can be in deep financial trouble. Private equity funds, sometimes called "vulture funds," specialize in finding distressed private or public entities, including entire countries, buying up their debt at bargain basement prices, and then trying to collect the original amount from the countries at the original price, and at a huge profit for themselves. One such company, Elliot Management, has had a drastic effect on the finances of Argentina, the Congo Republic, and Peru. In the Congo Republic, money that was to go for health care had to be diverted to satisfy Elliot's demands.

The big corporations of finance, industry, and retail sales can and do act on their own to enforce the neoliberal rules on the poorer countries, because the sheer scale of their operations sometimes dwarfs the size of the economies of fairly large countries of Asia, Africa, and Latin America. Walmart's revenue in 2010, for example, exceeded the gross domestic product of most countries around the world, including major ones like South Africa and Vietnam. Many see the only way out of all this is for the poor countries to move rapidly toward socialism, but that would have to happen in a very unfavorable international and national context. So the dilemma is likely to continue for a while.

Meanwhile, the world becomes more and more unequal as larger and larger fortunes accumulate in fewer and fewer hands due to the wonders of the twenty-first century neoliberal imperialism. Oxfam recently reported that just eight individuals of the 7½ billion on earth have more wealth than the poorest 50 percent of the world's population.

Instability and Crisis

This seemingly all-powerful world-scale structure of economic and political power is not, however, stable. Neoliberal imperialism, as a world system of integrated economic and political power, is subject to a series of increasingly serious crises. There is the profitability crisis. In order to keep profits up, corporations have to continue to find new sources of income. Many Marxist economists relate this issue to an old problem, the declining rate of profit. Corporations try to do this via new technology and via outsourcing of production to poor countries where they can find cheaper and cheaper labor and sources of raw materials, with fewer regulatory obstacles to profit making. But how long can they keep this up?

There is a crisis of excess financialization. Back in 1916, Lenin pointed out the rapidly increasing degree to which finance capital was becoming dominant over industrial capital. In our own time, this process has metastasized with a galloping increase of financialization of the world's economic life, with currently as much as 40 percent of all capital being in financialized form. The increase in global debt and the growing mobility of capital promote instability and accelerate the spread of crises, as shown by the financial crisis of 2007–2008 which spread rapidly from the United States to Europe and beyond. Capital that is diverted into financial speculation and accumulated wealth does not contribute to increased production, just to the wealth of already wealthy corporations and individuals. Extreme financialization contributes to the already sky-high level of inequality without proportionately increasing production and thus is a factor in recurring crises like the mortgage crisis of 2007–2008.

There is a food self-sufficiency crisis, as, in one poor country after another sees its ability to feed its people dwindle, in part because the actions of transnational corporations take food-producing farmland out of circulation either by reorienting agriculture to export crops or by diverting both land and water supplies to ecologically destructive mining operations. There is a potential world-scale public health crisis. As we saw with the 2015 Ebola Virus epidemic in West Africa, poor countries that lack the infrastructure and public health services to protect their own populations can serve as incubators of epidemics that could threaten people far beyond their borders. There is a worldwide migration crisis, with more people today displaced as economic or political refugees than at any time since World War II. In many rich capitalist countries, this migration crisis is being used by demagogues of the far right to build up their political power. Trump is only one example of this kind of opportunistic antimigrant demagogy.

And, finally, there is the climate change and global warming crisis, the biggest of them all, which is threatening an existential crisis to entire countries and, if not checked, will create economic devastation worldwide. The capitalist mode of production itself requires constant development, not to meet human needs but to meet the needs of capitalist corporations for more and more profits. There is no end to this within capitalism; it is the nature of the beast.

All of these things are either products of the current model of neoliberal capitalist production and distribution or at least exacerbated by it. They are the source of its instability as a world system, but it will not be replaced by something better without action at the base. Resistance to neoliberal imperialism is often thought of as a matter for workers and poor people in the poor countries of the world, but it should and can be a task for us all, even in the wealthy United States, because it affects us all. We must finish with neoliberal imperialism (which is capitalism of the twenty-first century) or it will finish with us.

RESISTANCE TO NEOLIBERAL IMPERIALISM

There have been many working class and grassroots protests against the ravages of neoliberal imperialism and structural adjustment programs specifically, some of them successful. For example, the Water War centered in Cochabamba, Bolivia, not only reversed a government plan to privatize the water supply and drastically drive up the price of water to the poor but also led eventually to a total political shakeup and the coming to power of a left wing, indigenous president, Evo Morales, in January of 2006. Protests against such policies also led to other advances of the "Bolivarian pink tide" electoral movement to the left in Latin American politics, starting with the election of Hugo Chavez as president of Venezuela in 1998. To a greater or lesser extent, the "Bolivarian" and left-center governments of Argentina, Bolivia, Brazil, Chile, Ecuador, Nicaragua, Uruguay, Venezuela, and some smaller states repudiated Structural Adjustment and tried to break away from the controls of neoliberal imperialism overall. They have had mixed success, and the "Bolivarian" project is currently in crisis, essentially because of the difficulty of breaking free from the neoliberal vortex.

To tamp down such protests, the wealthy countries have resorted to destabilization methods and have also propped up authoritarian right-wing governments, like the current ones in Honduras and Guatemala, which are willing to guarantee transnational monopoly capital the conditions for profit making. Yet resistance never ceases either, in spite of many setbacks and defeats.

IMPERIALISM AND WORKERS IN THE UNITED STATES

After Lenin's *Imperialism: The Highest State of Capitalism* was written a hundred years ago, there was considerable discussion in the world communist movement about how workers in the wealthy capitalist countries benefited—or not—from the super-exploitation of the workers in the colonies and semicolonies. This debate has now been superseded by events. It is quite clear that neoliberal, twenty-first-century imperialism harms workers in wealthy capitalist countries like the United States. It does so in a number of ways.

Most obviously, making workers in poor countries like Haiti or Bangladesh even poorer intensifies the tendency of capitalist corporations to move production away from the rich capitalist countries to those poor countries. This undercuts the position of workers in the rich countries while imposing heavier and heavier burdens on the workers in the poor countries. Even if factories do not close in the United States, Japan, or Britain, the mere threat of moving production to low-wage countries exerts a downward pressure on the wages in the former.

A second way in which workers in countries like the United States are harmed by the super-exploitation of workers in the poor countries is by greatly increasing the concentration of wealth in fewer and fewer hands—fewer and bigger monopolistic corporations richer and richer individuals. This increases the power, including the political power, of those corporations and individuals in our own country, with deleterious effects on all aspects of our society, including especially our electoral politics and labor relations. In recent years, U.S. elections have increasingly become matches between candidates who can line up the most corporate and billionaire campaign donors.

Now after the new Trump administration, we see the White House and the cabinet being taken over by tycoons in the oil industry (Exxon), in finance capital (Goldman Sachs), and in other corporate giants. These capitalist entities operate on a world scale, and their wealth and power comes not only from the exploitation of workers in the United States, but from the super-exploitation of workers all over the world, and from other profits they derive from the radical inequality among and within nations. These oligarchs have the power to buy elections, candidates, and officials, rework the laws to maximize their profits, control the media and weaken, and, if they could manage it, destroy labor unions.

A third way in which workers in the United States and other rich capitalist countries are harmed by today's neoliberal imperialism relates to the crises which this phase of capitalism has engendered. The financial, environmental, food security, public health, and other crises are a threat to ordinary people in rich countries as well as poor. The strengthening of tendencies toward military intervention goes hand in hand with the increasing scale and power of the armaments industry, with its close links to the top military brass—another threat to democracy and world peace.

For these reasons, it is essential that workers in the rich countries, in the United States also, find common cause with workers (and poor farmers) in the poor countries. We have the same enemy—twenty-first century neoliberal imperialism, which is the same as the twenty-first century capitalism—and face the same dangers.

One of the things that came out of Lenin's 1916 book was an emphasis in the world communist movement on connecting proletarian internationalism with a struggle against imperialism in all its forms. Today, we prefer to say, "working class internationalism" here in the United States but remember that the last words in the Communist Manifesto of Marx and Engels are "Workers of all nations, unite!" Today, we must add "against neoliberal imperialism."

Since people live, work, vote, and pay taxes here, and because the United States is by far the biggest state entity involved in modern imperialism, workers have a responsibility to convince fellow U.S. workers that it is in their own interests to join hands with other workers around the world to face the common enemy. The ruling class does everything in its power to convince U.S. workers otherwise, to tell them that workers in poorer countries are their "competitors" rather than potential allies. During the period in which the left was repressed, back in the days of Senator Joe McCarthy and the House Committee on Un-American Activities, organized labor's efforts to counter this nationalistic zero-sum propaganda were greatly weakened. However, since that time U.S. organized labor has become more open to a different approach that makes new initiatives in international labor, working class, and all people's solidarity possible. Every effort should be made to develop that solidarity, including especially bringing workers from the United States into direct face-to-face contact with struggling workers in every part of the world. In delegations, visits, conferences, and other contacts between workers of many nations, mutual understanding can be developed and mutual strategies for confronting neoliberal imperialism can be developed and implemented.

DO MIGRANT WORKERS HAVE LEVERAGE OVER NEOLIBERAL POLICIES?

Neoliberal imperialism is modern monopoly capital seen at the level of the entire globalized world. It is not a mere matter of decisions by this or that government in power. In our own country, it is a system supported by the most powerful sectors of both the Republican and the Democratic parties. But this does not mean that workers have no leverage over key policy decisions that affect the ability of workers in every country and worldwide to defend their interests and rights.

Among electoral politicians in Western countries, there are nuances of opinion, and they are also subject to pressure and influence. For example, not every electoral politician, or elected official, is equally keen on military interventions in other countries. So, when George W. Bush started the Iraq War, there was increasing opposition to this policy not only in the country but in Congress as well. There has also been opposition, mostly within some sections of the Democratic Party, to U.S. support for right-wing governments that acquiesce to neoliberal trade regimes imposed on poorer countries. For example, there is a strong current in the House of Representatives that wants to cut off U.S. military and security aid to Honduras (in Central America) because the corrupt right-wing regime in that country has been murdering human rights and environmental activists. The murders have been happening to prop up the people in power in Honduras, but also to guarantee profits for transnational mining corporations which are engaged in aggressive and invasive profit-seeking activities in that country.

Not every Democratic Party politician is strongly tied to all aspects of the neoliberal program, especially as it applies to the internal affairs of this country. Some strongly oppose privatization and austerity, for example, while others are almost as gung-ho as their Republican colleagues on these matters. In the recent elections (November 2016), one of the Democratic Party candidates for nomination, Bernie Sanders, came out very much against a domestic neoliberal approach, and even Hillary Clinton, like Sanders, eventually stated opposition to the neoliberal Transpacific Partnership. The party program of the Democratic Party for 2016 also diverged very much from the neoliberal approach to domestic affairs, reflecting the upsurge of popular support for Sanders and his non-neoliberal proposals such as free university and college tuition for all.

It is easier for electoral politicians to diverge from neoliberal policies on domestic issues than on international ones, because to a large extent mass public opinion, especially of the working class, is opposed to things like privatization and austerity. So, candidates for election and re-election are often in a position to be rewarded for anti-neoliberal and punished for pro-neoliberal attitudes on such matters.

It is harder by far to pressure our politicians to diverge from the neoliberal program at the international level, because most voters do not have a clear understanding of how such global patterns affect their lives and those of their families. This is why it has been possible for the fascist-trending ultra-right to demagogically use issues like international trade and migration to garner votes on the basis of fears of foreign threats—Mr. Trump being exhibit A in this country.

CONCLUSION

Although after the collapse of the Soviet Union and the Eastern European socialist states by the early 1990s, the U.S. imperialists suggested that there would be a so-called peace dividend. Nonetheless, the shareholders only found new ways to embark upon other wars. From Iraq, Afghanistan, Panama, Libya, Syria, Yemen, Sudan, and other geo-political regions, the wars of regime change have proven to be just as deadly and destabilizing as those of the previous century. A recent report by the United Nations Refugee Agency indicated that the number of Internally Displaced Persons (IDPs) and migrants are higher than any period since the conclusion of World War II. It is estimated that well over 50 million people have been dislocated with the largest segment of these populations emanating from the U.S.-instigated wars in Afghanistan, Iraq-Syria, and the Horn of Africa (Somalia, Ethiopia, Eritrea, Djibouti). The world is witnessing the impact of these dislocations in the Mediterranean.

Within the same region where the Atlantic Slave Trade was born, over 2,000 people have died at sea so far during 2015. This problem will not end until those people based in the Western industrialized states build a formidable anti-imperialist and anti-war movement in alliance with the peoples of the oppressed nations to end these modern wars of conquest and dispossession. The impoverishment of the nationally oppressed and working class in Europe and North America cannot be ended until imperialism is destroyed; therefore, global fate is linked with the status and future of the peoples of the world.

The reason is that what is being cast as a "migrant problem" is in fact a problem of imperialist rule and of the capitalist system. There are two root causes of the massive refugee crisis. The first is the growing number of predatory wars being conducted by the imperialist powers and their proxies. Indeed, the United States, backed by its allies, has now been involved in perpetual war since 1991 that has displaced entire populations and destroyed entire societies. The second major factor is the control and economic destruction of the planet by the major capitalist states that have plunged billions of people into abject poverty.

The European powers seek to insulate themselves from the results of the carnage they have wrought through the creation of a "Fortress Europe." At its June emergency summit on refugees, the EU washed its hands in the face of growing public revulsion at the deaths of thousands in the Mediterranean. They refused to set any quotas for countries to take in the increasing numbers of desperate refugees, agreeing to relocate just 40,000 refugees already in Italy and Greece.

Instead, all efforts are concentrated on strengthening border controls. Hungary's southern border marks the edge of the EU's Schengen Zone of passport-free travel. The right-wing government there is building a massive fence along its 109-mile border with Serbia. This week a prime ministerial spokesman said that the fence would be "defended" by thousands of police against "increasingly aggressive" migrants.

New meters-high fortified border fences, miles in length, have been built and strengthened by Greece, Bulgaria, Spain, the United Kingdom at the Channel Tunnel port of Calais, and by other countries. Under conditions in which the global economy is more closely interconnected and more complex than ever before in history, the capitalist system, based on the outmoded division of the planet into antagonistic nation-states and private ownership of the means of production, is creating hell on earth.

In the founding program of the Fourth International, the great revolutionary Leon Trotsky wrote on the eve of World War II, "Before exhausting or drowning mankind in blood, capitalism befouls the world atmosphere with the poisonous vapors of national and race hatred."

These words are as apt today as they were then. As with all the great problems facing humanity, the only rational solution that can prevent tens and hundreds of millions more becoming refugees is the unification of working people internationally in the struggle for a socialist reorganization of economic life. Socialism, a society based on fulfilling human need, not profit, would rationally use and develop the earth's abundant resources to provide a life worth living for everyone.

The connections of global resistance to IMF structural adjustment programs promoted by U.S. economic imperialism may not be readily evident, but the chain reaction is there. Thus, a global thread of economic exploitation binds the multitudes from the Global South to the 99 percent in the United States. Indeed, the fierce cries from the Global South resonate in the shouts propelling the Occupy movement into the streets and onto the path of radical resistance. What Occupy now shares with the Zapatistas and the Water War in Cochabamba is a distrust of and antagonism to the political system and the ruling elites and the expression of class and communal solidarity. Whether Occupy Wall Street, like the Zapatistas, can create autonomous and alternative institutions is still an open question. On the other hand, there is now no question about the growing resistance to global capital.

In pursuance of this goal of resistance and with all its collective strength, the working class must unswervingly defend the democratic rights of refugees and migrants to asylum and their right to live wherever they wish. The international working class, the only revolutionary force on the planet, must be mobilized in order to put an end to the horrors of imperialism and the capitalist warfarist system of accumulation by dispossession. This task requires the building of the International Committee of the Fourth International, the world Trotskyist movement.

NOTES

1. http://www.theguardian.com/world/2015/sep/03/refugee-crisis-syrian-boy-washed-up-on-beach-turkey-trying-to-reach-canada
2. http://www.thestar.com/news/canada/2015/09/04/parties-responses-to-refugee-crisis-show-stark-differences.html
3. http://www.globalresearch.ca/the-refugee-crisis-and-the-genocidal-nature-of-us-nato-interventions/5474296
4. Parenti, Michael. "The Terrorism Trap." Page 56. City Lights Books, San Fransisco, 2002.
5. http://www.globalresearch.ca/libya-ten-things-about-gaddafi-they-dont-want-you-to-know/5414289
6. http://www.infowars.com/us-nato-commander-admits-al-qaeda-linked-to-libyan-rebels/
7. http://www.ibtimes.com/four-years-later-free-syrian-army-has-collapsed-1847116
8. https://www.washingtonpost.com/posteverything/wp/2014/08/18/the-terrorists-fighting-us-now-we-just-finished-training-them/
9. http://www.wnd.com/2014/06/officials-u-s-trained-isis-at-secret-base-in-jordan/
10. http://www.nbcnews.com/storyline/isis-terror/turkish-jets-strike-kurds-iraq-complicating-anti-isis-fight-n398276
11. http://www.commondreams.org/news/2015/03/26/body-count-report-reveals-least-13-million-lives-lost-us-led-war-terror
12. http://www.aljazeera.com/news/2015/04/iom-mediterranean-death-toll-top-30000-2015-150421232012080.html
13. http://www.independent.co.uk/news/world/europe/refugee-beaten-unconscious-as-clashes-continue-with-riot-police-on-greek-island-of-lesbos-10488615.html
14. http://www.commondreams.org/news/2015/08/22/war-refugees-trapped-under-fire-trying-enter-macedonia
15. http://www.theguardian.com/world/2015/jun/16/italy-forcible-removal-eu-mediterranean-migrant-crisis-french-border-refugees
16. https://www.washingtonpost.com/world/europe/refugees-race-into-hungary-as-border-fence-nears-completion/2015/08/25/91f6e9c8-4aac-11e5-9f53-d1e3ddfd0cda_story.html
17. http://www.democracynow.org/2015/1/22/guantanamo_of_the_pacific_australian_asylum
18. http://www.smh.com.au/federal-politics/political-news/nauru-guards-paid-for-sex-with-asylum-seekers-and-filmed-it-social-worker-claims-20150620-ght36i.html

19. http://www.theguardian.com/australia-news/2015/jun/05/former-asylum-seeker-worker-tells-of-abuse-of-two-year-old-children-on-nauru

20. http://www.telegraph.co.uk/news/general-election-2015/politics-blog/11549721/The-900-refugees-dead-in-the-Mediterranean-were-killed-by-British-government-policy.html

REFERENCES

Armiero, M. (2008). Seeing like a protester: Nature, power, and environmental struggles. *Left history* 13 (1). https://lh.journals.yorku.ca/index.php/lh/article/view/24610.

D'Alisa, G., Burgalassi, D., Healy, H., & Walter, M. (2010). Conflict in Campania: Waste emergency or crisis of democracy. *Ecological Economics* 70, 239–249.

De Angelis, M. (1999). Marx's theory of primitive accumulation: A suggested reinterpretation. Manuscript, University of East London. Available at http://homepages.uel.ac.uk/M.DeAngelis/PRIMACCA.htm.

Demaria, F., & D'Alisa, G. (2012). Industrialización de la gestión de los residuos en Delhi (India): ¿cual es el futuro de los recicladores? *Ecologia Politica* 43, 37–46.

Etienne Balibar. (2009). In his "Reflections on Gewalt," Etienne Balibar has discussed the theoretical history of this concept. See, *Historical Materialism* 17 (2009), 99–125, especially the third paragraph.

Harvey, D. (2003). *The New Imperialism*. Oxford: Oxford University Press.

———. (2007). Neoliberalism as creative destruction. *Annals of the American Academy of Political and Social Science* 610, 22–44.

Martínez-Alier, J. (2002). *The Environmentalism of the Poor: A Study of Ecological Conflicts and Valuation*. Cheltenham: Edward Elgar.

Marx, Karl, *Capital* Vol. 1, Section 4.

Marx-Engels-Werke (MEW) Vol. 23, 788.

Petras, J., & Veltmeyer, H. (2007). *Multinationals on Trial: Foreign Investments Matter*. Burlington, Vermont: Ashgate.

Schindler, S., Demaria, F., & Bhushan, S. (2012). Delhi waste conflict. *Economic and Political Weekly* XLVII (42), 18–21.

Chapter 3

Citizenship as Commodity

A Closer Look at Birthright Citizenship

Philip Sutherland

Political membership based upon territoriality (*jus soli*) or upon parentage (*jus sanguinis*) is analogous to what Shachar (2009) called a "complex form of inherited property" (p. 22), and it partially contributes to the valuing of citizenship as a commodity. Commonly known as "birthright citizenship," this way of automatically allocating the goods of citizenship unjustly exacerbates global inequalities and contributes to a misvaluing of citizenship. Birthright citizenship ties the value of citizenship to one's unearned privilege of birth rather than to one's commitment to the political community. And much like other unearned privileges such as those tied to sex or race, people who possess them are often reluctant to share those privileges with others. In this way, these privileges are like property because their "owners" have the right to their exclusive use, and it is that restrictiveness that gives the property much of its value. Citizenship's value is further amplified by the boundary work it does in a society by separating those who truly belong from those who do not. Such division makes certain classes of people ripe for exploitation. Furthermore, such exploitation is combined with resource hoarding that funnels the goods of citizenship to a small number of people. Strict citizenship criteria thus contribute both to exploitation and resource hoarding, the combination of which inevitably will lead to social stratification. Social stratification in turn places some social groups above others in terms of their ability to access money and other social goods.

In order to make the case that citizenship is analogous to other forms of property, I will first discuss briefly the history of birthright citizenship and its different forms. Then, I will place birthright citizenship in the context of Cheryl I. Harris' (1993) article "Whiteness as Property" in which she argued that historically and legally whiteness has acquired many of the characteristics of intangible property even though its similarity to traditional forms of property is often overlooked. Similarly, I will argue that citizenship also shares many of these same properties, especially its value as a "status property." Once I have established that citizen is a valuable property that can be traded in a market, I will then use Shachar (2009) to discuss why we should resist this commodification of citizenship. Citizenship should be considered a good whose value is not reducible to the price it can get on the market. I will then conclude by suggesting that a framework of citizenship based upon active political participation can aid in resisting this commodification by transforming citizenship from unearned property to an earned privilege.

CITIZENSHIP AS COMMODITY

First, we must be clear about what birthright citizenship is. In the United States, birthright citizenship is guaranteed by the Fourteenth Amendment of the Constitution: "All persons born or naturalized in the United States, and subject to the jurisdiction thereof, are citizens of the United States and of the State wherein they reside" (Shacar, 2009, p. 217, n. 16). This was a post-Civil War amendment designed to insure the integration of former slaves into American society. This understanding of citizenship based upon territoriality (*jus soli* means "justice of the soil") has its roots in English common law that recognized the bond of "true and faithful obedience" between a monarch and all subjects born within his domain (Shachar, 2009, p. 114). Under *jus soli*, the *only* factor that determines citizenship is one's place of birth.[1] This principle was famously upheld in the Supreme Court case of *Wong Kim Ark* (1898) which upheld the citizenship of all people born in the United States regardless of the immigration status of their parents (Mendoza, 2017, p. 12). It is important to note that although current U.S. immigration law also confers citizenship to the children of U.S. citizens born abroad, this is not a constitutional right, but a civil right granted by the law. Thus, as opposed to a constitutional right, this transfer of citizenship by blood (*jus sanguinis*) could be repealed in the future by an act of Congress for all subsequent children of citizens born outside the territory of the United States. Although the United States and Canada grant citizenship to any person born within their territories, other countries such as Britain, Ireland, Australia, and New Zealand have combined the principles of *jus soli* and *jus sanguinis* so that the only people granted citizenship automatically are those born within their territories to at least one parent who is also a citizen of that country (Shachar, 2009, p. 116). The United States has moved slightly in this direction with the Child Citizenship Act (2000) which retroactively granted citizenship to foreign children who were adopted by United States citizens (Shachar, 2009, p. 119).

Jus sanguinis, by contrast, relies not upon where a child is born but to whom the child is born. Unlike the common law English tradition that informed *jus soli*, the Roman law tradition is the remote basis for attributing citizenship through familial descent (Shachar, 2009, p. 120). The modern manifestation of familial descent began with the post-French Revolution civil code of 1803 and spread to Continental Europe and beyond to its various colonies. At the time, such attribution of citizenship was considered "radically egalitarian" by linking citizens together and to their nation no matter where they resided (Shachar, 2009, p. 120). However, as Shachar (2009) pointed out, such citizenship on the basis of nationality has tended to reproduce divisions within society based upon ethnic, linguistic, religious, or other grounds (p. 121). When that happens, there is a large problem of underinclusion within the society, as anybody residing within the territory of the nation who is not of the proper familial lineage may have no hope of becoming a full member of the society through the bestowal of citizenship. In this way, *jus sanguinis* can quickly produce second-class citizens and encourage discrimination based upon nationality. Thus, countries such have Germany have since added a *jus soli* component to their immigration restrictions in order to include long-term residents of other nationalities (Shachar, 2009, p. 122).

The value of such citizenship is clear. Even the status of residence within developed countries is extremely valuable to most of the world that live on less than $2 per day. Around the world, governments have tried to use monetary incentives both as a funding mechanism and as a way to incentivize certain kinds of immigrants. In 1990, the United States Congress provided a special immigration visa to foreigners willing to invest $500,000: upon two years of residency and the creation of at least ten jobs, the foreigners would receive a permanent green card along with their families (Sandel, 2012, p. 62). In 2011, in order to boost the high-end housing market after the financial crash, two senators proposed a bill that *The Wall Street Journal* called "Buy House, Get a Visa" (Sandel, 2012, p. 63). Similar programs that offer residency in exchange for money have existed in Canada, Germany, Great Britain, Portugal, Malta, and various island nations in the Caribbean and the Pacific (Shachar, 2017, p. 791). Malta sold its citizenship (and thus also EU membership) beginning in 2013 for the low price of €650,000 (Hildalgo, 2016, p. 223).

These are just some examples of the marketization of more and more spaces of our public life. Markets *seem* like they are value-neutral (Sandel, 2012): "they don't ask whether some ways of valuing goods are higher, or worthier, than others" (p. 14). Sandel (2012) further remarked that markets don't pass judgments, they merely allocate resources using commodities (goods that can be bought and sold in a market) (p. 9). But markets are not value-neutral. They are necessarily built upon inequality and so raise questions of justice and fairness. Why should people not have access to commodities that are beyond their price range? And certain things (and people) are corrupted by being turned into a commodity. Otherwise, we would have no moral qualms about the black markets for children and organs. Instead, opponents of the commodification of human beings such as Sandel (2012) and Shachar (2017) have argued that markets value human life incorrectly. In order to answer these questions, we must make decisions about justice, value, and political arrangements. Unfortunately, as Sandel (2012) pointed out, we have neglected many of these normative questions by drifting from a society that *has* a market economy to a society that *is* a market economy (p. 10). We are so used to markets that we can forget to question the moral commitments that undergird them.

So how is it that citizenship specifically can be bought and sold like property? As the legal scholar Harris (1993) admitted, the "popular usage" of the term "property" applies to tangible "things" that are "owned by persons" (p. 1724). Such possession then entails certain rights with respect to that thing such as rights of use, disposition, alienability (transfer), and the right to exclude others (Harris, 1993, p. 1731). But property does not have to be physical. The courts have recognized intangible property such as jobs, entitlements, contracts, intellectual property, and even professional degrees or licenses (Harris, 1993, pp. 1728, 1733). Additionally, although property traditionally had to be alienable (transferrable), that is no longer the case. For example, government licenses are inalienable and yet also property. Similarly, medical degrees cannot be transferred, but their value can still be contested as marital property (Harris, 1993, pp. 1732–1733). Citizenship fits into this mold of intangible, inalienable property since one cannot transfer his or her citizenship to somebody else; only the state can confer or confiscate citizenship. And since citizenship is something of value on the open market, it is also a commodity. Commodification occurs when enough people value something that can be traded or sold for something else. In the case of citizenship, its value on an open market will be directly tied to contingencies such as the wealth, stability, and reputation of the country to which the citizenship is tied. This is why citizenship in a Caribbean nation is only about $250,000 while in the United States $1,000,000 will only buy a green card (Shachar, 2017, p. 791).

The modern concept of property focuses on its social and functional relations, as Harris (1993) pointed out (p. 1728). Shachar (2009) calls this "new property" (p. 29) after the legal scholar Charles Reich (1964) who identified much of government "largess" as a form of property that is tied to citizenship and residence within the United States (p. 733). These privileges supplied by the government can take the form of money, beneficial regulations and laws, contracts, franchises such as the limiting of taxi medallions in New York city, or licenses (Reich, 1964, p. 734). Unlike traditional forms of wealth such as income from a job or the owning of a house, this governmental "new property" places the citizen in a new social relationship of dependency. Just as such largess can be distributed favorably, so too can it be taken away by administrative fiat. Reich (1964) gives many examples of such governmental property that has been taken away with very little, if any, due process by administrative bureaucracies rather than through a judicial hearing. Whether it is a driver's license or a medical license, such property is treated by the courts as a privilege rather than a right, and thus the government has very little constraint upon its revocation of such privileges. This approach to the new property is summed up by Reich's quotation of one particular court case in New York State: "in accepting charity, the appellant has consented to the provisions of the law under which the charity is bestowed" (Reich, 1964, p. 741). Many forms of property are no longer rights but gifts bestowed at will by the government.

Functionally, property can confer certain privileges and benefits such as possession, use, and disposition. Even though new property granted by the government can be taken away by the government, it also gives the owner exclusive rights to its use to its benefit and to exclude others. Harris (1993) applies this idea of exclusivity to the privileges associated with the possession of whiteness as property that can be used to "fulfill the will and to exercise power" (p. 1734). Here, the focus is not upon whiteness as a physical object that can be bought and sold, but as an ascriptive identity conferred by society that carries with it specific social benefits. Certain privileges in the society of the United States were granted to whiteness that were not granted to people of other races. For example, white people could use certain restrooms, sit at certain tables, sit in certain places, and maintain their freedom from slavery. But there was also a social relationship that was attached to whiteness in American society—its "reputational interest." To be white was to have a certain status in society, which is why Harris (1993) called it a "status property." Courts have ruled that to call a white person "Black" is to defame the person, but the reverse occurrence was not considered defamation because of how American society assigned reputational interests to different races (Harris, 1993, pp. 1735–1736).

Citizenship around the world, but especially in the developed world, is similar to how whiteness was understood at one point in American history. Citizenship grants its possessor specific privileges in the political, economic, and social spheres. Specifically, the citizen of a state has power, access, and influence that other members do not have. Politically, the citizen is given the right to vote, the right to run for political office, the obligation and right to serve on a jury, and the right to all of the state's constitutional protections. Economically, it is much harder for undocumented migrants to find high-paying, skilled work than it is for citizens and documented migrants. And because citizens can vote, there is a level of social influence that non-citizens simply do not possess. In terms of reputation, there are clear parallels with race. For example, there has always been varying degrees of xenophobia in America, and the possession of an American passport smooths the way for travel to much of the rest of the world.

As with race, citizenship possesses a right to exclude others from the same privileges. Harris (1993) wrote that "whiteness became an exclusive club whose membership was closely and grudgingly guarded" (p. 1737). The "one-drop rule" in America made it very easy to be considered Black within the legal system and thus subject to the political, economic, and social inferiority that the status entailed. The value of whiteness was increased because it was restrictive. Like race, the value of citizenship rested upon its restriction to a limited group. Citizenship's value is directly proportional to the number of people with whom I share citizenship. In a liberal democracy, I have much more power, access, and influence when the population is smaller than when it is larger. Citizenship is most like a commodity because its value is directly proportional to its scarcity. It is the relative scarcity of any particular country's citizenship that is a major contributor (but not the only contributor) to the value of citizenship in that country, and it is this value that can be commoditized in an open market because there is a demand for its concomitant privileges. In these ways, citizenship is like the "new property" identified by Charles Reich (1964); however, while it can be conferred at will by the state upon whatever criteria it decides, it cannot be revoked as easily as most other government privileges. In this respect, citizenship is both a privilege, in that it is granted at will by the government but also a right, in that it cannot be arbitrarily taken away.

CITIZENSHIP AS BOUNDARY MARKER

This value to citizenship is further amplified by its function in society as a boundary marker between an "in" and an "out" group. Citizenship is both a "gate-keeper" and an "opportunity-enhancer" (Shachar, 2009, p. 33). The right to exclusion is a gate-keeping function that limits how many people possess this property since the government can pick and choose its citizens. Furthermore, Shachar (2009) wrote, the relatively lucky few who do get to be citizens of a well-off state are then able to take advantage of that state's robust conditions that create greater opportunities for its citizens than exist for citizens in poorer countries: effective government, the rule of law, domestic and international security, stable markets, and public investments in education, arts and culture (p. 37). This is citizenship's "opportunity-enhancing" function.

These traits of citizenship (gate-keeping and opportunity-enhancing) are aspects of "opportunity hoarding." Sociologists such as Douglas Massey (2007) have shown that the mechanism of resource hoarding works together with exploitation to create social stratification: the hierarchical ordering of social groups with respect to their ability to access social goods such as material wealth, social status, or even love (p. 6). Opportunity hoarding occurs when one social group restricts access to a scarce resource. Exploitation occurs when people in one social group possess a resource produced by another social group while simultaneously preventing those in the other social group from realizing the full value of their labor (Massey, 2007, p. 6). These mechanisms distort the effects of the market and create an unequal playing field between social groups. Massey (2007) stated, "depending on how a market is structured and organized institutionally, it can produce more or less inequality and lead to greater or lesser stratification" (p. xvi). Because of these mechanisms, decisions about who becomes citizens contribute directly to the social stratification that perpetuates global inequalities.

Massey (2007) pointed out how these sociological boundary markers interact seamlessly with the psychological phenomenon of "framing" (p. 242). Framing is the work of people to "convince others in society to accept a particular categorization of social reality" (Massey, 2007, p. 242). Massey (2007) pointed out that people are naturally prone to accept frames that give them "advantages and privilege their own access to material, symbolic, and emotional resources" (p. 242). In this way, it is no surprise that such divisions in society seem to form naturally, whether the categories that divide are based upon race, gender, or socioeconomic status. Citizenship allocation is one of the ways society supports the framing that is already done psychologically between those who belong within a particular community and those who do not. Importantly, the social mechanisms that do this kind of boundary work—whether they are laws and regulations are more informal such as gossip, ridicule, and ostracism—tend to perdure through time (Massey, 2007, p. 244). This is because of two other social processes: emulation and adaptation. Emulation is the transfer of stratification mechanisms across social settings so that the boundary differentiation spreads more deeply into the society (Massey, 2007, p. 244–245). For example, with regard to the boundary work accomplished by citizenship, immigration enforcement at the border is one social mechanism that supports the division between those who belong and those who do not, but so do employment laws and political rhetoric. Furthermore, the social process of "adaptation" is the "structuring of individual actions and expectations in ways that assume the continued operation of a particular stratification system" (Massey, 2007, p. 245). As the boundary work of many different social processes becomes integrated into society, such division seems more and more natural, as simply the way societies operate and thus appear beyond critique.

Many authors miss these hidden social mechanisms that contribute to global stratification and inequality. Authors like Michael Walzer (1983) argued that "across a considerable range of the decisions that are made, states are simply free to take in strangers (or not)" (p. 610). For Walzer (1983), there is almost no consideration of justice until after somebody is admitted into the territorial boundaries of the state (one exception is the case of refugees). By only focusing on the moment when one becomes a member of the political community, Walzer (1983) neglected the issues of international justice that are always present in the background between developed and developing countries. The resources of citizenship are continually funneled globally to a minority of people through the social mechanisms of exploitation and resource hoarding. Exploitation occurs when the state takes advantage of, for example, the labor of others without offering them just compensation. This is particularly true with undocumented immigrants whose labor and taxes contribute to the economy but who are not rewarded with the privileges that come along with citizenship in the developed world. Even if these migrants are paid a just wage, the goods of access, influence, and power within the political community are beyond the reach of noncitizens. Similarly, developed nations rely on the cheap goods imported from developing nations, but most of the economic benefit from the trade remains with the citizens of the developed nation. The laborers in developing nations do not get to share in the allocation of resources that go only to citizens of the developed nations.

This view of citizenship as unearned property also offers a unique perspective on the morality of immigration restrictions. When analyzing the morality of different immigration policies, it is helpful to understand what Mendoza (2017) referred to as the "liberty dilemma": the tension inherent in reconciling the commitments to democratic self-determination, individual freedom, and universal equality. Some scholars like Christopher Heath Wellman (2011) have emphasized democratic self-determination and have placed the sovereignty of the state as the primary value. By doing this, they conclude that the state has a right to freedom of association (or not) with those whom it chooses. Universal egalitarians like Michael Blake (2003) who are committed to individual freedom and universal equality have taken a contrary view and asserted that most philosophers fail to justify with nonarbitrary criteria the privileging of citizens over and against noncitizens (Mendoza, 2017, pp. 61–63). Such people have the right to the freedom of emigration and immigration, and some scholars such as Joseph Carens (1987) have argued that this right is absolute, while others such as David Miller (2016) have argued that this right must be balanced against the security, welfare, and cultural concerns of the receiving nation.

But both sides of this debate miss that when citizenship is viewed as a commodity, then there is a temporal element to the immigration debate. Underlying much of the angst about immigration may be a concern about lowering the value of citizenship. Those who are immigrants today may become citizens tomorrow. If immigration is not restricted, the privileges of power, influence, and access afforded to a country's citizens may quickly become diminished in a very short time. As the political winds change, new laws may be enacted granting citizenship to those who have lived within the nation's territory for a long period of time and thus dilute the value of citizen for the other citizens. Even immigrants who enter the country but never become citizens will have children who are citizens and who will compete for jobs and governmental benefits, vote and run for political office.

Again, we see the gate-keeping function and opportunity hoarding of birthright citizenship at play. Limiting automatic citizenship to territoriality (the gate-keeping function) greatly restricts how many people can join the political community by limiting the granting of citizenship through the naturalization process that strictly caps how many people are admitted every year. This gate-keeping restriction works in tandem with strict immigration laws to funnel the opportunities of citizenship toward the citizens and away from foreigners by preventing migrants who come to the United States from remaining in its territory for more than a short period of time. In this way, the opportunity-enhancing function of citizenship (security, economic resources, political access, and influence) remains with those who are already citizens and is not transferred either to the immigrants or to their children over time.

One possible counterargument to this perspective is that if the value of citizenship as a commodity is unnoticed but beneath the surface of the immigration debate, then why do most countries have birthright citizenship laws which automatically transfer such a valuable commodity? It would make much more sense to hoard this commodity and only transfer it to a limited number of worthy people every generation. One answer may be to look at the example of inherited property that gets passed down from one generation to another. Just as many wealthy people do not like the estate tax because they want to pass on their wealth to their children, so too citizens want to pass on their property of citizenship to their children. They want to give their children the privileges that they themselves possessed. There is familial self-interest in preserving the value of that citizenship by limiting citizenship to their heirs.[2] However, as with property inheritance law, the children do nothing to deserve the opportunities and security that citizenship provides. This is an affront both to libertarian theorists who want to tie rewards to merit and to universal egalitarians who see justice as tied to the fair treatment of all people (not just a country's citizens).

Birthright citizenship is thus one more mechanism of resource hoarding, and it is part of the political structure of most countries around the world. Its very ordinariness contributes to its invisibility because it seems so natural. But one must justify why birthright citizenship is a just political arrangement for allocating the goods that accrue to those who possess citizenship as an unearned privilege. Why should certain people possess the political, economic, and social privileges of being born into the political community of a developed country while others are excluded from those same privileges? Birthright citizenship, like the intergenerational transfer of wealth, is an institutionalized mechanism for hoarding the resources conferred by citizenship while excluding others. In the case of the developed world, this exclusion applies most perniciously to the developing world whose citizens lack the wealth, security, and other privileges that accrue to citizens in the global north.

OTHER WAYS OF ALLOCATING CITIZENSHIP

Citizenship as commodity raises important ethical questions. First, are we misvaluing citizenship by reducing it to a monetary amount? There are many goods in life that cannot be equated with what they are worth on an open market. Love, for example, cannot be bought or sold and still remain love. A friendship that is bought is not a true friendship. As Shachar (2017) stated, "citizenship as we know it . . . is comprised of *political* relations; as such, it is expected to both reflect and generate notions of participation, co-governance, risk-sharing, and some measure of solidarity among those constituting the body politic" (p. 805). If this is true, then these benefits are both incommensurable with a dollar value and corrupted when they become commodities. They are not the kinds of things that can be traded for profit and remain what they are. Furthermore, if citizenship is bought and sold, then it is not at all assured that the buyer will be fully engaged with the country as a co-participant, sharing in its governance and its risk, nor living in solidarity with other citizens. If somebody is rich enough to buy citizenship, he or she is probably rich enough to move when the economy slows down or when the political leaders draft their citizens into war. Citizenship as a commodity is a "hollowing out" of what citizenship is because then it is only self-serving and instrumental (Shachar, 2017, p. 805).

The commodification of citizenship in the developed world is also unjust because it is based upon a distorted market that is already biased against much of the rest of the world. As the economist Simon (1986) said in his editorial advocating for the commodification of citizenship, the market allows for "*anybody* in any part of the world the *same* opportunity to buy" an admission visa (p. 55, italics original). But this is clearly false. There are information and knowledge asymmetries across the globe (Shachar, 2009, p. 55). People without access to the media will not even know about the market, and most will not have the money to access it. So, if commodification of citizenship is not the answer to the global inequality exacerbated by citizenship, then is the solution simply to eliminate national citizenship altogether? No, we can eliminate much of the inequality while still preserving the advantages that come with national citizenship such as cultural and ethnic identity, national solidarity, democratic self-determination, a secure legal status, and an enforceable bundle of rights and responsibilities.

One way to address the global inequality that is exacerbated by citizenship is to make some of the goods that accrue to citizenship in the developed world more widely available to citizens of other countries. The developed world could act upon something like John Rawls' difference principle: all social inequality is justified only if it results in the greatest benefit to the least-advantaged members of society (Rawls, 2001, pp. 42–43). This principle would dictate not only greater equality in terms of the economic distribution of wealth, but it also would determine the institution of international policies that promote greater democracy and stability around the world. As other nations gained in wealth and security, their citizens would begin to enjoy roughly the same advantages that citizens of the developed world currently possess.

Such an international "difference principle" could take the form of a "birthright levy," as Shachar (2009) calls it (p. 70). In an analogy to inherited wealth, this "tax" on wealthier countries with birthright citizenship would then be dispersed to poorer countries around the world in an effort to curtail some of the monetary privileges and opportunities that accompany the automatic membership into a developed nation. From average income to life expectancies, there are many ways in which membership in a developed country is generally much better for its citizens than membership in a developing, less-wealthy country. As of 2005, for example, it was estimated that 45 percent of the world's population survived on less than $2 per day (Shachar, 2009, p. 24). Such a levy would serve both to address some of the global inequalities that result from the luck of where one is born while preserving many of citizenship's other nonmonetary advantages such as national affiliation and social cohesiveness: "The challenge for us is to target the injustice of a birthright-transmission system that permits morally arbitrary circumstances of birth to dramatically shape people's life chances while at the same time preserving the collective good of citizenship" (Shachar, 2009, p. 85). The amount of the levy would be whatever sum from all the developed nations was necessary to ensure a "threshold" or basic level of life prospects for those denied membership in the wealthier polities (Shachar, 2009, p. 86).

This birthright levy is a more direct and more practical way to address global inequalities than is only a policy of allowing in more immigrants from poorer parts of the world. First, merely allowing immigrants into a nation does not provide them with the benefits of political participation, access, and power that is granted to citizens. Residents also lack many of the constitutional protections that citizens receive by virtue of their legal status in the United States. Furthermore, the legal status of a resident is always precarious since the government can choose at any time to deport someone who is not a citizen. Citizenship, on the other hand, is irrevocable under most circumstances in the United States. Additionally, it would be impossible to let in enough people to meaningfully reduce global inequalities. Such a response may help temporarily, but it would not directly address the "push" factors responsible for driving people from their homes, and it may even hurt other nations by draining them of their own citizens who possess enough wealth and mobility to emigrate from their home country. As already discussed, opening one's borders to immigration does nothing for the vast majority of the world's population who either do not have the resources to emigrate or who do not possess the information that such emigration is even possible (Shachar, 2009, p. 84).

The birthright model also encourages an individualistic view of citizenship as a good that must be restricted rather than broadly shared. This "rivalrous" perspective sees property as something to be jealously guarded and only surrendered voluntarily (Shachar, 2009, p. 30). This view aligns with the traditional notion in political philosophy of negative liberty. As Mendoza (2017) pointed out, the primary role of the state in a framework of negative liberty is to protect the individual rights bearer from external interference (p. 28). The individualistic view of citizenship privileges self-interest and is most congruent with an understanding of citizenship as a commodity.

Conversely, the communitarian view can be associated with the traditional notion in political philosophy of positive liberty. The primary role of the state in a framework of positive liberty is to enable the citizen to contribute actively to the political life of the community (Mendoza, 2017, p. 28). Property in this philosophical framework is not an end but a means to advance the common good. This communitarian framework views citizens as "partners in a shared political community" (Shachar, 2009, p. 32). A country that conferred citizenship wholly by naturalization rather than birthright citizenship would support the view that citizenship is a public good, like park or road, which benefits all in the community and is the kind of thing that is meant to be shared. Public goods are valuable because they are shared equally, and the entire community has a stake in the resources they provide. This framework better supports a view of citizenship whose value rests not in its right to exclude others but in others' rights not to be excluded (Shachar, 2009, p.

32). The focus is placed upon citizenship as a shared resource rather than a privately reserved good.

Another way, then, to begin to level the global playing field would be the elimination of birthright citizenship altogether. This policy would be more congruent with the contractarian understanding of liberal society since Locke believed that every person is "naturally free" and that one's consent is sufficient to make one "subject to the Laws of any Government" (Locke, 1988, p. 347). Birthright citizenship, like its close cousin the hereditary disposition of wealth, was both foreign and antithetical to the values of America's founders (Shachar, 2009, pp. 38–39). Granted, this policy is not immune to unjust discrimination. The United States has a sordid history of denying citizenship to many different classes of people under birthright citizenship, so there is certainly no guarantee that a naturalization model would not unjustly discriminate as well. But if the proper criteria for citizenship were instituted, then the transferal of citizenship based upon choice and consent would reward those who have proved that they have the desire and the ability to contribute to the political community.

Shachar (2009) called this principle of grounded participation in the political community the principle of *jus nexi* (justice of connection) to distinguish it from *jus soli* and *jus sanguinis* (p. 164). Rather than a principle of birth, this way of allocating membership would be based upon a genuine connection to the political community. Such a model of conferring citizenship would start with the "social fact" of membership in the community as a prerequisite to being considered for full citizenship (Shachar, 2009, p. 165). Thus, *jus nexi* would address both the problem of overinclusion and the problem of underinclusion that can result within a system of birthright citizenship (Shachar, 2009, p. 165). Overinclusion is the problem of including too many people as citizens, even those with little or no connection to their country of citizenship. This can be the case if somebody chooses to leave their home country and live abroad, or if a child is born to American parents (perhaps on a military base) but never sets foot within one of the fifty states. But it is the case of underinclusion that is more relevant to our present-day context. There exist what Shachar (2009) calls "resident stakeholders" who participate meaningfully in the life of the polity but lack the ability to become citizens because they were not born in the territory of the United States (p. 165). This category would include so-called Dreamers (undocumented children brought to the United States when they were very young) as well as long-term residents (documented or undocumented) who have lived within the United States for decades. The moral intuition at work here is that citizenship is justly distributed to those who inhabit a place, share in its risks and rewards, and interact with others in the society (Shachar, 2009, p. 167).

Shachar (2009) gives many examples of how judicial systems and societies are beginning to tie citizenship to grounded participation in the political community. In the United States, there are elements of a *jus nexi* test with regard to conferring citizenship to those born abroad. A child born to American parents abroad only gains citizenship if one of the parents has resided in the territory of the United States before the birth. If one of the parents is not an American citizen, then the rules of residency for the American parent are even stricter (Shachar, 2009, p. 174). So there already seems to be a nascent concern within American citizenship law for making sure that the citizenship that is conferred by birth has a minimal connection to the larger political community, even if that connection is only territorial. The *jus nexi* test is even stronger in the case of deportation waivers that can be granted to residents on the basis of length of stay in the country, family ties, evidence of value and service to the community, employment, and extreme hardship that would befall family members such as small children (Shachar, 2009, p. 177). The recognition of a grounded participation in the larger community also is being recognized in various cities as noncitizens are being given limited rights to vote in local elections. For example, in New York noncitizens can vote in school board elections (Shachar, 2009, p. 229, n. 3).

A model of citizenship conferral based only upon naturalization would raise problems in the United States with the constitutional rights of children before they reached the age of majority and could choose for themselves to become citizens. However, this concern is mitigated by the present reality that the constitutional rights of children are already drastically curtailed. Whether it is their first amendment rights in school or their autonomy as dependents upon their parents, children already do not possess many of the rights that adults take for granted. One of the most important rights to preserve for all residents within the United States would be the rights to due process, protection against unlawful searches, and other rights that pertain to criminal procedure. But again, many of these rights are already granted to those arrested within the United States regardless of their legal status as resident, citizen, or undocumented immigrant. In the end, the legal changes that would need to be made to accommodate the conferral of citizenship only upon willing adults would be minimal, and the costs would be outweighed by a renewed understanding of citizenship as grounded in participation within the political community and based upon one's merits rather than an accident of birth.

Citizenship is a valuable commodity that people rationally desire both to possess and hold onto once they possess it. One reason that citizenship is so valuable in the developed world is because of its scarcity which rests upon the social mechanisms of resource hoarding and exploitation to funnel the goods of citizenship away from most of the rest of the world. At the same time, we can see that buying and selling citizenship misvalues and corrupts the nature of what citizenship is in the first place. Birthright citizenship is one way that resource hoarding occurs and exacerbates global inequality. The elimination of this system would return citizenship to its status as a shared public good that is earned rather than bestowed. It also would make citizenship more widely available to all who wish to immigrate. This availability would contribute to a reduction in global inequality by allocating the goods of citizenship in the developed world to more people.

NOTES

1. The one exception to this is the children of foreign diplomats who are not "subject to the jurisdiction thereof," see Shachar (2007), p. 218, n. 23.
2. Shachar (2009) estimates that Canada and the United States rarely fall below 85–90 percent of their population being native-born citizens rather than naturalized citizens (p. 33).

REFERENCES

Blake, M. (2003). Immigration. In R. G. Frey & C. H. Wellman (Eds.), *A companion to applied ethics* (pp. 224–237). Oxford: Blackwell Publishing.

Carens, J. H. (1987). The case for open borders. *The Review of Politics*, *49*(2), 251–273.

Harris, C. I. (1993). Whiteness as property. *Harvard Law Review*, *106*(8), 1710–1791.

Hidalgo, J. (2016). Selling citizenship: A defence. *Journal of Applied Philosophy*, *33*(3), 223–239. doi: 10.1111/japp.12117.

Locke, J. (1988). *Two treatises of government* (3rd ed.). P. Laslett (Ed.). Cambridge: Cambridge University Press.

Massey, D. (2007). *Categorically unequal: The American stratification system*. New York, NY: Russell Sage Foundation.

Mendoza, J. J. (2017). *The moral and political philosophy of immigration: Liberty, security and equality*. New York, NY: Lexington Books.

Miller, D. (2016). *Strangers in our midst: The political philosophy of immigration*. Cambridge, MA: Harvard University Press.

Rawls, J. (2001). *Justice as fairness: A Restatement*. E. Kelly (Ed.). Cambridge, MA: Belknap Press.

Reich, C. (1964). The new property. *The Yale Law Journal, 73*(5), 733–787.

Sandel, M. (2012). *What money can't buy*. New York, NY: Farrar, Straus and Giroux.

Shachar, A. (2009). *The birthright lottery: Citizenship and global inequality*. Cambridge, MA: Harvard University Press.

Shachar, A. (2017). Citizenship for sale? In A. Shachar, R. Bauböck, I. Bloemraad, & M. Vink (Eds.), *The Oxford handbook of citizenship* (pp. 789–816). Oxford: Oxford University Press.

Simon, J. L. (1986, January 28). Auction the right to be an immigrant. *The New York Times*, p. A25.

Walzer, M. (1983). *Spheres of justice: A defense of pluralism and equality*. New York, NY: Basic Books.

Wellman, C. H., & Cole P. (2011). *Debating the ethics of immigration: Is there a right to exclude?* New York, NY: Oxford University Press.

Chapter 4

Colonialism, Refugees, Migrants, and Human Tragedies

Fonkem Achankeng

Stephen Castles (2004) of the Refugee Studies Center at the University of Oxford made the strong point that it can be misleading to speak of a refugee or forced migration "crisis" in isolation because international migration is an integral part of relationships between societies. As the world watched with horror the thousands of refugees flooding the streets of Europe from postcolonial countries and the astounding numbers that perished at sea or in the desert trying to get to Europe in 2015 alone, and continue to perish, there was an outcry about a "refugee crisis" unlike anything the world had seen since World War II. In the wake of the events, there seemed to be a variety of factors to explain away the crisis. Scholars and observers alike linked "the refugee crisis" to everything, but the legacies of European colonialism and a flawed decolonization process. Some observers, for example, attributed the "crisis" and its attendant disasters to the concept of failed states and failed policies of the international community and the European Union (Miliband, 2015). Others like Ambassador Ford (2015), U.S. Ambassador to Syria from 2011 to 2014, blamed the crisis on President "Assad's brutality" on his people, while Richard and Elizabeth Cheney (2015) saw the crisis as an indictment of President Barack Obama's foreign policy in the Middle East. Yet, others including Richard Angel (2015), NBC Reporter in the Middle East, considered the crisis a result of the U.S. government "unraveling the old order" in the Middle East. This chapter contributes to the different perspectives on the 2015 refugee crisis by suggesting that the "refugee and migrant crisis" was and is an extension and a consequence of the legacies of European colonization and a flawed decolonization process. I focus on the living conditions in many postcolonial countries forcing people to flee as an extension of colonial rule in terms of a colonial inheritance of bad governance, repression, fratricidal wars, and the misery of people in postcolonial societies.

Although some scholars consider colonialism as all but vanished (Herbst, 2000; Roy, 2007), this chapter argues that colonial influences remain an important factor in postcolonial societies long after European colonization is said to have ended. The discussion in this chapter focuses on the legacy of colonialism and the nature of the decolonization process to understand the "refugee crisis" and its human tragedies. The chapter also argues that the people fleeing to Europe and other destinations from war-torn and poverty-ridden home countries in Africa and the Middle East escape from a situation also created for them, their families, and their home countries by colonial legacies in postcolonial states and the nature of the decolonization process. It claims that the global community and above all, many member countries of the European Union ignored the disasters (Muscat, 2015; Psaropoulos, 2016; Moulson, 2016), because the refugees/forced migrants remained for them mere "objects conceived primarily as incomplete or imperfect rather than as peoples of a comprehensibly distinct kind" (Thomas, 1994, p. 71). In view of the indecision of European Union leaders, even after thousands of desperate people drowned trying to reach Europe, the chapter points to the callousness of Europe toward the refugees and the forced migrants, a situation worsened by the Paris terrorist attack of Friday, November 13, 2015. The chapter finally claims that the world certainly misses out on effective conclusions on refugee/migrant issues each time we continuously focus on geopolitics and the indignity of "Others" in refugee and forced migration discourses.

To understand how colonial influences remain an important factor in understanding forced migration from postcolonial countries, this qualitative study analyzed the narratives of fifteen survivors collected purposively from media accounts on the 2015 refugee and migrant crisis. The following two questions guided the inquiry: What circumstances lead people to risk their lives on perilous journeys and how does the decision to flee from postcolonial countries leaving home, possessions, loved ones, and everything individuals knew relate to persisting colonial experiences in those societies? The first question leads us to explore the political and economic realities in postcolonial societies beginning from the decolonization process. In this regard, I premise the discussion on Nicholas Dirks' (1992) affirmation that "colonialism lives on in ways that perhaps we have only begun to recognize." To answer the second question, I build on studies that focus on the colonial past but also recognize the present implications colonialism continues to exert for colonized people (Nicholas Dirks, 1992, Nicholas Thomas, 1994, Bernard Cohn, 1996, and Susanne Mueller, 2014).

In terms of the delimitation, the discussion in this chapter consists of those postcolonial countries experiencing violent conflicts, bad local governance, and misery from which many refugees flee. Consequently, the discussion may not be generalizable to all postcolonial settings as other factors may also contribute to refugee flows from some other postcolonial countries. Furthermore, the discussion focused on the interpretations of one researcher and on data collected from archival material including newspaper articles. The discussion and interpretations in this chapter are thereby limited to this author's exploration of the beliefs, thoughts, feelings, and interpretations of the survivors as reported in the media. Before addressing the two questions, let us first consider the question of refugees and forced migrants as part of the global community.

SUMMARY OF RELEVANT STUDIES ON REFUGEES AND THE GLOBAL COMMUNITY

Refugees flee their home countries out of fear for their lives. The United Nations Refugee Agency reported that some 55 million people were forcibly displaced at the end of 2014. This number did not include the 5.1 million Palestinian refugees nor did the figure include the tens of millions more in poverty who voluntarily seek a better life elsewhere (Onyanga-Omara, 2015). In 2014, Syria overtook Afghanistan as the biggest source of refugees and Somalia came in third place (Onyanga-Omara, 2015). It became a fact that many more people from every corner of the globe were uprooted by war and persecution for the most part. Andrew Geddes (2015), co-director of the University of Sheffield's Migration Research Group, agreed that conflict and persecution remain the key forces driving the mass migration with much of the displacement occurring within countries or to neighboring countries where conflicts are raging. In this regard, if we consider the many conflicts (manifest or latent) and the chaos raging in postcolonial Africa and the Middle East as well as the distressed economic conditions in many of the postcolonial countries, forced migration across the globe from postcolonial societies may be around for a long time.

Stephen Castles has indicated that waves of refugees are nothing new (2004). For him, "Europeans, North Americans, or Australians, who rely on the tabloid press could well believe that their countries were under siege by others." Castles' critique focused on those prominent academics who argued that the world was in the throes of a "global migration crisis" recalling campaigns against Jewish immigrants in Britain in the 1880s, the U.S. Nativist movement of the 1920s, Asian flows into Australia in the 1960s, and more recently, the new wave of migrations experienced at the end of the Cold War. For Castles, "Europeans, North Americans, or Australians who rely on the tabloid press could well believe that their countries were under siege by others." There are some who consider the 2015 "refugee crisis" mainly as being about extreme right-wing parties mobilizing public opinion and racial prejudice across Western Europe to whip up anti-immigrant street protests with some states strengthening border controls (Harris & Jesko, 2015). The November 15, 2015, Paris terrorist attack only made the situation worse. In the United States, a total of twenty-nine governors mainly Republican, issued statements refusing that their states would not allow the federal government to settle the 10,000 refugees the Obama administration planned to bring to the United States. A presidential candidate on the Republican side, Donald J. Trump, promised to "ban all the refugees from entering the United States." In Germany, there were many street protests by PEGIDA, or Patriotic Europeans Against the Islamization of the West, against Angela Merkel's government for opening the borders of Germany to over a million refugees.

Years of war, oppression, and human rights abuses in refugee source countries like Syria, Libya, Eritrea, and Somalia are the main reasons for the mass sea-bound exodus across the Mediterranean. Some other refugee source nations include Egypt, Nigeria, Sierra Leone, Gambia, Guinea, Liberia, Mali, Niger, Somalia, Sudan, Cameroon, etc. Will Moore and Stephen Shellman (2004) have sought to understand the characteristics of the countries that produce large numbers of forced migrants and others that produce none.

One persistent idea is the continuous imagination of citizens of postcolonial nations about life in Europe and elsewhere as a contrast to the lived experiences in the home countries. Such imaginations remain sharpened by the hardships of repression, violent conflicts, and poverty, which continue to force citizens of postcolonial states to flee their home countries, not only to escape war-torn and poverty-ridden conditions in the home countries but also to seek what has become known as "a better life." Writing in the *Washington Post*, Anthony Faiola (2015) reported about "an increasingly deadly exodus to Europe from a host of war-torn poverty-ridden nations of Africa and the Middle East."

COLONIALISM, BAD GOVERNANCE, CONFLICTS, REFUGEES, AND MIGRATION

Analyses critical of colonialism and its forms of knowledge, including those of scholars such as Nicholas Dirks (1992), Nicholas Thomas (1994), and Bernard Cohn (1996), predominantly focus on the colonial past, but they also recognize the present implications of colonialism continues to exert for colonized people in former colonies. I agree with Nicholas Dirks (1992, p. 23) that "colonialism lives on in ways that perhaps we have only begun to recognize." In other words, colonialism is alive because, in the making of postcolonial states, many of the inequalities under colonial rule remained in the present. Writing about the case of postcolonial Kenya, for example,

Susanne Mueller (2014, p. 1) depicted the situation in the following words: "Much has changed since colonialism and independence, but much persists. The act of challenging the state continues to invite intimidation and repression. Earlier legacies continue to haunt the present. The state and its enforcers still use the carrot and the stick to entice or punish their opponents." She added that the state

> controlled both politics and the economy, leaving few avenues of dissent open for its subjugated population. Under colonialism, the government developed a highly authoritarian set of institutions, laws, and tactics designed to administer the country and repress emerging associations opposed to its rule. It was characterized by a centralized administration that was the arm of the executive. (Mueller, 2014, p. 1)

The situation is almost identical in many other postcolonial states of Africa and the Middle East even when the governments of such states profess to be democratic. Indeed, the reality of the postcolonial state is that the colonial experience remains key to understanding the image of things in the postcolonial state as many of the colonial features persist in postcolonial states defined geographically in the first place by the colonial administration, which also maintained a monopoly of force over the territory. The example of the cooperation agreements signed between France and her former colonies on the eve of the independence of the latter may be additional indication that colonialism never ended (Kamga, 2011).

As a concept, colonialism was and continues to be "associated with intrusions, conquest, economic exploitation and the domination of indigenous peoples by European people" (Thomas, 1994, p. 1). As he put it,

> The persistence of neocolonial domination in international and inter-ethnic relations is undeniable. The colonialism that is still with us is expressed in a plethora of crude and more subtle acts, nasty jokes and pervasive inequities, but is perhaps most conspicuous in the frequent military assaults against Third World states or groups within them, acts that aim to preserve spheres of influence, apparent political quiet, and conditions that favor investment. (p.1)

Political repression and nonrespect for human rights in postcolonial nations are synonymous with bad governance, a characteristic feature of colonial rule.

Many scholars consider colonialism as long ended and that the current woes of postcolonial societies remain the exclusive fault of such postcolonial societies. Such scholars, including Herbst (2000), on Africa, and Roy (2007), on India, contend that colonial rule plays only a minor part of what happens in postcolonial societies. De-emphasizing the impact of colonialism on institutions and state formation in Africa, Herbst argued, ". . . it was impossible for Europeans to have changed 'everything' in the few decades they ruled Africa" (p. 4). Although it is true that formal colonialism was limited in Africa, Latin America, the Middle East, and Southeast Asia, there is a large amount of historical and other evidence that European influence remained important in those parts of the world long after colonization. The cooperation agreements signed on the eve of independence provide enough evidence to support this assertion.

In addition, scholars, including Said (1978); David Prochaska (1990); Sandra Marker (2003); Nicholas Thomas (1994); Escobar (1995); Engerman and Sokoloff (1997, 2000); La Porta et al. (1998a, 1998b); Acemoglu, Johnson and Robinson (2001, 2002); Banerjee and Iyer (2003); Berkowitz et al. (2004); Sharp (2008); and Susanne Mueller (2014), for example, have argued that the impact of European colonialism was not limited to a few decades of colonial rule and that colonial rule has had very long-term consequences on postcolonial societies. For Susanne Mueller (2014) in her work in postcolonial Kenya, the repercussions of colonialism continue to be present in the postcolonial world. Like Mueller, other scholars contend that the idea remains that images of colonialism persist in the present. Concluding his book, *Colonialism's Culture*, Nicholas Thomas (1994) expressed the viewpoint that "[I]f we had transcended colonial images and narratives more comprehensively, perhaps we would not need to discuss them at all—but there is no emptiness at present in which such a confident silence can be heard" (p. 195). In Africa and Asia, in particular, these problems were inherited in postcolonial societies. Article 4 of the African Union Constitutive Act, for example, provides that all African countries would respect the boundaries inherited from colonialism. This is only one example of the colonial presence in postcolonial Africa, and one that remains very problematic as with many inter-state and intra-state conflicts that have resulted in refugee flows. Eritrea, South Sudan, Western Sahara, and Cameroon are a few examples in Africa producing many forced migrants resulting from conflict, violence, and political repression.

Political repression in postcolonial settings of Africa and the Middle East goes back to the colonial rule and its legacy. Colonial rule was the antithesis of democracy, because it was premised on the usurpation of the fundamental right of self-determination. As Okoyo (1977) put it, "whatever legitimacy colonialism possessed was derived not from any set of agreed rules or consensus, but from the monopoly of the means of coercion and violence, and by its divide-and-rule strategies aimed at intensifying the cleavages (class, tribal, religious) inherent in the social structure and prolonging its rule." Colonial rule never raised the issue of good government. The only issue was power and that remained the tradition of politics the new leaders in Africa and the Middle East took to independence in their respective nations. The new leaders of Africa and the Middle East did not only retain all state power but also continued to reinforce it, a situation which generated many conflicts producing refugees and forced migrants. Claude Ake (1985, 1213) remarked that "because many leaders in postcolonial states were insecure when they inherited power, they held tenaciously to the idea of the ruler's exclusive claim to power." The Assad family in Syria and the many years of civil war in that country provide a good example.

Research on specific aspects of, or institutions created by, colonial rule indicates the lasting effects on the people and nations the colonial masters had left after World War II and especially following the United Nations Declaration on Independence for Colonial Countries and Peoples (UNGA Resolution 1514 of December 1960). Engerman and Sokoloff (1997, 2000) and Acemoglu, Johnson, and Robinson (2001, 2002) have argued that property rights institutions created by colonial powers have had very long-term consequences in postcolonial societies. La Porta et al. (1998a, 1998b) and Berkowitz et al. (2004) also focused on the long-term effects of legal systems put in place by different colonial powers, while Banerjee and Iyer (2003) in their study of the role of British colonial land tenure systems in India revealed the lingering of the culture of colonialism in former European colonies.

As Gene Sharp (2008) stated, "[E]uropeans renamed, re-defined, and thereby controlled peoples, places, and things, into imperial colonies." The societal effects of colonialism—the imposition of a subjugating colonial identity—were harmful to the mental health of the native peoples who were subjugated into colonies. Fanon (1963), a foremost theoretician of colonialism, also wrote that the ideological essence of colonialism is the systematic denial of "all attributes of the humanity" of the colonized people. Living conditions in many postcolonial countries remain to this day an extension of colonial rule, in that in many of the former colonies the people and the places were renamed, redefined, and continue to be controlled. In many such societies, repression, bad governance, fratricidal wars, insecurity, and misery for the local people continue to force out many people from the postcolonial countries.

Colonialism was never about good governance. It was always about dominance, repression, and exploitation. Consequently, the new governments that succeeded colonial rule were just as repressive and exploitative of the people as the colonial situations they inherited. There is no doubt that there has been mass disillusion on the part of the people in postcolonial states in terms of the social, economic, and political lives of the people. Evidence of this situation is abundant in the literature on the political and economic tumults of postcolonial countries. As a result, many scholars have considered the numerous conflicts in postcolonial Africa and the Middle East as a natural consequence of the colonial rule. Some of the scholars include Gunter (2015), Ochonou (2015); Fonkem (2013); Mokwugo Okoyo (1977); Bonny Duala-M'Bedy

(1984); Claude Ake (1985); and Herman J. Cohen (1995). Okoyo (1977, p. 93) for example, posited that "political instability is rooted in the very structure of society and, for most new countries, in the colonial past." Ochonu (2015, p. xxi) also indicated that the troubled nations and home countries of the refugees "were founded on colonial logics without thc deliberative input of their constituent peoples."

In the case of Africa, Okoyo stated, "Africa's post-colonial present can be said to have been fashioned for Africa by Africa's colonial past." Subscribing to this viewpoint, Ambassador Herman J. Cohen (1995) asserted that "the sources and consequences of Africa's internal conflicts have their roots in colonialism, the subsequent processes of decolonization and state formation, and the ensuing crisis of nation building." For Cohen, the colonial state was fraught with contradictions. As he puts it, "The modern African state was created by colonial powers out of ethnic and regional diversities, and rendered conflictual by gross inequities in power relations, and in the uneven distribution of national wealth and development opportunities." Gunter and Bengio have advanced similar arguments in respect of the Middle East. In other words, the basis had been created for many of the conflicts that we experience in postindependence Africa and the Middle East producing many refugee flows. Duala-M'bedy (1984, p. 10) subscribed to the same viewpoint, when he asserted that "the problems being experienced by postcolonial states are based on our colonial experience."

Cohen (1995) also indicted the decolonization process in the many conflicts experienced by postcolonial countries. In Cohen's view, "the contradictions of the colonial state were passed on to the independent states through a flawed process of decolonization." He argued, that "conflict, recurring instability, and bad governance in Zaire (RDC), Rwanda, and Burundi can be traced back to the hasty and unprepared granting of independence by Belgium in 1960." He also considered the wars in Angola and Mozambique as arising out of "panic decolonization from a revolutionary and chaotic Portugal in 1974–75." Regarding the war in Sudan, Cohen traced it to "the manner in which the Anglo-Egyptian administration brought the North and the South together, but kept them apart under a separatist policy for most of the Condominium rule, and then left them in a centralized unitary state without constitutional guarantees for the disadvantaged South." In the case of Cameroon, the United Kingdom failed to nurture British Cameroons, an administered territory to statehood. Instead, the United Kingdom lobbied the United Nations to hastily lump together British Cameroons and the French-speaking Republic of Cameroon without constitutional guarantees for the disadvantaged former British Cameroons. While colonial decisions did not put together disparate peoples, they separated other peoples arbitrarily into different states. The more than 40 million Kurds are a striking case study, as their populations are found in four different countries today: Turkey, Syria, Iraq, and Iran. The culture of colonialism that always sought to perpetrate the control and exploitation of others put together and sustained states irrespective of the different nationalisms that may exist within such state boundaries.

The arbitrary bordering and clustering of different nations and groups in Africa first at the 1884 Berlin Conference into colonies, and after World War I and World War II into states was an attempt at making and building new states modeled after European experiences from Westphalia in 1648. Part of the vision of this chapter is the argument that the making of new states from the colonial "lumping together of disparate peoples" (Axel, 2001, p. 210) or separation of other groups like the Kurds was a flawed idea. It was also a recipe for the conflicts in such states. The different struggles to overcome such arrangements as is the case in postcolonial Cameroon remain intractable and will continue to produce refugee flows.

Cohen's assertion, discussed above, has an interesting implication for understanding the various conflicts and the fleeing of people from their home countries to Europe and other destinations. If the causes and consequences of the conflicts have their roots in colonialism, the processes of decolonization and state formation, and the ensuing crisis of nation-building, then any attempt to understand the 2015 refugee and migrant crisis must include the colonial legacy in postcolonial societies. Discussion of "internal or national governance" in postcolonial states cannot therefore exclude the nature of their independence, the state structure, and political leadership inherited from colonialism and sustained by colonial arrangements in the postcolonial countries. Former colonial masters were not in search of good leaders. The concern of the colonial powers at independence and decades after "independence" for the most part was to hand power to a group of cronies. The mission of such cronies was always not to "govern their people well," but to protect the economic and security interests of the metropole as demonstrated in the military and economic pacts concluded by French-speaking African leaders with France at independence as mentioned earlier. Similarly, the considerations of the United States in Iraq pre- and post-Saddam Hussein or Afghanistan were always more about the interests of the United States than about the respective peoples of Iraq and Afghanistan. It was not uncommon to hear the political right in the United States blame the Obama administration for overseeing the demise of the Egyptian dictator, Mubarak, in the wake of the increasingly degenerating security situation in the Middle East. Although a dictator, many among the political elite in the United States were always ready to wink as long as Mubarak was used to maintain the political balance in the Middle East. The same holds true for Western Sahara being part of Morocco against the wishes and aspirations of the Saharawi people. Colonial powers made these decisions to bolster their national interests and those of their allies, with no consideration for the interests of the indigenous people, the interests of peace and justice, and often, with no consideration for international law. As Zunes and Mundy (2010, p. xxii) pointed out in the case of Western Sahara, supported by the United States and France, "Morocco's acquisition of Western Sahara in 1975 added significant resources of revenue to state coffers." The colonial-style top-down arrangements employed in state-making have accounted for the bulk of the violent and latent conflicts experienced in postcolonial societies and elsewhere around the globe.

Another perspective from colonial studies indicates that colonial powers insisted on this arrangement first because colonizers considered it would facilitate postcolonial rule and access to economic resources, and second, because of the colonial disdain of colonized peoples and their cultures. There are reports of the inhumane treatment, over the years, of colonial people in distress by European officials. Jack Schenker (2011) recounted how passengers on a sinking boat made contact with a military helicopter and a warship that would not attempt to rescue them. The story goes that the passengers used the boat's satellite phone to call a priest, Father Zerai, their contact in Rome. Father Zerai in turn alerted the Italian Coast Guard to the boat's distress. Survivors reported that they were seen by a helicopter with the word "ARMY" spelled out on its side and that the helicopter lowered some water and biscuits into the boat but left without a trace. Shenker also mentions how the passengers tried to communicate with a military plane that was taking off from a nearby aircraft carrier, but it never tried to rescue the passengers even after they held two starving babies over their heads. *The Guardian* newspaper later ascertained that the aircraft carrier was likely to have been the French ship, Charles de Gaulle, which was operating in the Mediterranean on those dates (Shenker, 2011). The story identified the passengers as Ethiopians, Nigerians, Sudanese, Ghanaians, and Eritreans of both sexes and varying ages.

Let us briefly consider the basis of postcolonial nations or states. In Africa and the Middle East, the concept of state or nation is based on the colonial past of those regions. The nations and states of the postcolonial world are a creation of European colonial powers, which partitioned entire continents according to their whims and economic interests. The European concept of state had a strong influence on African and Middle Eastern countries and that concept of state led to the drawing up of arbitrary borders. Eurocentric thinking, reinforced by technological and scientific achievements in the West, continues to be very present in the former colonies. This is why citizens of the war-torn and poverty-ridden postcolonial nations yearn to flee to Europe in spite of the risks involved in crossing the Sahara Desert and the Mediterranean Sea (Faiola, 2015; Moulson, 2016) to get to perceived freedom and safety in Europe and a better life for themselves and their families.

DISASTERS ON MIGRANT ROUTES

It is important to note that forced migration figures stood at more than 20 million in 2003 (UNCHR, 2004; Weiner, 1995; Loescher & Loescher, 1994; Zolberg, Suhrke, & Aguayo, 1989). Over 7,000 of these people perished trying to get to Europe from former colonies of Africa and the Middle East. In 2011, the most severe incident took place in April, when more than 220 Somali, Eritrean, and Ivoirians drowned as their boat capsized 39 miles south of Lampedusa via Sicily (Fundamental Rights Agency, 2013, p. 31).

According to estimates by the United Nations High Commissioner for Refugees (UNHCR), 1,500 people lost their lives in the Mediterranean in 2011 alone, and "although precise numbers are notoriously difficult to establish, thousands more died since then in maritime accidents or of suffocation, hunger, and thirst on overcrowded boats" (Follis, 2015, pp. 41–62). In the wake of the 2015 crisis, many observers wondered why individuals would take the risk involved in the hazardous journey of crossing the Sahara Desert and the Mediterranean Sea especially considering the perilous nature of the venture as illustrated by the iconic picture of the little boy washed off the coast of Turkey (Parkinson, 2015). According to Al Jazeera's Hoda Abdel-Hamid (2015) "more than 10,000 migrants were plucked from seas between Italy and Libya in one week." News agencies including the *BBC, Washington Post, Newsweek, CNN, and Al Jazeera* reported the following disaster figures between February and April 2015 alone: On April 19, 2015, 700 were at risk of drowning off the coast of Malta; April 13, 2015, at least 400 dead and 145 survivors from a boat capsized off the Italian coast of Lampedusa; February 2015, 29 dead 300 missing as four boats began taking in water off the coast of Libya; 3,400+ drowned/missing at sea in 2014 (Chughtai, 2015). By April 2015, it was reported that "Up to 1,500 migrants were feared to have drowned in 2015 alone." The misfortune is that many hundred deaths were reported between 2015 and 2016. All the disasters came to be symbolized by the iconic photograph of a three-year-old boy washed ashore in Turkey, which exemplified the thousands of lives lost in the crisis in the Sahara Desert or in the Mediterranean Sea escaping from conditions in postcolonial societies.

In their study of forced migration from 1952 to 1995, Will Moore and Stephen Shellman (2004) tried to address the question why people would "abandon their homes in favor of an uncertain life elsewhere" with the short answer that "violence" was the explanatory variable. Escaping war, poverty, and repression, some of the 2015 refugees traveled for weeks to reach Libya—only to end up in detention centers after coastguards intercepted the boats the refugees hoped would take them to Europe.

On April 18, 2015, for example, news reports across the globe revealed the deaths by drowning in the Mediterranean Sea, of some 900 migrants, attempting to get to Europe (Wescott, 2015; Abdel-Hamid, 2015; Faiola, 2015; Chughtai, 2015). According to Alia Chughtai (2015), "Thousands of desperate people risk their lives crossing the Mediterranean to reach Italy. Many never make it." The UN's refugee agency, the UNHCR, believed that the April 18, 2015, incident was the deadliest on record. What probably alarmed the world the most at this time was the huge number of migrants in Europe and those who perished at sea. The International Organization for Migration (IOM) warned that, based on current figures, the migrant death toll in the Mediterranean could top 30,000 in 2015. IOM sources believed 1,727 migrants died in the first four months of 2015 trying to make the journey to Europe from North Africa, compared to just 56 at the same time in 2014. In all, The UNCHR estimated that there were 60 million refugees in 2015 and that estimate gave rise to the concept of the biggest "refugee crisis" since World War II.

METHOD

This qualitative study employed the phenomenological approach. Phenomenology is that form of interpretation that says that human consciousness is the key to understanding the world (Shank, 2006, p. 134). Phenomenological studies are interested in seeing how people interpret their worlds and how we can in turn interpret their interpretations. Researchers using the phenomenological approach seek to locate their participants through purposive sampling. In this sampling method, the researcher looks for people who have something important and informed to say on the topic of research. Once the researcher finds a few carefully selected participants, s/he expands the sample as he or she seeks to explore their beliefs and feelings toward the target concepts (Shank, 2006, p. 132). To use this method correctly, Groenewald (2004) recommended a process in which the researcher bracketed his or her own thoughts and interpretations as he or she pays particular attention to unique utterances and points of view.

This chapter analyzed studies on refugees in a global context, colonialism, and its legacies in postcolonial societies as well as media reports of the narratives of survivors of refugee route disasters collected through interviews in the media. In the analysis, I paid particular attention to what the survivors narrated in the media interviews I collected. I also took care of the issues reported, the frequency of the viewpoints expressed by the survivors, and the manner of statement as reported in the media to make sense of the beliefs and feelings of the survivors toward the circumstances that led them to risk their lives on perilous journeys and the decision to flee from their home countries leaving all behind.

DISCUSSION

Although in stating that "colonialism lives on in ways that perhaps we have only begun to recognize," Nicholas Dirks (1992) did not explicitly discuss the lingering colonial experiences in terms of refugee and forced migration flows from postcolonial societies, the discussion in this chapter suggests that there is a need to think with Dirks, beyond Dirks, and against Dirks. This suggestion is necessary to better account for the varied experiences of people in postcolonial societies generating massive refugee flows as the world witnessed in 2015 and on.

The data reproduced below illustrate the experiences that survivors draw on to make meaning of their lives. In the analysis that follows, I explore the narratives of survivors on the persisting colonial-type conditions in their home countries to spotlight the lingering experiences in the postcolonial societies forcing citizens to flee at the risk of their lives. The basis of my discussion here is Marita Eastmond's (2007) work on narratives in forced migration research. As theorized by Eastmond (2007, p. 250), "narratives can help us explore the radical discontinuities in the lives of displaced people, as well as the struggles to make sense of disruptive change." Some of the themes for this discussion are persisting colonial legacies; determination to flee; disasters of refugee routes; lamentations on the decolonization process; what survivors want Europe to know; and European and Western responses to the crisis.

PERSISTING COLONIAL LEGACIES

The narratives on persisting colonial legacies did not only answer the research question but also more specifically addressed the political and economic conditions in the home countries forcing out the refugees. In the experience of the refugee, they narrated that colonial control over them simply transferred from European to new local masters who were their neighbors and who continued the colonial traditions of bad governance, violence, and repression. As one survivor put it,

> *The métropole and the colony are right here at our doorstep. The empire is now people who want us to consider them as our brothers and sisters. They see us as a colony and a farmland to exploit in true colonial tradition. They have never considered us part of them. And true enough, we are different. We have every right to stand up for what is ours rather than staying enslaved in a foreign country . . . where we cannot move an inch without the police and the military harassing us and where we cannot express our political ideas without being arrested and incarcerated. (Emphasis added)*

To understand the persistence of the colonial legacy in postcolonial settings, the work of Susanne Mueller (2014) on postcolonial Kenya is very instructive. According to Mueller (2014, p. 1), "Much has changed since colonialism and independence, but much persists." The Kenyan example is very similar to that of many African countries where "Under colonialism, the government developed a highly authoritarian set of institutions, laws, and tactics designed to administer the country and repress emerging associations opposed to its rule." These conditions remain in postcolonial states and continue to generate refugee flows.

DETERMINATION TO FLEE WHATEVER THE OUTCOME OR RISKS

Explaining the risks the refugees had taken, another refugee said, *"The risk leaving is great, but it is even more risky to stay."* Mohamed Hussein, a twenty-one-year-old philosophy student from Aleppo, Syria, who looked exhausted, approached the first-aid station with a group of his friends. *"We were arrested in Hungary and held for three days,"* he said. *"We were mistreated. We were hurt."* But, he said, *"I'm here now, and that is the past. I can't think about yesterday, because it hurts. I want to think about tomorrow, and the day after."*

Many survivors of the different perilous trips include refugees from Nigeria, The Gambia, Sudan, Libya, Eritrea, Ethiopia, Cameroon, Western Sahara, Yemen, Syria, and Iraq. Survivors narrated their stories and also responded to interviews with the news media and security officials after following disasters such as the drowning of as many as 800 people in Lampedusa in just one day. Judie, a widow from Eritrea, aged twenty-five, said she first went to Khartoum and was smuggled into Libya from there. She was caught while crossing the desert in the south of the country. She said, *"yes, it's dangerous. I know I can die. If I get a chance to live, OK, better. But if I die, that's also OK. I cannot go anywhere else to change my life. I can't change it in my country and that is why I want to leave."*

DISASTERS ON REFUGEE ROUTES

Disasters on refugee routes were/are frequent in the narratives of survivors. Notwithstanding such disasters, the survivors were determined to continue to look forward to the future despite the traumas they went through losing loved ones or seeing fellow refugees perish at sea or in the desert. In one interview, survivors told authorities that between 700 and 950 people were on board a boat from the coast of Libya and that *"we were only the lucky ones who survived after the overloaded boat overturned in the high sea"* . . . *"many of the passengers drowned including young children."* Another migrant from Bangladesh told Italian prosecutors that *"plenty"* of them had been locked in a hole by smugglers. Stories of these kinds of disasters were not only regular in media reports but also in the narratives of survivors collected for analysis.

Although IOM Director General, William Lacy Swing, advocated for a need to reinstate a program on the scale of Mare Nostrum as a response to refugee disasters stating, "All of us, especially the E.U. and the world's powers, can no longer sit on the sidelines watching while these tragedies unfold in slow motion," EU and indeed Western leaders continued over the years to do little more than deplore the rising death toll and to mark tragedies with moments of silence and wreaths instead of fundamental action.

LAMENTATIONS ON THE DECOLONIZATION FLAWS IN REFUGEE FLOWS

The data under the theme of decolonization flaws was very recurrent in the narratives of some of the refugees. Such narratives were driven by the belief of the survivors that their woes originated from the fact that they were fleeing from countries, which were in fact not their countries as perceived by many in the global community. As they identified in the media interviews, they originated from countries including Eritrea, Syria, Iraq, Cameroon, Bangladesh, and others. These refugees believed the homeland was misrepresented by the history of colonialism and its effects on the countries in which they lived. For such refugees, the unease of the past is present in their history and lived experiences spanning from the conduct of the United Nations regarding the independence of such countries. Such independence was effected without consideration of the incompatibility theory of plural states (Fonkem, 2013). As one survivor told the press in a voice of focus and conviction,

> *As a people, who had been self-governing or quasi-independent and sovereign between 1954 and 1961, we have leverage at the level of the United Nations and cannot understand why our country was not granted her independence in accordance with the UNGA resolution 1514 of 1960 on the granting of independence to colonial countries and peoples. (Emphasis added)*

The question of an independent statehood or nationalism for some of the refugees was paramount in their minds. These refugees stated unequivocally, "*We prefer to die on our feet than live on our knees forever.*" From the viewpoint of these groups of the refugees, this chapter is significant for understanding the perspectives of groups of refugees yet to be more purposefully addressed by refugee scholarship. As Ladislav Holy (1998, p. 111) stated, "Although all nationalisms share common features, each of them has also its own particular characteristics, determined by the historically specific context in which the nationalist ideology emerged and the specific circumstances in which it persists."

Some research on the relationship between refugees and the home country does not appear to include one phenomenon: it is that some refugees do not recognize as their country of origin or the countries believed to be theirs. In the twenty-first century, such refugees from Africa come from ex-British Somaliland, ex-British Cameroons, Eritrea, and Western Sahara, which are either not recognized as independent countries but as integral parts of nation-states within the global system. Mainstream perspectives on refugees do not capture the experiences of this particular subset of political refugees from some of these non-nation-state origins. Until Eritrea, Namibia, and East Timor gained independence, they belonged to this category of nations and peoples found, respectively, within the borders of Ethiopia, South Africa, and Indonesia. Drawing from the example of British Southern Cameroons, a territory in postcolonial Cameroon Republic and that of Western Sahara in Morocco that continue to produce refugees, I argue that the non-nation-state origins of some refugees should be a consideration in refugee and forced migration studies. Further research in this area will be important in explaining the situations in such countries causing increasing numbers of refugees, who do not consider the countries as their "home." Such a study would build on work by Al-Ali and Koser (2002) and Rapport and Dawson (2005) in exploring the relationship between migrants and home. Considering that there are things humans believe they need and have a right to demand, it is important therefore for future research to explore why some of the refugees' narratives in this study indicated that an independent homeland would relieve their colonial woes and considerably stem refugee flows.

WHAT THE SURVIVORS WANT EUROPE TO KNOW

In a sea disaster that may have killed 500 migrants in the Mediterranean, Mr. Mahmud and another survivor of the shipwreck recounted grim details of the sinking of their boat. Mr. Mahmud told the French radio station RFI. "*We said please help us, but the boat's pilot refused, brandishing a knife and threatening to kill him.*" The smuggler said that if they took on more people, their boat would sink, too. "*He started the motor,*" Mr. Mahmud said. "*He left all those people in the water.*" For those who survived the journey to Europe, responding to a journalist's question about what he wanted the people in

Europe to know about them, one refugee said, "*We want them to know we're human beings. We did not want to be here.*"

According to Rishi Iyengar (2015), most people attempting the perilous crossing are fleeing poverty or violent conflict in their native countries and are attempting to reach Europe, where they seek asylum and better employment opportunities. Such misery and violent conflicts are generally viewed as colonial legacies in postcolonial settings (Duala-M'bedy, 1984; Anyang Nyongo, 1991; Cohen, 1995; Fonkem, 2013; Mueller, 2014).

EUROPEAN AND WESTERN RESPONSE TO THE CRISIS

The refugee experience placed the individuals and/or groups face to face with major risks not only in their home countries, on the forced migration escape routes often littered by hazardous and tragic circumstances as discussed earlier, but equally when and if they arrived in Europe and the West. According to estimates by the UNHCR, 1,500 people lost their lives in the Mediterranean in 2011, and "although precise numbers are notoriously difficult to establish, thousands more died since then in maritime accidents or of suffocation, hunger, and thirst on overcrowded boats" (Follis, 2015, pp. 41–62).

If survivors succeeded in arriving in Europe, they were met with major hostilities from some Europeans although International Human Rights Law determines the obligations of states toward all human beings. In the pictures that came through the evening news, some refugees were seen being hit, kicked, and tripped by a journalist in Hungary (Mackey, 2015; HuffPost, 2015). With anti-immigrant parties on the rise in Europe, considering the longstanding perception of the refugees and people from the Middle East and Africa as racially inferior, divisions remained over longer term proposals, ranging from dealing with people smugglers and African migrant camps to how to redistribute asylum-seekers around twenty-eight nations. "This is not a problem for Italy, Spain [or] Malta, but a European problem," said Giordano. "At the end of the day, the problem is for all countries."

As stated earlier, for several years, EU leaders did little more than deplore the rising death toll and mark tragedies with moments of silence and wreaths instead of fundamental action. Until the tens of thousands of refugees flooded the European streets, the European Council released a 10-point plan of immediate action ahead of their meeting in Brussels. The plan included reinforcing the EU's maritime patrol operations and extending the area it covers, as well as fingerprinting all migrants and refugees creating a pilot project on resettling refugees. There was also the preference in the European media to characterize the crisis more as a migrant crisis than as a refugee crisis. This preference, if intended, meant to blame the migrants rather than evoke compassion for the refugees escaping wars and repression.

The European 10-point plan: (1) Increase financial resources, (2) Capture and destroy vessels used by smugglers, (3) Gather information on smugglers and trace their funds, (4) Help Greece and Italy in processing asylum APPLICATIONS, (5) Ensure fingerprinting of all migrants in member-states, (6) Consider options for an emergency relocation mechanism, (7) Offer a NUMBER of places to persons in need of protection, (8) Establish a new program for the rapid return of irregular migrants, (9) Engage with countries surrounding Libya initiatives, and (10) Gather intelligence on migratory flows

Dutch prime minister Mark Rutte for example, insisted that Europe should not take the brunt of blame. As Prime Minister Rutte (2015) put it, "We ask that Africa, the source of the problem, also collectively takes up its responsibility," arguing that the "last time (he checked) Libya was in Africa, not Europe." French president Francois Hollande saw the problem from a different perspective. According to Hollande, the problem involved "fixing yesterday's errors." For Italian prime minister Matteo Renzi, it was a question of the urge for Europe to take "measures to prevent migrants in Libya from leaving their countries in the first place." Prior to these major incidents, there had been several reports, over the years, of migrant deaths both at sea and in the Sahara Desert. In the ten-point plan discussed by European Union leaders, none raised the colonial connection to the huge wave of refugees and migrants.

British prime minister David Cameron seeking to fend off anti-immigration populists as he faced an election just two weeks away, pledged a warship, helicopters, and support craft. But he stressed that people picked up would not automatically be given refuge in Britain and would mostly be delivered to Italian authorities to DEAL with.

"What is happening now is of epic proportions," Maltese prime minister Joseph Muscat told BBC News. "If Europe, if the global community continued to turn a blind eye . . . we will all be judged in the same way that history has judged Europe when it turned a blind eye to the genocide of this century and last century." The leaders said they would aim for long-term solutions, such as easing poverty and war in the Middle East and Africa, giving people in need a chance to ask for asylum before reaching Europe and opening possible legal routes to migration for some. German chancellor Angela Merkel, whose country along with Sweden took in a large proportion of asylum-seekers, called for a change in the EU's system of managing asylum claims to better distribute the pressures across the bloc.

In the wake of antirefugee street protests across Europe, the decision of some European states to triple naval search missions in the Mediterranean, for example, restoring funding to the 2014 level appeared to be a mere face-saving operation. A criticism from the United Nations went that the European Union's response needed to go beyond the minimalist approach . . . focusing primarily on stemming the arrival of migrants and refugees on its shores. In the wake of the April 22, 2015, great disaster and many others at sea since 2011, the political elite in Europe saw the problem differently, especially after the Paris attack of November 13, 2015. While the world community was reflecting on what to do with the refugees, the two attacks demonstrated the double standards of Europe and the West in general. Islamic State terrorists struck in Beirut, Lebanon, on Thursday, November 12, 2015, killing a total of forty-three people and in Paris, France, the day after. While the tragedy in Paris dominated the news agenda for days in the West, the Beirut attacks made only a few headlines. In the United States, Presidential Candidate Marco Rubio issued a campaign advertisement in which he used the attack in Paris to demonize the refugees a week after the attack, Donald J. Trump, another candidate, stated he would ban the refugees from coming to the United States, and thirty-nine state governors refused to settle the refugees in their states. In the face of this disparity in media coverage of similar attacks, Emma Gatten (2015) commented on how *"it is easier to feel empathy for those closest to us and whose lives appear to be more like ours."* Why Europe and the West would identify with Paris in a way they could not with the Lebanese capital can also be perceived from the perspective of the colonial culture (Thomas, 1994).

Stephen Keller (1975), using general theoretical aspects originally developed by disaster researchers, explored the reaction to threats and the impact of stress and trauma on behavior. Keller argued strongly that the trauma of flight produces residual psychological states in the refugee that will affect the behavior of refugees for years to come as can be evidenced in some of the narratives reproduced above. Of particular interest in the discussion in this chapter is the refugees' perception of danger, threat, and the future recurrent in the narratives explored. These were only a few examples of the kinds of stories the refugees and forced migrants had about their lives and the perceptions of how they saw their existence. The examples provide some insight into the minds of refugees and forced migrants in general as well as the perceptions of Europe and the West of refugees and migrants.

CONCLUSION

The purpose of this chapter was to link the "2015 refugees and migrant crisis" to colonialism and the nature of the decolonization process. The chapter argued that the refugees flocking to Europe and other parts of the world from war-torn and poverty-ridden nations of Africa and the Middle East were fleeing from a situation created for them and their countries by colonial rule and the nature of the decolonization process. In arguing this position, I discussed the colonial legacy in postcolonial states, because in the making of postcolonial states, many of the elements of colonial rule remained in the present. The chapter also highlighted the disasters on refugee routes, underscored the responses of Europe to the 2015 refugee crisis, and discussed the narratives of some survivors. The claim in the discussion was that the global community and above all, the European Union turned a blind eye to the disasters (Muscat, 2015), because the refugees remained mere "objects conceived primarily as incomplete or imperfect rather than as peoples of a comprehensibly distinct kind" (Thomas, 1994, p. 71). In view of the indecision of European Union leaders even after thousands of desperate people drowned trying to reach Europe the discussion pointed to the callousness of Europe toward the refugees, a situation that worsened after the Paris terrorist attack of Friday, November 13, 2015. Finally, the chapter maintained that the world certainly misses out on effective conclusions each time we continuously focus on geopolitics rather than on human lives and human dignity.

For the refugee narratives collected and analyzed, the hardest part is that the individuals taking the risk to flee have almost no choice but to leave their homes and home countries and go to somewhere new without any time to plan. When the individuals arrive in a foreign place, there is no guarantee that they can stay there. The pain of escaping one's home, leaving one's country, or losing one's family and friends can be understandable, and should also form the basis of understanding the narratives of refugees in general. Focusing on keeping people out by cutting their only existing routes with the walls erected at some European borders and anticipated by the Trump administration in the United States would only push people fleeing for their lives to find alternative routes, potentially even more dangerous ones.

REFERENCES

Abdel-Hamid, H. (2015, April 22). UN: The number of Syrian refugees passes five million. *Al Jazeera.*

Acemoglu, D., Johnson, S., & Robinson, J. A. (2001). The colonial origins of comparative development: An empirical investigation. *American Economic Review* 91(5), 1369–1401.

Acemoglu, D., Johnson, S., & Robinson, J. A. (2002, November). Reversal of fortune: Geography and institutions in the making of the modern world income distribution. *The Quarterly Journal of Economics* 117(4), 1231–1294.

Ake, C. (1985). Why is Africa not developing? *West Africa* 1985, 1212–1214.

Anyang' Nyong'o, P. (1991). The implications of crises and conflict in the Upper Nile Valley. In Francis M. Deng & I. William Zartman (eds.), *Conflict resolution in Africa*, Washington, D.C.: Brookings Institution, pp. 95–114.

Angel, R. (2015). Report on NBC, Sunday, September 13.

Banerjee, A., & Iyer, L. (2003). *History, institutions and economic performance: The legacy of colonial land tenure systems in India*. Mimeo.

Bhatt, A. (2013). Unequal global exchange: Colonization, politics, and economics. *Office of Minority Affairs & Diversity*. http://www.washington.edu/omad/ctcenter/projects-common-book/mountains-beyond-mountains/unequal-global-exchange/.

Berkowitz, D., & Clay, K. (2004). Initial conditions, institutional dynamics and economic performance: Evidence from the American states. Mimeograph. William Davidson Institute Working Paper Number 615, October 2003 SSRN Electronic Journal, https://papers.ssrn.com/sol3/papers.cfm?abstract_id=485003.

Castles, S. (2004). Migration fundamentals: Confronting the realities of forced migration. *Migration Information Source*. Retrieved from www.migrationinformation.org/feature/display.cfm?ID=222.

Cheney, R., & Cheney, L. (2015a). *Exceptional: Why the world needs a powerful America*. Threshold Editions.

Cheney, R., & Cheney, L. (2015b) Interview on Fox News Sunday, September 6.

Chughtai, A. (2015, April 20). The ongoing tragedy of migrants and the Mediterranean. *Al Jazeera*.

Cohen, H. J. (1995). Conflict management in Africa. *CSIS Africa Notes*, 181, February.

Cohn, B. S. (1996). *Colonialism and its forms of knowledge: The British in India*. Princeton: Princeton University Press.

Dirks, N. B. (Ed.). (1992). *Colonialism and culture:* University of Michigan Press.

Duala-M'bedy, B. (1984). African problems: Any links with the past? *Cameroon Tribune*, Wednesday, 6 June, p. 10.

Eastmond, M. (2007). Stories as lived experience: Narratives in forced migration. *Journal of Refugee Studies*, 20(2). See more at: http://www.forcedmigration.org/digital-library/journals/journal-of-refugee-studies#sthash.zSLOcTJv.dpuf.

Engerman, S. L., & Sokoloff, K. L. (1997). Factor endowments, institutions, and differential paths of growth among new world economies: A view from economic historians of the United States. In Stephen Haber (Ed.), *How Latin America fell behind: Essays on the economic histories of Brazil and Mexico, 1800–1914*. Stanford: Stanford University Press.

Engerman, S. L., & Sokoloff, K. L. (2002). Factor endowments, inequality, and paths of development among new world economies. *Economia* 3(1): 41–109.

Escobar, A. (1995). *Encountering development: The making and unmaking of the third world*. Princeton: Princeton University Press.

Esteva, G. (1998). Beyond development, what? With M. S. Prakash. *Development in Practice* 8(3), 280–296.

Faiola A. (2015, April 19). Calls for action in Europe after migrant disaster in the Mediterranean. *The Washington Post*.

Follis, K. S. (2015). Responsibility, emergency, blame: Reporting on migrant deaths on the Mediterranean in the Council of Europe. *Journal of Human Rights* 14(1): 41–62.

Fanon, F. (1963). *The wretched of the Earth*. Présence Africaine, New York: Grove Press.

Fanon, F. (1967). *Black skin, white masks*. Trans. Charles Lam Markmann. New York: Grove Press.

Fonkem, A. (2013a). Conflict and conflict resolution in Africa engaging the colonial factor. *African Journal on Conflict Resolution* 13(2): 11–38.

Fonkem, A. (2013b). De facto association, forced assimilation and a nationalist conflict in the Cameroons: Perspectives from the incompatibility theory. *Journal of International Studies and Development* 3(Spring), 142–168.

Ford, R. S. (2015). Interview on *Meet The Press*, Sunday, September 13.

Fundamental Rights Agency. (2013). Fundamental rights: challenges and achievements in 2013—Annual report 2013. European Union Agency for Fundamental Rights, p. 31.

Gatten, E. (2015, November). Don't forget Beirut; we are grieving, too. *USA Today*.

Groenewald, T. (2004, April). Phenomenological research design 2. *International Journal of Qualitative Research Methods* 3(1), 1–26.

Harris, D., & Jesko, J. (2015, December 21). Anti-immigrant protests grow as thousands of refugees flood Europe. *ABC News*. http://abcnews.go.com/International/anti-immigrant-protests-grow-thousands-refugees-flood-europe/story?id=35888428.

Herbst, J. I. (2000). *States and power in Africa: Comparative lessons in authority and control.* Princeton: Princeton University Press, pp. x–280.

Holy, L. (1998). The metaphor of 'home' in Czech nationalist discourse. In N. Rapport & A. Dawson (Eds.), *Migrants of identity: Perceptions of home in a world of movement.* Oxford: Berg Publishers, pp. 501–502.

Huffington Post. (2015). Family members of Syrian refugees abused by Hungarian journalist tell their story, September 11.

Iyengar, R. (2015). What you need to know about the E.U.'s refugee crisis. *Time*, April 20.

Kamga, L. K. (2011). President Sarkozy and Franco-Cameroonian relations. *Dynamiques Internationales*, CEAN-IEP Bordeaux, Issue 4, May.

Keller, S. L. (1975). *Uprooting and social change: The role of refugees in development.* Delhi: Manohar Book Service.

Kidder, T. (2003). *Mountains beyond mountains: The quest of Dr. Paul Farmer, A man who would cure the world.* New York: Random House.

Loescher and Loescher. (1994). *The global refugee crisis: A reference handbook.*
ABC-CLIO (December).

La Porta, R., Lopez-de-Silanes, L., Shleifer, A., & Vishny, R. W. (1998a). Law and finance. *The Journal of Political Economy* 106(6), 1113–1155.

La Porta, R., Lopez-de-Silanes, L., Shleifer, A., & Vishny, R. W. (1998b). The quality of government. *Journal of Law, Economics and Organization* 15(1), 222–279.

Mackey, R. (2015). Hungarian Journalist, Petra Laszlo, Fired for Kicking Migrants on Camera. *New York Times*, September 8.

Marker, S. (2003, November). Effects of colonization. *Beyond Intractability*. http://www.beyondintractability.org/essay/post-colonial.

Miliband, D. (2015). Interview on *Meet the Press*, Sunday, September 6.

Moulson, G. (2016, August 28). Europe's refugee crisis simmers despite efforts to solve it. *The Washington Times*.

Mueller, S. D. (2014). The resilience of the past: Government and opposition in Kenya. *Canadian Journal of African Studies*, 8(1), 25–42

Ochonu, M. (2015). Foreword. *Nationalism & intra-state conflicts in the postcolonial world.* Lexington Books.

Okoyo, M. (1977, October). Africa and political stability. *Africa* (74), 93–96.

Onyanga-Omara, J. (2015, November). 55 Million people were forced from their home by end of 2014. *USA Today*.

Parkinson, J. (2015, September). Image of drowned Syrian boy echoes around the world. *Wall Street Journal.*

Prochaska, D. (1990). *Making Algeria French: Colonialism in Bône, 1870–1920.* Cambridge University Press.

Psaropoulos, J. (2016, January). Greece reacts to EU's hard line on refugees. *Aljazeera.*

Roy, T. (2007). *Traditional industry in the economy of colonial India.* Cambridge University Press.

Said, E. (1978). *Orientalism.* New York: Vintage Books.

Shank, G. D. (2006). *Qualitative research: A personal skills approach.* Second Edition. Columbus: Pearson.

Sharp, J. (2008). Chapter 1, on orientalism. *Geographies of Postcolonialism.* SAGE Publications.

Shenker, J. (2011, May 8). Aircraft carrier left us to die, says migrants. *The Guardian* (Online). Available: http://www.theguardian.com/world/2011/may/08/nato-ship-libyan-migrants accessed August 30, 2013.

Thomas, N. (1994). *Colonialism's culture: Anthropology, travel and government.* Princeton: Princeton University Press.

UNCHR. (2004, May). http://www.unchr.ch/ accessed June 5, 2017.

Wescott, L. (2015, April 23). Why are so many migrants crossing the mediterranean? *Newsweek.*

Weiner, M. (1995). *The global migration crisis: Challenges to states and human rights.* New York: Happer Collins.

Zolberg, A. R., Suhrke, A., & Aguayo, S. (1989). *Escape from violence: Conflicts and the refugee crisis in the developing world.* New York: Oxford University Press.

Chapter 5

Refugees and Immigrants

The Tragedy of Arab Politics in the Early Twenty-First Century

Ali R. Abootelabi

The Arab World since the end of the Cold War has experienced accelerated political decay and a crisis of governance. The so-called Arab Spring since 2011 has already been derailed with detrimental results for Arab politics. The United States and its allies' disastrous policy of intervention and regime change in the Middle East and North Africa since 2001 has produced damaging results also: either the collapse of the old regime with widespread devastation and millions displaced or consolidating authoritarian rule and hastening further political decay. The movement of Syrian and other refugees into Europe since 2011 has been the most recent manifestation of both the crisis of governance and Western intervention. As such, the leading NATO (European Union) members, along with the United States, must share the burden of responsibility for refugee stream into Europe, with all its real, legal, and ethical responsibilities attached.

The flow of people out of war zones and economically depressed areas is only natural, as the world has repeatedly experienced such episodes since World War II. This time around, war and economic miseries in Afghanistan and many Arab countries in the Middle East and North African region (MENA) are forcing millions to leave their home countries of birth in search of "human security." The refugee crisis during and after World War II was only one episode in many more such mass movements of displaced people in the coming decades. What makes the current refugee flow since the 2001 U.S. invasion of Afghanistan different is not its scale but its causes and timing. Millions of people have become national and international refugees, the causes of which essentially boil down to "misguided Western policies" and "ineffective, authoritarian governance." The United States' injudicious policies of direct and indirect intervention into the affairs of MENA countries, assisted by its regional and European allies, have translated into disastrous outcomes across the region. Specifically, the policy of "regime change" in Afghanistan, Iraq, Libya, and Syria and "regime preservation" in Egypt, Saudi Arabia, Bahrain, Qatar, Kuwait, the United Arab Emirates, and Yemen before the end of Ali Abdullah Saleh's three-decade rule have contributed to either wars and refugees or further consolidation of authoritarian rule. Since 2011, only Tunisia's popular resistance has created some prospects for responsible politics and political opening, although Tunisia's future still remains tenable. Saudi Arabia's overt military invasion of Yemen, with the tacit support of the United States and without a United Nations' Security Council resolution, has led to similar national devastations as in Syria.

Ironically, the current refugee crisis in the MENA region rides on the shoulder of what was supposed to be an "Arab Spring" movement to end authoritarian rule and to empower "the New Arabs."[1] The shattering of the Arab peoples' dream for political opening and democracy is not accidental; it is the result of domestic and foreign forces trying to maintain the national and regional sociopolitical and economic status quo in favor of the conservative, pro-Western Arab regimes. As such, the United States and its NATO allies must share the responsibility, with the autocratic Arab regimes, for the ongoing humanitarian disaster that began with the U.S. invasion of Afghanistan and has intensified over the years, culminating in region-wide disastrous refugee crisis since 2011.

REFUGEES AND MATTERS OF GOVERNANCE

The twenty-two-member-Arab League in 2016 remains as divided as ever on central issues pertaining to matters of national governance and regional issues. The central players, namely Egypt, Saudi Arabia, and the Persian Gulf Arab States (The United Arab Emirates, Qatar, Kuwait, Bahrain, and Oman) remain at odds over regional issues that can ultimately overshadow their internal political stability and social order. They remain divided over policy preferences and approaches regarding, among others: the security threat of the so-called the Islamic State in Iraq and Syria (ISIS), hitherto the *Daesh*, and al-Qaeda and other radical militant Muslim groups; the legitimacy and popularity of some Islamist movements like the Muslim Brotherhood; the civil wars in Libya, Syria, and Yemen; the rise of Iran and the Shi'a power in Iraq, Lebanon, and Yemen; their respective relations with the United States; and the rise of a new assertive Russian power. The Arab countries have also responded differently to the rise of more aggressive Turkish diplomacy and projection of its power, the division in the Palestinian leadership and the worsening life conditions for millions of the Palestinians in the occupied territories, and of course the ongoing refugee crisis. The drastic decline in oil income that provides for the lion's share of many Arab States' national income has only made matters worse. The Arab economies are struggling with their economic balance sheets while the human and material cost of conflicts and instability in Libya, Syria, Egypt, Yemen, Iraq, Bahrain, and Somalia are staggering. The October 2015 International Monetary Fund report for Arab countries in transition (ACT) reminds us of the political dimension of Arab economies:

> Several of the ACTs have also suffered from intensifying and spreading conflicts that cause widespread human suffering and sizeable economic challenges. Libya and Yemen are directly affected, while spillovers from these conflicts and the civil wars in Iraq and Syria weigh on Jordan and Tunisia, as well as other countries in the region (e.g., Lebanon, Djibouti), Turkey and Europe. These spillovers come most prominently in the form of large refugee flows, deteriorating security, and pressures on economic infrastructures and labor markets.[2]

Arab Countries in Transition

The tragedy of the refugee crisis cannot be exaggerated. Contrary to migrants whose departure from their place of residence is presumably driven by choice in search of better lives outside their place of birth—the pull factor—refugees are forced to leave their place of residence—the push factor. The sheer number of Syrian and other refugees is overwhelming, and the vast majority of these refugees are internally displaced in Syria or are living in the neighboring Turkey, Jordan, and Lebanon. This is while the world's attention seems zoomed on the refugees trying to reach Europe via Greece and the Mediterranean. Germany and Sweden received the lion share of the refugees, when the proposed German "quota" system for admission of refugees into all European Union member-states was swiftly rejected. The majority of the twenty-eight member-states have bickered over their international and humanitarian responsibilities.

The International Organization for Migration's Displacement Tracking Matrix 2015 report indicated that a total of 990,671 migrants and refugees entered Europe in 2015 from (North) Africa and the Middle East by a combination of irregular land and sea routes, and the number was expected to reach over 1 million.[3] Until 2015, the rise in Mediterranean Sea arrivals was seen primarily in Italy. Over the course of 2014, it received over three-quarters of all arrivals by sea (170,000). During all of 2014, 34,442 people arrived in Greece, less than one-fifth of the total number of arrivals. In 2015, that picture changed. During the first six months of 2015, 70,354 people arrived in Italy, while 69,000 arrived on the Greek islands—more than the number for whole of 2014.[4] In the first four months of the 2016 alone, as IOM reported on April 15, 2016, some 177,207 migrants and refugees had arrived in Europe via Mediterranean Sea routes, with deaths of 732 men, women, and children in 2016.[5]

Europe because of its proximity and the promise of economic opportunity and better future has been the natural destination for millions fleeing wars and instability, although Turkey, Jordan, and Lebanon are hosting many more Syrian refugees because of their geographical locations; Syrian refugees had started arriving in Jordan, Lebanon, and Turkey in late 2011. Turkey in October 2015 was hosting over 1.9 million (2.5 percent of the population)[6] of the 4 million[7] Syrians who had fled war, while Lebanon had about 1.1 million refugees[8] and Jordan housed 630,000.[9] Overall, according to a 2015 study by UNICEF, four-and-a-half years into the crisis, four out of five Syrians are estimated to be living in poverty and 7.6 million people were internally displaced.[10]

Since 2015, refugees living outside refugee camps in Jordan have seen World Food Program food stipends reduced from $28 per person to as low as $14 each. Meanwhile, cuts to stipends from the World Food Program have left refugee families more vulnerable. For example, across Jordan, nearly half of all Syrian refugee households said they rely partly or entirely on income generated by a child (UNICEF, 2015).[11] The tragedy is worsened when many refugee children born in the past five years are without documents, making them ineligible to schooling, as in Jordan. In the countries neighboring Syria, including Jordan, Lebanon, and Turkey, an estimated 700,000 Syrian refugee children are out of school, according to a UNICEF report.[12] This is in spite of UNICEF's help in mobilizing the largest humanitarian operation in history, supplying food, water, education, clothing, and critical immunizations in Syria and neighboring countries. By the end of 2014, 2.3 million children had been vaccinated against measles. Nearly 17 million people had received clean, safe water; 400,000 children were to attend school through a UNICEF-supported home-based program.[13]

It seems the promise of globalization, transnationalism, and universalism has quickly been abandoned. States that have until recently been preaching others to respect human rights and freedom of speech and expression have, in the face of economic slowdown since 2007, turned their backs on refugees. Many Western newspapers have also done a major disservice to the cause of human solidarity by referring to refugees (migrants) fleeing violence as a "flood,"[14] or an "Islamic invasion,"[15] or a "swarm,"[16] as the British Prime Minister commented in an interview, though retracted later. These refugees are, however, the creation of the leading NATO members of the European Union's foreign policies; namely, the United Kingdom, France, and Italy, whose interventionist policies in support of the United States in Libya, Syria, Iraq, and Somalia have had severe catastrophic consequences for the peoples in these countries. This is a failure of responsible democratic governance in pursuit of political expediency and proclaimed national interest.

Similarly, the rich Persian Gulf Arab States, fearing the crumbling of their own sociopolitical order, have closed their doors to refugees, and instead have enflamed the ravages of ethnic and sectarian conflicts for the sake of staying in power. This is the result of the failure of governance in oil-rich Arab countries in self-serving policies, geared at regime survivability and sociopolitical status quo.

While the moral case for taking these refugees is overwhelming, it is not difficult to argue that there are important economic benefits that come with accepting refugees, as many of the destination countries suffer from an ageing and declining population.[17] Refugees to Europe would ultimately benefit the countries they go to, in the medium and long term. Mette Foged and Giovanni Peri, for example, have found that refugees raised the wages, employment, and occupational mobility of low-skill Dane when Denmark, between 1994 and 2008, admitted over 80,000 refugees from former Yugoslavia and Somalia, and later from Iraq and Afghanistan, tripling the share of its population born outside the EU. The refugees actually help push Danes into more complex tasks and jobs, complementing many refugees' more basic skills.[18]

GOVERNANCE AND THE ARAB STATES

In 2016, many Arab States remain in the midst of political chaos and uncertainty and are vulnerable to regional events, including the cross-border movement of hundreds of thousands of displaced populations. If Lebanon, Jordan, and the non-Arab state of Turkey have accepted millions of Syrian refugees by default, the richer Arab Persian Gulf States, especially Saudi Arabia and Qatar, have avoided the issue and have actually contributed to the refugee problem by instigating organized political violence against the Syrian regime of Bashar al-Assad. The reversal of the Arab Spring movement in Syria into an armed confrontation between the regime and the opposition since 2011 has led to a brutal civil war and millions of refugees because of the regime's incapability to respond positively to popular demand for political opening and also because of regional and extra-regional interventions either in support of or against the Syrian regime. Regardless of the political debate designating blames on the opposite sides of the conflict and their supporters,[19] the human cost and the material destruction of the Syrian war has been unprecedented since World War II. Much of the blame for the deterioration of the early peaceful demonstration in to open conflict goes to the nature of the regime and its institutional inability to manage people's demand for wider political participation and to accommodate political opposition in orderly and peaceful fashion. In other words, Syrian regime at the time ached from similar shortcomings many other Arab States continue to suffer today—a chronic problem with effective governance.

It is only natural to think of national governments once the question of governance comes up. After all, national governments are endowed with tremendous power, legitimate or not, and resources to govern over matters of significance to the population, including law and order, national security, social and economic development, and the preservation of cultural heritage and overall social harmony. At its most basic level, however, governance is also about local neighborhoods and communities organizing themselves into more effective units in dealing with local issues, whether in cooperation with agencies of the national and local governments or with private individuals and agencies of civil society or a combination of such forces. The prevailing historical and cultural characteristics and forces present in any given community can also help the cause of local organizing, for example, tribal order and affiliation or community mosques as places of both worship and mobilization and networking.

Authoritarian rule by definition and nature is antithetical to long-term good governance and is more prone to corruption and abuses of power. On the other hand, political democracy, if understood as a means to an end, offers the best chance for social organization and governance at local or national levels. At its core, political democracy would require the presence of free, fair, and frequent elections to gage the health of the relationship between the governed and the governors. Political democracy also is about a continuous process of push and pull between the state and society, as structural and cultural changes always require "political adjustments" to meet the ever-changing societal needs and demands. The presence of viable political institutions such as political parties and independent legislative and judiciary branches of the government help solidify the legitimacy of the political system, resulting in better governance. So, governance[20] is really about the ability of the political system to continuously respond and adjust to the parameters of authority as the society becomes wealthier, healthier, more educated, more sophisticated, and better organized.

Good governance and democratic rule are not about culture or religion *per se;* it is about the management of political power and the competition over socioeconomic resources[21] within agreed-upon normative principles and values and institutional arrangements, whereby individual citizens through elections and other forms of political participation determine their own choices through elected representatives. In other words, political democracy is (can be) an instrumental method in the resolution of "identity conflicts" over cultural and nationalistic issues by providing legal and institutional venues for resolution of differences and conflicts to groups in competition over socioeconomic resources and political power.

The separation of Church and the state and the evolution of the modern state as it happened in the Western experience since 1648 has been unique in certain ways. Secularism and liberalism may have proven instrumental in the evolution of political democracy and civil liberties in the Western tradition, but they should not be considered as preconditions for the inauguration and the evolution of democracy elsewhere. Recall also that the appearance and the evolution of political democracy in Europe took centuries and remains, and also will persist as an ongoing process. Every society must formulate its own strategy and travel toward political democracy and determining the levels and degrees of civil liberties within its defined particular cultural and socioeconomic milieu. That is, the parameters of democracy in a Muslim country may differ from those of the Western societies. If so, the gates of experimentation with Islamic governance and popular participation, for example, an Islamic Republic,[22] are wide open. My contention here and throughout this chapter is that political democracy and effective governance are positively correlated. This correlation may not be a causal one, but democratic states have proven over past centuries as more effective in matters of governance. Furthermore, the presence of democracy can alleviate the potential challenge political Islam poses to effective governance. That is, if political violence in Muslim countries has been attributed to the presence of political Islam and Islamic groups, the real problem rests with the absence of legal and institutional venues that only political democracy provides for orderly political bargaining, and not Islam per se.

The competition among cultural groups in a given society is not so much about the superiority or inferiority of certain value system or way of life *per se* but how the competition translates into control over local, regional, and national resources while realizing the ambitions and aspirations of all cultural groups. This is especially true, where legal and institutional venues for dispute settlement and conflict resolution and power sharing among competing cultural groups are weak or are seriously lacking. In such cases, it becomes "natural" for a dominant culture trying to impose its ethos and belief systems, through cooperation or coercion, on minority groups, monopolizing control over socioeconomic resources and political power.

Frustration and anger over inept and corrupt political leadership, widespread inequality in wealth and income, and significant poverty in countries rich in minerals, wealth, and even human capital can also result in anger and even violence, but not always. The degree of regime repressiveness can go far in suffocating popular sentiments and preventing mass mobilization in pursue of some cause, albeit in support of the regime or its slogans; for example, Mobutu in Zaire; Marcos in the Philippines, South Korea under President Park, Mubarak in Egypt, and Saudi Arabia. The late Edward N. Muller of the University of Arizona and Erich Weede,[23] Universität zu Köln, among others, have conducted extensive research on regime repressiveness, poverty, and inequality and political violence across large sample of countries, refuting any significant positive correlation between inequality and violence but observing the correlation between the level of regime repression and present or absence of violence. Similarly, weak governments— legitimate or authoritarian—can prove ineffective in controlling popular sentiments in either support of, or in opposition to, the regime and its slogans because of the regime's institutional and/or legal shortcomings.

It is not surprising that more widespread violence and death have occurred precisely in countries weak in their institutional/legal and political structure (e.g., Pakistan, Afghanistan, Somalia, Libya, Syria, Yemen, and Iraq). In contrast, demonstrations in Iran, Turkey, and Lebanon, where the state's effective power is legally and institutionally more organized have been more orderly. The state in most Arab countries has also tried to redirect people's anger toward the "enemy"—the West and Israel, and more recently the threat from the "Shi'a Crescent" of Iran, Iraq, Lebanon, and Syria—and away from domestic socioeconomic and political problems.

The Arab regimes have relied on different tactics to dominate political power and to endure: Relying on Rentierism and patrimonial rule, foreign security and financial assistance, and foreign migrant workers, as in Saudi Arabia and the Persian Gulf States, Egypt, and Jordan; sheer brutality, as in Iraq under Saddam Hussein, Qaddafi's Libya, Egypt under Mubarak, and Syria under the military rule of the Assad family; corruption, nepotism, and patrimonialism, as in Yemen under Ali Abdullah Saleh, Tunisia under Bin Ali, and Morocco's king Hassan. Arab regimes, and particularly the Rentier states with abundant oil and financial resources, have used cooptation of the opposition to silence civil society. Whether through privileged access to the state's coffers or participation in lucrative state business enterprises, social opposition often is weak and coopted into the system. In the case of oil economies and traditional patrimonial states, excessive wealth and cooptation have been central instruments in keeping the state running while avoiding major concessions to societal forces in competing for political power and resources. The state tools of oppression and control in turn are heavily subsidized through a generous share of national budgets and foreign supporters. For example, as Bruce K. Rutherford remarks that in Egypt, Mubarak's regime had "used cooptation and coercion with equal skill to build a wide circle of supporters and to keep opponents at bay."[24]

Saudi Arabia and the Persian Gulf family-ruled city-states are the quintessential examples of patrimonial, Rentier states supported by the United States. The state apparatus remains dominated by the al-Saud family and its extended subjects. The system has proven stable since its modern inception and has relied heavily on support and protection from its Western supporters, in general, and the United States, in particular. The ruling family and its cohorts have continued to control all political, security, and economic institutions in Saudi Arabia, effectively eliminating the chance for a rebellion or overthrow. As Jennifer Gandhi and Adam Przeworski discuss In *Authoritarian Institutions and the Survival of Autocrats*, the necessary step for an autocrat to remain in power is through its institutional control at a time of struggle. Gandhi and Przeworski propose that by institutionalizing, and through a system of sharing rewards, an autocrat can stay in power by retaining the good will of the citizens.[25]

The presence of the U.S. 5th fleet naval forces in Bahrain further strengthened the regime's resolve in the suppression of any social demand for popular participation and regime accountability. The GCC countries relying on oil rent and an army of migrant workers and a network of blood kinship and patrimonial rule continues to "ignore" popular demand for greater participation in sociopolitical and economic decisions. The UAE has since 2011 brought dozens of alleged Muslim Brotherhood members to trial, including Emirati, Qatari, and Egyptian citizens.[26]

In Bahrain, "The military, like all institutions in the country, is penetrated and controlled by the thousands of princes who constitute the broader backbone of the royal family; more than seven hundred are direct descendants of Ibn Saud, and approximately four hundred are key."[27] Bahraini Shi'a population leadership is portrayed as "agents of a foreign power," code name for Iran and the popular legitimate protests for political opening is suppressed. The decision by Manama to ask for help from its powerful neighbor led to a Saudi intervention that goes on until today. Haas and Lech explain Saudi action, stating that

> It lent the Saudi-backed, Sunni monarchy in Manama the muscle it needed to keep control of its Shia-majority population and, in turn, it should on power. More importantly, Saudi intervention stifled momentum in Saudi Arabia's oil-rich eastern province among the newly restive Shia minority, who might have sought a repeat performance of what was occurring in Bahrain.[28]

On the surface of it, limited political liberalizations in Arab countries have helped open up more space for nongovernmental organizations to receive legal recognition. Egypt parliamentary elections (1984, 1987, 1990, 1995, 2000, 2005, 2010), Yemen parliamentary elections (1993, 1997, 2001, 2003), and Algeria's parliamentary elections in 2002, 2007) provided examples of such regime opening. Among monarchies, Morocco (1993, 1997, 2002, 2007); Jordan (1989, 1993, 1997, 2003, 2007, 2010); Kuwait (regular elections since independence, with two periods of suspension in 1976–1981, 1986–1992); and Bahrain (2002, 2006, 2010) all held contested but managed elections to their parliaments over the past two decades or more. In all such elections, the state restricted the opposition independence and effectiveness through new legal frameworks.[29] Therefore, the notion that the regime-constructed political parties could actually aggregate popular demand and interest is convincing to none. Instead, such political parties across the Arab World, where they existed at all, became a focal point for regime supporters to help coopt opposition and thus help the cause of regime stability. Political parties like the National Democratic Party in Egypt, or the General People's Congress in Yemen, or the Ba'ath in Syria only have helped the creation of a top-down bureaucratic, corrupt state supported by the forces of the status quo and their foreign supporters.[30]

The rise of Daesh represents the frustration of the Arab population with powerlessness in the face of inept, authoritarian Arab regimes, and their Western supporters, who since the 1940s have promised a lot and delivered meagerly. It also represents the failure of the Sunni religious leadership, in general, and in the Arab World, in particular, to present itself as a viable, functioning alternative to the "secular" state. Whether Muslim Brotherhood prior to Mubarak's demise, al-Shabab in Somalia in 2006, Boko Haram in Nigeria, FIS or the National Salvation Front in Algeria in the 1990s, the Daesh today, or a host of militant groups in Pakistan, they all represent the failure of the mainstream Sunni religious leadership in these countries to organize themselves into viable opposition to the state. True, the authoritarian Arab States have prevented the rise of religious groups into national political prominence and thus prospects for a peaceful takeover of the state by such groups. But, the unpreparedness of the Sunni Islamic movements to be in charge of the state itself has cost them their relevance and demise, for example, Muslim Brotherhood in Egypt; or, their degeneration into militant, violent movements, including the Daesh.

Gilbert Achcar in *The People Want: A Radical Exploration of the Arab Uprising* sums up the state of Arab political economy. He observes that almost all Arab States take their place on a scale running from patrimonialism to neopatrimonialism regimes, further accentuated by their Rentier economies (p. 59). Sociopolitical instability and the absence of any real rule of law in virtually all Arab countries means the development of speculative or commercial capitalism with the specific variant of the capitalist mode of production being politically determined. So, the peculiar modality of the capitalist mode of production—a mix of patrimonialism, nepotism, and crony capitalism pillaging of public property, swollen bureaucracy, and generalized corruption, against a background of great sociopolitical instability and the impotence or even nonexistence of the role of law—is dominant in the Arab region (p. 74). The state itself is merely a cash cow (p. 63).[31] It is all about governance with all its political intricacies and engineering, especially in heterogeneous and divided societies.

Given the above, it is not surprising why the Persian Gulf Arab States have not opened their arms to refugees from Syria, Iraq, and the Palestinians from Syria, and Somalia, despite the religious and linguistic and cultural commonalities. The regimes in these countries are concerned to the point of paranoia that changes in the sociopolitical status quo will breed instability, threatening the status quo and their rather "cozy" political arrangements. The larger Arab States in North Africa like Algeria and Morocco feel vulnerable because of instability in Libya and the threat of spillover effect. Egypt after the failure of the Arab Spring movement and the military coup d'état and the suppression of the democratic movement under General Abdel Fatah al-Sisi remains economically weak and dependent on largesse from Saudi Araba, Qatar, and the United States. Egypt is under a de facto military regime, fearful of Muslim Brotherhood and the threat of violence and with no appetite for helping the fellow Arab refugees. So, the neighboring Lebanon, Jordan, and Turkey have hosted the bulk of the Syrian refugees while Iraq is being avoided by the Syrian refugees for the obvious reasons of its internal instability and its own refugee problem.

THE WEST AND THE ARAB STATES' POLITICAL DECAY

The end of the cold war initially meant the unparalleled supremacy of the United States in military, technology, economy, and finance. President George Herbert Bush's vision for a "New World Order" upon the defeat of Iraqi army in the Persian Gulf War in 1991 proved as simplistic as early assumptions over his chances for presidential reelection in the same year. Only a decade later, the September 11 terrorist attacks on America set a new *"security-first" tone* in America's foreign policy establishment. Initially, however, the neoconservative foreign policymakers in the United States saw an opportunity for the country to dominate and even direct world affairs to an unparalleled degree. Thus, writing in 2011, Jack Smith of Global Research observed,

> The U.S. inherited this position two decades ago upon the implosion of the Soviet Union and the socialist camp and is hardly prepared to step aside. The policy Washington adopted at that time, and which remains in force today, is to prevent the emergence of any powerful rival or military force potentially able to undermine American dominion.[32]

Specifically, the "Defense Planning Guidance on Post-Cold-War Strategy," and prepared under the supervision of Paul Wolfowitz—the then Pentagon's undersecretary for policy—was disclosed in March of 1992 by the *New York*

Times. After the first invasion of Iraq, it became known as the *Project for the New American Century*, publicly released from 1997 to 2000 prior to the September 11 attacks. Item 6 of the strategic plan defined the agenda in general terms: "In the Middle East and Southwest Asia, our overall objective is to remain the predominant power in the region and preserve U.S. and western access to the region's oil."[33]

The convergence of interest of local Arab States elites and the U.S. strategy for dominance in MENA since 1990, and especially since 2001, drastically contributed to increasing popular opposition in Arab streets to Western domination and "Arab humiliation" and the Arab Spring movements since December 2010. As John Waterbury observed as early as in 2003:

The post-9/11 terrorist attack on American forces in Iraq has also revealed that al-Qa'ida is really a multinational network of dedicated radical militants from all over the Muslim world, committed to an anti-Western, and especially anti-American, campaign. The ultimate goal of al-Qa'ida is the eradication of Western influence and control over Muslim countries, especially the oil-rich Middle East. But equally important to al-Qa'ida operatives is the overthrow of "corrupt" governments in the Middle East and elsewhere in the Muslim world, who, with the support of the West, have abandoned the *will of Allah*—the establishment of just and viable Islamic governments. The U.S. support of the "illegitimate" state of Israel in its conflict with the conquered Palestinians, the U.S. military presence in Saudi Arabia and the Persian Gulf States and support for their corrupt regimes, and the long-standing U.S. sanctions against innocent Iraqi people have been cited by Osama bin Laden as the fundamental reasons behind his strong anti-American stance.[34]

The United States' military presence and close support for authoritarian Arab regimes, especially since the September 11, 2001, attacks, has exacerbated seemingly sectarian and ethnic rivalries, evident in violent clashes, among others, in Iraq and Syria. The phobia over a rising Shi'a state blending Islam and Republicanism after the Iranian Revolution alarmed the political elite in conservative Arab States as a threat to the status quo, who then utilized their wealth to shore up religious sectarianism in the name of national and international security. Billions of Saudi dollars helped spread Wahhabism in Pakistan, giving rise to the al-Qaeda and the Taliban, and all of it with the help of the Central Intelligence Agency and the Pakistani ISI. Only Saudi Arabia, the United Arab Emirates, and Qatar recognized the Taliban rule, where an estimated 40 percent of their supporters studied in Saudi maintained religious school in Pakistan.

The U.S. invasion of Iraq in 2003 under false pretenses and its imbalanced approach to central issues of concern in the MENA region stood contrary to peoples' interest, if not the regimes'. These concerns included: the U.S. support for abusive, authoritative regimes while preaching democracy and human rights; preferential treatment of the state of Israel vis-à-vis Palestinian national aspirations; and the duplicitous approach in the treatment of Israeli and Iranian nuclear programs, pressuring Iran for a civilian program while totally ignoring the Israeli possession of nuclear arsenal. Therefore, as one observer points out, the threat to the United States does not stem from the militant terrorists but from the larger group of Muslim Middle Easterners who express anger toward the United States and evince some sympathy for bin Laden: "This group's members are afflicted by middle-class frustrations, governed by political systems that give them no voice, and burdened by economies that offer them few opportunities." They are witnessing a conflict over land and sacred places in which they perceive the United States as applying two standards of equity and two standards of measuring violence, each in favor of Israel. That resulting frustration and anger leads to expressions of sympathy for those who resort to violence against the United States.[35]

Furthermore, the all-inclusive definition of al-Qaeda also served as the ever-convenient ruse to justify American involvement. Al-Qaeda has been used by Washington to rationalize the establishment of the U.S. Africa Command (AFRICOM); it was set up in 2008 to manage U.S. military interests in the whole continent with the exception of Egypt. The U.S. State Department claimed that AFRICOM "will play a supportive role as Africans build democratic institutions and establish good governance across the continent."[36] The Arab Spring initially promised prospects for political revolution, as in Tunisia and Egypt or political reform from the above. However, the Saudi and the Persian Gulf Arab States' (GCC) response to the Arab Spring came through a combination of tightening security and oppression and financial largesse, quieting the otherwise complacent population. The United States' assurance to retain its military presence and political support only further facilitated regime resistance to popular call for political opening, and in the case of Bahrain and Yemen actually gave tacit support to the Saudi invasion of these two countries. Saudi Arabia sent in its troops to Bahrain in 2011 to help the ruling family suppress the popular movement, although the GCC countries' unanimous decision on the matter testifies to the shallow nature of the state structure in these family-rule sheikhdoms, where the country is treated as a "real estate" and citizens are in reality only subjects. Popular movement in Bahrain for political opening in Bahrain was portrayed as an "Iranian-back" Shi'a insurgency![37] Saudi Arabia began its military campaign in Yemen in March 2015.

President Obama's handling of the Arab Spring has also proven insensitive to popular demands in the Arab streets and only called for political opening and democracy, while continuing with a priority policy of regime stability, secured oil flow, and a secured and dominant Israel. So, the United States' support for monarchical and family regimes in the name of stability stands in contradistinction to its political rhetoric in support of democratic values and human rights. The U.S. and NATO military support and intervention has been mainly in support of the old regimes' political elites, as in Bin Ali's Tunisia, Mubarak's Egypt, Ali Abdullah Saleh's Yemen, Saudi Arabia's al-Saud family, Kuwait's al-Sabah family, the UAE's al-Nahyan family, Bahrain's al-Khalifa family, and Qatar's Kalifa bin Hamad's family. Marc Lynch, writing on the U.S. relations with Arab Gulf monarchies observes that there are policy implications attached to the "belief in a 'monarchical exception.' It may be useful for the monarchs in their efforts to deflect domestic challenges, reduce expectations of potential change, and maintain international support. [But] It may also contribute to a certain complacency among their foreign allies, who may be relieved at not seeing the need to plan for the possible loss or transformation of such useful partners." Marc Lynch's concludes that "the monarchies look like fairly typical Arab authoritarian regimes, surviving because they enjoy greater financial resources, less demanding international allies, and powerful media assets to perpetuate their legitimation myths" remains valid.[38]

One group of refugees suffering from both displacement and occupation is of course the Palestinians. The Palestinian issue, however, has been "put on the back burner" since the United States' declared war on terrorism. Millions of Palestinian refugees in Lebanon and Syria have once again become refugees, and millions of others in Gaza, Libya, and in the Persian Gulf region have experienced hardship in recent years, particularly suffering since 2001, and more recently since the advent of the Arab Spring in 2011. The Obama administration's lip service to the Palestinian issue also has meant the deterioration of lives for millions of Palestinians and more intrusive and damaging Israeli policy. The early appointment of Dennis Ross and the appointment of former British prime minister Tony Blair, as the Middle East point man to restart negotiations between Palestinians and Israelis were merely window-dressing. Aside from Obama's 1967 borders remark, all his comments just before and during Netanyahu's 2011 self-serving visit were paeans to Israel and pledges of America's support. . . . Obama (1) refused to call on Israel to stop building settlements in Palestinian territory; (2) omitted mention of Israel's illegal demand to annex all Jerusalem; (3) did not refer to the Palestinian refugee situation; (4) insisted that the PA withdraw its application for statehood set to be debated at the UN in September, with a good chance of General Assembly approval (though an inevitable U.S. Security Council veto will obviate the vote); (5) opposed the unity moves between Fatah/PA in West Bank and Hamas in Gaza.[39] Absence of a serious and full-time U.S. commitment to a viable two-state solution, an emboldened Israeli leadership under Prime Minister Netanyahu has pursued a policy to kill any chances for a two-state solution to the conflict.

CONCLUSION

Arab regimes' ineptitude in dealing with effective governance is well apparent in events in the region that have resulted in harsh authoritarian rule, severe socioeconomic problems, and Western interventionism to the detriment of native population. Arab peoples' demand for empowerment and dignity has, for the most part, not been realized. The neo-patrimonial and Rentier nature of Arab political economy, though with varying degrees, persisted throughout the Cold War and only worsened in its aftermath. The Post-September 2001 events further revealed the "shallow" basis of power of the Arab political elite and their clumsy attempts at building modern, prosperous, Islamic societies. El-Din Shahin wrote in an edited volume that, "[T]here is no dissent in this volume from the view that the existing regimes (in the Arab world) are deeply entrenched and that tentative steps toward liberalization hardly amount to a move toward democratization." . . . .While their authors noted some "pockets of liberalization" in more critical local media, a young generation of Internet activists, increasingly experienced NGOs, and a few protest movements, in general, saw a "weak, fragmented, and passive civil society" and "very low political participation and public apathy" as major obstacles to democratic change.[40]

The authoritarian Arab States have prevented the rise of civic and religious groups into national political prominence and preventing prospects for a possible peaceful takeover of the state by such groups. Sociopolitical movements like the Islamic movement since the 1980s, including the Taliban, the militant terrorist groups like the al-Qaeda, and the Daesh and a plethora of other militant movements in the past few decades have all emerged to fill in the political vacuum and to restore "Islamic governance." That is, the failure of politics and political leaders in the Arab States in securing legitimate, popular participation in national and local governance galvanizes radical thinking and the emergence of militant groups, all in the name of Islam. This is nothing but a crisis of governance.

Persistent Western intervention has been detrimental to Arab politics: it has basically supported the family and elite-dominated authoritarian regimes at the expense of political development toward democracy and popular empowerment. The spillover effect from Iraq and Afghanistan in the 1980s—and one can add the 1976–1990 civil war in Lebanon—was the consolidation of Shi'a-inspired anti-Western "resistance ideology" and the Sunni-inspired "anti-Modern" ideology. The U.S. support for the Iraqi regime in the 1980s and support for the Mujahedeen fighting the Soviet invasion of Afghanistan in the 1980s had resulted in the prolongation of Iran–Iraq war, with incalculable sufferings on both sides and the training and breeding of a new generation of fighters inspired by religious zealotry in Afghanistan and Pakistan. The

MEA region has experienced widespread instability and misery since 2001 and the U.S. declared war on terrorism. Either the policy of regime change in Afghanistan (2001), Iraq (2003), Libya (2011), and Syria (still ongoing) or regime preservation in Egypt, Saudi Arabia, and other GCC states since the advent of Arab Spring has contributed to intensified regime repressiveness, chaos and war, and refugees.

There are consequences to every policy, especially one with "imperial designs" while preaching democratic rule and human rights. As Gregory Gause referring to Washington's dilemma over matters of security and democracy in Saudi Arabia and Bahrain and elsewhere in the region rightly points out,

> I think you are trying to have it both ways here, "Liberal vision" AND the existing security structure of American regional policy. I don't think that you can have both. The middle ground of talking about pushing for reform and the like in Saudi Arabia without really doing anything about it opens us up to legitimate charges of hypocrisy.[41]

Recent research overturns the standard narrative that addressing migration crises mainly means curtailing the conflict and poverty that "push" migrants away from home and slashing the excessive generosity that "pull" them into other countries. Instead, pragmatic and self-interested policymakers should consider that they often waste resources when trying to reduce push factors, and they can spark an inhumane and inefficient race to the bottom by acting individually to reduce pull factors. Through broad international cooperation to get people out of camps and into the labor force, though, they can transform refugees from a burden into an investment.[42] Rich countries, it is also proposed, could reduce onward flows of refugees by compensating third countries—elsewhere in the region or even far away—for the upfront costs of permanently resettling and integrating them.[43] But, this is only a "buck-passing" solution to the problem that was actually prompted by the very rich countries of the West who are accomplices in the U.S. regime change policy since 2001, not to mention the rich Persian Gulf Arab States who often try to pour money on any inflaming issues seemingly threatening their regimes and who have also been accomplices in the creation of the current refugee crisis, namely, Saudi Arabia and Qatar.

In the end, if there will be those who lose economically from an influx of refugees, but Europeans must open their borders and show compassion because it is the right thing to do, and also because they are partly responsible, through their open and complicit cooperation with the United States' failed, aggressive policies, for the political disarray in Syria, Libya, Iraq, Yemen, Somalia, and Afghanistan. The EU's failure to agree on a simple, equitable quota system to embrace most recent refugees since 2011 may will be remembered in the future as a turning point contributing to the weakening or even ending the European project. The economic and financial crisis since 2008 may be the real force threatening the survival of the EU. But, shutting the doors on people in dire need of help is the real moral and legal failure of these "democratic, liberal, humanitarian states." Aside from Germany and Sweden, the failure of the EU members, especially the "Eastern European" members, is only outdone by the Australian government. Tony Abbott's Australian policy of shutting down the door to refugees was a shameful rejection of Australia's international responsibilities: as unauthorized seaborne arrivals reached to almost zero in 2014 from about 20,000 in 2013, as patrol ships turned back migrant boats even if they appeared at risk of sinking.[44]

NOTES

1. Juan Cole (2014). *The New Arabs: How the Millennial Generation Is Changing the Middle.* New York: Simon and Shuster.
2. International Monetary Fund (Oct. 8, 2015). *Economic Outlook and Key Challenges.* Washington, DC. http://www.imf.org/external/np/pp/eng/2015/100815a.pdf
3. International Organization for Migration (Dec. 18, 2015). *EU Migrant, Refugee Arrivals by Land and Sea Approach One Million in 2015* http://www.iom.int/news/eu-migrant-refugee-arrivals-land-and-sea-approach-one-million 2015
4. For Italy, the main countries of origin during the first half of 2015 were: Eritrea (18,676), Nigeria (7,897), Somalia (6,334), Syria (4,271), Gambia (3,593), and Sudan (3,589). See International Organization for Migration (Jul. 10, 2015). *Migrant Boat Arrivals in Europe Top 150,000 in 2015.* http://www.iom.int/news/migrant-boat-arrivals-europe-top-150000-2015
5. International Organization for Migration (2016). *Mediterranean Migrant Arrivals in 2016: 178,882; Deaths 737 IOM,* April 19. http://www.iom.int/news/mediterranean-migrant-arrivals-2016-178882-deaths-737
6. United Nations Human Rights Commission (2016). *Syria Refugee Response. UNHCR, April 11.* http://data.unhcr.org/syrianrefugees/country.php?id=224
7. United Nations Human Rights Commission (2016). *Syria Refugee Response. UNHCR, April 25.* http://data.unhcr.org/syrianrefugees/regional.php
8. United Nations Human Rights Commission (2016). *Syria Refugee Response. UNHCR, March 31.* http://data.unhcr.org/syrianrefugees/country.php?id=122
9. United Nations Human Rights Commission (2016). *Syria Refugee Response. UNHCR, April 19.* http://data.unhcr.org/syrianrefugees/country.php?id=107
10. UNICEF (2015). *Small Hands, Heavy Burden: How the Syrian Conflict Driving More Children into Workforce.* July 2. https://www.unicef.es/sites/www.unicef.es/files/child-labour-final.pdf
11. UNICEF (2015). *Small Hands, Heavy Burden: How the Syrian Conflict Driving More Children into Workforce.* July 2. https://www.unicef.es/sites/www.unicef.es/files/child-labour-final.pdf

12. Samantha Schmidt (2016). "How to Educate a Generation of Syrian Refugees? Makeshift Classrooms and the Teacher Next Door," *Yes Magazine*, April 12. http://www.yesmagazine.org/peace-justice/how-to-educate-a-generation-of-syrian-refugees-makeshift-classrooms-and-the-teacher-next-door-20160412

13. http://www.juancole.com/2014/12/refugees-struggle-winter.html

14. Anthony Faiola and Robert Samuels (2015). "As Human Flood Continues, Germany Slaps Controls on Border with Austria," *Washington Post*, September 13. https://www.washingtonpost.com/world/migrants-coming-into-europe-reach-record-highs/2015/09/13/5c2732e9-dc33-4528-850d-94361c7b0917_story.html

15. Yoruk Bachceli. (2015). "Wilders Tells Dutch Parliament Refugee Crisis Is 'Islamic Invasion'," *Reuters*, September 10. http://www.reuters.com/article/us-europe-migrants-netherlands-idUSKCN0RA0WY20150910

16. British Broadcasting Corporation. (Jul. 30, 2015). "David Cameron Criticised Over Migrant 'Swarm' Language," http://www.bbc.com/news/uk-politics-33716501

17. Michael A. Clemens and Justin Sandfur. (2015). "A Self-Interested Approach to Migration Crises: Push Factor, Pull Factor, and Investing In Refugees," *Foreign Affairs*, September 27. https://www.foreignaffairs.com/articles/central-europe/2015-09-27/self-interested-approach-migration-crises See also, Europe should welcome more refugees and economic migrants—for the sake of the world and itself, The Economist, Sep 12th 2015 http://www.economist.com/news/leaders/21664136-europe-should-welcome-more-refugees-and-economic-migrantsfor-sake-world-and

18. Mette Foged and Giovanni Peri (2015). "Immigrants and Effect on Native Worker: New Analysis in Longitudinal Data," *Institute for the Study of Labor*, IZA. March. http://ftp.iza.org/dp8961.pdf

19. James Corbett (2013). "Syria Is Not a Civil War, It Is a Foreign Intervention," *Global Research*, October 4. http://www.globalresearch.ca/syria-is-not-a-civil-war-it-is-a-foreign-intervention/5352926

20. Governance and Democracy. https://www.giz.de/en/ourservices/governance_and_democracy.html

21. Ali R. Abootalebi (2000). *Islam and Democracy: State Society Relations in Developing Countries, 1908–1994*. Taylor and Francis Group.

22. Ali R. Abootalebi (2009). "Iran's Tenth Presidential Elections: Candidates, Issues, and Implications," *Rubin Center or International Affairs Research,* September 1. http://www.rubincenter.org/2009/09/abootalebi-2009-09-01/

23. Erich Weede and Edward N. Muller (1998). "Rebellion, Violence and Revolution: A Rational Choice Perspective," *Journal of Peace Research*, vol. 35, no. 1, January, pp. 43–59.

24. Bruce K. Rutherford (2012). "Egypt: The Origins and Consequences of the January 25 Uprising," In *The Arab Spring: Change and Resistance in the Middle East.* Boulder, CO: Westview Press, 35. Print.

25. Jennifer Gandhi and Adam Przeworski. (2013). "Authoritarian Institutions and the Survival of Autocrats," *Comparative Political Studies*. n. page. Web. Dec. 5. https://uwec.courses.wisconsin.edu/d2l/lms/content/viewer/main_frame.d2l?ou=2184483&tId=13270024

26. Elizabeth Dikinson (2014). "How Qatar Lost the Middle East," *Foreign Policy*, March 15. http://www.foreignpolicy.com/articles/2014/03/05/how_qatar_lost_the_middle_east

27. Haas, Mark L. and David W. Lesch (2012). *The Arab Spring: Change and Resistance in the Middle East*, p. 107.

28. Haas, Mark L. and David W. Lesch (2012). *The Arab Spring*, p. 103.

29. Steven Heydemann, "Upgrading Authoritarianism in the Arab World," *Saban Center Analysis Paper* No. 13 (Washington, DC: Brookings Institution, October 2007); Ellen Lust-Okar. "Divided They Rule: The Management and Manipulation of Political Opposition," *Comparative Politics*, vol. 36, no. 2 (January 2004); Lisa Blaydes, *Elections and Distributive Politics in Mubarak's Egypt* (Cambridge: Cambridge University Press, 2011).

30. Jason Brownlee (2007). *Authoritarianism in an Age of Democratization.* Cambridge: Cambridge University Press.

31. Achcar, Gilbert (2013). *The People Want: A Radical Exploration of the Arab Uprising*, tr. By G. M. Goshgarian, Berkeley: University of California Press.

32. Jack Smith (2011). "Obama's Foreign Policy Objectives: The Geopolitical Middle East, North Africa, Central Asia Mosaic," *Global Research*, June 1. http://www.globalresearch.ca/obama-s-foreign-policy-objectives-the-geopolitical-middle-east-north-africa-central-asia-mosaic/25077

33. John Mc Murtry (2013). "The Moral Decoding of 9-11: Beyond the U.S. Criminal State, The Grand Plan for a New World Order," *Global Research*, February 19. http://www.globalresearch.ca/the-moral-decoding-of-9-11-beyond-the-u-s-criminal-state-the-grand-plan-for-a-new-world-order/5323300 For original analysis, see Journal of 9/11 Studies Volume 35, February 2013 http://www.journalof911studies.com/resources/2013McMurtryVol35Feb.pdf

34. John Waterbury (2003). "Hate Your Policies, Love Your Institutions," *Foreign Affairs*, vol. 82, no. 1, January/February, pp. 58–68: 58.

35. John Waterbury (2003). "Hate Your Policies, Love Your Institutions," *Foreign Affairs*, vol. 82, no. 1, p. 58.

36. Ramzy Baroud (2012). "West Africa, Next Stop for War on Terror," *Press TV*, Tuesday, Dec. 18. http://www.presstv.com/detail/2012/12/17/278485/west-africa-next-stop-for-war-on-terror/

37. Ethan Bronner and Michael Slackman (2011). "Saudi Troops Enter Bahrain to Help Put Down Unrest," *New York Times*, March 14. http://www.nytimes.com/2011/03/15/world/middleeast/15bahrain.html?_r=0

38. Marc Lynch. (2012). *The Arab Monarchy Debate*, March 16. http://lynch.foreignpolicy.com/posts/2012/12/19/the_arab_monarchy_debate

39. Jack Smith. (2011). "Obama's Foreign Policy Objectives: The Geopolitical Middle East, North Africa, Central Asia Mosaic," *Global Research*, June 1. (http://www.globalresearch.ca/obama-s-foreign-policy-objectives-the-geopolitical-middle-east-north-africa-central-asia-mosaic/25077

40. Nathan J. Brown and Emad El-Din Shahin. (2010). "Conclusion," in Brown and Shahin (eds.), *The Struggle Over Democracy in the Middle East.* New York: Routledge, pp. 186–187.

41. Gregory Gause is the author of the December 2011 Council on Foreign Relations task force report "Saudi Arabia in the New Middle East," see Marc Lynch (2013). "Debating the Saudi Exception," *Foreign Policy*, Friday, January 25. http://lynch.foreignpolicy.com

42. Michael A. Clemens and Justin Sandfur (2015). "A Self-Interested Approach to Migration Crises: Push Factor, Pull Factor, and Investing In Refugees," *Foreign Affairs*, September 27. https://www.foreignaffairs.com/articles/central-europe/2015-09-27/self-interested-approach-migration-crises

43. Ryan Bubb, Michael Kremer and David I. Levine (2011). "The Economics of International Refugee Law," *The Journal of Legal Studies,* vol. 40, no. 2, June, pp. 367–404.

44. Timothy J. Hatton (2015). The Mediterranean boat people: What can be done? *VOV CPER's Portal Policy*, June 5. http://voxcu.org/article/dealing-mediterranean-boat-people

Chapter 6

Beyond Resettlement of Internally Displaced Persons in Bakassi

Challenges and Vistas

Osita Adah

Cameroon and Nigeria are African states on the West Coast of Africa. These countries have adjoining coastlines within the waters of the Gulf of Guinea. On March 29, 1994, Republic of Cameroon being anxious to avoid any armed conflict arising between it and Nigeria approached the International Court of Justice (ICJ) Holden at The Hague on the question of sovereignty over Bakassi Peninsula. Cameroon asked the court to determine the course of the maritime boundaries between it and Nigeria beyond the line delineated by the Maroua Declaration of June 1975. Memorial, counter-memorial, reply, and rejoinder were settled, filed, and exchanged by the parties to the dispute. At the close of exchange of the documents, the matter went to trial during which parties adduced oral and documentary evidence in support of their respective cases. One of the issues that arose for determination by the court from the evidence tendered is whether sovereignty over the Peninsula of Bakassi is vested in Cameroon or Nigeria (Cameroon *v* Nigeria, 2002).

At the close of the written and oral submissions by counsel to the parties, the ICJ on October 10, 2002, handed down its judgment on the Bakassi case. The court declared *inter alia* that sovereignty over Bakassi Peninsula lies with Republic of Cameroon as the successor of German position. Consequently, the court ordered that the Federal Republic of Nigeria should expeditiously and unconditionally withdraw its administrative and its military and police forces from the territories that fall within the Sovereignty of the Republic of Cameroon. The judgment was principally based on the March 11, 1913, Anglo-German Agreement, other events and documents that bear their origin from the Anglo-German Agreement. Nigeria did not appeal against the judgment as specified in Article 61 of ICJ Statute (Adah, 2022; Agwu, 2012).

On June 12, 2006, Nigeria and Cameroon under the auspices of the United Nations (UN) entered into the Green Tree Agreement. The essence of the Green Tree Agreement (GTA) as can be gleaned from its Articles 3 and 7 is to set out the modalities for the implementation of the ICJ Judgment of October 10, 2002, and the guarantee of the fundamental rights and freedoms of the internally displaced persons (IDPs) in Bakassi who were conceded the opportunity of choice of residing in the Bakassi Peninsula after its eventual transfer to Cameroon (Adah, 2022). On August 14, 2008, final transfer of sovereignty over Bakassi to Cameroon by Nigeria was made. By the transfer, Nigeria thus complied with the ICJ Judgment of October 10, 2002, and the provisions of the Green Tree Agreement of June 12, 2006. The Bakassi people not long after the ICJ Judgment began to suffer in the hands of the Gendarmes of Cameroon incessant attacks, raids, raping of women and girls, and human right abuses. They therefore took the option to return to Nigeria. This provoked population movement and forced migration from Bakassi Peninsula to Nigeria. Nigeria resettled the displaced people of Bakassi Peninsula in "New" Bakassi in Ikot-Effiom/Obutong in Akpabuyo Local Government Area of Cross River State. The place of resettlement now named "New" Bakassi was in memory of their ancestral home "Bakassi Peninsula." The resettlement of IDPs in "New" Bakassi has with it the attendant implications that border on social, political, and economic challenges that are brought to bear on the IDPs in "New" Bakassi, Cross River State, Nigeria (Dakas, 2012).

But, the displacement and resettlement dislocated the IDPs from the source of their economic activity, and this rendered the IDPs vulnerable. The negative impacts of displacement, resettlement, and dislocation include exposing the victims to environmental and health hazards, human right abuses, social disarticulation, and unemployment. The unemployment results in loss of income, poverty, and destitution has the potency to activate terrorism (Ngalim, 2019; Usang, Ikpeme & Amimi, 2014).

Several scholars have addressed the question of the accommodation, health, and general living conditions of the IDPs (Uttah, Ogban & Ukpong, 2013; Ntui, 2015) in "New" Bakassi. Others have reflected on the challenges of displacement and effective resettlement strategy (Onwe & Nwogbaga, 2015). None of these scholars raised the issue of socio-political and economic effects of the resettlement on the IDPs. They failed to address the question why Nigeria has neglected to provide the social, economic, and political needs of the IDPs or achieve durable solution for their displacement since 2007. Of course, Nigeria has the duty to provide the welfare and security needs of the displaced population resettled in "New" Bakassi until durable solutions are achieved within the context of their displacement. Displacement is only required to endure within the period allowed by the circumstances (Brisibe, 2017; Bukar, 2012; McDowell & Morell, 2007).

Since 2007, when the displaced population of Bakassi Peninsula was resettled in Bakassi in Akpabuyo Local Government Area of Cross River State, Nigeria, durable solution with regard to their displacement has not been attained. The IDPs in "New" Bakassi do not enjoy minimum standard of living. The houses provided by Government to accommodate them are not sufficient and are in poor conditions. The IDPs do not live in clean, safe, and satisfactory environment as the camp is surrounded by bushes and IDPs are exposed to sanitation and waste disposal challenges. They have no access to essential food and are exposed to inadequate and unsafe water supply. There are no schools and healthcare facilities in the camp. Many of the IDPs are disenfranchised either because they cannot cast their votes at elections for lack of adequate facilities or that they have not been registered as voters since 2007 by the Independent National Electoral Commission (INEC) (Shebbs, Agbor & Uduma, 2022; Adah & Sodipo, 2021; Fonkeng, 2019). This chapter addresses the question as to why durable solution has not been achieved for the IDPs in "New" Bakassi with regard to their displacement since 2007.

Until the socio-politico and economic needs of the IDPs are met or durable solution is achieved with regard to their displacement, the plights of the population will remain a burning question. Thus, the principal objective of the chapter is to identify the various international, regional, and municipal instruments that impose on Nigeria the duty to achieve durable solution for IDPs; determine the necessary measures taken by Nigeria to enable it to achieve durable solution for the IDPs; and assess the degree of performance by Nigerian government of its duty to achieve durable solution for the IDPs.

INTERNALLY DISPLACED PERSONS

There is generally accepted definition of what constitutes IDPs. The United Nations Guiding Principles on Internal Displacement 1998 (GPOID) gives the notion of IDPs which is meant to be descriptive rather than normative. This notion has gained acceptance and is generally used within the international community (Kälin, 2014). The team internal displacement since it was first coined by Eugene M. Kulischer in 1960 has gained prominence in conflict and humanitarian agenda (Osah & Ogu, 2020). It has as well assumed different definitions, but the most prominent being the United Nations Guiding Principles on Internal Displacement, 1998 (GPOID). Its introduction defines IDPs as:

> A person or groups of persons who have been forced or obliged to flee or leave their homes or places of habitual residence in particular as a result of or in order to avoid the effects of armed conflicts, situations of generalized violence,

violations of human rights, natural or human made disasters and who have not crossed an internationally recognized state border.

Similarly, African Union Convention for the Protection and Assistance of Internally Displaced Persons in Africa 2009 popularly known as "Kampala Convention" adopts verbatim the definitions of IDPs offered by the GPOID, 1998, on IDPs, but goes further to say that internal displacement is "The involuntary or forced migration, evacuation or relocation of persons or groups of persons within internally recognized border." These definitions show two clear characteristics of internal displacement and IDPs. First, internal displacement is an involuntary movement or forced migration of persons or groups of person. Second, while on forced migration from their homestead or places of habitual residence, the IDPs have not crossed internationally recognized state border.

Adedayo (2015) noted that those classified as IDPs has increased exponentially and far out-number refugee figures globally. He further noted that by the year 2000, the number of IDPs had reached 25 million. The UNHCR in 2014 reported that the IDP figures globally had risen to 59.5 million. That 2014 figure were the highest since the World War II, which was more than a 100 percent increase. Africa is also reported as having the highest figure with one-third of the world's refugees and IDPs, and the numbers have largely remained on the rise with the endemic nature of conflicts in the continent.

Cohen and Deng argued as early as 1998 that IDPs now constitute one of the largest populations at risk and the figures are on the increase yearly. Displaced persons are mostly vulnerable and defenseless and easy target of the poverty and human rights abuses, hence the need for not only protection and assistance from their own government but from the international agencies as well. Today, most of the world's countries produce refugees and IDPs, yet it is arguable whether the United Nations High Commission for Refugees (UNHCR) should provide the same level of assistance to IDPs as to those others who have crossed an internationally recognized border (Özerdem & Jacoby, 2007).

Though the causes of internal displacement vary between natural disasters and man-inflicted such as armed conflicts, others like those of Bakassi were an aftermath of the judgment ceding Bakassi Peninsula to the Cameroons. The people of Bakassi Peninsula now in "New" Bakassi are IDPs, in that they were forced by the ICJ Judgment, the GTA, and final transfer of Bakassi Peninsula by Nigeria to migrate to "New" Bakassi in Cross River state, Nigeria. They did not cross any internationally recognized state border, in that prior to their forced migration Bakassi Peninsula remained under the sovereignty of Nigeria.

The challenges of IDPs lead to Resettlement (Ekoh, Okoye, George, Chukwuemeka & Agbawodikeizu, 2022; Gurung, 2022). Resettlement within the context of IDPs and internal displacement means the processes and arrangements that enable or provide the opportunity for the IDPs in the exercise of their volition to return to their homes or places of habitual residence and re-unite with their families or provide them the opportunity to integrate into another community or a place within the territory of Nigeria other than their place or places of original displacement for the purpose of achieving durable solutions in the affairs of the IDPs (NPIDP, 2012). It means the processes and arrangements undertaken by a national government, international community, or nongovernmental organization to protect the rights and provide the welfare and security needs of the IDPs by integrating them in a different environment and providing them land, modern homes, assets, sources of sustenance or livelihood, access to resources, and services so as to provide enduring solutions to their problems (Onwe and Nwogbaga, 2015).

To achieve the resettlement of the IDPs, host communities become very relevant (Jafer, Imana, Doda & Lemessa, 2022). A host community within the context of internal displacement and IDPs refers to a community that is not itself displaced but experiences the effects or results of displacement, in that it has to accommodate or host a reasonable number of IDPs either in camps, collective centers, and informed settlement or by directly integrating them into households (Bakare, Khan & Akash, 2022). Host community may also refer to a community that has to receive and integrate formally displaced persons who decide to return to their homes or places of habitual residence or who have decided to settle permanently elsewhere in Nigeria (NPIDP, 2012).

According to Inter-Agency Standing Committee, Internally Displaced Persons Protection Policy (1999), IDPs are entitled to the right of protection. Protection means all activities aimed at obtaining full respect for the rights of the individual in accordance with the letter and the spirit of the relevant laws (i.e., Human Rights Law, International Humanitarian Law, Refugee Law). Protection therefore involves creating an environment conducive to respect for human beings, preventing and/or alleviating the immediate effects of a specific pattern of abuse and restoring dignified conditions of life through reparation, restitution, and rehabilitation (NPIDP, 2012).

The efforts of resettlement of IDPs are expected to lead to durable solutions. Durable solutions refer to a situation or circumstance in which the IDPs no longer have any specific assistance and protection needs that are linked to their displacement and can enjoy their human rights without discrimination on account of their displacement. This requires a comprehensive approach encompassing voluntary return, local integration, and resettlement (Onwe and Nwogbaga, 2015).

IMPACT OF RESETTLEMENT ON THE IDPS OF THE "NEW" BAKASSI

The International Court of Justice (ICJ) in its judgment of October 10, 2002, declared that: "the boundary between Cameroon and Nigeria in Bakassi is delimited by Articles XVIII to XX of the Anglo-German Agreement of 11th March 1913, and that sovereignty over the peninsula lies with Cameroon."

The court ordered that: "the Federal Republic of Nigeria is under an obligation expeditiously and without condition to withdraw its administrative and its military and police forces from the territories which fall within the sovereignty of the Republic of Cameroon."

On June 12, 2006 Cameroon and Nigeria under the auspices of international community entered into the GTA aimed at setting up modalities for the implementation of the ICJ Judgment, and on August 14, 2008, Nigeria formally transferred the sovereignty over Bakassi territory to the Republic of Cameroon. The declaration and order made by the court, the modalities set up for the implementation of the judgment, and the subsequent resettlement have political, social, and economic impacts on the IDPs resettled in Bakassi in Akpabuyo Local Government Area of Cross River State, Nigeria (Aluko & Obodo, 2018; Okoi, 2016; Dakas, 2003).

POLITICAL DIMENSIONS OF THE RESETTLEMENT

By the force and operation of the ICJ Judgment, Bakassi ceases to be a Local Government Area in Cross River State, Nigeria. The loss affects the right of the Bakassi population to vie to or be represented in Cross River State House of Assembly, House of Representatives, and Senate at the federal level in Nigeria. This is the reason notable politicians from the Bakassi population seem to have disappeared from Nigeria political theatre. The loss also affects the size of the constituencies in House of Representatives and Senate (Ugwuka, Adesegun & Adam, 2016).

A weighty implication of the ICJ Judgment is that the indigenous people of Bakassi have their group identity effaced or obliterated from the global map. The judgment also dismantled and swept away all the electoral words, constituencies, and structures created by Nigerian government and disfranchised the population of Bakassi Peninsula, until institutional arrangements are made by Nigerian government (Adah, 2022).

This is because the judgment and the modalities for its implementation provoked forced or involuntary migration or resettlement with its attendant consequences. The IDPs may exercise the option to remain in Bakassi Peninsula and change to nationals of Republic of Cameroon. They may choose to remain in Bakassi and retain their citizenship of Nigeria. In this case, they will be treated as aliens and subjected to the requirement of resident permits and visa among others (Dakas, 2003; Ugwuka, Adesegun & Adam, 2016).

Social Implications of the Resettlement

The displacement and resettlements of the Bakassi Population have their attendant social implications. A common thread that runs through or a malady that affects all the IDPs across the globe including those in Bakassi, Nigeria, is “vulnerability” (Osah & Ogu, 2020). The vulnerability is caused by the displacement and resettlement of the IDPs in a new or foreign environment. The vulnerability also stems from the dislocation of the IDPs from the source of their domestic economy or livelihood (Agba, Akpanudoedehe & Ushie, 2010).

There exists no hospital or a functional health center in Bakassi. The available hospital is situated at Ikot-Ene in Akpabuyo Local Government Area, about an hour drive in a car from the settlement. It was the lack of these amenities that led to the death of Mrs. Eno Asuquo Etim in 2018 during child birth (Uttah, Uttah & Okonofua, 2012). There are no social amenities and common facilities in Ikot-Effiom/Obutong. There are no primary and secondary schools located in Bakassi where the IDPs are resettled. The nearest primary school in Bakassi is located in the host community at Bakassi market which is about fifteen-minute drive on a motorcycle (motorbike) from the settlement. The nearest secondary school to the settlement is also located in the host community at Obot-20-Ikang, about forty-five-minute drive from the IDP settlement. The schools do not have sufficient facilities to accommodate both the children of the IDPs and the host community (Bakassi people) together (Ekezie, Siebert, Timmons, Murray & Bains, 2022; Brisibe, 2017; Fayomi, 2012).

Bakassi where the IDPs are resettled has no efficient system of adequate and continuous water supply. It lacks sanitary facilities and electricity supply, and the camp is surrounded with bushes. The system of water supply provided by the Cross River state government is dysfunctional. The only source of water supply that is functioning is the World-Bank-type hand-pump. The system does not supply water to the available water closet toilets. The IDPs therefore use water from the hand-pump to manually depose of their human wastes. The IDPs also need water for drinking, personal sanitation, washing of clothes, food preparation, and household hygiene, to prevent death from dehydration, and reduce the risk of water-related disease. Furthermore, the IDPs need water for subsistence farming, to secure their livelihood, lead a life in human dignity, and achieve adequate standard of living (Adah & Sodipo, 2021; Kamta, Schilling & Scheffran, 2020; Ngalim, 2019).

The houses in Bakassi are not adequate and sufficient to accommodate the IDPs. The total number of houses provided does not satisfy the housing requirements of the IDPs. The current population size of IDPs in Bakassi is 4,717 comprising 2,214 households. The population figure took into account the fact that many of the IDPs have fled to other parts of Nigeria while others have returned to Bakassi Peninsula to seek means of earning income in order to live. The total number of houses provided is about 3 percent of the housing requirements of the IDPs. The houses lack modern facilities such as mosquitoes screen, showers, and hot water systems. The environment is covered with bushes and is in poor sanitary condition (Onuoha & Chukwu, 2022; Kamta, Schilling & Scheffran, 2021).

ECONOMIC IMPLICATIONS OF THE RESETTLEMENT

The Bakassi Peninsula has mangrove vegetation rich in oil mineral, fish, shrimps, and varied array of other marine life. The original inhabitants of Bakassi Peninsula now resettled in Bakassi are skilled fishermen. The Bakassi Peninsula is a fertile area for the business of catching fish or fishing expedition. By resettling the IDPs in Bakassi, they have been dislocated from their age- long fishing business in the sea. This means loss of income, unemployment, and destitution. It also entails loss of good will and customers, and it will take a pretty long time for the IDPs to acclimatize themselves in the new environment (Aghemelo & Ibhasebhor, 2006; Isokon, Ekeh & Icha, 2014).

The judgment of International Court of Justice (ICJ) delivered on October 10, 2002, extinguished the customary title of the IDPs over their ancestral lands and vested same on the Republic of Cameroon. The Republic of Cameroon has neglected to give a measure of compensation to the IDPs to assuage them for the injury. Land has commercial value. The IDPs having been divested of their ancestral lands have therefore suffered economic loss (Ugwuka, Adesegun & Adam, 2016).

According to Onwe and Nwogbaga (2015), no matter the dimensions and causes of displacement, its impact on the displaced persons is enormous and includes loss of land, loss of employment, loss of shelter, marginalization, increased morbidity and mortality, greater food insecurity, loss of access to common property/services, and social disarticulation. Similarly, Agba, Akpanudoedehe, and Ushie (2010) noted that social change is inevitable in resettlement. They assert that the provision of modern houses in twenty-one resettlement sites in Jebba was one of the positive outcomes of resettlement. They argue that in-spite of the provision of these modern houses that brought positive structural change in Jebba, many families suffered occupational dislocation and disruption of sources of domestic economy. In their assessment of camp condition of the IDPs in Bakassi thus, Uttah, Uttah, and Okonofua (2012) averred that the IDPs in Bakassi were fishermen and fisherwomen carrying on the business of fish catching in the Bakassi Peninsula. Their camp assessment shows that these fishermen and fisherwomen since their resettlement in Bakassi have remained idle and do not carry on their fishing business. And according to Ntui (2015), the IDPs in Bakassi being fishermen and fisherwomen who have spent a greater part of their lives fishing in the sea and river are now beginning to acclimatize themselves to a "new mode of survival on land."

Uttah, Uttah, and Okonofua (2012) carried out an assessment of camp condition and medical complaints by Bakassi Resettlees attending Approved Hospitals in Cross River state, Nigeria. The study revealed that the Internally Displaced Persons (IDPs) were exposed to poor water supply, overcrowded environment, poor feeding, and paucity of social amenities such as schools. Many of the houses had no mosquito screens. The camp is surrounded by bushes and no electricity supply.

Resettlement is a precursor or forerunner to health hazard, outbreak of resettlement- related diseases. The health hazards common among displaced persons are those associated with overcrowding, poor accommodation, inadequate and unsafe water supply, sanitation, and waste disposal challenges. Others include poor sewerage system, under-nutrition, paucity of water, and poverty (Eweka & Olusegun, 2016; Uttah, Uttah & Okonofua, 2012).

NATIONAL OBLIGATIONS TO THE IDPS

The Universal Declaration of Human Rights 1948 (UDHR), Article 25; International Covenant on Economic, Social, and Cultural Rights 1966 (ICESCR); The Guiding Principles on Internal Displacement 1998 (GPOID), principles 3 and 25(1) and the African Union Convention for the Protection and Assistance of Internally Displaced Persons in Africa 2009 (Kampala Convention), Article 5(1) place on the national authority the primary duty and responsibility to provide protection and humanitarian assistance to the IDPs within their internationally recognized borders. The purpose is to enable the national authorities to achieve durable solution for the IDPs in their jurisdictions. The GPOID, 1998, and Kampala Convention, 2009, cloth the IDPs with the right to request and to receive protection and humanitarian assistance from the national authorities and the national authorities are to refrain from punishing the IDPs for making such a request.

In the domestic arena, it is the primary responsibility of the Nigerian government under Section 14(2) (b) of the Kampala Convention to provide the security and welfare needs of her citizens including the IDPs in Bakassi. The national authorities faced with the phenomenon of internal displacement are to enable them to strictly comply with their obligations. The Brookings

Institution–University of Bern, 2005, has since 2005 developed a framework for national responsibility which set the standard and provided the specific and necessary guidance for the governments of the national authorities to address the phenomenon of displacement (Mooney and French, 2005). The relevant areas or functions to be executed for Nigeria to achieve durable solution for the IDPs in Bakassi are hereby discussed:

ADEQUATE DATA COLLECTION PROCESS

To execute laws and government policies so as to meet the security and welfare needs of the Bakassi population and other IDPs in Nigeria requires the gathering of accurate or correct information on the number, location, and condition of the displaced persons. A reliable database on the Bakassi population and other IDPs in Nigeria will ensure that the proper execution of the IDP laws and the management and prudent allocation of the scarce resources to the security and welfare needs of the population. It will also ensure that the specific needs of the vulnerable subgroups of the IDP population are addressed. Data gathering on the IDPs should begin as soon as displacement occurs and continue until durable solution is achieved. This will provide the opportunity to eliminate or correct false information already gathered and takes note or records of changes in the IDP population (Onuoha & Chukwu, 2022; Kälin, 2004). Nigeria therefore has the accrued obligation to provide an accurate or a reliable database for the IDPs in Bakassi and in other part of Nigeria.

NATIONAL IDP-SPECIFIC INSTITUTION

The African Union Convention for the Protection and Assistance of Internally Displaced Persons in Africa, 2009 (Kampala Convention) provides in its Article 3(2)(b) thus: State Parties shall:

> Designate an authority or body, where needed, responsible for coordinating activities aimed at protecting and assisting internally displaced persons and assign responsibilities to appropriate organs for protection and assistance, and for cooperating with relevant international organisations or agencies, and civil society organisations, where so such authority or body exists.

Drawing from Article 3(2) (b) of this Kampala Convention 2009, Nigeria as the national authority has the accrued obligation to establish an authority or a body to secure the rights of IDPs in Nigeria. In the alternative, the ambit of the National Commission for Refugees can be expanded to include the IDPs in Nigeria. A National IDP-specific institution is essential to promote attention and facilitate effective coordination of various interventions on issues of IDPs in Bakassi and other parts of Nigeria. The institution should be charged with the duty to:

i. collate the figures of the internally displaced persons (IDPS) in Bakassi and other parts of Nigeria from the moment the displacement occurs until durable solution is achieved;
ii. cater for security and welfare needs of Bakassi population and other IDPs;
iii. effectively coordinate the various interventions from the tiers of government, various government agencies and Human Rights Institutions on the issue of IDPs in Nigeria with particular reference to Bakassi Population;
iv. train skilled workers or experts in the management of the concerns generated by the phenomenon of internal displacement. This will give the IDPs specific institution the maximum capacity to manage and resolve IDP issues; and
v. Achieve durable solution for the IDPs in Bakassi and other parts of Nigeria. (Brookings Institution, 2008)

NATIONAL LEGAL FRAMEWORK

The first obligation accruing to Nigeria is to take legislative action to create national legal framework in accordance with the benchmark or the set standard by international law and the Guiding Principle on Internal Displacement, 1998. The legal framework and policies should secure the rights of the Bakassi population and other IDPs or address issues arising from their resettlement. The laws should provide for an efficient government system or approach and structure to coordinate the interventions of the federal, state, and local governments and other agencies and institutions on IDPs questions. The legal framework should also facilitate the responses of humanitarian and development actors providing assistance to the IDPs and ensure that sufficient funds are allocated through national budgeting and international aid to advance the process of achieving durable solution. Nigeria also has the duty to adopt and domesticate International Human Right Law, International Humanitarian Laws, the Guiding Principles on Internal Displacement, and the Kampala Convention 2009 (Inter-Agency Standing Committee 2010; Adah, 2022).

EFFECTIVE MONITORING OF IDPS

Monitoring of IDPs including Bakassi population is essential to ensure that the manifest or real conditions of the IDPs are in strict accordance with the national legal framework and policies, and also the international human rights standards which provide for the exercise. Monitoring is also important to identify the strength and weakness of the existing legal framework and policies. The Federal Government of Nigeria, the state and local government, and the international community bear the duty and responsibility to create an efficient system to monitor the process of determining and achieving durable solution for the Bakassi population and other IDPs. The IDP laws and policies should contain clauses that consider or take into account the vulnerable subgroups of the Bakassi population and other IDP population such as women, children, the old people, the physically challenged, and the marginalized. The laws should also provide for internal mechanism for accountability and external monitoring process. Nigeria has the obligation to clothe the national human right commission with the duty and responsibility to monitor the execution of the legal framework and policies on the IDPs or the respect and protection of the IDP rights. To ensure effective monitoring, the Office of Attorney General of the Federal of Nigeria can be mandated to assist in the monitoring exercise (Adah, 2022).

ALLOCATION OF SUFFICIENT RESOURCES

Article 3(2) (d) of the African Union Convention for the Protection and Assistance of Internally Displaced Persons in Africa (2009) (Kampala Convention) places a duty on Nigeria to provide, to the extent of its resources, the necessary funds for the protection and assistance of the IDPs in Nigeria including the Bakassi population without prejudice to receiving international support or cooperation. In the same vein, the International Covenant on Economic, Social, and Cultural Rights (1966) (ICESCR) enjoins Nigeria to take adequate measures to the extent of its available resources or seek international assistance and cooperation to enable it to progressively achieve durable solution for the IDPs in Nigeria including Bakassi population.

Allocation of sufficient funds to implement the national legal framework and policies or the strategies and programmed designed to achieve durable solution for the IDPs in the country in particular the Bakassi population is essential. For effective national response, it is obligatory on Nigeria to allocate sufficient funds within the limit of its resources to address the concerns of IDPs in Bakassi and other parts of Nigeria. Consultation with the Bakassi population and other IDPs to understand their essential needs and priorities is important to ensure that the available or scarce resources are properly managed and prudently allocated to meet the prioritized needs of the Bakassi population and other IDPs in Nigeria.

LEGISLATIVE MEASURES

An obligation is imposed on Nigeria to achieve durable solutions for Bakassi population in Bakassi within a reasonable time frame as required by the circumstances. Achieving durable solutions for the IDPs entails resolving all issues arising from their displacement or the satisfaction of their rights and welfare needs to the extent that the cause of their discrimination no longer exists (GPOID, 1998 Principle 6(3), 28). From 2007 till date is sufficient a period for Nigeria to have long achieved durable solutions for the IDPs in the New Bakassi.

Nigeria is required to adopt legislative measure to achieve durable solution for the IDPs. Examination of the relevant domestic and international instruments will give credence to this assertion. The preamble to the Constitution of the Federal Republic of Nigeria (1999), Section 4(2), Chapter 2, and item 60(a) of the Exclusive Legislative List of the Constitution shows that Nigeria can adopt legislative measure to achieve durable solution for the IDPs in Bakassi and in Nigeria. A combined reading therefore of Section 4(2), Chapter 2 and item 60(a) of the Exclusive Legislative list of the Constitution shows clearly that Chapter 2 of the Constitution can be enforced by Nigerian government using legislative process to achieve durable solutions for the Bakassi population. In the case of *A-G Ondo State v A-G, (2002: 2008)* Federation, the Supreme Court stated thus:

> I must state that Section 15(5) of the Constitution must be read together with item 60(a) of the Second Schedule of the Constitution, the provisions of which I have set out above. When these two provisions of the Constitution are read together, the clear conclusion that must be reached is that the National Assembly has the legislative power to make laws, in the words of item 60 for:
>
> The establishment and regulation of authorities for Federation or any part thereof:
>
> (a) To promote and defend the Fundamental Objectives and Directive Principles contained in this Constitution.

In Shidali v F.R.N (2008:421), the Supreme Court held that the combined effect of the provisions of Sections 4(2) and 15(5) of the 1999 Constitution and item 60(a) of the Exclusive Legislative list of the Constitution is to empower the National Assembly to make laws for the peace, order, and good government of the federation with respect to any matter included in the Exclusive

Legislative list. It therefore follows that the National Assembly has power to legislate under item 60(a) for the purpose of establishing and regulating the law and order for the federation. In a similar vein, the National Assembly has the power to legislate under item 60(a) of the Exclusive Legislative list for the purpose of providing national legal framework, specific institutions, reliable Database for IDPs; domesticating the Guiding Principles on Internal Displacement 1998 and the Kampala Convention 2009, and taking other legislative steps that can lead achieving durable solution for IDPs in Bakassi and Nigeria.

International Covenant on Economic Social and Cultural rights 1966 (ICESCR) Art 2(1) imposes a duty on Nigeria as a state party to the covenant to adopt legislative measures to progressively achieve durable solution for the IDPs in Bakassi. Nigeria can through legislative measure establish National Legal Framework on IDPs or expand the ambit of the National Commission for Refugees (Establish) Act Cap 21, laws of the Federal of Nigeria 2004 to accommodate the IDP issues. By the same measure, Nigeria can establish an institution with a mandate to manage IDPs issues from inception of disaster till durable solution are achieved or in the alternative expand the powers of the Natural Refugee Commission to include the power to manage IDPs issues in the country including the Bakassi population. It is therefore humbly submitted that Nigeria as a national authority has the primary duty and responsibility to take legislative measures to ensure that durable solutions are achieved for the Bakassi population in Bakassi.

ADEQUATE STANDARD OF LIVING WITHOUT DISCRIMINATION

Principles 18 and 23 of the Guiding Principles on Internal Displacement, 1998 (GPOID), require that Nigeria should provide an adequate standard of living at the minimum for the IDPs in Bakassi by ensuring that the IDPs have access to:

(a) Essential food and potable water
(b) Basic shelter and adequate housing
(c) Appropriate clothing
(d) Essential medical services and sanitation
(e) Primary education

Nigeria should recognize the right of every IDP in Bakassi to adequate standard of living for themselves and their families including adequate food. It should also recognize the right of the IDPs to be free from hunger. The right of the IDPs to food is captured by the Universal Declaration on the

Eradication of Hunger and Malnutrition, 1974; Article 4 of the Declaration makes it the responsibility of the state parties including Nigeria to remove the obstacles to food production and to provide proper incentives to agricultural producers. To attain these objectives, the state parties should adopt the measure of agrarian tax, credit, and investment policy reform and reorganization of rural structure. The key role of women in agricultural production and rural economy should be recognized. It is also necessary to ensure that appropriate education, extension program, and financial facilities are made available to women on equal terms with men.

With regard to basic shelter and adequate housing, Nigeria at minimum should recognize the right of the IDPs in Bakassi to basic shelter and adequate housing and take the necessary measures to address the housing needs of the IDPs in Bakassi (Brookings Institution, 2008). The following obligations are imposed on Nigeria with regard to rights to health and medical services: by the provision of Section 17(3) (c) and (d) of the Constitution of the Federal Republic of Nigeria, 1999 (CFRN) and principles 18 and 19 of the Guiding Principles of Internal Displacement, 1998 (GPOID), Nigeria has a duty to provide health facilities and underlying determinants of health located in the camp or within safe physical or reasonable distance from the camp. Mrs. Eno Asuquo Etan in April 2018 lost her life during childbirth in the camp because health facilities or underlying health determinants are not within safe physical reach of the IDPs.

Designated government agencies such as the Ministry of Health or organization such as the Red Cross Society should be clothed with the duty to provide essential health services to the IDPs in New Bakassi since the amp is located at a far distance from the existing health facilities and services in Calabar that cannot be physically accessed by the IDPs. And to ensure that the IDPs in Bakassi exercise their right to education during and after displacement as enshrined in international legal instruments and Nigerian law, Nigeria should discharge the following duties.

Nigeria should recognize the right of the IDPs in Bakassi to education without discrimination on the basis of their status as IDPs. They are entitled to enjoy their right to education as do all other citizens. To give effect to the right of the IDPs to education without discrimination, Nigeria should direct its policy to ensure that the IDPs in Bakassi have equal and adequate educational opportunities and that illiteracy is eradicated in IDPs camp. To achieve this objective, Nigeria should ensure that the internally displaced children should receive:

1. (i) Free, compulsory, and universal primary education
   (ii) Free secondary education,
   (iii) Free university education, and
   (iv) Adult IDPs should be protected.

2. Adult illiteracy program be instituted in the IDP camp and adult IDPs should benefit from the program. (CFRN 1999, S.18 and42; GPOID, 1998, principle 23)

Build primary and secondary schools and institute adult illiteracy program in Bakassi and remove administrative constraints such as formal documentation and local registration that may limit access to schools by internally displaced children and to adult illiteracy program by the internally displaced adults. In the alternative, the internally displaced children should be permitted where possible to enroll in the local educational facilities in their host community. Qualified teachers from among the IDP camp or community should employ, and the women among them who are qualified to teach should be encouraged to become educators along with men (Brookings Institution, 2008).

Nigeria as the national authority bears the main burden of ensuring at the minimum, at all times and without discrimination, that these basic needs of the IDPs in Bakassi do not go unmet. Nigeria has the right and freedom to enlist the cooperation of international humanitarian organizations and development actors in order to address these concerns of the IDPs in the event that the resources at its command appear inadequate (UDHR 1948, Article 25; ICESCR, 1966 Article 11; Kampala Convention, 2009 Article 9(2) (b); Kälin, Williams, Koser & Solomon (2010).

LIVELIHOOD AND EMPLOYMENT

Nigeria bears the primary obligation to ensure that the Bakassi population regain their fishing business or acquire new skills or are trained and equipped in new vocations or professions and adapt to new economic activities or employment (GPOID 1998, Principle 21(1) (b); Brookings Institution, 2008; Kälin, Williams, Koser and Solomon (2010) in compliance with international, regional, and domestic instruments. International Convention on Economic, Social, and Cultural Rights (1966) (ICESCR, Article 6 (1)) imposes a duty on the state parties to recognize the right to work, which includes the right to everyone to the opportunity to gain his living by the work freely chosen by him and to take appropriate measures to protect the right. The same duty is imposed by the Universal Declaration of Human Rights (1948) (UDHR) in Article 23(1), African Charter on Human and Peoples' Rights (1981) (ACHPR), Article 15, and the Guiding Principles on Internal Displacement 1998, Principle 22(1) (b). The Constitution of the Federal Republic of Nigeria (1999) (CFRN), Section 16(1) (d) guarantees the right of every citizen to engage in any economic activities of his choice, outside the major sectors of the national economy. Section 17(3) (a) of the same Constitution of Nigeria guarantees to ensure that all citizens, without discrimination on any group whatsoever, have the opportunity for securing adequate means of livelihood and opportunity to secure suitable employment.

PERFORMANCE OF OBLIGATION

The Universal Declaration on Human Rights, 1948 (UDHR), was adopted on December 10, 1948, but the same has not been ratified by Nigeria. The International Covenant on Economic, Social, and Cultural Rights, 1966 (ICESCR) entered into force on January 3, 1976 and was ratified by Nigeria on July 29, 1993. The UDHR, 1948 and ICESCR, 1966 are International Human Right Laws. They are, however, not specific legislations on internal displacement. The Guiding Principles of Internal Displacement, 1998 (GPOID) is an international instrument dealing specifically with the dilemma of the IDPs across the globe. The instrument does not have binding force on states but serves as guide to states, other authorities, organizations, groups, or persons striving to combat the phenomenon of internal displacement. It has not been ratified by Nigeria. The African Union Convention for the Protection and Assistance of Internally Displaced Persons in Africa, 2009 (Kampala Convention) is a specific legislation on internal displacement, ratified by Nigeria.

The UDHR, 1948, ICESCR, 1966, GPOID, 1998 and the Kampala Convention, 2009 have not been domesticated by Nigeria. These instruments are not enforceable in Nigerian courts because of the provision of Section 12 (1) of the Constitution of the Federal Republic of Nigeria, 1999 which provides that: "No treaty between the Federation and any other country shall have the force of law except to the extent to which any such treaty has been enacted into law by the National Assembly."

It necessarily follows that until the foregoing instruments or treaties are domesticated or made part of Nigerian law by the National Assembly of Nigeria, they remain unenforceable in Nigerian court. Since achieving independence in 1960, Nigeria has always been faced with the question of IDPs. In-spite of the numerous cases of IDPs across the country, Nigeria has no law that guarantees the rights and protection of IDPs. There exists in Nigeria the National Emergency Management Agency (NEMA) Act Cap 34 LFN 2004. The NEMA has the mandate to provide emergency relief to IDPs within the first two to four weeks of the emergency leading to the displacement. The NEMA Act does not specifically provide for the IDPs in Nigeria. The act does not guarantee the rights nor provide for the welfare and security needs of the Internally Displaced Persons in Nigeria from the point of its eruption until lasting or permanent solutions are put in place without discrimination. The agency as a body corporate does not possess the power to manage the affairs of the Internally Displaced

Persons in Nigeria in the context of their rights, welfare, and protection or security from the beginning of the crisis until durable solutions are achieved. This study therefore agrees with Ladan (2013) that there exists in Nigeria no specific legal framework that guarantees the rights, protection, and management of IDPs (Kolawole, 2013; Tatile & Bello, 2015; Obikaeze & Onuoha, 2016).

According to Adah (2022), the Federal Government of Nigeria charged with the primary duty and responsibility of achieving durable solutions for the IDPs in Bakassi has not released any fund for that purpose. All the entreaties made by the IDPs to the Federal Government of Nigeria for assistance measures have remained painfully unavailing. There is no reliable data on the number, profile, needs, and vulnerability on the IDPs in Bakassi. The federal government and Cross-Rivers state government have not carried out the gathering of relevant and accurate information on the IDPs in Bakassi. The result is that it is now difficult to gather accurate data on the IDPs in Bakassi because many of the IDPs have taken refuge with friends and families in the host community and other areas outside Bakassi.

There is no sea, neither are there rivers, creeks, and channels or streams in Bakassi in Cross-Rivers state where the IDPs can practice their fishing business. The IDPs have not been trained or equipped to undertake an alternative venture. The failure or neglect has propelled many of the IDPs including youths to flee from the settlement to Bakassi Peninsula and other environments in search of employment opportunities. The neglect also breeds unemployment and poverty.

The Federal Government of Nigeria has not through the Independent National Electoral Commission (INEC) provided sufficient polling units or necessary facilities to enable the IDPs in Bakassi already registered in Bakassi Peninsula and in possession of their voters' cards cast their votes and stand elections in their new constituency (Bakassi). Again voters' registration exercise has not been carried out in Bakassi by INEC since 2007 to enable children born at the time to exercise their voting rights and contest elections in the constituency.

IMPLICATION OF LACK OF PERFORMANCE

Failure to provide the socio-political and economic needs of the IDPs in Bakassi or achieve durable solution with regard to their displacement means that the concerns of the population will remain a burning national question. It also means a denial or deprivation of the universal or basic needs of the IDPs in Bakassi. It should be noted that the failure by the government to provide the basic needs of the IDPs may cultivate a niche for conflict (Cunningham, 2003; Woodhouse, 1999). The deprivation would instill in the IDPs a sense of social, political, economic, and historical injustice and failure to address the wrongs that has the tendency to activate structural or institutional conflict (Osah & Adah, 2017).

The failure by the Nigerian government to provide employment opportunities for the IDPs in Bakassi will provoke structural or institutional conflict or terrorism. When conflict or terrorism is structural or rooted in institutional arrangement, it will be difficult to curb it. Unemployment and poverty though have no causal link with conflict and terrorism, the interlaced phenomena provide favorable conditions for the growth of terrorism and other violent crimes in Nigeria (Adah & Sodipo, 2021).

CONCLUSION

The chapter highlighted that the IDPs in the New Bakassi do not enjoy their social, political, and economic needs, such as potable water, basic shelter, essential medical services, clean and safe environment, and opportunities for employment. There are no primary and secondary schools and health facilities in the New Bakassi. Unfortunately, Nigeria has no comprehensive legal framework on internal displacement; there are also no designated institutions with the capacity to manage IDPs affairs and no accurate data on IDPs in Bakassi. Thus, beyond the resettlement scheme, the Nigerian government should show commitment to the basic needs of the IDPs by making specific budgetary allocation for IDPs not only in the New Bakassi but all IDP camps nationwide to ensure availability of funds. More so, the government should seek financial assistance from international bodies and collaborate with international humanitarian organizations and stakeholders to achieve durable solution for the IDPs. The Nigerian government should also take legislative measure to provide comprehensive legal framework to specifically deal with issues of IDPs in Bakassi and Nigeria. This should include the domestication of the Guiding Principles on Internal Displacement, 1998 (GPOID) and the Kampala Convention, 2009. By the same measure, the government should establish institutions specifically clothed with the power to manage issues affecting IDPs in Bakassi and Nigeria.

The government should make the necessary institutional arrangements to address the lack of social amenities in Bakassi and the rights of the IDPs to vote and participate in public affairs and economic activities in Nigeria.

REFERENCES

A.G. Ondo State *v* A.G of the Federation (2002) FWLR pt 111.

Adah, O. (2022). Legal Social and Political Rights of Internally Displaced Persons in Bakassi; An unpublished PhD Thesis, Ilishan, Babcock University.

Adah, O. & Sodipo, B. (2021). Bakassi Population (IDPs) in Ekpiri-Ikang and the Right to work. *KIU Journal of Social Sciences* 7(3): 75–83.

African Charter on Human and Peoples Rights, 1981.

African Union Convention for the Protection and Assistance for Internally Displaced Persons in Africa, 2009 (Kampala Convention).

Agba, A. M. O., Akpanudoedehe, J. J. & Ushie, E. M. (2010). Socio-Economic and Cultural Impacts of Resettlement of Bakassi People of Cross-River State Nigeria. *Studies in Sociology of Science and Technology* 1(2): 50–52 www.oscanada.org.

Aghamelo, A. T. & Ibhasebhor, S. (2006). Colonialism as a Source of Boundary Dispute and Conflict among African States: The World Court Judgment on the Bakassi Peninsula and its implications for Nigeria. *The Social Science Journal* 13(3): 177–181.

Agwu, F. A. (2012). The ICJ Ruling and the Appeal that Never Was. *Nigerian Journal of International Affairs* 38(3): 51–63.

Aluko, B. A. & Obodo, N. N. (2018). International Court of Justice Judgement on the Nigeria-Cameroon Borderland Conflict: Implications on Bakassi People. *KIU Journal of Humanities* 3(3): 21–36.

Bakassi; An unpublished PhD Thesis, Ilishan, Babcock University.

Bakare, N., Khan, F. & Akash, S. A. (2022). Beyond Return and Resettlement: The Impact of Exposure and Interactions on the Post-Conflict Development of North Waziristan. *Migration Studies* 11(4): 28–45.

Brisibe, W. G. (2017). Trapped in Impermanence. *Journal of Internal Displacement* 7(1): 4–15.

Bukar, B. A. (2012). Nigeria Needs to Take Responsibility for its IDPs. *Forced Migration Review* 40: 44.

Case Concerning the Land and Maritime Boundary between Cameroon and Nigeria (2002) ICJ Report.

Cunningham, W. G. (2003). Terrorism and Typologies. In *Terrorism: Concept, Causes and Conflict Resolution*. Available See No. 10.

Dakas, C. J. D. (2003). *International Law on Trial: Bakassi and the Eurocentricity of International Law*. Lagos: St. Stephen Bookhouse Inc.

Danielsen, G. (2005). Meeting Human Needs, Preventing Violence: Applying Human Needs Theory to the Conflict in Sri Lanka. USAL. https://silo.tips/queue/meeting-human-needs-preventing-violence-applying-human-needs-theory-to-the-confl?&queue_id=-1&v=1664890983&u=MTk3LjIxMC43OC42MQ== Accessed 18 July, 2018.

Ekezie, W., Siebert, P., Timmons, S., Murray, R. L. & Bains, M. (2022). Exploring the Influence of Health Management Processes on Health Outcomes Among Internally Displaced Persons (IDPs). *Journal of Migration and Health* 6: 100124.

Ekoh, P. C., Okoye, U. O., George, E. O., Chukwuemeka, E. & Agbawodikeizu, P. U. (2022). Resettlement of Internally Displaced Persons (IDPs) in Nigeria: The Housing Problems Facing IDPs in Abuja Camps and the Risk of Homelessness and Secondary Displacement. *Journal of Social Distress and Homelessness*, 1–9. DOI :10.1080/10530789.2022.2027069.

Eweka, O. & Olusegun, T. O. (2016). Management of Internally Displaced Persons in Africa: Comparing Nigeria and Cameroon. *African Research Review* 10(i): 193–210. http://dx.doi.org/10.4314/afrrev.v10i1.15

Faleti, S.A. (2006). Theories of Social Conflict. In Shedrack Gaya Best (Ed.), *Introduction to Peace and Conflict Studies in West Africa*. Ibadan: Spectrum Books Ltd, 35–37.

Fayomi, O. O. (2012). Displacements in the Context of Social Crises in the Oil-Rich Niger-Delta of Nigeria and Oil-Rich Bakassi Peninsula in Cameroon. *Journal of History and Social Sciences* 3(2): 1–15.

Federal Republic of Nigeria. (1999). *The Constitution of the Federal Republic of Nigeria*. Lagos: Government Press.

Fonkeng, P. (2019). Insecurity, Forced Migration, and Internally Displaced Persons along the Cameroon-Nigeria Border, 2003–2018.

Guiding Principles on Internal Displacement, 1999.

Gurung, S. (2022). Rehabilitation of Internally Displaced Persons and the Support of Nepal Peace Trust Fund in Gorkha District. *Journal of Political Science*: ISSN: 2362–1273, 26–39.

Inter-Agency Standing Committee. (2010). IASC Framework on Durable Solutions for Internally Displaced Persons. In *IASC Framework on Durable Solutions for Internally Displaced Persons*, 57–57.

International Covenant on Economic, Social and Cultural Rights, 1966 (ICESCR).

Isokon, B. E., Eke, J. E. & Icha, C. I. (2014). Fishing as a Source of Livelihood and Sustainable Growth in a Resettlement Scheme: The Case of Bakassi Resettlement Programme in Cross-River State, Nigeria. *Journal of Sociology and Social Work* 2(1): 9–20.

Jafer, E., Imana, G., Doda, Z. & Lemessa, A. (2022). Post Conflict-Induced Displacement: Human Security Challenges of Internally Displaced Persons in Oromia Special Zone Surrounding Finfinne, Ethiopia. *Cogent Social Sciences* 8(1): 2103252.

Kälin, W. (2004). *Addressing Internal Displacement: A Framework for National Responsibility*. Washington, DC: Brookings Institution–University of Bern Project on Internal Displacement.

Kälin, W. (2014). Internal displacement. In *The Oxford Handbook of Refugee and Forced Migration Studies*. Oxford University Press, 1–10.

Kälin, W., Williams, R. C., Koser, K. & Solomon, A. (2010). Incorporating the Guiding Principles on Internal Displacement into Domestic Law: Issues and Challenges. *American Society of International Law Studies in Transnational Legal Policy* No. 41. Washington, DC. https://www.refworld.org/docid/4b6c164e2.html

Kamta, F. N., Schilling, J., & Scheffran, J. (2020). Insecurity, Resource Scarcity, and Migration to Camps of Internally Displaced Persons in Northeast Nigeria. *Sustainability* 12(17): 6830.

Kamta, F. N., Schilling, J., & Scheffran, J. (2021). Water Resources, Forced Migration and Tensions with Host Communities in the Nigerian Part of the Lake Chad Basin. *Resources* 10(4): 27.

Kolawole, A. A. (2013). Towards the Evolution of Legal and Institutional Framework for the Protection of Internally Displaced Persons (IDPs) in Nigeria. *International Journal of Sustainable Development* 6(5). http://www.ssm.com/link/OIDA-Intl-Journal-Sustainable-Dev.html

Marker, S. (2003). What Human Needs Are, Beyond Intractability. http://beyondintractability.org/m/human-needs.jsp. Accessed June 10, 2017.

McDowell, C. & Morell, G. (2007). Development and Displacement: Institutionalizing Responsibility. *Development* 50(4): 33–38.

Mooney, E. & French, C. (2005). Barriers and Bridges: Access to Education for Internally Displaced Children. *The Brookings Institution-University of Bern.*

National Commission for Refugees (Establishment Act, Cap 21) LFN 2004.

National Emergency Management Authority Act Cap 34 LFN 2004.

Ngalim, A. N. (2019). Post-Conflict Experiences of Resettled Bakassi Peninsula People, 2006–2016. *Asian Journal of Peacebuilding* 7 (1): 105–123.

Ntui. (2015). Financing Libraries and Information Centres for Internally Displaced Persons in Nigeria: The Bakassi Case. *Journal of Economic and Sustainable Development* 6(16). www.iiste.org.

Obikaeze, V. C. & Onuoha, C. B. (2003). The Nigerian State and Management of Internally Displaced Persons (IDPs) from 2012–2016. *African Journals of Polices and Society (AJPS)* 4 (1): 12–24 (January–February 2023).

Okoi, O. (2016). Limits of International Law: Settlement of the Nigeria-Cameroon Territorial Conflict. *International Journal on World Peace* 33(2): 77.

Onuoha, C. E. & Chukwu, N. N. A. (2022). Challenges of Internally Displaced Persons (IDPS) in Bakassi IDP Camps in Cross River State: The Roles of Social Workers and Non-Governmental Agencies. *International Journal of Sociology and Anthropology Research* 8(1): 10–23.

Onwe, S. O. & Nwogbaga, D. M. E. (2015). Reflections on the Challenges of Displacement and Effective Resettlement Strategies. *JOSR Journal of Humanities and Social Sciences (JOSR-JHSS)* 20(3): 51–56. www.josrjournals.org

Osah, G. & Adah, O. (2017). Community Policing: An Essential Strategy for Checkmating Crime and Terrorism in Nigeria: A Case Study of Gombe State. *KIU Journal of Social Sciences* 3(2): 231–243.

Osah, G. & Ogu, M. (2020). Conflicts and Internal Displacement in Nigeria. *FUWUKARI Journal of Politics and Development* 4(2): 37–51. https://www.fuwjpd.com.ng/journal-articles-detail/22.

Shebbs, E. U., Agbor, U. I. & Uduma, D. O. (2022). Local Government as Potential Leverage for the Management of Internally Displaced Persons in Nigeria: Study of Bakassi Local Government Area of Cross River State. *International Journal of Public Administration and Management Research* 7(6): 18–32.

Sheehan S. (2003). The Need for Multi-Paradigmatic Analysis and Multi-Dimensional Strategy. In *Terrorism: Concepts, Causes and Conflict Resolution.* http://edocs.nps.edu/dodpubs/org/DTRA/Jan03_terrorism_concepts.pdf. Accessed 18 July 2018.

Shidali *v* F.R.N (2008) All FWLR pt 431.

Tatile, J. O. & Bello, W. O. (2015). Managing Internally Displaced Persons in Nigeria: The Case of Insurgency in the North-East Geo-Political Zone. *International Journal of Development Strategies in Humanities, Management and Social Sciences* 5(2): 145–166.

Ugwuka, A. C., Adesegun, A. A. & Adam, E. M. (2016). Historical and Legal Implications of the ICJ Judgment on the Bakassi People of Nigeria. *Babcock Journal of History and International Studies* 3(1): 1–24.

Universal Declaration of Human Rights, 1948 (UDHR).

Universal Declaration on the Eradication of Hunger and Malnutrition, 1974.

Usang, E. E., Ikpeme, N. J. & Amimi, P. B. (2014). Challenges of Mobilization and Participation for Community Development: A Study of the Internally Displaced Person of Bakassi Peninsular, Nigeria. *Journal of Education and Practice* 5(7): 158–165.

Uttah, E. C., Ogban, E. & Ukpona, G. I. (2013). Clinical Malaria: Aspects of Demographic and Health-Seeking Characteristics on inmates of New Bakassi Resettlement in Ekpiri-Ikang, Nigeria. *International Journal of Scientific and Research Publication* 3(6). www.ijsrp.org

Uttah, E. C., Uttah, C. & Okonufua, C. (2012). Assessment of Camp Conditions and Medical Complaints by Bakassi Returnees Attending Approved Hospitals in Cross River State, Nigeria. *The Pacific Journal of Science and Technology* 13(2). http://www.akaiuniversity.US/PJST.htm

Chapter 7

Refugees with or without Papers

Stories of Persecution, Flight, and Resettlement in the United States

Donald F. Hones, Mayra Pasayes, and Txerthoj Vang

As 2015 wound down to a close the United States, like countries in Europe and elsewhere, continued to grapple with the arrival of children and adults seeking refuge from violence in their countries of origin. In the aftermath of the Paris bombings, President Obama stood by his pledge to welcome thousands of refugees from war-torn Syria despite strong opposition in Congress and public opinion polls (Beinart, 2015). In contrast to his support of the Syrians, Obama approved Immigration and Customs Enforcement raids aimed at deporting hundreds of undocumented families who had fled the upsurge in violence in El Salvador and elsewhere in Central America (Homeland Security to begin raids in order to deport hundreds of families who fled the violence in Central America) according to Markon and Nakamura (2015). Clearly the president of the United States made the distinction between refugees, who he deemed worthy of asylum, and undocumented immigrants, who he deemed worthy of deportation. Yet, were the stories of danger, persecution, and exile so very different for Central Americans and Syrians, especially from the perspective of the human rights and human dignity?

The 1951 Refugee Convention of the United Nations defined a refugee as a person who "owing to a well-founded fear of being persecuted for reasons of race, religion, nationality, membership of a particular social group or political opinion, is outside the country of his nationality, and is unable to, or owing to such fear, is unwilling to avail himself of the protection of that country" (Convention and Protocol Related to the Status of Refugees, 1951: 3).

The United Nation High Commissioner for Refugees (UNHCR) differentiates between economic migrants, who choose to move to better their economic situation, and refugees, who move to save their lives and their freedom. The UNHCR explains further the situation of refugees:

> They have no protection from their own state—indeed it is often their own government that is threatening to persecute them. If other countries do not let them in, and do not help them once they are in, then they may be condemning them to death—or to an intolerable life in the shadows, without sustenance and without rights. (UNHCR, 2015)

If people are fleeing their homelands because of persecution, because they have no protection from their own state or indeed are persecuted by their own government, such people fall under the definition of refugee as mentioned above. Yet, the United States government has not defined refugees in this way for the purposes of granting asylum. The history of the past fifty years has shown that refugee status in the United States is granted most frequently to persons fleeing from a country that is unfriendly to the United States. During the Cold War, this usually meant fleeing communist regimes in the Soviet Union, Cuba, Vietnam, and elsewhere (Newland, 1995). After the passage of the Refugee Act of 1980, the interpretation of who could be a refugee broadened somewhat, yet remained governed by political, not humanitarian considerations: "Admissions . . . shall be allocated among refugees of special humanitarian concern to the United States in accordance with a determination made by the President after appropriate consultation" (Refugee Act of 1980).

For persons fleeing countries that are supported by the United States, often with weapons and advisors, refugee status has not been an option. Such persons, if they were able to make it to the United States, are labeled "illegal aliens" and, if not deported, are condemned, in the language of the UNHCR, "to an intolerable life in the shadows, without sustenance and without rights." In the 1980s, after the passage of the Refugee Act, over 1 million Central Americans from Guatemala and El Salvador fled violent civil wars in their countries and came north to the United States, seeking asylum as refugees. The Reagan administration, however, denied the human rights violations perpetrated by the governments of El Salvador and Guatemala and deemed persons fleeing those homelands as "economic migrants" (Gzesh, 2006). Thirty years later, according to the American Immigration Council, tens of thousands of children and adults fleeing and upsurge of violence in Central America and Mexico continue to be denied asylum because of an ever-narrowing definition of what constitutes credible fear of persecution:

Despite reports of horrific violence, most Mexican and Central American claims continue to be rejected. Some Mexican journalists and human rights activists have been granted asylum, as have family members of law enforcement and union activists and Central American family members of murdered or tortured persons. But many claims asserted by Central Americans are based on forced gang recruitment, and many claims presented by Mexicans are based on violence, including torture and murder, resulting from resistance to extortion or kidnapping by cartels, military, government officials, and sometimes by a combination of all three. Those claims do not fit neatly within the ever-narrowing definitions established by the Board of Immigration Appeals through its decisions, of political opinion or membership in a particular social group (American Immigration Council, 2014).

In this chapter, two coauthors share their immigrant stories of persecution and flight to the United States. Txerthoj Vang is a refugee from Laos who supported the United States as part of the Hmong secret army during the Vietnam era. Mayra Pasayes is an immigrant from El Salvador who fled that country's civil war during the 1980s. Though they each faced a high level of violence in their home country, Txerthoj was granted official refugee status. Mayra was not and only later obtained residency. The granting, or denial, of asylum to each would have major impacts on their lives and their perspectives. They each continue to support refugees with or without papers in their work as educators in public schools. Their individual stories mirror those of hundreds of thousands of others who fled Laos and El Salvador during the 1970s and 1980s, running from crisis and war, taking arduous journeys, and resettling, with or without official status, in the United States.

Dangerous Departures, Doubtful Arrivals

In "Along the Way to the Mekong," a collection of memories of first-generation Hmong Americans, Mai Neng Moua describes in very personal details the war and flight of people out of Laos:

> My father was killed two years before we left Laos. My older brother was five, I was three, and my younger brother was a few months old. I carried a pot of rice. I don't remember what my little brother carried. (Moua, 2003: 57)

For the hundreds of thousands of people who fled the wars in Laos and El Salvador in the 1970s and 1980s, the decisions to embark on dangerous journeys into exile were marked with very personal details. Born in the Ban Vinai refugee camp near the Thai border with Laos, Kao Kalia Yang provides an account of a Hmong family's journey in *The Latehomecomer: A Hmong Family Memoir* (2008). Mario Bencastro uses fictional characters to write about the truths of the civil war and exodus of Salvadorans in Odyssey to the North (1998). A review of these two works can be organized into three stages, like the journey of a refugee: The first stage, the crisis in the homeland from which one flees; the second stage, the flight to safety, which may include stops in camps and detention centers; and the third stage, a doubtful arrival and adjustment in a new land.

First Stage: Crisis in the Homeland

In 1961, the United States CIA began a relationship with Vang Pao, a Hmong officer in the Royal Laotian Army. This relationship would see the creation of a Hmong guerrilla army numbering at its peak 30,000, raised to fight against the Pathet Lao and North Vietnamese communists moving weapons and troops along the Ho Chi Minh trail (Quincy, 2000). Over the next fourteen years, tens of thousands of Hmong fighters would die, with boys as young as ten replacing their fathers and older brothers in the army. Yang writes:

> In old photos they hold guns in their small, dirty hands. Sometimes, with big smiles on their young faces. I know that their mothers waited by empty doorways for their return. (Yang, 2008: 8)

Hundreds of Hmong villages were destroyed, and villagers moved from place to place looking for shelter. Many sought refuge at Long Cheng, the airstrip in the mountains that had been built for the American warplanes, and Vang Pao's headquarters. In 1973, the United States signed a peace agreement with the North Vietnamese, and in 1975, the Vietnamese and their Pathet Lao allies gained control of Laos. Long Cheng was surrounded by battalions of the North Vietnamese Army, and Vang Pao and other members of the leadership took the last planes out of the country into exile. When the communist soldiers arrived, Hmong who had been village leaders or officers in the army were invited to "seminars" from which they did not return. Yang writes from the perspective of those who were left behind:

> When the Americans left Laos in 1975, they took the most influential, the biggest believers and fighters for democracy with them, and they left my family and thousands of others behind to wait for a fight that would end for so many in death. A third of the Hmong died in the war with the Americans. Another third were slaughtered in its aftermath. (Yang, 2008: 3)

From Spanish colonial times until the 1980s, fourteen families controlled the lands and destiny of El Salvador, largely through a series of military dictatorships. The vast majority of the population, indigenous and mestizo, were reduced to poverty. In 1932, Farabundo Marti and others led a rebellion in Izalco and nearby towns in response to a rigged election. As Galeano writes, the campesinos controlled the region for three days, and then came the reprisals:

> Three months of slaughter follow. Farabundo Marti and other communist leaders face firing squads. Soldiers beat to death the Indian chief Jose Feliciano Ama, leader of the revolution in Izalco. They hang Ama's corpse in the main plaza and force school children to watch the show. Thirty thousand campesinos . . . dig their own graves with their hands. (Galeano, 1988: 91)

By the late 1970s, the activities of left-wing guerrillas and right-wing death squads were leaving little room for compromise in El Salvador. When Archbishop Oscar Romero, a champion of the poor, was assassinated in 1980, it provoked a full-scale civil war that would last the entire decade and lead hundreds of thousands to flee the country for their lives (Center for Justice and Accountability, 2015; Galeano, 1988; Allison, 2012).

In Odyssey to the North, the character Calixto represents the everyman of El Salvador, caught in the middle of a civil war, suspected by both sides. With his friend Lencho, he leaves an impoverished village to make his way to the capital and "a short time later their village is destroyed in a bloody battle between the army and rebel forces" (Bencastro, 1998: 12). One day his wife comes running to his workplace to inform him that armed men are looking for him, and this dialogue ensues:

> *"Someone reported you as an enemy of the government!"*
> *"It can't be! I'm not involved in politics, you know that!"*
> *"You have to get out of here and hide, before they find you!"*
> *"But it must be a mistake!"* insisted Calixto. *"Or someone's slandering me. One or the other."*
> *"Go!" his wife begged him.*
> *"Where?"*
> *"To Lencho's house!"*
> Quick as a cat, Calixto jumped into the bushes and disappeared (Bencastro, 1988: 11).

Like hundreds of thousands of others in Laos and El Salvador, the Yang family and Calixto would soon be on the run, beginning the dangerous journey into exile.

Second Stage: The Dangerous Journey

When the Pathet Lao came to power in Laos in 1975, their agenda was announced in the party newspaper: "It is necessary to extirpate down to the root the Hmong minority" (Yang, 2008: 7). Tens of thousands of Hmong fled the country that year and in succeeding years. Those who remained behind fled to the remote area around Phu Bia mountain (Quincy, 2000). Yang writes that "the day my father met my mother was a normal day of scavenging for food in the jungle" (Yang, 2008: 12). They married, and a few months later, they were ambushed by government troops:

> My mother remembers the moment of stillness before the smell of guns and the echo of artillery filled the air, when confusion struck amid the rising smoke. In an instant, families were separated. Little children ran after people they thought were their parents, mothers ran back and forth finding this child or that one . . . The men tried to protect the women and children with their arms. They knew that there would be no fighting back. (Yang, 2008: 20–21)

It was decided that the women and children would surrender, while the few remaining men would look for survivors in the jungle, and then find a way to liberate their captured families. After six months of captivity in an abandoned village, the men returned and escaped with their families into the jungle. Yang's father met his baby daughter for the first time. Like thousands of Hmong before them, they made their way to the Mekong River, the frontier with Thailand, patrolled by soldiers in gunboats. Yang describes how they swam the river, tied together:

> When my father's feet touched the river bottom, he did not know if they were far underwater or close to shore. He walked on the shifting pebbles, and he pulled, for all the years of running through the jungle, the weight of his wife, his mother, and his child. He looked behind him. There were men on the other side with guns, firing. He could not hear sounds. There was silence in his ears. (Yang, 2008: 38)

Part of Yang's family had been captured by Laotian soldiers in gunboats. The rest made their way slowly toward the Thai soldiers, who led them to the refugee camp at Ban Vinai. The family hesitated before entering the forbidding gates of the camp, surrounded by a barbed wire fence. Yang describes what happened next to her father:

A Thai soldier punched him and he fell to the ground. The man kicked him. My father got up as fast as he could. Not to hit the man back, but because he did not want my mother and grandmother to see him on the ground. My father looked at the man and did nothing. (Yang, 2008: 44)

Ban Vinai Refugee Camp would be their home until 1987. Kao Kalia Yang was born there and would grow up with the dirt, the hot wind, the inadequate food, the overcrowding, in this place where so many were born and so many would die. When the family were granted asylum in the United States, they were translated first to Phanat Nikhom, a transition camp for those going to the United States. Then the day came to board the bus to the airport in Bangkok and the plane that would take the Yang family to Minnesota:

> The bus to America was full of many Hmong families, pregnant mothers, little boys and girls my age, some still suckling on their mother's breasts, and others looking almost grown up with their hair pulled back, with straight spines, all of us in our newest clothes. Old grandpas and grandmas with steady eyes that blinked back the past and tried to focus on a future they couldn't see. (Yang, 2008: 114)

In El Salvador, "nighttime was horrifying in the city because it belonged not to people but to the shadows that played with the destiny of human beings" (Bencastro, 1998: 17). Calixto, on the run from the armed men, is advised by his friend Toño to hire a coyote to take him north to the United States. When asked why Calixto cannot just get papers to enter the United States legally, Toño replies:

> Because, to give you a visa, the U.S. Embassy has a lot of requirements that poor people like us can't meet. Like having a good job, money saved in the bank, good personal references, a round trip ticket, proof that the people we're going to visit in the United States are well-off financially and reside their legally, and other requirements. But with a coyote, you can do it without so much paperwork. (Bencastro, 1998: 20)

Calixto gathers the $400 needed for the coyote and arrives at the outskirts of San Salvador at the appointed meeting place. Then the guide and his deputy arrive:

> The smugglers looked over the group and with crude, indiscreet stares examined the young women, who turned toward their companions to make clear that they were not traveling alone. No one complained or said anything.
> "*Do you have the money?*" asked the one with the broken arm.
> "*Yes!*" the men and women answered.
> "*Very good,*" he said. "*Because you know that without the money no one goes anywhere.*" (Bencastro, 1998: 46)

The group left by rental cars and then by bus and crossed their first border at Guatemala. At certain points, the bus was stopped in the night and Guatemalan soldiers ordered everyone off, searching each passenger carefully. They crossed into Mexico and twenty-four hours later arrived at the Central Camionero del Norte, the major bus terminal to the north:

> In the business of the trafficking of undocumented persons, the Central Camionero del Norte represented the center of the world. All those headed to the United States stopped there. . . .The walls and benches of the terminal witnessed so much sadness, despair and fear. They listened to the countless stories of the great Latin American exodus, the stories of millions of human beings who were

fleeing from the misery and violence in their countries, in search of the promised land. (Bencastro, 1998: 86–87)

After avoiding the immigration authorities in the bus terminal, the group finally boards their bus for the crossing point at Ciudad Juarez. As they get close to the border, the smugglers demand more money from each of the passengers, and then have all but ten of the passengers get out and walk around a final checkpoint inside Mexico. Walking through the desert night, one of the travelers collapsed in pain and told the others to continue on without her. A former soldier in the group approached her:

> "*No, no one is staying behind.*"
> "*But I can't walk anymore,*" she said sadly.
> "*You'll forgive me for touching your legs,*" the soldier said resolutely, "*but I'm going to carry you on my back.*"
> He picked up Elisa, and they continued on their way. They passed the checkpoint and continued about a kilometer beyond, and stopped to wait for the bus (Bencastro, 1998: 95).

After a week waiting in a hotel in Ciudad Juarez, the group heads out, divides into three, runs through the desert for a stretch, occasionally crouching down when a helicopter passes overhead, and then crosses the shallow Rio Grande, entering the United States. They climb into two vans and headed to Silver City, New Mexico. Shortly thereafter, they are captured by border patrol and sent to the detention center at El Corralon, near El Paso:

> No one knew how long they would have to remain in the prison. Their length of stay depended on many factors: the attorneys, the money their relatives had available for bond, and luck. (Bencastro, 1998: 141)

Calixto, the soldier, and another friend were released on bonds that had been paid by relatives. The detention center kept their passports, but they were supplied with papers explaining that they were on bond awaiting a deportation decision. When the soldier greeted his brother at the airport in Washington, D.C., he said:

"*I don't have much time. In a few months I have to go to Immigration Court, and they'll decide my case. I hope they don't deport me.*"
"*Forget that,*" said the brother. "*Most people don't even show up for court.*"
"*But then they'll issue an arrest warrant. And we'll lose the bond money.*"
"*Among so many millions of people they'll never find you. And you can pay me back the bond money whenever you can. The important thing is that you made it.*" (Bencastro, 1998: 191)

Third Stage: Adjustment in the New Land

The Yang family arrived in St. Paul, Minnesota, and moved into the McDonough Housing Projects, built for veterans returning from World War II. Yang describes the projects, her new home:

> Everything was cold and strong, meant to last a long time. And they they had, and they had waited for us, soldiers from a different war, not returning to families but to remnants of them. (Yang, 2008: 131)

For the children, there was school, for the adults, there was a limited time of welfare and the pressure to get jobs, for the elders, there was disability, and for everyone, there was learning English. Yang remembers how the sameness of Hmong families' lives matched the sameness of the project architecture:

> Each family caught up in school and English, each family visiting thrift stores and driving used cars, living on the monthly welfare and disability checks from the government. The truth was dawning: the lives we were living in America were far from the life that the adults had imagined from the camps of Thailand. (Yang, 2008: 131–132)

There is no public housing, public benefits, or adjustment time for Calixto when he arrives in Washington, D.C. He must find a way to make a living, even when this means living a life in the shadows. Odyssey to the North opens with a workplace accident that leaves a coworker dead, and Calixto knows that he can neither come forward with evidence about the dangerous working conditions, nor ever go back to that job. At his new job at a restaurant, Calixto manages to escape from an immigration raid. With his coworkers, he discusses the challenges of living in a one-bedroom apartment with twenty people:

> There was no privacy. Families would gather in the corners
> of the apartment and arrange their belongings there.
> And where did you all sleep?
> People would sleep and eat in the same little corner. They would
> discuss family matters in a whisper, but everyone would hear.
> How could you all share the bathroom?
> We always had to wait in line. Maybe because the situation
> made us nervous, people were always sick to their stomach
> and used the bathroom often. (Bencastro, 2008: 14)

Yet, Calixto and his apartment mates at least have their lives. This is not the case for Theresa, whose appearances before an immigration judge over a period of months form a subtext to Calixto's story. In the end, her pleas for asylum are denied and she is sent back to El Salvador. Within a short time, she is found murdered on the outskirts of the city (Bencastro, 1998).

In 1984, approval rates for asylum seekers from Guatemala and El Salvador were under 3 percent, while rates for Iranians fleeing the Khomeini regime were 60 percent and Afghans fleeing the Soviet occupation were 40 percent. Furthermore, those arrested near the U.S.–Mexico border were crowded into detention centers and pressured, without legal advice, to agree to "voluntary return" to their homelands. Gzesh concludes:

> Considering the widely reported human rights violations in El Salvador and Guatemala, the treatment of these migrants constituted a violation of U.S. obligations under the 1951 Refugee Convention. (Gzesh, 2006)

A movement in support of those fleeing repressive Central American regimes came together in the 1980s and 1990s to provide sanctuary to individuals and families, especially in churches. Nevertheless, a life in the shadows was the lot for most Central Americans until the opportunity for some to obtain legal residency came with the Immigration Reform and Control Act of 1986 (Badger, 2014).

Narrative Inquiry of the Immigration Experience

Txerthoj Vang, a Hmong refugee, and Mayra Pasayes, a Salvadoran immigrant, have come together to share their stories of civil war in their homelands, dangerous journeys into exile, and adjustment to life and work in the United States. A questionnaire developed and administered by coauthor Hones was sent to Vang and Pasayes by email. Although both coauthors addressed the same general questions, questions were made specific to the country of origin as well as some of the life experiences of the coauthors of which I was already aware. Examples of questions asked include the following (the complete questionnaire can be found in Appendix):

> What are some of your earliest memories of growing up? What was the name of your town? How big was it? Is that the only town you lived in your country?
>
> Tell me about your family: Your mom, dad, brother, extended family. What are some memories of family that you have from growing up?
>
> When did you first become aware of the war in your community? How did it affect your family and community?

Following email responses to these questions, audiotaped interviews with Vang and Pasayes were conducted to explore issues in more depth. From the written responses to the questionnaire and from the audiotaped interview transcripts, narrative portraits of each of these coauthors have been constructed. It was important that Vang and Pasayes helped in the editing of their portraits to final form. In this process of narrative inquiry, fidelity to their own words has been the goal of the research (Polkinghorne, 1995; Hones, 1998; Clandinin, Davies, Huber, Rose, and Whelan, 2001; Benei, 2010; Elbaz-Luwisch, 2010), wherein stories of individuals, groups, and communities are central to the interpretation. Through a process of interpretive interactionism (Denzin, 1994) and grounded theory (Glaser and Strauss, 1967; Strauss and Corbin, 1994), important themes are examined that emerge from the portraits of these coauthors.

Leaving Laos: Txherthoj Vang

> I tell you this is the last word for this war.
> This little side war we were the center of.
>
> —Bryan Thao Worra, "The Last War Poem" (Moua, 2003: 98)

At the local high school in Oshkosh, Wisconsin, eighteen students sit around a horseshoe shaped table. Six are from the Congo; four are from Myanmar; four are from Iraq; and four are from South Korea. Most are refugees who have lived in the United States for at most two years or as little as one month. Some struggle to ask questions in survival English, yet they are pushed to adapt to a highly academic curriculum. Yet this is the English Learner (EL) room, their safe space. American-born teachers work to help them make the transition from lives on the move or in refugee camps to life in an American school. Their greatest ally, however, and the one who pushes them the most, is a fellow refugee. After almost thirty years in the United States his hair is now turning from black to gray, but his eyes are clear, and he stands straight as a soldier. He knows exactly what these newcomers are going through.

My name is Txerthoj Vang. My nationality is Hmong. My birth name was Her Vang. I was born on September 15, 1956 in a small house at a small valley called Hav Fijkas, Ban Haithey, Mueang Samnuea, Houaphan Province in Laos. My family members were farmers and life was very peaceful in the green mountains of our home.

Altogether there were thirteen people in my family, but my dad and my adopted mom passed away five years after I had to part from my family. My father had four wives. His first wife was a Lor, and she died childless. His second wife died childless as well. Next, my dad married his third wife, Poshoua Lee, my adopted mother. She had no son, but she had five daughters, two who passed away and three who married (two died in Laos and one in the

USA). She then adopted her first son, Txhiajcawv. Last, my dad married my mother, Mai Xiong, his fourth wife. When my mother gave birth to me, she gave me to my adopted mother, so I am the second adopted son. My mother had ten children, three sons and seven daughters. My oldest sister (Vah) and my oldest brother (Char) passed away before I was born. My three younger sisters from my mother died during the Vietnam War because we kept moving a lot and there was no medical treatment. Two younger sisters are married and still living in Laos.

My older sister Yee married Captain Zakhue Lor and they had seven children. Captain Zakhue served the CIA during the secret war in Laos. He died from chemicals sprayed from the air by the communist Lao government in 1979 in Mueng Phoon Hong, Vientiane province, Laos. Next, my sister took her children and moved to Paksan province and living there for a short of time. Then she escaped across the Mekong to Thailand in November 1982. After that, she took her family to the United States. Yee became my co-sponsor to come to this country. Now my two older sisters and my older brother are here. They all are on disability except me. My two younger sisters are living in Laos and they are married. Eight family members are deceased.

Joining the Secret Army

Shortly after I was born, my family moved to Ban Hoy-An, Hoychian, Louangprabung province. In 1965, I attended my first school and I learned to read and write the Hmong Pahawh.[1] The next year the war came to our village of Xam Pak Kham, and my adopted mother, my sister Der, my older brother Chuetong, and I fled to Shee Nyao for a short time. In 1967, we moved from Hoy-An to Ban Phou Chan and in 1968 we moved to Phou Koom. The war was all around us, and there were few places of safety in those years.

Early in 1969, at the age of thirteen, I was ordered to serve in the CIA secret army. That same year my brother Txhiajcawv died in the battle. The next year my brother Xiacher was killed in the battle at Phou Koom. In September 1971, I left my parents at Phou Koom and flew to Long Chieng, General Vang Pao's headquarters, for Laotian schooling (second grade) and also army training. I was fifteen years old when I left my parents behind. Later that year, the Pathet Lao and North Vietnamese Army attacked Long Chieng for the second time, and I fled to Phakay village with my sister's family. In September 1972, I moved from Parkay to Phouhey to continue my schooling there while still carrying out my duties as a soldier there. I graduated from Hongnon High School in 1975.

I joined the army with the rank of sergeant. After military training at Long Chieng, I earned the rank of sergeant major and after the operation at Phou Hey I achieved my final rank of warrant officer. I served in the United States

Special Forces under General Vang Pao, Colonel James William (Bill) Lair, and CIA Agent Jerry Daniels in Laos during the Vietnam War for six years, from 1969 to 1975, and for three additional years of resistance fighting after the United States withdrew from Laos. My oldest brother and my wife's oldest brother were killed in a battle fought in my village. My older brother and I got shot and wounded.

In 1973, a peace agreement between the Royal Lao and the Communist Lao was signed in Paris to provide for a cease-fire in Laos. American troops and Vietnamese troops would withdraw from Laos and let the Royal Lao and Communist Lao get together to form their own government, but the Pathet Lao communists and North Vietnamese violated the cease-fire agreement by seizing power in 1975. When the Pathet Lao came to power in Laos, it led to persecution and execution of the Hmong who served the Americans during the war in Laos. May 8th to 14th, 1975 were the days that tears fell, foretelling shadows of dread and fear for the Hmong. All things came to a disappointed and hopeless end. At noon on May 14th, 1975 General Vang left in the last C-130 airplane with other Hmong leaders and some of their people and departed Long Chieng airport, bound for Thailand. A Pathet Lao battalion arrived the following day to take control of Long Chieng.

A few weeks later, Pathet Lao soldiers came over to my village, Phou Hey and started to investigate the Hmong people who worked alongside the CIA and who should go to the "seminar" camp. This caused us to leave our homes, farms, and animals and flee into the jungle. Thousands of Hmong people were moving from one village to the next, seeking shelter. When I got to another village, the people in that village said "Oh No! All these people will come to share our food." When we got there, I said, "We are starving! Our kids have had no food for many days, and they will die, can you share with us just a little and we will pay you? Please." "No," they responded, "we just have enough for us you can go to another village." "I don't think you take your rice with you when you leave your village!" I said. "We are running away like you guys!" they said. Then we moved forward to another village. When we got there, I asked the same thing and they were so nice to share their food with us. "We are sure that we may follow you and we will share our food equally with you and then we can go together," they said. Three days later, the Pathet Lao came to shoot the people in the first village and some were killed, and the rest escaped and followed us without any food.

Refugee

In 1978, the Lao government used airborne chemicals to spray Hmong people in their villages. My sister's husband died from chemical poisoning. We ran out of weapons, supplies, food, clothing, and medicine; so my brother, his wife and I decided to seek refuge in Thailand. Finally, my brother Chuetong, his wife, and I decided to leave my sister Yee Vang's family at Mueang Ow and join a huge group that would try to make it to Thailand. We took nine days walking and guided by my compass through the jungle to the Mekong River. On the first day, we caught up with my cousin, Nyia Vah's family and three other families at Nam Sang. Nyia Vah asked us to take his older son, Porze with us to Thailand. On the second day, we caught up my wife's group at Phou Nasai. On the third day, I met my wife and on day four we rested at Nam Lerk with my wife's family. On the fifth day, we got lost for a while and separated from my wife's group. On the sixth day, we slept in a cave because of the danger of wild elephants. On the seventh day, we came across Chao Xiong's group of about fifty people, we slept in the rain, and I ate termite-flies for food. On the eighth day, we slept close to a Lao temple, and we cut bamboo to make bundles to help us swim across the Mekong River. On the ninth day, we went into the water in the evening and swam across the Mekong River to Thailand.

I had already met my future wife, Kia. In 1977, we left each other in different areas because we were not married yet so we each had to go with our own families. Eleven months later, we came across again for only four days in the jungle. I had decided to go to Thailand with my brother, but Kia had to stay with her family. The night before I left her, I said *"Kia! I know you cannot go with me because we are not married, but I hope one day you might follow me to Thailand."* Kia said *"I don't know, but please remember me."* In Hmong culture, if we are not married, we cannot hold hands or talk face to face, so when I left her, I looked in her eyes and I said in my heart *"we will never see each other again."* I left her in the jungle, and I was on my way to Thailand. Fortunately, about two months later, Kia showed up at the Nong Khai camp where I was living. That made me so happy.

After five months in Nongkhai Camp, we moved into Camp Ban Vinai. We were to live there for nine years. After our first year at Ban Vinai, Kia and I decided to get married in May 1979. Our eldest daughter, Hlee, and our sons Chan and Leng were born in the camp. For four years I was a team leader on an effort to find out about American soldiers missing in action (MIA). I interviewed arriving refugees who might have information about American MIAs in Laos.

Arrival in the United States

For nine years, we lived within the barbed wire of Ban Vinai. I knew that we would never have a chance to go back to meet with my parents again. Therefore, on March 13th, 1987, I decided to take my family and we were transferred to Phanat Nikom for American culture orientation. We were there five months, then at Chonburi transit center for two days. I was chosen to be the group leader and led my group from Chonburi to Don Mueang International Airport, Bangkok, on August 27, 1987, and after one day at the airport, we flew to Tokyo, Japan, and then to Seattle-Tacoma International Airport, on August 29, 1987. When we got to Seattle, my group scattered, and I didn't know where they were. Fortunately, a Hmong refugee staff took my family to stay overnight in a hotel in Seattle. The next day we flew to O' Hare International Airport in Chicago and finally we flew to our destination, Whitman Airport in Oshkosh. Our sponsors Dorothy and Mike Stratz, my sister Yee with her family, my sister Der and her husband, Nhiavang Lor with her family plus many other relatives came to welcome our family. This was the end of my refugee journey.

I was apart from my family in Laos from the age of fourteen until the age of forty-nine. I very much regret that I never had a chance to say goodbye to my dad, my adopted mom, and my younger sister who passed away in Laos.

I am proud to have served on the side of the United States of America. I am fortunate to be here and begin a new life in the United States where there is freedom and opportunities for me to grow and use my abilities to better myself and contribute to the life of our communities. I continue living in Oshkosh, Wisconsin. I have worked with refugee and immigrant students in the public schools since 1997. I am vice president of the Wisconsin Lao Veterans of America. I also teach Hmong language and literacy at the university. I have seven people in my immediate family including my wife, two daughters, three sons, and myself. We all are American citizens now.

In today's society, teens like to be alone and forget about their culture. Some of their parents may not know how to teach them to respect family, and culture, and these young people may feel lost. Therefore, in our family, we get together with the kids and talk with them at least once a month about our culture, our future, what we have done, and what we want for the future and how we will catch up in this technological society.

I want to be a Hmong language teacher and Hmong culture specialist so that I can help Hmong people and others to understand what it means to be Hmong. I will encourage Hmong not to live in isolation, but to cooperate with others, to be flexible and be good citizens for the country in which we are living.

Out of El Salvador: Mayra Pasayes

And then comes the killing of the tribes. This is how they died: when there was just one person out walking, or just two out walking, it wasn't obvious when they took them away . . ." A jaguar has been eating," was all that was said, because the tracks were like a jaguar's tracks when they did their deed. They did not reveal themselves. Many people were abducted.

—The Popol Vuh (Dennis Tedlock translation, 1996: 165)

I met Mayra Pasayes at a fundraiser for Latino students headed for college and got to know her in her work as a counselor and liaison between Latino students, the Appleton high schools, and the technical college. When I first came back from doing humanitarian relief on the Arizona border with Mexico, Mayra invited me to speak to a few students about it. Over forty showed up, in the middle of a school day, and their questions and comments made it clear to me that many had entered the United States on foot through the Sonora desert. She has spoken passionately to my classes about the military and gang violence in her home country of El Salvador, yet her joy of life and her big smile come shining through.

I am from a small town or colonia called Solorzano. The population was very small, perhaps 500 people or less. Everyone knew everyone else, if someone was sick or if a person was doing something bad, the colonia would also know about it. I remember that when we moved there in 1980, my dad was very happy that he had to purchase a lot to build his family a home. We had moved three times since I was born. This was the first time that my dad saw the possibility to create a home for us, the way he had always envisioned. After work, he would work on building his masterpiece (our home), and mom used to take us to visit. In the beginning, the place was full of coffee plants, an avocado, lime, and mango tree. Five years earlier, my grandparents had purchased a similar lot closer to the main road but in the same block. So, while dad worked at the house, my mom would bring us to grandma's house. Their home was a huge room made of lamina material, no electricity at first, but very airy so we did not need fans. There were no divisions among rooms; everything was in one room together. There was a living room made of concrete material, but the rest of the place looked more like a big barn. There was just a dirty floor. Every morning, my cousins swept the place and put water to keep the dust on the floor down. Then outside the house, they had a dining room table for ten, and a huge table made of cement, sand, and hay to do the cooking. This would hold the big pots and the comal where my grandma made the tortillas. There was also a lavadero where my grandma washed clothes for the army, a small space attached was designed to take showers and another to do the dishes. The backyard was filled with coffee plants, guava, avocado, lime, pepeto, and mango trees, but also peppers all kinds, squash and other vegetables. I loved to visit their home as it was full of the country life that I enjoy.

The house did not have electricity at that time, so there was no refrigerator or TV until later days. My grandpa made these hanging containers so grandma could preserve food by hanging it from the ceiling. Sometimes the food was so high that we had to climb on the table (when no one was looking) to take food, sometimes a piece of meat or chicken that was left over. The family did not have access to beef that often but when it was available it was definitely a feast. The environment inside of the house was very peaceful. Grandpa turned on the radio as soon he got up in the morning to get ready to go to work. Then, the radio would stay on all day. I remember listening to the radio, but it was usually Christian music. Once in a while, when grandma was gone, my cousins used to flip to the regular music stations. As a kid, our life was about playing outside and getting dirty, as my cousins and I would go and play with the rest of the kids from the *colonia*. If our grandparents would give us permission, we used to go to the only place that had a television and we would watch it for thirty minutes only, because the television used to overheat very quickly. We loved to climb the jocote trees, even if there was no fruit. The leaves of the tree were kind of sour, and we used to cut, wash, and mix them with lime juice and salt and drink it. Sometimes, we would add ice when it was available.

My mom loved the house that dad was building. The only problem was that there was a vacant land next to us that people used to use as a short cut to another street, and she was not used to having people coming and going right outside. She was always afraid at night because there were nights that my dad had to work late or do an overnight shift and we stayed alone.

My dad had three jobs as far as I remember, but he also used to do side jobs at home. He drove a city truck early in the morning picking up trash from different communities, and then he used to come home, take a shower and get dressed to go to his second job as an ambulance driver for the local private hospital. Then he volunteered at the Red Cross also driving an ambulance. He was certified as a mountain rescuer and a lifeguard. At night, when he was home, after we went to bed, he did accounting for a small business and/or did small appliance repairs for the neighbors. My dad was what the locals call *siete oficios catorce necesidades*, [seven jobs for fourteen needs]. One time, dad came home talking about a new job as a lifeguard at the beach every Saturday. I was so happy because I love the beach and now we would go with him to work. The best memories of spending time with dad were the ones when we took this trip every weekend to the beach. Since he drove a truck, he used to pack all the kids from the *colonia* plus my cousins, mom, and us. Mom would pack a lunch while he packed the truck; the kids from the neighborhood got ready with their parents to come along, too. My dad's truck was small, but since in our countries everyone travels standing up in the back of the pickup, there was lots of room for anyone wanting to come. We would leave around 6:00 am and come home at dawn.

I learned to have a respect for the ocean. My dad used to take us to the *reventazon de olas*, the place where the waves break, and he used to tell us either you jump them or swim under. I always preferred to jump them, since there was always one after another. In one of those lessons, he used to tell us that the ocean was very dangerous and that every time we go in, we have to be aware of what is happening around. He said not to go in drunk, because many people had died in that way.

Civil War

In 1979, I started to notice that dad was spending less time at home. Mom told us that he was saving lives because there were many people hurt. I remember the first time that I felt the pressure of the war. We went to visit my dad's father in our neighborhood. Dad told mom to go inside of grandpa's house because there was trouble. Very close by, there was an army station and that day, it was being taken by the guerrillas. There were shootings everywhere, people running to find shelter, some running to find their children, calling them by names. Ambulance sirens were all around. People were screaming, dying, and going insane when they could not find their children or because they would find them dead. Grandpa got us inside his house. I did not want my dad to go, but his duty was to help with the ambulance. We could not leave the town because it was being taken by the army: Roads were closed, so the only way out was if you were taken by ambulance, hurt or dead. We were so scared, and we wanted to go home, so dad hid us inside the ambulance and took us off like there was someone hurt inside. I was so happy when we got home but dad had to go back to help people. I remember that night so vividly: I slept in my mom's arms next to my little brother.

Things got worse after that. The military would come to the schools to recruit students. They did not ask for permission to take you: They would select a group of boys, grab them, and take them to the military station. Days later, we would see them with guns patrolling the streets. There was not parent consent, no questions asked, just pure evil. On occasions, the guerrillas would also come to school to do the same thing, pick boys to fight. We would go home, tell their families that their son was taking by someone, but we could not know which side it was because they always came in army clothes.

One day in the middle of April we got a visitor, a cousin from the United States, who came to get his legal documentation in order. Dad was supposed to take him to the immigration center the following week. So on April 29, 1979, my dad started his daily routine. He got up early, cut some avocados from the tree, took a shower and said goodbye to my mom, and gave us a kiss because we were still sleeping. He went to work to pick up his check and buy some stuff that he needed for a trip that we were taking that day. For the first time in a while, he had taking time off from work during the week to help his nephew with the documentation required to obtain his residency in the United States.

Dad never came home. Around 9:00 in the morning, some officials from the Red Cross came to tell mom that she was needed to identify his body which was lying in the middle of a main road. I could not believe the impact that it caused to hear the news. I begged my mom to take me with her, so I could see for myself that my dad was really dead. My mom did not want to take me but I grabbed her arm so hard that she didn't have a choice. We arrived at the scene and I remember my mom recognized his shirt. She did not want to get close, so she moved her head admitting that yes, indeed, that was her husband lying in the middle of a lagoon of blood. She knew it because she was the one who advised him to wear the clothes that he was wearing; my mom always said that my dad could not combine his clothes, so she took it upon herself to arrange his clothing so that he matched. So that morning, while dad was in the shower, she had taken the outfit out and laid it in the bed with his socks, shoes, and belt.

I did not have the same reaction, I had to see the body to believe, so I got close and there he was, my hero, dead. Inside his truck there was another passenger, a woman. The next day the newspaper said that she was his lover, and that it was a love triangle. The woman's husband was in the military, so they assumed that he sent out people to kill my dad. She was a nurse at the hospital where he worked. There were reports by people that said that they had seen when he was killed: The woman hid in the truck, but she was shot there, while my dad was left dying on the street. His body was picked up right after that and taken to the Red Cross where he was going to be shown. Mom did not want to do it, she was in shock; but the arrangements had to be made since the funeral was going to take place that night.

That night was the worse night of my life. My mom was trying to be strong, but she was lost somehow. People kept asking questions, but she only moved her head yes or no. She did not know what to say or do. Everything was slipping away. Family was calling from the United States wanting to know what had happened. I remember that I kept looking at the casket, and seeing my dad there was very painful. He had a bullet that had entered through his left side of the face by his chin, but I know that the one that killed him was the one to his heart. He used to carry many forms of identification in his left shirt pocket and when the Red Cross gave mom his belongings, the ones that he carried in his left pocket had a bullet mark on them. The next day, twenty ambulances were at the front of his funeral procession, sirens wailing all the way to the cemetery. Mom could not handle it and she fainted. Someone took care of my brother and one of my cousins was with me because I wanted to go with dad. I did not want to let him go. I remember that I attempted to throw myself into the ground where the casket was being buried. Mom was taken in an ambulance so she did not get to pay her last respects to dad.

Something else happened on the day of the funeral: There were two other girls there saying that he was their dad, too. So, I was not the only girl or the oldest in the family. The oldest one of my sisters was ten years older than me. I was so angry to find that out, but it was more painful to know that I had lived all this time without knowing about them.

After the funeral, we came back to an empty house. Everything was happening too fast, I became very depressed, and all I wanted to do was sleep. I used to pray to God to let me talk to my dad in my sleep, but he never came. He used to come to play with my brother at night; he was only four, and he would laugh and laugh and say: "no daddy that tickles. Stop it, stop it!" I was always angry because his spirit could play with my brother but did not want anything to do with me.

Since mom was a homemaker, and we did not an income now, mom had to find a job. The only thing that she knew was how to run a store, so with the little money that the insurance gave mom, she purchased some counters, and she started to sell stuff at home. It was a very small store: the customers were people that came to purchase an egg, a piece of cheese, ten cents of gas to start a fire, a small bag of laundry detergent or a pencil. However, with this small amount of money mom served us food every day.

I continued to go to school but the toll of dead people kept growing. While walking I would encounter dead bodies, and sometimes parts of a body, a leg, an arm, a head. There were times that you would find entire families dead in their homes. Every night, my family used to sleep between four walls just in case there was a shooting. During the night, we would hear people screaming, being chopped alive, or killed on the spot. Some people used to help when it was known that there was a dead body or family in need. We had made some cans for people to donate money so the bodies could be buried.

Mom always said that I was very smart, and every year since I started school, I received a prize for having some of the highest grades in the classroom. However, when dad died my studies went to hell. I had just started sixth grade and things were not going well at all. All year I struggled with school. Mom was willing to tell the teachers that I should stay behind due to the grades, but my teacher was so confident that I could pull it through. My teacher passed me to seventh grade because she knew that I was capable of doing the work but because of the tragedy, it was going to take a while to get back on track. Before I started seventh grade, my mom took me to a friend that is a psychologist to do some testing. Mom wanted to know if I was going to be okay starting seventh grade or should I go back to sixth. Testing came back normal and I enrolled in seventh grade. It was a nightmare! I did not want to go back to school, but I also did not want to stay home. Mom told me to try my best and that was what I did.

There were days that the streets were closed, that the schools were also closed or taken by the guerrillas or the army, and buses burned or destroyed by the opposing sides. Mom spoke with one of my aunts in California to see if they could sponsor me to attend private school. Mom's intention was for me to continue my education since she only went to school for four or five years. At that time my brother was doing really well at school too, so the pressure was on me to do better since he was the one getting the rewards for being the best in the class. My brother started to learn how to make shoes at the age of eight. Mom asked a couple of friends to take him under the wing, so that they could teach him things that mom could not. He was really good about learning new things, and always wanting to learn more.

Many times, my girlfriends would come and spend time at home with me. Some of those times they slept over, and we used to do homework together or study for a test. There were times that we needed to drop them back at their home but since we did not have a car, a group of my mom's friends used to walk them back safe to their homes. One particular night, one of them came to drop off some stuff that I needed for school the next day. She stayed for dinner and then asked if we could drop her off. I asked mom and she told me to ask her friends if they would be able to go with us. Some of them were not home yet and some of them were really busy. So, my mom and I decided to walk her home ourselves.

The walk was approximately twenty minutes along some dark paths, but it was the only way to be connected to the main road. I remember mom asked what time it was because she wanted to be back in time for her soap opera. I told her that it was 7:20 p.m. So, she said, "Let's go so we are not out too late at night." We dropped my friend off at her house and on the way back, we decided to take a short cut because it was getting dark. There was a small path through a coffee farm that the same community had made so people did not have so walk far. Mom told me, *"Look, there is a guy walking the path, maybe if we hurry up we can catch up with him, so we do not have to walk it alone."* We followed the guy, but it turned out that he lived in one of the houses right at the beginning of the path. I asked, *"What are we going to do now?"* She said: *"We are already here, let's prayed to God to protect us so we can be home soon."* We started to walk together, we were holding each other close, and then we heard a noise, like someone had slipped down to the ground between the trees. We got really scared when a man appeared, took out a gun and said: "I was waiting for you." He put the gun to my forehead.

My mom told me to just listen and do what he told us to do. He threw my mom on the ground and he told her to stay there for now, then he told me to tie her to the tree facing north. Later he did the same to me facing south. He told us that he had a series of questions that we needed to answer the same way. If we disagreed, he was going to kill us right there.

Sometime later, he told us to wait for a signal. If he heard a whistle we were to continue, but if we heard a shot then he was going to kills us. We started to walk, mom told me to go ahead of her so that the gun was pointed to her. She said: *"Keep praying, God was protecting us and that it was not going to be the end for us, He had better plans for us."* With that in my head, we continued to walk. He told us to sit again, and mom told him that she was thirsty and tired. His answer was that if she wanted, he could put her out her misery. He began to hit her really bad and I could not do anything about it. I started to cry silently, asking for forgiveness because I thought that it was going to be the end for us. After he finished with my mom, he came to me, placed his gun between my legs and started to touch me. I did not want him to touch me so he hit me really hard with his gun, and I did not know what happened next. He told us to keep walking, my mom was hurt but we were okay. I was in a lot of pain mainly because I was raped by him at gunpoint.

Finally, he let us go. Mom could hardly walk but she was happy that we would make it home. He told us that if we mentioned anything to anyone about what had happened, he knew exactly where we slept and next time he was not going to have any compassion. He also told us that it was better for my brother not to mention anything to anyone either. We got home around four or five in the morning. Grandpa was waiting for us. I remember throwing myself in bed crying, but grandpa made me stand up to pray thanking God that we had made it home. A couple of days later, my friend came to visit me asking why I had not been to school and that I was to bring the homework the next day. I could not tell anyone what had happened that night, but mom and I had nightmares. I was so scared, but mom made me do my daily routine, as if nothing was out of the ordinary. The only thing that she did that same night was to call my aunt in California to ask for help to get me to the United States because I was in danger. We could not say too much because we did not know if the lines were tapped.

Journey to the United States

My mom and I celebrated when I got my next period, as she was worried that I was going to be pregnant. My relatives in California collected money to help pay for my trip and sent it to my mom. Five months later, it was my turn to leave my country and my family. I would never forget the day that I left: My mom was still at home taking care of a customer in the store. I told her that

I was going to be back. I gave her the biggest hug that I could at that time. I wanted to cry and not to let go but I had to leave.

I was told how to dress, what to bring, and what house to meet at for the journey. There were twenty-one people in the group. I was acquainted with one woman who was traveling with her child. We made our first payment to the coyotes, and they gave some of it back to us in quetzales, for Guatemala, pesos for Mexico, and dollars for the United States. We left by bus, crossed Guatemala as if we were tourists, and then arrived at the Mexican border. We were taken to a hotel in Mexico and held there while the coyotes "negotiated" with the local authorities. We were told to pool together all of our remaining money so that our group would be allowed to continue. Everyone reached into their socks, their shoes and all of their hiding places, and we made a pile of money. The Mexican official looked at it and said it was enough. From there, our bus went to Mexico City, and we were kept in a hotel near Plaza Garibaldi for fifteen days while the coyotes contacted our families to ask for more money. Here, we were joined by many more people traveling north. We would go out at times to explore the plaza in small groups and listen to the mariachi music. The coyotes had arranged for a commercial flight to take us to Tijuana, but I was one of the few who did not make it on. Instead, I traveled overland to Tijuana. Fortunately, one of my aunts from California met me there, as her husband's family had some relatives living there.

I stayed in Tijuana for one month. I watched as the group I was traveling with was loaded into the back of a semi-trailer, sitting with legs open, one person in front of another. I think that they made it across, but I also remember the trucks full of bodies that have been found abandoned in the desert. I was able to walk across the border, pretending to be the daughter of another family. I was taught how to talk like a Mexican, and the local geography I should know when they asked me for my address. The lady I was crossing with said, "Do what I do. If they stop you, pretend you don't know me. I will come back for you." When I got to the customs official, he asked me where I was going. I looked across into San Ysidrio and saw a restaurant.

"I am going to the Burger King," I replied.

"What are you going to get there?"

"A cheeseburger."

"With fries?"

"Yes."

He smiled, waved me through and said, "Bring me back a medium order of fries, too."

I arrived in California in May 1989, after being in the road for a few months. I missed my mom so much and I cried every time I talked to her. The phone calls kept getting longer and longer, I wanted to go home but knowing how bad was at home, I kept telling myself that it was going to get better.

I lived with relatives in the Los Angeles area for a while, moving around because the places were small. Sometimes I slept in the bathtub, sometimes on the floor. When it was time to enroll in high school, I moved in with an uncle in North Hollywood, away from the gangs in other schools. While I finished school, I also had an active asylum application, but while that was being processed, I would report every six months to extend my temporary visa. We had to carry our documents all of the time because the INS could stop us in the street and demand to see them.

I moved to Phoenix, Arizona, after high school and stayed with a friend for a while, then on my own. I barely had money for a small apartment, and little for food. I was able to eat popcorn at my job at a gas station. I met my ex-husband and eventually agreed to go out with him. When his grandmother got sick, he wanted to return to Wisconsin to help take care of her and asked me if I would like to come with him. I agreed, we were married, and I soon landed in Appleton, Wisconsin. His grandmother helped sponsor me and I became a permanent resident.

I got a job as a bank teller, and soon long lines of Spanish speakers were waiting for me to cash their checks. Soon, they were asking for help in other areas. I realized that I wanted to do more than cash checks: I was ready to help the community. After a job as a bilingual interpreter for the Green Bay schools, a job opened up as liaison to the Latino community, working half-time at the Appleton high schools and half-time at Fox Valley Technical College.

My boss recently asked me what I like best about my job: I told him that it was seeing young people walk across that stage and get their diplomas and degrees. I have struggled very hard to get to where I am today, and I encourage the students I meet to never give up, to keep their dreams alive. I did it. So can they.

I still have nightmares, post-traumatic stress, and anxieties. It is hard to go back and remember those times I have lived through. But I take each day as it comes, with gratitude.

Themes in the Narratives

There are many similarities in the exile experiences of Txerthoj Vang and Mayra Pasayes. Each remembers fondly the beautiful countryside and the connection to family and community in their homelands of Laos and El Salvador. For Txerthoj, this was a farming community in the steep hills of Laos, his many siblings, and the role played by not just his mother, but his adopted mother, both of whom were married to his father. For Mayra, this was a colonia on the edge of the capital, a place where everyone knew each other, and where, at her grandparents' house, "the backyard was filled with coffee plants, guava, avocado, lime, pepeto, and mango trees, but also peppers all kinds, squash and other vegetables."

War entered the lives of Txerthoj and Mayra while they were still young. Txerthoj writes of a constant moving from village to village, seeking refuge, and losing family members along the way because "we kept moving a lot and there was no medical treatment." His older brothers fought and some died as soldiers in a secret army raised by the American CIA, and at the age of thirteen, Txerthoj was asked to become a soldier himself. Mayra remembers how her father was always working as an ambulance driver as the civil war escalated in El Salvador, the bodies in the streets, and how the army would arrive at school, "select a group of boys, grab them, and take them to the military station. Days later, we would see them with guns patrolling the streets." Like the Hmong secret army, the Salvadoran military, trained by the United States, had the habit of recruiting child soldiers.

Violence perpetrated by both individuals and governments led Txerthoj and Mayra to leave behind their loved ones and make a journey that would eventually lead them to the United States. Txerthoj describes the desperation of Hmong communities when the Americans and the Hmong military leadership headed by Vang Pao left Laos, and also the purges carried out by the Pathet Lao regime against America's Hmong allies: "Thousands of Hmong people were moving from one village to the next, seeking shelter." Within a few years, the Hmong people still resisting in the mountains were being bombarded by yellow rain, chemicals dropped by government planes on their villages, and Txerthoj decided to make the journey through the forests and across the river into Thailand. Mayra witnessed and heard the bombings and shootings at night, saw the corpses in the street, and her classmates forcibly recruited. At a very personal level, she experienced the murder of her father, an ambulance driver, and the sexual assault on herself and her mother as they were walking home one night. The perpetrator "told us that if we mentioned anything to anyone about what had happened, he knew exactly where we slept and next time he was not going to have any compassion."

Where the stories of Txerthoj and Mayra differ the most is in their route to the United States. Txerthoj reached a refugee camp in Thailand, continued to work to support the Americans shot down and MIAs, and eventually gained asylum to the United States with his family. Like many fellow Salvadorans, Mayra made a long, overland journey by bus and on foot to reach the United States, without official asylum. Yet, as can be seen by her account, her life was in danger, as were the lives of hundreds of thousands of other Salvadorans, from their own government that was supported militarily by the United States. It was only much later that she would obtain official residency in the United States after a long effort to get her asylum application considered.

Refugees With or Without Papers

If our era had a name, it could be "The Time of the Refugee." Millions of men, women, and children are displaced in Asia, Africa, the Middle East, and Latin America. Despite opposition in Congress, the United States president, Barack Obama, at least recognizes the reality and desperation of the millions fleeing civil wars in the Congo, Iraq, Syria, Burma, and elsewhere. What has not been officially recognized is the right to asylum for the hundreds of thousands fleeing the organized violence of drug cartels and criminal gangs in Latin America.

This is particularly troublesome, in that the roots of the gangs such as the Mara Salvatruchas in El Salvador can be traced back to the streets of Los Angeles and other cities: A previous generation of Central Americans arrived, traumatized by civil war, hungry and desperate, and some of their children took to gang life. Unwanted in either country, these gangs have flourished, developed, and soon began to hold sway over schools and neighborhoods in Guatemala, El Salvador, and Honduras. Arana (2005) reports how this has shaken the lives of citizens in these countries:

With the United States preoccupied elsewhere, the gangs have grown in power and numbers; today, local officials estimate their size at 70,000–100,000 members. The marabuntas, or maras, as they are known (after a deadly species of local ants), now pose the most serious challenge to peace in the region since the end of Central America's civil wars (Arana, 2005).

Now it is the children from schools, neighborhoods, and communities controlled by gangs who are fleeing north, seeking asylum from organized violence (Nazario, 2014).

The United States trained the soldiers who committed some of the worst atrocities in the Central American civil wars of the 1980s. Many of our urban neighborhoods have proven as dangerous for immigrants as the countries that they have left behind. Rather than deal with gangs here, we have often exported the problems back to the very countries in which we have previously supported dictators and their death squads. The tragic irony for Central Americans fleeing violence is all too apparent: Just as in Laos, in Syria, and elsewhere, we have had a hand in creating a refugee crisis. It is time that we take responsibility, grant asylum to those who have fled to our land for shelter from the storm, and seek ways to integrate traumatized children and adults more fully into our society.

NOTE

1. The *pahawh* was a Hmong written language developed by Shong Lue, whom some considered a prophet. He attracted many followers in Vietnam and Laos, was

persecuted by both sides in the war, and was murdered. His followers continued to spread the *pahawh* and other beliefs and led the *Chao Fa* resistance after the departure of the Americans in 1975 (Quincy, 2000; Vang, Yang and Smalley, 1990).

REFERENCES

Allison, M. (2012). El Salvador's Brutal Civil War: What We Still Don't Know. *Aljazeera*, March 1. http://www.aljazeera.com/indepth/opinion/2012/02/201222812312297 5116.html

American Immigration Council (2014). Mexican and Central American Asylum and Credible Fear Claims: Background and Context. Special Report. http://immigrationpolicy.org/special-reports/mexican-and-central-american-asylum-and-credible-fear-claims-background-and-context

Arana, A. (2005). How the Street Gangs Took Central America. *Foreign Affairs*, May/June. https://www.foreignaffairs.com/articles/central-america-caribbean/2005-05-01/how-street-gangs-took-central-america

Badger, E. (2014). What Happened to the Millions of Immigrants Granted Legal Status Under Ronald Reagan? *Washington Post*, November 26. https://www.washingtonpost.com/news/wonk/wp/2014/11/26/what-happened-to-the-millions-of-immigrants-granted-legal-status-under-ronald-reagan/

Beinart, P. (2015). Why Obama Is Standing by the Syrian Refugees. *Atlantic Monthly*, November 23. http://www.theatlantic.com/politics/archive/2015/11/obama-syrian-refugees/417222/

Bencastro. (1998). *Odyssey to the North*. Houston: Arte Publico Press.

Benei, V. (2010). To Fairly Tell: Social Mobility, Life Histories, and the Anthropologist. *Journal of Comparative & International Education*, 40(2), 199–212.

Center for Justice and Accountability (2015). El Salvador: Twelve Years of Civil War. http://www.cja.org/article.php?list=type&type=199

Clandinin, D., Davies, A., Whelan, K., Huber, J. and Rose, C. (2001). Telling and Retelling Our Stories on the Professional Knowledge Landscape. *Theory and Practice*, 7(2), 143–156.

Denzin, N. (1994). The Art and Politics of Interpretation. In N. Denzin and Y. Lincoln (Eds.), *Handbook of Qualitative Research* (pp. 500–515). Thousand Oaks, CA: Sage.

Elbaz-Luwisch, F. (2010). Narrative Inquiry: Wakeful Engagement with Educational Experience. *Curriculum Inquiry*, 40(2), 263–280.

Galeano, E. (1988). *Century of the Wind (Memory of Fire Series)*. New York, NY: W.W. Norton and Company.

Glaser, B. and Strauss, A. (1967). *The Discovery of Grounded Theory: Strategies for Qualitative Research*. New York, NY: Aldine de Gruyter.

Gzesh, S. (2006). Central Americans and Asylum Policies in the Reagan Era. *Migration Policy Institute*, April. http://www.migrationpolicy.org/article/central-americans-and-asylum-policy-reagan-era

Hones, D. (1998). Known in Part: The Story, the Teller, and the Narrative Researcher. *Qualitative Inquiry*, 4(2), 225–248.

Joint Fact Sheet on Unaccompanied Children. http://www2.ed.gov/about/overview/focus/rights-unaccompanied-children-enroll-school.pdf

Markon, J. and Nakamura, D. (2015). U.S. plans raids to deport families who surged across border. *Washington Post*, December 23. https://www.washingtonpost.com/politics/us-plans-raids-to-deport-families-who-surged-across-border/2015/12/23/034fc954-a9bd-11e5-8058-480b572b4aae_story.html

Moua, M. N. (2003). Along the Way to the Mekong. In M. N. Moua (Ed.), *Bamboo Among the Oaks*. St. Paul, MN: Minnesota Historical Society Press, 57–62.

Nazario, S. (2014). *Enrique's Journey: The Story of a Boy's Dangerous Odyssey to Reunite with His Mother*. New York, NY: Random House.

Newland. (1995). Impact of U.S. Refugee Policies on U.S. Foreign Policy: A Case of the Tail Wagging the Dog? In M. S. Teitelbaum and M. Weiner (Eds.), *Threatened Peoples, Threatened Borders: World Migration and U.S. Policy*. New York, NY: The American Assembly. http://carnegieendowment.org/1995/01/01/impact-of-u.s.-refugee-policies-on-u.s.-foreign-policy-case-of-tail-wagging-dog

Polkinghorne, D. (1995). Narrative Configuration in Qualitative Analysis. In J. Hatch and R. Wisniewski (Eds.), *Life History and Narrative*. Bristol, PA: Falmer, 5–23.

Quincy, K. (2000). *Harvesting Pa Chay's Wheat: The Hmong and America's Secret War in Laos*. Spokane, WA: Eastern Washington University Press.

Refugee Act of 1980 (1980). Public Law 96-212:103. https://www.gpo.gov/fdsys/pkg/STATUTE-94/pdf/STATUTE-94-Pg102.pdf

Strauss, A. and Corbin, J. (1994). Grounded Theory Methodology: An Overview. In N. Denzin and Y. Lincoln (Eds.), *Handbook of Qualitative Research*, 273–285. Thousand Oaks, CA: Sage.

Swoyer, A. (2015). Donald Trump: Humane Deportation Plan for Illegal Immigrants Will Work, September 27. http://www.breitbart.com/big-government/2015/09/27/donald-trump-humane-deportation-plan-illegal-immigrants-will-work/

Tedlock, D. (trans.) (1996). *The Popol Vuh: The Definitive Edition of the Mayan Book of the Dawn of Life and the Glories of Gods and Kings*. New York, NY: Touchstone.

UNHCR. (1951). Convention and Protocol Related to the Status of Refugees. http://www.unhcr.org/3b66c2aa10.pdf

UNHCR. (2015). Refugees: Flowing Across Borders. http://www.unhcr.org/pages/49c3646c125.html

Worra, B. T. (2003). The Last War Poem. In M. N. Moua (Ed.), *Bamboo Among the Oaks*. St. Paul, MN: Minnesota Historical Society Press, 98–99.

Yang, K. K. (2008). *The Latehomecomer: A Hmong Family Memoir*. St. Paul, MN: Minnesota Historical Society Press.

Chapter 8

Rudolphs Searching for Sleighs

Parallels, Paradoxes, and the Emotional Challenges of Standing Out without a Stage

Patience E. Fonkem

IMMIGRANTS ARE RUDOLPHS SEARCHING FOR SLEIGHS

Inspirational Background: The Rudolph in Immigrants

This narrative, metaphorical study is inspired by the November 27, 2018, controversy over the holiday classic *Rudolph the Red-Nosed Reindeer*. It was described by some viewers as being "seriously problematic" (Huffington Post, Dec. 5, 2018). The analyses and comments from different viewers on either side of the argument irrespective were very insightful and reawakening. Reflecting on the lyrics of the Christmas Classic ignited some perspectives and the need to rethink the metaphorical connotations of *Rudolph the Red-Nosed Reindeer* and its respective themes. Rudolph's experiences do not only represent the psychology of the society that produced him as was revealed in the several tweets and articles that emanated from the controversy but also depict how nonconformity and diversity are acknowledged and understood in our society today. Among others, the tweet describing the classic as "a parable of racism & homophobia . . . and seriously problematic" is very compelling and insightful and forms the basis on which this study is conceived. In this chapter, I examine and question why and what about the classic could be problematic? Is Santa, whom I perceive as "the Good Samaritan" the problem? Is Rudolph, the red-nosed reindeer who reminds me of the "sins" of the outsider, those who do not need a stage to standout, the problem? Or, is it about the fact that the Rudolph was given the stage, a different stage, one that brings his other side, his best qualities and make him shine, the problem? These questions summarize the major concepts and assertions that surround immigration policies today and the implications and will be discussed in this chapter.

Leaning on the above premise is important because just as the controversy over the classic, the whole issue of immigration is dividing the world and most especially the United States of America today than never before. First, statistics from the Council on Foreign Relations on the immigration debate state that immigrants together with their U. S. born children comprise about 27 percent of the U. S. population and form about 20 percent of the U.S. workforce. A 2017 gallop poll revealed that 71percent of Americans believe that their country is a country of immigrants and that immigrants contribute in positive ways to the country's economy. The former president of the United States of America Donald Trump supported by a handful of nationalists, defines immigrants as criminals, outcasts, and enemies to the society and was bent on implementing policies that will selectively discourage immigrants from certain parts of the world. Usually, the president and his cronies targeted current immigrants who look differently from the privileged class.[1] This chapter argues that the current controversy on immigration and the fear of what the other is capable of doing limits the potential for individuals to actively participate and strive for social justice more, especially because the abovesaid controversy has contradictions with truth in a way that justice means differently for many individuals, across different communities, social classes, age, genders and races. In other words, this study is significant because there continues to linger some level of subtle misunderstanding that is maligner and needs to be dissected among activists to smoothen their part to establishing a socially just community.

More importantly, this author comprehends that Robert May wrote this Christmas Classic to comfort their daughter with no intention to incite the perceptions that have built up over the years especially in relation to how immigrants are viewed and understood in our communities today. This study aims at kindling the notion that like Rudolph, many immigrants, especially non-white immigrants, while learning to brace their fears and integrate in gainful ways are sadly challenged not by the traumas of the horrors and hardships they experienced on their fight for survival (especially in the case of forced migrations) or from the losses incurred from the life they have abandoned (voluntary migrations). The research done on this topic reveals that most immigrants irrespective of the cultural dissonances are mainly challenged by the mere fact that they are different. It is disturbing that being different should be that stressful given the uniqueness of our human character. The chapter articulates the irrespective or the pull and push factors, most immigrants, no matter their country of origin, are motivated by the notion that faraway hills are greener. Most of them irrespective of societal misrepresentations and the philosophy of fear mongering that describe immigrants as "rapist, drug dealers, thieves and killer," thrive on the hope that there are still some who believe in the dignity of humans and will take the time to understand who they are before judging them. It is with this motivation that they continue to yearn for sleighs to illuminate their potential. They approach their new setting with high expectation and with the ambition to contribute to their communities in mutually beneficial ways. Most immigrants are challenged with the sad realization of the labels, suspicion, and baggage of misinformation and mistrust that define them. The implications of this realization may be worse than the hardships they encountered before their flight to "freedom-land." The emotional infliction on the self-image paradoxically interferes with the abilities and productivity of the immigrants and unfortunately impedes their ability to function as useful and productive members of their communities. This chapter highlights that the most inflicting of the challenges immigrants in our communities face today is the disturbing knowledge of how they are viewed and defined, the thought that they are less of a human because mostly because of circumstances out of their control. These emotional challenges constitute the frame of what this chapter refers to as the invisible challenges faced by most immigrants. Understanding what these emotional challenges are firsthand, that is, from the immigrants who are the victims, is not only compelling but is emancipatory and transformational.

THE PURPOSE OF UNDERSTANDING EMOTIONAL CHALLENGES OF IMMIGRANTS FIRSTHAND

The intent of this chapter is to situate the emotional challenges immigrants from non-white origins go through to motivate activists to rethink their human engagement and reflect on how misunderstandings, mistrust, and misinterpretations of each other's motives can blur and obstruct equity and social justice. The chapter argues that the current controversy on immigration is related to an ego-based human dysfunction whose main intent is to untie the human thread that interconnects the human family by creating fear and distrust among groups. The study assumes that this conscious manipulations, mischaracterization, and misrepresentation of immigrants not only create lack of respect for immigrants but also limit the society from benefiting from the talents of the immigrants. Most significantly, this perceived mischaracterization also damages the self-esteem of immigrants.

This chapter gleans on the views of activists in the fight for social justice who uphold that there is only one race, the human race. The study maintains that irrespective of the countless differences and numerous tensions present in our world today, the entire planet is almost paradoxically striving toward harmony. This fact is best expressed by Congress Woman and Speaker of the House, Nancy Pelosi when she explains:

> Our Nation's immigrants are the constant reinvigoration of America. Each wave of newcomers brings their patriotism, bravery and determination to succeed to our shores—and in doing so, makes America more American. As students and service members, entrepreneurs and public servants, parents and neighbors, these new Americans affirm our country's fundamental, founding truth: that in diversity, lies strength.[2]

As part of contributing toward this global harmony, the study endeavors to bring visibility to the emotional struggles these immigrants go through using case study narrative and critical theory analysis. While acknowledging the extensive work of prohumanitarian organizations, the study projects the evils of mutual mistrusts and misinterpretations and their emotional impact that continue to linger and present obstacles to global harmony. The claim is that confronting these misunderstandings in a manner that promotes lasting cross-generational interconnectivity of humankind is essential and could be likened to Rudolph's sleigh. It highlights the fact that immigrants may be underdogs but should not be underestimated. Although some of our leaders may shun immigrants because they are different, given the right opportunity, communities would realize the mighty potentials because no one knows who will grow up to be a great success. Lastly, the study recommends that these mutual mistrusts and misinterpretations need to be identified, examined, and analyzed to successfully pave the way forward to global harmonization.

The Exigencies of Firsthand Understanding of the Emotional Challenges of Immigrants

Have you ever been in a room and discovered you looked different from everyone else? I understand teachers are usually in rooms with students younger than they are but I mean, against the norm. For example, you find yourself underdressed or overdressed, went to a night club with your spouse and noticed it was a teenage party and/or shopping for a present for your wife and discovered you were the only male in Victoria Secret? Or, even better, have you been stopped on your way out of a department or grocery store and asked to show your receipt when every other shopper is going passed without question? Better still, have you noticed individuals double-clicking their car locks as they leave their cars just because they noticed you pulled and packed your car by them? Has someone refused to get into the elevator even though he was waiting for one and you were the only other passenger? How did that make you feel? Imagine living that experience every day. As unimaginable as it can be, immigrants today, especially those who look different from the ruling class, live life with a burden; a sentence that defines them as criminals. Walking the parking lot and hear car keys double-clicking, watching women grabbing tight their purses, cleaning other's mess in a common restroom because it would be assumed you made the mess, your son being tracked and questioned because he is pushing a cart with your purse in, while you are on a different aisle, are all examples of some of the emotional challenges' immigrants in the United States in the twenty-first century.

Paradoxically, America is a land of immigrants, and immigrants of color turn to remain immigrants for life just because of who they are. As humans, we understand what the natural tendency is for us when they approach criminals or danger. Imagine being considered a criminal or dangerous. This metaphorical narrative therefore explains that immigrants of color, Rudolphs' spend their livelihood struggling hard to blend while standing out and it is for this reason that they yearn for sleighs to stand out in a bright manner. This is significant because as this study explains emotional imbalance is a silent killer, one that is worse than any enemy the immigrants may have fled from.

To better understand the nature of this silent killer, Frank Baum in *The Wonderful Wizard of Oz* (1991) provides helpful hint that exemplifies the current emotional conundrum of immigrants in our society today. According to Baum, "no matter how dreary and gray our homes are, we people of flesh and blood would rather live there than in any other country, be it ever so beautiful. There is no place like home" (Baum, 1991). Have you ever wondered why Moses, who was brought up as the child of the Princess of Egypt and possible heir to the throne chose to align with the "slaves" when he learned he was biologically an Israelite? Home is home! The same goes for most immigrants. Irrespective of their reason for migrating, irrespective of where they are coming from, the push and pull factors; leaving their homes was not an easy decision. This study highlights that irrespective of whether they come from homes described as "*S...hole countries*" Leaving home, "a place where the heart is," is an opportunity cost whose sentimental value cannot be fully assessed. In most cases, individuals leave their homes because they have approached breaking point and to them it is a life or death situation. They approach their receiving countries with plethora of hope that the new pastures are greener. They are looking for progress not for problems. They yearn for safety and are not sellouts. They plan to contribute and live as useful and acceptable members in the new communities and grow the economy. They come in with no weapons because in most cases they are fleeing from weapons. They are mostly armed with gratitude and yearn for love.

Sadly, on arrival, they are looked upon with disdain and fear. It is a very uncomfortable feeling to live with, and the emotional toll is enormous. It is therefore inhumane for example, the 2019 State of the Union address to congress, when the president of the United States of America spent 20 percent of the air time on immigration most of which describing immigrants as:

> . . . putting the ruthless coyotes, cartels, drug dealers, and human traffickers out of business . . . This is a moral issue. The lawless state of our southern border is a threat to the safety, security, and financial well–being of all Americans. We have a moral duty to create an immigration system that protects the lives and jobs of our citizens . . . Tonight, I am asking you to defend our very dangerous southern border out of love and devotion to our fellow citizens and to our country . . . working class Americans are left to pay the price for mass illegal migration – reduced jobs, lower wages, overburdened schools and hospitals, increased crime, and a depleted social safety net. Tolerance for illegal immigration is not compassionate—it is cruel. One in three women is sexually assaulted on the long journey north. Smugglers use migrant children as human pawns to exploit our laws and gain access to our country. Human traffickers and sex traffickers take advantage of the wide-open areas between our ports of entry to smuggle thousands of young girls and women into the United States and to sell them into prostitution and modern-day slavery. Tens of thousands of innocent Americans are killed by lethal drugs that cross our border and flood into our cities—including meth, heroin, cocaine, and fentanyl. The savage gang, MS-13, now operates in 20 different American States. (President Donald Trump, State of the Union, 2019)

The president of the United States (2019) rightfully declares that immigration is a moral issue thereby concurring with the Unitarian Universalist Association 2013 "statement of conscience" and its emphasis on the inherent worth and the dignity of every person.[3] The president in his speech also agrees with Speaker Pelosi's assertion that immigrants affirm the strength of our country's diversity as a fundamental, founding truth. Irrespective of the moral affirmation, the president addressed the immigrant problem in terms of caravans and safety treats and the need to build walls and stop ICE to protect Americans. He contradicts his former claim and asserts that tolerance for immigrants is "not compassionate" because immigrants, he posits, are criminals. This declaration exposes his lack of respect for the dignity of every person from backgrounds different from his. The president's ideas also contradict that of the speaker of the house, in that he refuses to acknowledge immigrants and their experiences and to reaffirm and promote a flourishing human family. He thereby shows very little respect for the Universal Declaration of Human Rights assertion that "everyone has the right to leave any country, including his own, and to return to his country" (Article 13.2).

This study encourages the adoption of "the love your neighbor" mentality and promotes the need for institutions and individuals to recognize the opportunities and challenges of human migration by caring for and valuing each other, diversity, and our immigration systems. It calls for all to be "Good Samaritans" and decease from the politics of fear mongering that define immigrants as criminals. It calls for immigrants to be treated with love as they come protected by a greater power, the power of the good. Like Good Samaritans, we should understand that "a heart is not judged by how much you love, but by how much you are loved by others" (Baum, 1991). Stemming from the common denominator, that immigration is a moral issue, "We have a moral duty to create an immigration system that protects the lives and jobs of our citizens" (Trump, 2019) irrespective of who we consider are our citizens because, there is only one human citizen, the humankind. This is primordial because the benefits are mutual. According to Chaudry (2018):

> The United is engaged in an intense debate about immigration policy, particularly with regard to unauthorized immigrants . . . today there are an estimated 5.5 million children with unauthorized immigrant parents, about three-quarters of whom are US-born citizens. The nation builds its own future by investing in the futures of children, spending billions of dollars annually on education and health care, preventing abuse and neglect, and supporting when necessary their basic needs for housing and food. Yet, unlike other children in this country, the children of unauthorized immigrants live with the fear that their parents might be arrested, detained, or deported.

Kumar (2019) in like manner states that "there is no living thing that is not afraid when it faces danger and the moral imperative lies for us to be decent and fair." Kumar also states that it was inhumane for the president in the State of the Union address to paint the picture that the people on the southern border are trying to cross without rights when they are actually asylum seekers. The fact is that legally by international law, crafted by the government of the United States, states clearly that individuals have the right to legally seek asylum. This is saddening because as Chaudry (2019) reported, the federal government spends billions each year to arrest, detain, and deport immigrants many of whom are parents. By one estimate, in the last 10 years, over 100,000 immigrant parents of U.S. citizens have been deported from the United States.

These are hard issues especially when leaders are all divided on issues and the subjects are caught between analyzing what is fact or fake and depending on their analysis, it would determine if they adopt the Outsider or the Samaritan Syndrome. The situation is even worse for the immigrants who have been condemned as criminals, some even before their arrival. Imagine the feelings of worthlessness and the emotional impact. Understanding this invisible weapon targeting immigrants is important for all supporters of social justice and human rights, and hence the significance of this study.

RESEARCH QUESTION

The main purpose of the chapter was to provide a forum for immigrants' voices to be heard. Immigrants today especially those who do not need a stage to stand out are experiencing untold emotional distress than have ever been recorded in history. They live life with a burden; a sentence that defines them as criminals. And the natural human tendency when they approach criminals is fear, distrust, dislike, and sometimes even hate. Understanding that when individuals know that they matter does not only result in emotional balance but is emancipatory and transformative, this study provides an opportunity for first-generation immigrants to voice their challenges as they strive to integrate as useful and acceptable members of their respective communities. The research question to guide this process was: How do first-generation immigrant adjust emotionally to life in the United States? To solicit answers to this question, the researcher formulated three open ended sub-questions to drive the discussions.

Sub-Questions

- What are some of the challenges that you face and how do they affect how you live life?
- What have been helpful for you this far?
- What would make life better for you?

The summary of these semi-structured and informal interviews are reported and analyzed under data analysis as individual case analysis.

THEORETICAL FRAME AND REVIEW OF RELATED LITERATURE

The theoretical frame and related literature of this study are based on the emotional theory of mattering and marginality, the critical race theory, and the theory of fear. This section of the chapter discusses these theories and their related literature within the frame of emotional challenges of immigrants, especially in the United States during the Trump regime.

Rudolphs Searching for Sleighs: The Theory of Mattering and Marginality

Schlossberg (1989) states that the theory of marginality and mattering refers to the state of perceiving oneself as not fitting in well, not making friends, feeling like no one cares about you and what you do, not believing yourself to be important, and so on, whether true or not, impacts a person's feeling of marginality. In other words, "mattering is a motive: the feeling that others depend on us, are interested in us, are concerned with our fate, or experience us as an ego-extension, exercises a powerful influence on our actions" (Rosenberg & McCullough, 1981, p. 165). The present situation of immigrants especially immigrants of color in many ways give them many reasons to feel like they do not matter. This study claims that this is a moral and social justice issue. The sad realization is that immigrants today, especially those who do not need a stage to stand out, live life with a burden; a sentence that defines them as criminals. The effect is emotionally draining and emotional imbalance as most psychologists would agree is a silent killer, one that is worse than the enemy the immigrants fled from. More compelling, this study provides an opportunity for first-generation immigrants to voice their challenges as they strive to integrate as useful and acceptable members of their respective communities. This study upholds that knowing that you matter does not only result in emotional balance but is emancipatory and transformative.

Generally speaking, emotions are considered ubiquitous and are instrumental in determining factors in social life. They are very necessary in locating and orienting individuals' personal and relational interactions. This makes emotion especially important for any social understanding of human nature. In *Re-Reading Sociology Via the Emotions,* Hochschild (. . .) describes Marx's conception of human nature to include human passions and emotions as the fundamental integrative aspects of our social nature and the capacity for free conscious activity. He argues that in our human ability to react upon and act within our experiential life, we are both social general beings and particularly, physical and psychical beings grounded in particular contexts. The essence of humanity is that each individual objective sensuous, suffering human being should be able to feel human suffering by being in unity of the particular and the general. According to Hochschild, time of rapid economic and cultural change especially as it concerns issues like immigration creates more complicated relations between acknowledged and unacknowledged feelings between apparent ideologies and their emotional anchors. He also emphasized that because human beings appropriate their integral essence in integral ways as a total person, it is essential that this appropriation of human reality is approached in a manner that transcends and estranged existence and open the possibilities of living truly human lives.

Standing Out without a Stage and the Theory and Politics of Fear and Manifest Destiny

Contemporary psychiatrist and psychologists in agreement with the larger community describe fear as maladaptive to the human condition because it restricts freedom of action (Kagan & Schulkin, 1995, Harvard Review of Psychiatry). In a similar light, American sociologist Barry Glassner (2010) describes the culture of fear as "the concept that people may incite fear in the general public to achieve political or workplace goals through emotional bias." Current happenings in our society reveal that fear has long served as a viable weapon to the elites. The elites usually rely on fear to keep and expand their privileges and control the masses. According to Glassner, the elites shape these fears intentionally so people look to authorities for security. This just gives permission for the extension of apparatuses of coercion like police and military forces.

In situating the debate that surrounds the migration issues and dynamics in our globalized world, Yuval Harari (2018) explained that as more and more migrants search for jobs and better security there is also a growing need to confront, assimilate, or expel immigrants leading to strain in political systems and collective identities across and within national borders. Many consider the effects of the increasing controversies on migration as a fabric of social justice and injustice whose history and situational analysis strive to motivate activists to rethink their human engagement and reflect on how misunderstandings, mistrust, and misinterpretations of each other's motives can blur and obstruct equity and social justice. In the United States, for example, more and more Americans are becoming racially and ethnically diverse than in the past with projections reflecting an even more diverse society in the future (PEW Research Center).

Research also highlights that the immigration controversy seems to be selective and connected to an ideology whose agenda seeks to keep America white. According to Lubich, the term social justice was enacted based on the fictitious assumptions, misconceptions, and false fears about the "other." Lubich's writings highlight that most often, the roots of social injustices stem from our differences because, humans generally appear to be wired to fear what is different. This idea is also stressed by Bangou and Austin's (2000) in their article on "Collaborative boundaries in power relations" when they stated that humankind's complex understandings are informed through a confluence of racialized expectations. For example, statistics from the PEW Research Center seems to have rejuvenated a new wave that is scary and dangerous in our communities today. According to the PEW Research Center:

> By 2055, the U.S. will not have a single racial or ethnic majority. Much of this change has been (and will be) driven by immigration. Nearly 59 million immigrants have arrived in the U.S. in the past 50 years, mostly from Latin America and Asia. Today, a near-record 14% of the country's population is foreign born compared with just 5% in 1965. Over the next five decades, the majority of U.S. population growth is projected to be linked to new Asian and Hispanic immigration.

This projection has been taken seriously in, especially by some who believe and preach the doctrine of manifest destiny. They consider themselves superior and cannot see themselves controlled by groups they consider lesser than them. This author is also convinced that it is with the same consideration that it would appear, certain borders, certain programs, certain countries are more targeted than others on border control and issuing asylum and even visitors' visas to certain regions or groups. It is for this same reason that this study argues that the current controversy on immigration is related to an ego-based human dysfunction whose main intent is to untie the human thread that interconnects the human family by creating fear and distrust among groups thereby linking the current immigration issues to issues of social justice and racism. The above situation is supported by the idea that news briefs from the institute of Foreign Policy in Focus and their allegation that:

> Trump can only win by using fear and racism. . . . He wants to create an atmosphere of chaos and panic that allows him to act more forcefully (sending troops), speak more rashly (terrorists are coming!), and present himself as the country's savior (*apres moi, le deluge*). He's a grandstanding nationalist who has finally found his calling: to preserve white dominance in the United States and prevent the country from becoming part of a multicultural world . . . (Feffer, Nov. 2018)

Fredrickson (2003) in his work on the history, origins, and development of racism asserted that "racism exists when one ethnic group or historical collectivity dominates, excludes, or seeks to eliminate another on the basis of difference that it believes are hereditary and unalterable." Fredrickson's analysis objects all activities that define and judge individuals or groups by race. He upholds that individuals are prejudiced about others different from them mostly because of a lack of understanding or knowledge and traits that the individuals have no control over. Similarly, Memmi (2000) defined racism as "a cultural disease that prevails because it allows one segment of society to empower itself at the expense of another" (p.16). Memmi explained that everyone may have some prejudice (which is not worth condoning) but racism is worst because it moves beyond these individual prejudices and questions social behavior and social responsibility. This definition of racism also insists on the fact that racism thrives on four different structures: differences, negative valuation imposed on others who are different, the generalization of the negative values to an entire group, and the use of generalization to legitimize hostility. Defining racism this way also assumes that for racism to be eradicated, it is necessary for anti-racists to understand the various forms of racial manifestations that give power and tenacity to the perpetrators. Understanding this negative valuation and the emotional turmoil on its victims is very important for social justice and human flourishing.

Critical Race Theory, the Outsider Syndrome, and the Intersectionality of Racism and Immigration

The critical race theory provides a framework or set of basic insights, perspectives, methods, and pedagogy that seeks to identify, analyze, and transform those structural and cultural aspects of education that maintain subordinate and dominant racial positions in and out of the classroom (Crenshaw, Gotanda, Peller, & Thomas, 1995; Matsuda, Lawrence, Delgado, & Crenshaw, 1993; Tierney, 1993). The theory is committed to social justice and offers a liberal and transformative response to racial, gender, and class oppression. The theory also recognizes that the experiential knowledge of people of color, their lived experiences are legitimate, appropriate, and critical to understanding, analyzing the concept of a deficit-informed ideology that silences and distorts the experiences of minorities.

Race, in other words, encompasses both overt and subtle forms of normalized biases against the powerless, mostly minority groups, through spoken and unspoken languages and also and most often, through creating conscious and unconscious hierarchies of qualifications between and among humans in ways that perpetuate, normalize, and justify class differentiation for profit. It is from this standpoint that Tatum (2007) explained that racism cannot be fully explained as an experience of prejudice alone but as system of advantage based on race; more precisely, prejudice plus power. This definition of racism, as a systemic evil, exists because prejudice when combined with social power (access to social, cultural, and economic resources, and decision-making) leads to the institutionalization of racist policies and practices (p. 8). It is this universal and intersectional human problem called racism that Tatum (2013) compares to smog; "sometimes it is so thick it is visible, other times it is less apparent but always, day in and day out, we are breathing it in" (p. 6). Tatum believes that irrespective of individuals' views of the problem, all humans, privileged or underprivileged experience the evils of racism.

The understanding gained from the aforementioned definitions is that racism is a universal problem that intersects and permeates the fabric of our humanity. In addition, racism projects the eminence of the double standards apparent in America's democracy and freedom. This institutionalized racism is also emphasized by the activist, Paulo Freire. Freire (1990) in *The pedagogy of the oppressed* professed that ". . . to glorify democracy and at the same time silence the people is a farce; to discourse on humanism and also negate people is a lie because freedom is not an ideal located outside of man; nor is it an idea with the potential of becoming a myth. Freedom, he posited, is the indispensable condition for the quest for human completion" (p. 84). Freire confirmed the conscious and unconscious manifestations of racism that continue to linger in America, the beacon of democracy today. He believed that, for America to function as a true democracy, freedom should be a right to all because it is a human need. Similarly and in more emphatic terms, West (1994) in *Race Matters* asserted that ". . . the aim of a constitutional democracy is to safeguard the rights of the minority and avoid the tyranny of the majority" (p 102). This chapter contends that irrespective of all the attempts by activists to advocate for social justice for all, their efforts are mitigated by mistrust and misunderstanding of each other's motives. Understanding immigrants' challenges becomes a necessary step in the process of forging a sound, equitable, and sensible immigration policy.

This chapter relies on the belief that true social justice activism can only prevail on the basis of universal justice, one based on human values, the belief that irrespective of individual differences, there is only one race, the human race. Throughout this chapter, the claim is that confronting these misunderstandings in a manner that promotes lasting cross-generational interconnectivity and commitment is transformative. Such understanding is humanly plausible from a participant research methodology.

In addition to Christian views, this perspective is also provided by Plato, in the *Republic*. Plato contended that justice is indispensable to the soul and is necessary both for the individual and the state. He also contended that justice cannot be practiced at the individual level because of its social value, and the pursuance of justice is a necessary objective to restore peace in both the society, the individual, and all human institutions. Common to these authors is the recognition that when racial attitudes permeate institutional practices in ways that ratify rather than condemn racial injustices, social injustices become invisible, remain unchecked, and consequently, such practices become the norm. The authors underscore the need for deliberate effort for mutual and collaborative understanding of effects of racism as social injustice on both America's human and institutional existence.

One of the ways of doing this is to seek understanding rather than breed in fear of the unknown. This is why this study is significant. It thrives on the notion that "It's easy to judge and more difficult to understand because understanding requires compassion, patience and a willingness to believe that good hearts can sometimes make poor choices through judging we separate, through understanding we grow" (Zantamanta). Listening to the voices of immigrants, understanding their plight will humanize immigrants for who they are and dislodge the discourse that defines them as criminals today. The study also has therapeutic values as immigrants carry emotional burdens, invisible swords and feel committed to prove to the world their self-worth. Like Rudolph the Red-Nosed Reindeer, they are yearning for sleighs to project their true value. This study serves as a starting point for such conversations because as immigrants find their voice in telling their story, they will experience emancipatory transformation. Such an empowerment is emotionally therapeutic.

Method of Investigating the Current Perspectives and Controversies on Immigration

This qualitative metaphorical study utilized phenomenological and psychoanalytic ideals to forge an understanding of immigrants' intent and the paradox that other immigrants perceive current immigrants as criminals. The chapter sets to illuminate that immigrants like Rudolph the Red-Nosed Reindeer are simply armed with the hope to live as useful and acceptable members of the new communities. The study is influenced by the author's need to provide greater understanding of the current enigma, immigration, as well as offer explanations for the current prevailing extenuating events. In keeping with Shank (2006) phenomenological ideals, this study as with any qualitative study, does not dwell on having the right meaning, but rather on having enough meaning, resulting in understanding social settings and activities viewed from the perspective of the research participant(s).

Through personal case narratives, the chapter's purpose is to understand firsthand the emotional challenges immigrants experience because of the mistrust and misinterpretations of their intentions mostly motivated by racism and xenophobia. Appreciating these emotional challenge, conscious and unconscious biases is beneficial for social activists and other policy-makers in their quest for social justice and provides them with the opportunity to reexamine their attitudes and behaviors. Equipped with such recognition, social activist would hopefully pursue the changes that create structures designed to facilitate the development of positive insights from immigrant and enable them to exhibit control over emotional challenges they experience and be able to function comfortably as useful and acceptable members of their respective communities.

The chapter also explored procedures that relied on the participants' experiences given that such procedures describe in detail the content of individual consciousness and capture the diversity of personal experiences consequently illuminating the essential meaning of the immigration phenomenon (Creswell

& Clark, 2007). In other words, the manner in which a phenomenological approach is structured enables the researcher to explore the essence of the phenomenon and at the same time perceive reality through the minds of the respondents. Phenomenological studies also expose the possibilities of developing meaning out of social interactions and relations (Amin, 2005). More explicably, the phenomenological approach was elected for this study because, through such an approach, human experiences are expressed consciously and are understood through the views of those who lived the experiences.

Another goal of this study therefore is to provide an empowering, emancipatory, and transformative opportunity for immigrants considered as misfits, rapists, drug dealers, thieves, and criminals. The knowledge claims in this study are primarily based on constructivist and participatory perspectives (Marshall & Rossman, 1999). Although all research is interpretive, this approach is preferred because unlike quantitative approaches to inquiry that have silenced many marginalized and oppressed groups and made them passive, this qualitative research encourages critical perspectives that are openly ideological, empowering, and democratic. This introspective methodology draws on the basic understandings of human nature and is informed by participant observed experiences and worldview. Having their voices heard does not only provide emotional therapy to the immigrants but also to those who claim to be the only rightful citizens of America. Understanding the views of the current immigrants helps in dislodging the myths that cause some individuals in the human family to be looked upon as criminals and promote the politics of fear. Especially those who strive for social justice, understanding the experiences of immigrants will help them understand how to rightly treat and view immigrants. This understanding will hopefully lead to the creation of the right settings that meet the needs and interests of all humans irrespective of their background of origin.

As a first-generation immigrant, I recognize my biases and predispositions and the need to set them aside my preconceived ideas about immigrants from my personal experiences. By acknowledging these inadequacies and by self-examining my circumstances and coming into terms with myself was not only emancipatory but was instrumental in transforming me as a researcher at the onset of this project. This is important because doing so allowed the researcher to develop the mindset necessary for adequate understanding of others' perspectives, and consequently, the necessary understanding and adequate interpretation of the data. Moustakas (1994) argued that the awareness of our world is not only limited to our worldview but is greatly dependent on our ability to consciously self-reflect and recollect representations of our reflections. In addition, the greatest insights of this study come from immersing the data by sifting and resifting the evidence until a pattern becomes visible (Macleod, 2009). The analysis also depended on the conscious interplay and reexamination of the data that opened up new awareness and gradually connected all the parts of the immigrant experiences into a unified whole. The analysis and discussions in the chapter emanated from the combination of my personal understandings obtained during the reduction process, the theoretical basis of this phenomenon, and the presuppositions of the study and in comparing with the respective themes reflected in the results of the case study narratives in a dialectical fashion.

Immigration, Emotional Challenges: Personal Reflection, Perception, and Data Analysis

The data that later formed the analysis for the study emerged from eleven immigrants: nine persons of color from varied countries of origin; Africa, Asia, Haiti, and Mexico, and two from Europe. The semi-structured interviews are based on the research question: How do first-generation immigrants adjust emotionally to life in the United States?

Sub-Questions

- What are some of the challenges that you face and how do they affect how you live life?
- What have been helpful for you this far?
- What would make life better for you?

The summary of the result of these interviews is analyzed and reported directly as individual case analysis.

DATA COLLECTION PROCEDURES

This chapter seeks to understand the emotional challenges immigrants, especially those who "stand out without a stage" experience in the United States. The study seeks to answer the question: How do first-generation immigrants adjust emotionally to life in the United States? The process of data collection was mainly through informal conversations with first-generation immigrants. The discussions took place both as focus group conversations or individual one-on-one conversations. The four sub-questions that emanated from the research formed the base of the discussions. Although the population for the study was mainly from experiences of individuals in Midwest America, these experiences are not unique to the individuals who express them. Immigrants all over the United States especially first-generation immigrants from Africa and South America may share similar experiences or may benefit from learning about the experiences of others who look like them. The author believes that like Rudolph the Red-Nosed Reindeer, immigrants are peaceful, hardworking individuals who will flourish if "Santa" comes along and ask them to lead.

I initially started the process just by working with a focus group but as I encountered many other self-acclaimed and proud first-generation immigrants and engaged in insightful conversations, the population and study expanded to include both African Americans and Latino Americans. Thus, the data for this study is a representation of the emotional challenges that African Americans and Latino Americans experience as they strive to adjust to life in the United States.

Focus Group Participation

As part of the therapeutic process, first-generation immigrants from one of the countries in West Africa get together on the last Saturday of every month to bond and discuss issues about home. Inspired by "the Rodolph controversy," I was motivated to learn more about the emotional challenges of first-generation immigrants as myself. Consequently, during our subsequent end of month meetings (December, January, February, and March), I deliberately asked questions that would solicit emotional challenges members of the group are experiences. Though consciously and deliberately in my questions, participants were not aware of the object of my questions. I chose the medium because I wanted their sincere stories since this was quite a touchy feelings topic in our community. The answers to the narratives are reported as summaries of individual case studies.

One-on-One Participation

Between December and the end of March, in my daily activities, be it in beauty salons, church, or grocery stores, I deliberately forged conversations to include emotional challenges faced. Four first-generation African Americans and four first-generation Latino Americans were involved during this period. Again conversations were informal, and participants were not aware of the informal interviewing. However, they were later on made to understand that I found the conversations very enlightening and would be using the information for a book chapter on immigrants. They were equally excited and appreciative that their stories can be heard. The process was very emancipatory and transformative because just informing them that I intend to

Table 8.1 Summary of Personal Narratives

Sub-Question 1	*Summary of Responses*
What are some of the adjustment challenges you face?	• Just because I do not speak English which I totally understand every word doesn't make me stupid. People treat me as if I am stupid, sometimes I look like I am maybe. But it is hard blending in, so I just blend out. I stay where people value me and relate with me in a respectful way not in a patronizing manner. Thirty years, I continue to work in a factory. My wife has never worked. All because of language barriers. Good thing is that my children have grown and I have grand children now. They speak English and are doing very well. *(Latino American Gentleman was helping to install a faucet in my kitchen, his middle school age son was his interpreter because he speaks only Spanish fluently. Very intelligent guy but limited by language.)* • My accent seems to be a hindrance. I do not mind repeating myself many times if someone is sincerely paying attention. I try and would like to integrate. However, there are aspects about me that I have no power to change no matter how hard I try. This day at work we were having a nice conversation with this coworker. I said something and she did not understand because of my enunciation. I have trouble pronouncing the "r" like most Americans do. When I explained that I understood why it was hard for her to understand what I was saying because of the handicap I have, she said something that changed the whole conversation. She said, ". . . don't worry, with time you are going to be and speak like us." Not sure why but I did not like her answer. I told her there is nothing about her that I admire and would like to emulate. It became a hot back and forth conversation which did not go well. She was fired at the end but I am not sure if I overreacted or not. You see statements like that get on me in a way that I think she is looking down on me. She thinks she is better than me although I am more educated (in terms of schooling) than she is. Statements like that are hard to not answer back. However, even when I do answer back, I go home hurt. Hurt at the thought that this is what may be hidden on the minds of most of the people I interact with and call my friends. Then, I shrink. I chicken out attending events and stay and wallow in my small space. This makes adjustment very difficult. I wish I could just turn a blind eye, pretend I do not hear some of the stuff especially on the news. Stuff like that really gets me . . . *(African American first-generation immigrant as part of a focus group conversation)*. • We lived here for 19 years. When we just moved many people were asking us if people are being nice to us. If we are noticing any signs of racism and I was very quick to say no. Sometimes ignorance could be a blessing. For example, I did not know what the middle finger means so there was no way I could feel offended or even notice. Moreover, I lived with my family in Chicago and it was an American who insisted and encouraged and made it possible for me to move with my family to the Fox Valley. No way I would even think that they

wouldn't want me here. These Caucasian families whom I owe my stay here to, are like my family. So, I had no reason to even think that some people were not wanted. Well, TV news was not good but I could tell I was well trusted especially by my new-found families. I was fine and comfortable and feared nothing. Now it is different. Every indication from the top-down is showing how unwanted people of color are irrespective of whether they are here legally or illegally. I have to prove that I am not a criminal. I get the looks, I feel them, I hear them. Sometimes right to my face, "Go back to Africa" Why? I have even been given a nickname, Ebola. What did I do wrong? I just came like history said most Americans came. I am not looking to harm anyone. I buy groceries, I am stopped at the door to show my receipt even in stores where that is not a requirement. Do I really look like a criminal. How do I fix this? *(African American first-generation immigrant in focus group conversation).*

- Being talked down on as if I am a child. I went to this event: one lady asked my last name, after I spelt it out and handed her my ID, she described my last name as interesting. Not sure what could be interesting in a two syllable six letter word. She even demanded that I pronounce my middle name to her. I then asked her if this was part of the identification procedure they were doing and she said no and I did not have to if I did not want to. I did not. I left that day and wondered, was she trying to be relational? Was I rude to her? However, I have learned that even when your name is Grace, an English word, people find it difficult to pronounce it when you are a person of color *(focus group conversation).*
- Having to start life all over. I was a respectable person in my country and then the war. I came here, couldn't speak English, had to take language lessons and care for my family. I thought it would be easier to find something to do to help my children so they could go to school. I already had an education so this is their turn. To find a job that was good enough with my qualification was not easy because of language barriers so I found job at a factory where I talk to machines and not people. I have lived here for more than 20 years. I understand English but very hard for me to speak fluently. My daughters are also having a hard time at school although they were born here and speak English and Spanish fluently. One told me that the teacher is a racist. When asked if she has spoken to the school authorities she said it will only make things worse for her. She doesn't want the teacher to even hate her more. The daughter who was present and mostly speaking for her mother took over at this point and explained that statements like where is your green pass? You know, green pass, green card? You don't get it? (sounded frustrated). Sometimes when I asked a question about something because everyone was laughing and I did not find it funny. The teacher said, "Oh I understand why you asked that question. I was in Mexico and you know, they do not have a sense of humor." That is not all. We watch CNN news every day in my class. When we are watching news and stuff about immigration comes up every one looks at me and I could feel the stare and them grinning in a mocking way and the teacher does nothing. *(Latino American first-generation immigrant, and former neighbor).*

(continued)

Table 8.1 Continued

Sub-Question 1	*Summary of Responses*
	• You may find this strange and confusing but accepting help becoming an object of charity. I am used to being the one who gives. So hard for me to have people helping me. I do not only reflect on how I helped out but also how those I helped out felt. People are being nice to me and every time they do so I cry. I wish it was easier to adjust and be a bread winner than receive from people. It hurts that I cannot fern for my family and I am a grown man *(African American first-generation immigrant who stopped at my desk during parent teacher conferences and somehow, this conversation emanated).* • People feeling sorry for me and treating me like a disease. For example, I met this guy waiting for the elevator. I joined him. I said hi and he just muttered as if he was even wondering why I should talk to him. You know sometimes when the mirror is not around, I forget that I look different and I am very quick to engage people in conversations. This is part of my way of getting to understand the new culture. Well, he wouldn't get into the elevator with me either. I went in, I thought he was just being a gentleman, ladies first. No, he just stood there although he could visibly see I was holding it open for him. I continued that whole day wondering. Sadly enough, instead of wondering about him, I kept looking inwardly and asking myself, what is wrong with me? Then when I see the stuff on the news describing African countries like S-hole countries, and immigrants as criminals . . . I wonder (*Focus group conversations*). • I just want to study hard and to take my parents out of this situation. Our neighbor treats us really bad and tell my sisters and I to leave the neighborhood. If he steps foot at our doorstep again he will regret it. You know I do not like to discuss things about my family in public. You know my parents do not yet have their papers. If I call the police, we get into even more trouble. I am waiting for the DACA stuff to go through. Right now I just work with my father on a pig farm. R & I are getting married. Remember my boyfriend from high school. He works really hard and he is going to the tech for welding. You know he was born here but I came here when I was one year old. If the DACA stuff doesn't work, then I may get papers through him. We are both living with my parents now. *(Former high-school Latino student—conversation at the grocery store).*
Sub - Questions 2, 3 & 4	Summary of Responses
How do these challenges affect how you live life?	• When I am with my people I am okay? My children are teaching me English. Right now I am not working, working. I help out working on somebody's farm. I feed the pigs. He gives me money under the table. That is okay for now. I wish I knew English so I can get a better job and better pay. • I do not know if it was ignorance or it was a consequence of the situation then. It was great around here. Although it was not as diverse as it is today, people were generally warm. Our common saying was: it is cold around here but people are warm. Now it seems colder and less warm. Things started changing when President Obama became president. It is worse

	now. Most of the same smiles are no longer there. I instead get the looks. Strange to say I am more a stranger to my community now than I was many years ago when I arrived. Either I am a disease (Ebola) or I am a criminal or a drug addict. It is hard, I go around as if I am less of a human being. Have you seen the news? Do you know what the president calls our countries of origin. Do you see what the police is doing with our children. It is very hard and drains on me emotionally. I wonder if that is why my health is struggling at this time. I had to stop working fulltime which makes it even harder again financially and an additional source of stress. It is indeed hard to wear the skin I am wearing. • It is hard to live life knowing that everyone is thinking that you are a criminal when you are not. I just hope one day, they will come to understand that we are just as human as everyone else. • You know when people treat you like a nobody, after a while you start feeling like one. I am fighting not to let those who think I am a nobody wins. Not to tell you a lie, it does gets under my skin. I just wish people do not generalize, try to get to know me better before they judge and not judge me for someone else's crime. Can you imagine if we consider every Caucasian to think like Donald Trump? Hmm! • I came to America to look for a better life. Now I cannot say I am safer or wealthier. This is sad. But I know America is a great country. When elections are held and the current president is dethroned, I believe all will be well. • I am glad that people are able to help. I just wish I was in a situation that I could help myself instead. I feel like I am a failure. Then when the news talk about lazy, druggies and the rest, I feel like I am one of those statistics. I do not want to be one. It is hard just thinking that coming to America is like leaving a frying pan and jumping into fire. Not sure which is better but it is tough.
What has been helpful for you this far?	• Knowledge that there are still some good people especially when I watch the news and realize that not everybody agrees with Donald Trump's ideology. There are many people out there fighting for people like us. • Here you can complain and speak out and play tough and survive. I couldn't say all the things I am speaking to you about and go free in my country. That is why I still hope for a better tomorrow. • My faith because going to church sometimes and sitting there and listening to sermons that sometimes seems to be looking at America as a victim and how other nations pry on America is not helpful. It makes you even question God. But I hold strong and pray always that my faith in the Ultimate Good is right.
What would make life better for you?	• See me like a human being. Understand that I am not less of a human because I speak with a different (thick) accent. • Do not talk to me as if I am a child. • Do not treat me or view me as a criminal. • Understand that I did not leave my country to come here to commit crimes. I came to look for a better life. Why then should I be the one ruining the life?

publish their stories made them expand more on the topic. Table 8.1 presents a summary analysis of the personal narratives.

CONCLUDING ANALYSIS

The Samaritan Ideology vs the Fear of Your Neighbor Ideology in the Manifest Destiny and the Outsider Syndrome

Following the current events in our news media, Donald Trump's America is drilling wounds especially those that were not completely healed from racism. The discussion in this chapter builds on the controversy that Americans are hurting as the scars of racism are reincarnating into wounds and the whole civil rights struggle is back in full force. Accordingly, Moore Jr. E., Penick-Parks, M. W, & Michael, A. (Eds.). 2016 p.158), if our goal is to build an inclusive society and eliminate all forms of racism, we have to use strategies that create inclusive structures; change consciousness, educate, train, and mobilize people into specific projects, campaigns, and movements; challenge power; and attack specific forms of exploitation and segregation. Stated differently, the need for the fight against social injustice is more obvious today than it has been anytime during my lifetime. Interestingly enough, most people join the fight with different motivations; some from a position of power and some from a position of no power, some as privileged and some as underprivileged. The argument here is that because of the differences in motivations and intents, because of the differences with experiences in race and race relations, because of our differences in endowment, our approaches are bound to be different, and these differences in approaches are subject to different interpretations. In addition, some activists, especially the privileged engage in the fight from a position of guilt and shame just because they belong to the privileged class. The main objective of the discussion in this chapter was to highlight that irrespective of the positions we have, we are all victims of this dilemma and no one should engage in this war from a position of shame or guilt. Inasmuch as socialization is a human trait, justice is the most essential ingredient. Ferber in *Everyday White People Confront Racial & Social Injustice: 15 Stories* (2015) in the "Knapsacks and Baggage" asserted that, "for inclusive social justice to prevail, every oppressed person is likely to benefit from some form of privilege, and we all need to start speaking from our positions of privilege." Feber believes that "there is no system of ism that will be destroyed without the involvement of the privileged, and there is no system of ism that will be destroyed alone." According to Ferber, the kaleidoscopic nature and uniqueness of a multiracial society is the combination of assets that each group adds to the table. It is only in recognizing these gifts that we can build on each other's strengths. The fear of being judged by the other, the fear of what the other is capable of doing, the fear of what the other thinks about you limits our potential to actively participate in the war for social justice. Indeed, justice means differently for many individuals, across different communities, social classes, age, genders, and races. The main problem in social justice activism lies in the current climate of mutual misunderstandings of what social justice is and should be.

Living in a just community benefits everyone, even those in a position of power. Kivel had to leverage his privileges, not out of charity or compassion, but because he considered that it was his life, his community, and his world. He understood he is responsible for being present, for leading a life of integrity, and for doing what is within his capacity to bring healing and justice into the world (p.158). Therefore, efforts at advancing anti-racism advocacy should be approached within the context of dismantling sexism, heterosexism, ableism, and any other repressive ism, because every voice is needed.

The understanding gained from the transcripts of immigrant narratives about their emotional experiences in this chapter is that the long-standing problem of institutional racism cannot be solved by paying attention to issues at the surface of the wound. The premise is that, for a wound as wide and as deep as the silent killer, the emotional challenges immigrants face today arrive at a long-lasting solution, it is necessary to uncover the roots of the issue. Approaching the challenges of immigrants from a firsthand perspective will help expand our hearts about the struggles of others and also understand individual and personal limitations, struggles, and anxieties in regard to our daily and unique encounters and relationships with others. It is important and necessary for social justice activists to understand the different faces of immigrant discourse in order to be able to approach the issues surrounding it with the dexterity necessary.

Today, even after the abolition of slavery in 1865, the citizens of the United States are not only confronting the scars of racism but are hurting from old scars that have turned into new wounds and from wounds that were never healed. This chapter concludes that it is in the interface of this misunderstanding of what is right and what is wrong, what may be right but just politically incorrect, what may be correct but not entirely true, or on the being right and getting it wrong that entangles our current society from living the true nature of its creed, that all humans are created equal and should be presented with the same opportunities and choices. Like Kivel (2015) asserted, "We are all in the same boat, we may be on different decks. We may even have different access to benefits on the same deck. But the boat has a massive hole in it, and it is sinking." And when it sinks, we will all drown, both citizens and noncitizens, black, brown, red, yellow, or while because I believe there is only one race, the human race and when one falls, we all fall. It is time we all realize that the issue of immigration is not just for noncitizens, it is an American problem and know we are not in it to just save others, but in trying to safe others, we are rescuing ourselves and our society. We will be living up to the nation's creed, that all men are created equal. Doing so, we will be discarding the politics of fear that encourages individuals to be "fear their neighbor and embrace the Samaritan Ideology" of "love thy neighbor as thyself."

NOTES

1. https://www.cfr.org/backgrounder/us-immigration-debate-0
2. https://www.speaker.gov/issue/immigration-reform/
3. socialjustice@uua.org

REFERENCES

Bangou, F., & Austin, T. (2011). Revisiting collaborative boundaries - Pioneering change in perspectives and relations of power. *Journal of Urban Learning, Teaching, and Research* 7, 41–48.

Bonilla-Silva, E. (2000). *Racism without racists: Color-blind racism and the persistence of racial inequality in the United States*. Lanham, MA: Rowman & Littlefield.

Chaudry, A., Capps, R., Pedroza, J. M., Castaneda, R. M., Santos, R., Scott, M. M., & Urban Institute. (2010). *Facing our future: Children in the aftermath of immigration enforcement*. Urban Institute. Retrieved from http://www.remote.uwosh.edu/login?url=http://search.ebscohost.com/login.aspx?

Chiva, R. (2008). Emotional intelligence and job satisfaction: The role of organizational learning capability. *Personnel Review* 37(6), 680–701.

Ewing, M. (2018). Rudolph the Red-Nosed Reindeer sparks debate over bullying, bigotry. Cox Media Group National Content Desk, Boston News. December 3, 2018.

Feffer, J. (2018). Trump's only election strategy was racism: Republicans can only win by racial gerrymandering and voter suppression and Trump can only win by using fear and racism. https://globalnews.ca/news/4747488/un-migration-pact-signed/

Freire, P. (1990). *The pedagogy of the oppressed*. New York: Continuum.

Irizarry, J. G., & Kleyn, T. (2011). Immigration and education in the "supposed land of opportunity": Youth perspectives on living and learning in the United States. *The New Educator* 7(1), 5–26. https://doi.org/10.1080/1547688X.2011.551731

Lubich, C. (2007). *Essential writings: Spirituality, dialogue, and culture*. Hyde Park, NY: New City Press.

Macedo, P. F. (2006). *Literacies of power: What Americans are not allowed to know*. West View Press.

Memmi, A. (2000). *Racism*. Minneapolis, MN: University of Minnesota Press.

Masaiti, A. E., & Keaten, J. (2018). 164 Countries sign non-binding UN migration pact amid international controversy. Associated Press. Retrieved October 4, 2019, from https://globalnews.ca/news/4747488/un-migration-pact-signed/

Moore, E., Pennick-Parks, M. W., & Michael, A. (2015). *Everyday white people confront racial & social injustice: 15 stories*. Sterling, VA: Stylus.

Novak, M. (2017). Social justice: Not what you think it is. *The Heritage Foundation*. N.p., n.d. Web. July 4, 2017.

Smith, A. M. (2007). *The careful use of compliments*. Isabel Dalhousie Series, Anchor Books.

Tatum, B. D. (1993). *Racial identity development and relational theory: The case of black women in white communities*. Wellesley, MA: Stone Center, Wellesley College.

Tatum, B. D. (2017). "*Why are all the black kids sitting together in the cafeteria?": And other conversations about race*. New York: Basic Books.

West, C. (1994). *Race matters*. New York: Vintage Books.

Weyher, F. L. (2012). Re-reading sociology via the emotions: Karl Marx's theory of human nature and estrangement. *Sociological Perspectives* 55(2), 341–363. https://doi.org/10.1525/sop.2012.55.2.341

Chapter 9

The Hmong American Experience

The Shifting, Cultivation, Transformation, and Preservation of an Ancient Culture

Pao Lor

Hmong Americans are originally a preliterate, semi-nomadic, animistic, and agrarian ethnic hill tribe that prior to 1975 primarily resided in southern China, Laos, Vietnam, Thailand, and Laos. In broad strokes, I share some key highlights of their four-decade quest to reestablish their cultural identity in the United States.

The highlights were abstracted and refined using these five perspectives: (1) my personal and professional experience having been a part of the four decades of the Hmong American experience, (2) my ethnographic observations of such time, (3) personal conversations and dialogues I had with Hmong individuals, (4) research I have conducted on the Hmong American experience, and (5) other research and resources on the Hmong American experience.

The highlights then were framed around these four guiding questions: How did the Hmong end up in the United States? What is the status of the Hmong Americans' four-decade experience? What are some lessons other U.S. refugees from developing countries can learn from the Hmong American experience? What does the future look like for Hmong Americans?

HOW THE HMONG ENDED UP IN THE UNITED STATES

Migration is a part of humanity. It happens for political, economic, environmental, cultural, or social reasons and has different time periods—sometimes lasting for years or sometimes lasting for decades. Also, the geographical ranges of each migration are vastly different; it could occur within a country—India, Korea, and Vietnam, out of a country—European Union or across continents and countries—Asia to North and South Americas.

In the case of Hmong Americans, they migrated from their ancient world cocooned in the jungles of northern and central Laos to reestablishing a new life in the United States. They left their birth country and migrated across countries and continents for political, cultural, and social reasons. Their migration lasted for almost four decades, from 1975 to 2011.

So, how did this happen?

Most Hmong Americans can trace their ancestral roots to Laos. Their ancestors started arriving to northern Laos around the mid to late 1800s. Prior to that, they resided in mainland and southern China. In China, for centuries, their ancestors resisted and fought against Chinese ideological coercion and oppression. When their resistance was weakened, facing ethnic persecution, many Hmong migrated to and resettled in southern China while others continued to live in Vietnam, Thailand, and Laos.

From the 1930s to the 1950s, French colonization of southeast Asia, particularly in Laos, began to affect their sophisticated and delicate ancient way of life. The French introduced them to formal education, modernized bureaucracies, and governmental infrastructure—the beginning of their transition to the modernized world.

After the French left southeast Asia in the late 1950s, the United States stepped in.

In the early 1960s, the United States recruited the Hmong and other ethnic minorities to establish a paramilitary to fight The Secret War, which was a clandestine military effort inside of Laos. The Secret War was unbeknown to many Americans and the world. The goals of The Secret War included fighting North Vietnamese insurgence in Laos, disrupting the Ho Chi Mien Trail and rescuing shot-down American pilots. The United States established the paramilitary to circumvent the 1962 Geneva Accord Agreements, which states that fourteen countries including Laos were not to establish any military bases inside of Laos' borders. In other words, North Vietnam didn't comply with the Accord and the United States found a loophole in the accord.

Some Hmong joined the United States with the belief that by winning the war the Hmong would have more influence in the political, educational, and economic landscape of Laos. The Hmong, like many minority groups in Laos, had been historically disenfranchised by the Laotians. Nevertheless, not all Hmong shared such sentiment, with some joining the Pathet Lao, the opposing communist regime.

When the United States pulled out of southeast Asia in 1975, the Hmong became targets of ethnic persecution for having supported the Americans during The Secret War. As such, from 1975 to the early 1990s, many Hmong fled Laos seeking refuge in Thailand. There were many tragedies during the two-decade exodus. Some were killed and wounded by landmines. Some drowned while crossing the Mekong River. Some died of starvation. Others were shot and killed. Some were captured and tortured.

In 1975, Hmong refugees in Thailand were granted "refugee status" to relocate to developed countries including the United States, Australia, France, Canada, Germany, Argentina, and New Zealand. For various reasons, some chose to leave while others chose to stay behind.

For those who decided to leave, they saw the opportunity for a new life and an escape from the communist regime. In many instances, in the middle of the night, many Hmong families boarded the "bell" of the "iron eagle" and headed to worlds some believed to be "heavenly kingdoms above the clouds."

For those who stayed behind, particularly the adults, there was a sense of uncertainty about going to a new strange land and there was the belief that one day they could take back Laos, go back to Laos, or at the very least, they were still close to home; their position was then validated and supported with financial, leadership, and military backing by those who had already gone abroad.

The first Hmong arrived in the United States in 1975, followed by several distinctive waves of Hmong refugees (late 1970s, 1980s, and early 1990s), with the last wave from 2004 to early 2010. The last wave included the Hmong who were living in Wat Thamkrabok, Thailand.

For many Hmong Americans who arrived in the United States in the 1970s and 1980s, they encountered many new life experiences for the first time. Some saw snow for the first time. Some worked in manufacturing for the first time. Some went to school for the first time. Some saw other races such as Hispanics and African-Americans for the first time. Some saw a bathtub and a shower for the first time. Some lived in a city for the first time. Some saw traffic and six-lane highways for the first time. Some tried a hamburger and fries for the first time.

Four decades later, some Hmong have acclimated well to the American landscape while others continue to struggle to find their place. Regardless, there is one thing that is certain: in the last four decades, Hmong Americans have established a good roadmap in moving forward.

STATUS OF THE HMONG AMERICANS' FOUR-DECADE EXPERIENCE

In the last four decades, many individuals and organizations (including both Hmong and non-Hmong) have used various "canons" to capture the Hmong American experience and share it with the public. These individuals and organizations include Hmong tribal and political leaders, scholars, Hmong organizations, conferences, community events, educational systems, and so forth. Some of the "canons" include traditional Hmong chanting, poems, research, books, social media, such as YouTube and Facebook, movies, radio conferences, websites, plays, documentaries, community events, and so on.

There are of course many reasons for these relentless efforts including improving race relations, preserving and advancing the Hmong cultural heritage, and promoting cultural efficacy and empowerment. For my purpose, in my attempt to capture some of the highlights of the Hmong American experience over the last four decades, I used these nine lenses: demographics, education, research, community and civic engagement, entrepreneurial achievement, socioeconomic status, political contributions, and cultural transformation and preservation.

Demographics

According to the 2010 Census, there are over 260,000 Hmong Americans (HND, 2003, 2013).

Over the last four decades, the demographics of the Hmong American experience have shifted and transformed. The shift and transformation have several key distinctive phases which are shaped and defined by various factors including business, education, agricultural, manufacturing, lifestyles (rural, suburban, and metropolitan life), and density of Hmong population or *cultural cohesion.*

The first phase took place from the mid-1970s to the mid-1980s. This phase encompasses the geographic regions where some of the first Hmong Americans were initially resettled in the United States and why they were resettled there. Mainly, Hmong Americans were first resettled on the east coast (Connecticut, Pennsylvania, and Rhode Island), west coast (California and Washington), and Midwest (Minnesota, Wisconsin, and Illinois) and into metropolitan areas, mid-size cities, and rural communities. Some of the first Hmong Americans were also resettled in Colorado, Texas, Kentucky, South Carolina, and Michigan. These early resettlements were connected to who and what sponsored them; potential sponsors were churches or family members. As early Hmong Americans would quickly discover, which state they were resettled in determined the types of opportunities they could take advantage of. For instance, in states like Minnesota and Wisconsin, Hmong American adults had opportunities for learning English, getting job training, and getting an education, whereas in other states Hmong adults were often put into the workforce shortly after arrival.

The second phase took place in the mid-1980s to the mid-1990s. This second phase was greatly influenced by Hmong Americans communicating with each other after their arrivals. More than anything else, they quickly learned about the different aforementioned opportunities because of their locations. Giving that, some Hmong began to migrate across the United States from their initial relocations. They migrated because of jobs, to join other Hmong or family members, education, job trainings, entrepreneurial opportunities, or public assistance programs. For example, some Hmong migrated to Wisconsin to take advantage of small town life, educational opportunities, and work training programs. Some Hmong migrated to California to take advantage of the agricultural opportunities and public assistance programs. Some Hmong moved to the Minnesota to take advantage of the entrepreneurial opportunities and to join other Hmong. Not surprisingly, some Hmong migrated to North Carolina, South Carolina, and Georgia to take advantage of rural lifestyles and agricultural opportunities.

The third phase started in the late 1990s and would continue to the present. In this phase, some Hmong began to move for professional or job opportunities or their life styles. Case in point, with more Hmong college graduates, the one point five and second Hmong generations began to move to where they can find jobs—this could mean moving to larger cities like Los Angeles, Chicago, Miami, or New York. Another example involves Hmong families that have the financial backing moving to states such as Oklahoma, Kansas, Arkansas, Missouri, and Texas to take advantage of the poultry business, to Michigan to take advantage of the restaurant business, or to California to take advantage of the marijuana industry. In some instances, some individuals move for a change of lifestyle, including moving from wintry states like Wisconsin and Minnesota to warmer climate states like Georgia, Florida, Texas, or California.

Today, the four states with the most Hmong Americans are California, Minnesota, Wisconsin, and North Carolina. Each of these states provides a good balance of economic and educational opportunities, diverse lifestyles, and high density of Hmong population. Hmong Americans reside in every state including Puerto Rico except Wyoming.

Moving forward, as for the next phase of Hmong American migration, I believe it will involve Hmong Americans moving abroad for entrepreneurial and work-related purposes or for lifestyles. Few Hmong Americans have already returned to and work in Thailand or Laos while others live abroad because of work or service.

Education

Being a preliterate society, formal education was introduced to the Hmong in the 1930s during French colonization when the Lyfoungs, while residing inside of Laos, sent their children to attend schools in Vietnam. In fact, it wouldn't be until the early 1950s when the current Hmong writing system (Romanized Popular Alphabets) was developed by Christian missionaries. From the 1930s to the 1960s, schools were built in Hmong tribal villages to promote literacy and nationality. In the 1960s, Hmong students started attending colleges and studied abroad, and it wouldn't be until 1972 when the Hmong have their first doctorate graduate—Dao Yang. After The Secret War, education continued to play a critical role for Hmong refugees in Thailand.

Today, the current landscape of the Hmong American educational experience is captured by two reports generated by the Hmong National Development (HND). Using Hmong American educational data from the 2000 and 2010 censuses, HND points out that in 2000, about 45.3 percent of the Hmong American population have no formal education as compared to only 1.4 percent of the total U.S. population, along with only about 27 percent of the Hmong American population having a high-school diploma, 11.7 percent with associate's or bachelor's degrees, and only 1.5 percent with graduate degrees. In 2010, only 14.5 percent of the Hmong American population above the age of twenty-five have attained a bachelor's degree or higher, lagging behind 31.4 percent of non-Hispanic whites, 18 percent of non-Hispanic Blacks, and 50.2 percent of non-Hispanic Asians.

Pfeiffer, Chiu, and Yang (2013) also provide a critical window to current status of the Hmong American educational experience, expanding on what Hmong American college graduates have done with their educational achievements. The progress looks promising with education paving the way for many Hmong American professionals to move into politics, education, business, and leadership positions.

Another brushstroke of the landscape is the number of Hmong Americans who are between the ages of eighteen and twenty-one and are attending college in the five most populated states: California (76.3 percent), Minnesota (54.9 percent), Wisconsin (73.1 percent), North Carolina (73.8 percent), and Michigan (49.5 percent), and as for the rest of the states, it's 83.6 percent (Xiong, 2012).

A common theme emerging from these studies on the Hmong American educational experience is the Hmong American cultural identity, and Hmong American diaspora continue to influence many Hmong American students' educational achievement. As such, beginning in the 2000s, charter schools with curriculum driven by the Hmong American cultural experience emerged, adding new dynamics to address and to advance the Hmong American student experience. Today, there are eight schools in Minnesota, Wisconsin, and California with curriculum that are driven by the Hmong American cultural experience. As Hmong Americans transitioned into the middle decades of the twenty-first century, giving the current Hmong American educational landscape, there is a wide belief, acceptance, and nurturance in the Hmong community that a college education will be crucial for sustaining a good life in America.

Research

Research on the Hmong before their relocation to the United States and other countries includes Goldstein (1985), Long (1993), Yang (1993), Quincy (1995), Hamilton-Merritt (1999), and Hillmer (2010) and could also be abstracted from other research where historical background is provided. Some of the early research on the Hmong American experience started in the late 1980s (Conquergood, 1988) and into the early 1990s (Hutchinson, 1994, 1997; Koltyk, 1997).

Since then, research on the Hmong American experience has exponentially expanded with earlier research being mainly anthological and historical in nature and then later research shifting to include topics such as Hmong American education (O'Reilly, 1998; Thao, 1999; Ngo, 2000; Lee, 2002; Depouw, 2003, 2006, 2012; Huffcutt, 2010; Lee, 2002, 2008; Lee, 2001; Lor, 2008; Vang, 2001, 2003, 2004, 2005; Xiong, 2010, 2012a, 2012b; and Innarelli, 2013), Hmong women (Vue, 2008; Lee, 2009; Lor, 2013), leadership (Lor, 2009, 2012), politics (Hillmer), Hmong children and adolescent (Hutchinson and McNall, 1994; Thao, 2000; Yang, 2004; Woo, 2007; Xiong and Huang, 2001), Hmong teachers (Root, 2000; McClain-Ruelle and Xiong, 2005; Upadhyay, 2009; Lor, 2010), Hmong parents (Lee and Green, 2008), Hmong from Wat Thamkrabok (Lor, 2009), among others.

In addition to the research, other informative resources about the Hmong American experience are available in and outside of academia. The resources include Hmong academic minors and Hmong Studies Centers in Wisconsin, Minnesota, and California; an emergence of Hmong and non-Hmong scholars in the United States and abroad who are focusing and establishing their research interests on various aspects and dynamics of the Hmong American experience; and books, articles, websites, conferences, organizations, documentaries, and academic journals, particularly the *Hmong Studies Journal*.

Community and Civic Engagement

Community and civic engagement are the essence of the Hmong life.

Living in the highland of Laos and remote tribal villages in the jungles of Laos, the Hmong, isolated from modernization, relied on each other for a variety of support. They helped each other with agriculture needs, wedding, funeral, resolving conflicts, building houses and tribal huts, hunting, fishing, and so forth.

More specifically, as for agricultural needs, families living in the same or nearby tribal villages would gather together and go from farmland to farmland throughout the harvesting season completing various tasks until all are done. These communal agricultural tasks might include chopping down trees, using "slash and burn" method to make the land suitable for farming, planting, and harvesting. Funerals, in particular, are similar to agricultural needs, with an entire tribal village and those nearby gathering together and supporting the family of the deceased in various ways until the funeral is done.

In the last four decades, though Hmong Americans are scattered in the vast United States and live in a different cultural context, the essence of the Hmong community and civic engagement has remained intact. In other words, many have not abandoned their commitment and loyalty to advance the well-being of their fellow Hmong members and their Hmong communities. Today, such commitment can be seen in the work advanced by Hmong organizations, Hmong professionals, Hmong businesses, Hmong leaders, Hmong conferences, Hmong community events, Hmong churches, among others.

Entrepreneurial Achievement

Before leaving Laos, the majority of the Hmong were semi-nomadic agrarian, hunters, and gatherers living in remote tribal villages across Laos. Only a small percentage of Hmong were entrepreneurs, mostly as street vendors selling products such as clothes, farming equipment, vegetables, meat, and other household items.

In the last four decades, Hmong Americans have made enormous progress. Today, there are many Hmong American entrepreneurs owning businesses including restaurants, law firms, insurance agencies, real estate, grocery stores, poultry farms, entertainment agencies, farmer's market vendors, and so forth.

Today's Hmong American entrepreneurial spirit can be traced to their early days in refugee camps in Thailand when Hmong families began setting up street vendor shops selling various products.

A dimension of the entrepreneurial achievement that is starting to expand is the global influence. With the financial foundation established and with a greater understanding of the business infrastructure, it is inevitable that Hmong businesses will eventually become a part of the global landscape.

Socioeconomic Status

From the mid-1970s to the early 1990s, Hmong Americans were on public assistance or had general labor jobs in agricultural, food and restaurant, or manufacturing. All were renters with many living on public housing and assistance. Consequently, many lived in poverty.

From the 1990s to the 2000s, some Hmong Americans began to move into the lower end of the middle class. They did so due to better jobs with increased pay in manufacturing, owning their own businesses (stores, restaurants, and small businesses), or holding professional jobs in education, social welfare, and health, among others. Not coincidentally, this change also aligned with the Hmong's rapid transition from being renters to being house owners.

According to the 2010 Census, socioeconomically, the Hmong still lag behind other racial and ethnic groups in the United States, but in terms of where they started and where they are at today, they made enormous gains.

Political Contributions

Politics are not new to Hmong Americans. For centuries to the present, they use a tribal clan system to resolve intra and inter-clan conflicts and to advance their social, cultural, and economic well-being. Some key intra and inter-clan conflicts that often need to be resolved include marriages, tragedies, property ownership, adultery, community events, and funerals.

From the 1930s to the 1970s, during French colonization, with access to education, military, and other modernized political and social infrastructures, the Hmong's tribal clan system began to shift and transition into mainstream politics, specifically, into the Laotian political landscape. A few examples of Hmong families that played critical roles during such times included the Lyfoung, Lo, and Moua, and of course, individuals like Vang Pao and Yang Dao.

In the last four decades, such political spirits and ambitions have seeped into the American political landscape. Across the country, especially in Minnesota, Wisconsin, and California, Hmong American members have gotten elected to the city council, state senate, and school boards. Some have also utilized their leadership skills serving on nonprofit organization boards and community committees while others have become activists establishing coalitions and professional networks that help to inform and shape law enforcement, law, education, and public policies.

Cultural Transformation and Preservation

The cultural transformation and preservation of the Hmong cultural identity and heritage can be viewed through several key lenses: changes to ancient practices, different assimilation process, religious continuum, tribal clan system, and global connections.

At one time, the Hmong practiced similar ancient rituals and ceremonies. These included the birth of a child, funeral, wedding, New Year, soul calling, and shamanistic rituals, among others. Though there were slight differences to how some of these ceremonies and rituals were performed, the essence remained the same (to achieve harmony with oneself and with one's family, tribal clans, the community, and the world of spirituality). Over the last four decades, due to changes in cultural contexts and ways of living, the Hmong have made adaptations and accommodations to these ceremonies and rituals. If needed, funerals can be shortened. Most, if not all, traditional weddings now follow the guidelines established by the eighteen clans. Speaking of weddings, a couple can have two weddings if they so choose to: a traditional one and an "American" style one. In other changes, women can now sit with men at mealtime during these ancient ceremonies and rituals; ritualistic rounds of drinks and their significance can be shortened and bundled to be more efficient (four rounds of drinks and their significance can be reduced and bundled to two rounds); and even content and context of blessings and wishes at these ancient ceremonies and rituals (such as at baci ceremony) are also changing.

In a mere four decades, unlike their ancestors who were able to keep their cultural identity and heritage stagnant for centuries, the Hmong American experience has transformed and expanded across the continuum of various assimilation theories: Anglo-conformist, process theory, melting pot, segmented labor market, or multiculturalism. The continuum began to expand in the early 1980s. Whereas some Hmong families began to assimilate into mainstream American life, others continued to practice, preserve, and advance their ancient practices as well as continuing to use the tribal clan system to manage, lead, and solve many challenges within and outside of the clan system. Simply put, whereas some Hmong families began to expand their community life other Hmong continued to isolate themselves.

Religion plays a critical role in the Hmong cultural transformation and preservation. Prior to the introduction of Christianity to the Hmong in the 1930s, the Hmong collectively practiced one main religion: animism or shamanism. In the last century, because of migration to various countries and the consequent exposure to multiple religions, Hmong Americans practice many religions including Christianity, Buddhism, and Atheism, among others.

Perhaps the most critical and influential aspect of the Hmong cultural transformation and preservation is that it has expanded globally. Four decades ago, most Hmong Americans' world didn't expand beyond their tribal villages, horizon, the sky above, and their ancient society. Today, more than ever, technology, social media, transportation, and financial resources have allowed the Hmong to seamlessly connect, and more important, to become more a part of the international landscape and conversation.

SOME LESSONS OTHER U.S. REFUGEES FROM DEVELOPING COUNTRIES CAN LEARN FROM THE HMONG AMERICAN EXPERIENCE

I believe there are four critical lessons that other U.S. refugees relocating from developing countries to developed countries can learn from the Hmong American experience.

First and foremost is education. For many refugees who lived in poverty in their native land, formal education is often a privilege and is revered. In contrast, in the United States and in other developed countries, formal education is an opportunity given to all. Access to education has given many Hmong Americans access and a pathway for social mobility and a better life, as indicated by the number of high-school graduates, college graduates, and professionals.

The second lesson is opportunity. More specifically, in addition to education, the opportunity to improve their socioeconomic status, intellectual capacity, psychological well-being, and self-efficacy.

The third lesson is cultural preservation. Protected by the U.S. Constitution, many refugees can continue to practice, advance, and preserve their cultural ways of life including religions in which they could continue to practice it, convert to new ones, or even not adhere to any religions at all. This particular human right has been most critical for many Hmong Americans.

Lastly, the pursuit of happiness: may it be in business, education, politics, or others; may it be living in the desert, in the heartland, on the east coast, on the west coast, or in Hawaii; may it renting or owning; or may it be a lifestyle preference.

It is important to note that the aforementioned does not at all imply that the transition or assimilation will not be without challenges; how far a person gets in life depends on many other variables as well including expectations, motivation, ability, and other unexpected circumstances (medical, family emergencies, inheritance, governance, etc.).

IMAGINING THE FUTURE FOR HMONG AMERICANS

Over the last four decades, the Hmong have made critical contributions to the American tapestry, and consequently, they have also become more visible in the global context.

The Hmong's past, which isn't too distant away, is defined by several key historical events: their migration out of China, their history in Laos, their involvement with France, their involvement with the United States, their refugee years in Thailand, and their American experience (from strangers to allies, from allies to neighbors, and from neighbors to citizens).

From such past, given the tribulations they experienced and their capacity to overcome such tribulations, the Hmong can be described as a resilient, forward-thinking, and well-adapted people.

As such, as Hmong Americans move forward, if their past is any indication of their future, they will continue to progress, particularly in areas of education, civil and political engagement, entrepreneurial contributions, community engagement, professional upward mobility, leadership capacities, global influences, and so forth.

In regard to their cultural heritage and history, they will continue to find ways to preserve, advance, and transform their cultural identity. At the same time, along such journey, there will inevitably be conflicts and disagreements about the essence of how such cultural preservation and transformation should take form. This cultural sifting, winnowing, and vetting is nevertheless good and necessary.

FINAL THOUGHTS

Each Hmong generation and each Hmong individual are defined, shaped, and transformed by their historical circumstances. Our ancestors and their generations were by their resistance in China and their eventual exodus. Our great grandparents, grandparents, and parents and their generations by their resiliency in times of self-sustainability, war, political, and civil unrests in Laos and their eventual exodus out of Laos and relocation to another country. As for my generation, we are defined, shaped, and transformed by our transition into the modernized world. And then as for our children's generation and the subsequent Hmong generations, theirs will be by their infusion into a global world.

Within these generational and historical contexts, there are divisions within the Hmong experience. Case in point, in China, whereas some Hmong remained loyal to their ancestral roots, others sided with the Chinese. In Laos and Thailand, whereas some sided with communism others sided with democracy. In addition, there are divisions in religions, political affiliations, philosophies, and lifestyles. There are Hmong Americans who are democrats, republicans, independents, Christians, Muslims, Buddhists, Atheists, and so forth.

Nevertheless, regardless of these generational, historical, and individual differences, we all are seamlessly connected to our common cultural roots. In other words, at one time or another, our ancestors speak Hmong. At one time or another, we were once a part of an oppressed minority. At one time or another, we had to leave our ancestral homeland. At one time or another, we had to assimilate into a different culture, which is often times assimilating, adapting, or accommodating into a dominant culture. At one time or another, our cultural identity triumphed and transformed, in my opinion, for the better. Retrospectively and introspectively, in many ways, I believe the aforementioned has been good and healthy for our cultural identity and heritage; they advance the limitless of what it means to be a Hmong.

REFERENCES

Conquergood, D. (1988). Health theatre in a Hmong refugee camp: Performance, communication, and culture. *TDR* 32(3), 174–208.

DePouw, C. (2003). *Familiar foreign: Hmong American students engaging and resisting America.* Champaign, IL: University of Illinois at Urbana-Champaign.

———. (2006). *Negotiating race, navigating school: Situating Hmong American university student experiences* (PhD Dissertation, University of Illinois).

———. (2012). When culture implies deficit: Placing race at the center of Hmong American education. *Race Ethnicity and Education* 15(2), 223–229.

Goldstein, B. L. (1985). *Schooling for cultural transitions: Hmong girls and boys in American high schools* (Ph.D. Dissertation, University of Wisconsin).

Hamilton-Merritt, J. (1999). *Tragic mountains. the Hmong, the Americans, and the secret wars for LJIOS, 1942–1992.* Bloomington, IN: Indiana University Press

Hillmer, P. (2010). *A people's history of the Hmong.* St. Paul, MN: Minnesota Historical Society Press.

Hmong National Development. (2003). *Hmong 2000 census publication: Data and analysis.* Washington, DC: HND-Census-Report.

Hmong National Development. (2013). *The state of the Hmong American community.* Washington, DC: HND-Census-Report.

Huffcutt, M. (2010). American Hmong youth and college readiness: Integrating culture and educational success (University of Wisconsin-Stout).

Hutchison, R. (1997). *The educational performance of Hmong students in Wisconsin.* Thiensville, WI: Wisconsin Policy Research, Inc.

Hutchison, R. and McNall, M. (1994). Early marriage in a Hmong cohort. *Journal of Marriage and the Family,* 56, 579–590.

Iannarelli, C. (2013). Socialization and Hmong student success in career and technical education (U.W.-Stout Master's Thesis).

Koltyk, J. A. (1997). *New' pioneers in the heartland: Hmong life in Wisconsin.* Allyn and Bacon.

Lee, J. K. (2002). Levels of education actual and expected achievement between older and younger generations of Hmong children in the U.S.A (M.A. Thesis, Lakeland College).

Lee, J. K., & Green, K. (2008). Hmong parental involvement and support: A comparison between families of high and low achieving high school seniors. *Hmong Studies Journal* 9, 1–27.

Lee, S. J. (2001). More than "model minorities" or "delinquents": A look at Hmong American high school students. *Harvard Review* 71(3), 505–528.

———. (2009). The road to college: Hmong American women's pursuit of higher education. *Harvard Education Review* 67(4), 803–828.

Long, L. (1993). *Ban Vinai, the refugee camp.* New York, NY: Columbia University Press.

Lor, P. (2008). Key life experiences contributing to Hmong students' matriculation. *Multicultural Education* 16(1), 39–47.

———. (2009a). A photo essay of the Hmong experience at Wat Thamkrabok in Thailand. *Hmong Studies Journal* 9, 1–41.

———. (2009b). The minority administrator. *The American School Board Journal* 196(8), 24–26.

———. (2010a). Commentary: A Framework for a Twenty-First Century Hmong Leadership. *Hmong Studies Journal* 13(1), 1–20.

———. (2010b). Hmong teachers: Life experiences and teaching perspectives. *Multicultural Education* 17(3), 36–40.

———. (2013). A Hmong professional woman's reflections and perspectives on the influences affecting the changing roles of Hmong women in America. *Journal of Cultural Diversity* 20(1), 40–48.

McClain-Ruelle, L., & Xiong, K. (2005). Continuing the promise: Recruiting and preparing Hmong-American educators for Central Wisconsin. *Hmong Studies Journal* 6, 1–16.

Ngo, B. (2000). *Obstacles, miracles, and the pursuit of higher education: The experiences of Hmong American college students* (University of Wisconsin, Master's Thesis).

Ngo, B., & Lee, S. J. (2007). Complicating the image of model minority success: A review of Southeast Asian American education. *Review of Educational Research* 77(4), 415–453.

O'Reilly, T. M. (1998). *An investigation of Hmong students' academic success in Eau Claire, Wisconsin* (PhD Dissertation, University of Minnesota).

Pfeiffer, M. Chiu, M., & Yang, K. (2013). *Diversity in diaspora: Hmong Americans in the twenty-first century.* Honolulu: University of Hawaii Press.

Quincy, K. (1988). *Hmong: History of a people.* Washington, DC: Eastern Washington University Press; First Edition.

Root, S., Rudawski, A., Taylor, M., & Rochon, R. (2003). Attrition of Hmong students in teacher education programs. *Bilingual Research Journal: The Journal of the National Association for Bilingual Education* 27(1), 137–148.

Thao, D. (2000). *Hmong parents' perceptions toward their children's education in Minneapolis, Minnesota.* M.S. Thesis, University of Wisconsin-Stout. Retrieved December 9, 2008, from http://www.uwstout.edu/lib/thesis/2000/2000thaod.pdf

Thao, P. (1999). *Mong Education at the Crossroads.* New York, NY: University Press of America.

Upadhyay, B. (2009). Teaching science for empowerment in an urban classroom: A case study of a Hmong teacher. *Equity & Excellence in Education* 42(2), 217–232.

Vang, C. T. (2001). *Histories and academic profiles of successful and unsuccessful Hmong secondary students* (Ph.D. dissertation, University of California, Davis and California State of University, Fresno).

———. (2003). Learning more about Hmong students. *Multicultural Education* 11(2), 10–14.

———. (2004). Hmong American K-12 students and the academic skills needed for a college education: A review of the existing literature and suggestions for future research. *Hmong Studies Journal* 5, 1–31.

———. (2005). Hmong-American students still face multiple challenges in public schools. *Multicultural Education* 13(1), 27–35.

Vue, P. P. (2008). Factors that contribute towards and/or impede Hmong women from obtaining a higher education degree. *Dissertation Abstracts International Section A: Humanities and Social Science* 68(8–1), 33313 0419-4209.

Woo, A. S. (2007). The socioeconomic attainments of second generation Cambodian, Hmong, Laotian, and Vietnamese Americans. *Sociological Inquiry* 77(1), 44–75.

Xiong, Y. S. (2010). State-mandated language classification: A study of Hmong American students' access to college-preparatory curricula. *AAPI Nexus Journal* 8(1), 17–41.

———. (2012). Hmong Americans, ducation of. In J. A. Banks (Ed.), *Encyclopedia of Diversity in Education*. Thousand Oaks, CA: SAGE Publications, Inc, 1078–1081.

———. (2012). Hmong Americans' educational attainment: Recent changes and remaining challenges. *Hmong Studies Journal* 13(2), 1–18.

Xiong, Z. & Huang, J. (2011) Predicting Hmong male and female youth's delinquent behavior: An Exploratory study." *Hmong Studies Journal* 12, 1–34.

Yang, D. (1993). *Hmong at turning point.* Minneapolis, MN: WorldBridge Associates.

Yang, K. (2004). Southeast Asian American children: not the 'model minority'. *Children of Immigrant Families* 14(2), 127–133 Summer.

Chapter 10

Involuntary Migration and Human Security in Africa

Exploring Legal Frameworks and Regional Infrastructure for Refugee Protection

Goodnews Osah, Abiola Abayomi Isikalu, Nwadiuto Franca Nwakanma, and Uzzibi Methuselah Irmiya

INTRODUCTION

In this chapter, we attempt to investigate the linkage between involuntary migration (which is also referred to as forced migration) and human security. Specifically, the study explores the legal and regional structures aimed at the protection of refugees in Africa and interrogates the degree to which these legal and regional frameworks sufficiently promote the human security of displaced individuals. The chapter proceeds first by exploring a number of previous literatures on the refugee crisis, the instrumentality of available international politico-legal frameworks in protecting the rights, and promoting the security of refugees and displaced individuals. Second, the chapter examines the impacts of forced migration on human security, it basically asks: while international conventions and laws normatively provide for the protection of the rights of refugees and the promotion of their human security, are these reflected in practice through policy implementation? In the third section, the chapter primarily assesses the international legal framework on the question of involuntary migration. In the fourth section, a comparative analysis of the policy frameworks of the Economic Community of West African States (ECOWAS) and the Southern African Development Community (SADC) is carried out to examine the manner in which subregional groups deal with migration and the refugee crisis in the African region. The fifth section concludes the chapter by advocating for an African Union (AU) framework for tackling the region's refugee crisis, with an emphasis on the promotion of human security.

Before going any further, it is necessary to provide clarification on the nature of involuntary migration, as well as on the refugee crisis. Involuntary migration, also referred to as forced migration, and sometimes as forced or involuntary displacement (with distinctions usually noted between "conflict-induced" displacement—caused by humans, and "disaster-induced" displacement—caused by natural disasters) (Migration Data Portal, 2021). It is worth noting that while defining these terms are analytically convenient, practically, the lines between them may be distorted. For instance, certain disputes over natural resources such as land may trigger conflict, while other human endeavors, may sometimes result in the occurrence of a natural disaster, such as a landslide. The International Organization for Migration (IOM) defines forced or involuntary migration as a "migratory movement which, although the drivers can be diverse, involves force, compulsion, or coercion" (IOM, 2019, p. 77). However, the glossary by the IOM notes that, "while not an international legal concept, this term has been used to describe the movements of refugees, displaced persons (including those displaced by disasters or development projects), and, in some instances, victims of trafficking" (IOM, 2019, p. 77). Nevertheless, at a global level, the use of the phrase "forced migration" remains a matter of contention, primarily because there is a general consensus that there is a "continuum of agency," rather than the often deployed forced/voluntary dichotomy, which has the likelihood of weakening the present international legal frameworks that serve to protect refugees (IOM, 2019). The 1951 United Nations (UN) Convention regarding the Status of Refugees as well as its 1967 Protocol defines refugees as individuals who flee their countries as a result of "well-founded fears" of persecution as a result of religion, race, nationality, belonging to a social group, or having a political opinion, who have left the confines of their country of nationality or have abandoned their permanent residence, and also because of their fear are refusing to go back.

Indeed, the number of individuals who have forcefully, or attempted to forcefully leave their homes due to one challenge or the other, has significantly been on the rise in the past few years. According to Knoll (2016), a large number of refugees and "irregular" migrants often come from, or through Africa, with hopes of getting to Europe. In trying to tackle the refugee crisis, Europe has tended to look to Africa in a bid to tackle the root drivers of involuntary migration. While both regions have been working to find a solution for the crisis, progress has been slow, particularly because both regions often adopt very distinct approaches to dealing with the situation (Knoll, 2016). News reports these days continue to capture images of desperate refugees and migrants trying to cross the Mediterranean to Europe from Africa, a situation that according to Williams (2019) has come to define the "African migration crisis." It is estimated that since 2014, on average, 86,000 African migrants have attempted to enter Europe without a visa annually (Williams, 2019). This crisis is occurring within the broader phenomenon of forced displacement. It is estimated that on average, around 1.6 million Africans have been displaced forcibly annually since 2014; while the alarming figure of 25 million African refugees, internally displaced persons (IDPs), and asylum seekers recorded in 2018 represents about a five-fold increase from just about 5 million displaced Africans as at 2005 (Williams, 2019). Beyond these figures and the politics of the so-called "African migration crisis" lies the question of the welfare of refugees, particularly, as this chapter seeks to now investigate, the degree of dignity that refugees and IDPs are able to enjoy. That is, the question of their human security. In the section that follows, the chapter explores two kinds of literatures: that on Africa's migration crisis, and the other on the protection of the human security of involuntary migrants and forcibly displaced people.

AFRICA'S REFUGEE CRISIS, HUMANITARIAN REGIME, AND INVOLUNTARY MIGRATION

Nindi (1986) and Anthony (1991) have considered Africa's refugee crisis from a historical perspective and attempted to outline pointers for the future, while Harrell-Bond (1988) consider the refugee crisis as a "twentieth-century phenomenon." Nindi identifies three primary challenges, that involving difficulties in estimating the number of refugees; that involve the causes and sources of refugees from an historical perspective; and lastly, that which involves the issue of self-settlement as against settlements. Starting from 1945, the struggles of refugees seemed to have tilted from Europe to Africa, with refugee rights often conferred initially on the basis of national interest or where a refugee-receiving government expected to receive financial aid for accepting refugees (Nindi, 1986). Similarly, Harrell-Bond (1988) argued that the emergence of African refugees had created an economic dependence between poorer countries and richer ones, through the advent of an industry of humanitarian organizations. This humanitarian regime created a nexus between host governments, international donors, and local agencies. Thus, it can be suggested that the humanitarian regime economy is "itself responsible for extending and perpetuating the unique status of of the refugee" (Harrell-Bond, 1988, p. 1). It is indeed interesting that in present times, the migration of refugees remain a highly contested matter, as host countries are only willing to accept refugees and displaced persons under certain conditions of national interest.

Furthermore, refugees are thought to be reflective of a disordered world, representing the "deep moral and spiritual crisis of a civilization which tolerates conditions which continue to generate them" (Nindi, 1986, p. 105). Nindi further argued that refugees were likely to remain a constant "by product" of the extant disordered world, until nations resolve to address the underlying causes. For Anthony (1991), the primary source of Africa's refugee crisis was internal warfighting, particularly during Africa's post-independence state-building efforts. The decision by a number of African governments to replace politics with war drove most African countries to conflict, and subsequently drove the continent into the production of refugees. While the number of intrastate conflict has declined over the years in Africa, new actors have emerged, including terrorists, extremists, bandits, and more, who through their activities continue to fuel Africa's refugee crisis. These actors, coupled with intrastate conflict in a few countries, seem to have worsened Africa's refugee crisis over the past few decades. However, some things are different today. We are able to better estimate the number of refugees or IDPs situated in a particular country or even camp and as shall be discussed subsequently, there are international laws and organizations that primarily serve to cater to the needs of refugees, and refugees throughout the world today remain an important aspect of conversation among governments, particularly pertaining to their welfare.

For Abdullahi (1994) however, Africa's refugee crisis is a problem of the institution of the state. The African state, he argues, has been modeled on the colonial state and its institutions, accordingly, the African state has failed to reach viable functionality in terms of satisfying the needs of the people, as well as in enjoying unrivaled legitimacy because of its inability to equitably distribute state resources among various ethnic groupings. The challenge of African states in nation-building persists today and the swelling in the figures of refugees is reflective of the fact that African governments are still not getting it right. In a bid to get it right, the chapter recommends the creation of an AU framework for dealing with the refugee crisis, with a mandate that focuses on improving the capacity of the state by restructuring how the state functions to meet the realities of contemporary African societies.

Williams (2019) seems to correlate earlier studies on the causes of involuntary or forced migration, as well as highlights new and emerging structural drivers. These drivers include rising population numbers in African countries, environmental pressures which continue to displace individuals, while consequently, migration as a result of population swelling has given rise to criminal networks. Despite international efforts being better than in the past, current policies remain inadequate, especially with regard to emphasis on short-term fixes, which usually lead to further long-term challenges. In addition, while the AU has deepened rhetoric on the need to curb the migration crisis and improve the well-being of refugees, policy action has largely been inconsequential (Williams, 2019). However, as this chapter proposes, the AU, through proactive measures can be a catalyst for arresting Africa's migration crisis.

Furthermore, the African migration crisis may well be a "European problem." Banchio (2021) argues that the movement of people from other regions of the world such as Africa, to Europe is a result of the global inequalities that were earlier established by European powers. The colonization of the rest of the world by Europeans and the history of using migrants as a "disposable labor force" have all contributed to the development of the ongoing migrant crisis, both from an African viewpoint, as well as from a European perspective (Banchio, 2021).

Following, forced or involuntary migration has immense negative consequences for migrants or refugees and IDPs. They usually find that their human rights are rampantly violated, and they often fall prey to infectious diseases and malnutrition, while simultaneously lacking access to any form of healthcare; migrants or refugees and IDPs usually have to also deal with threats to their personal security, including incarceration when in transit and on arrival in host countries, violence, restrictions of their freedom of mobility, as well as on their right to gainful employment (Martin, 2020). Similarly, in studying the intersection between the plethora of factors that lead people to forcibly or involuntarily migrate by drawing on trafficking data in Pakistan, Yousaf (2017) finds that most people who migrate are often susceptible to exploitation. Yousaf notes that marginalized groups often go through multiple channels of migration, during which they might suffer episodes of sex trafficking, forced labor, or slavery, as well as trafficking for other purposes. Indeed, there is a disconnect between policies and the realities of the plight of refugees, and current interventions have not done much to protect the human security of these individuals. Vietti and Scribner (2013) have argued that the state-centric security practices that have been applied to deal with the refugee crisis are inadequate and that the human security paradigm is more suited to dealing with the present crisis. In the section that follows, the chapter examines the impact of forced or involuntary migration on human security and further highlights the instrumentality of the human security approach to dealing with Africa's refugee crisis.

FORCED MIGRATION AND IMPACT ON HUMAN SECURITY

As Williams (2019) shows, there are about 7 million refugees in the African region, with about 60 percent of these individuals living in camps. Unfortunately, a majority of refugees are hosted by only a few countries in the region, with Ethiopia, Uganda, the Democratic Republic of the Congo (DRC), and

Sudan hosting majority of refugees and IDPs. As at 2017, Uganda was hosting around 726,000 refugees from neighboring South Sudan, making them the largest host nation of refugees in the region. The 2016 World Economic Forum Global Risks Report outlined three primary elements that heightened the dangers of involuntary migration, including longer stays by migrants in host countries; inadequate international humanitarian support to meet the long-term needs of refugees, especially concerning reintegration efforts; and, because a large majority of refugees live in already struggling countries, majority of them do not have access to basic amenities (World Economic Forum, 2016). Indeed, the risk factors that make the migrant crisis a global conundrum are the same ones that increase the threats to the human security of migrants.

For the United Nations High Commissioner for Refugees (UNHCR), there has been a shift on the definition of protection—that is, the protection of refugees, which is now defined as "security of refugees," and the security of refugee operations (Adelman, 2001). Security itself is undergoing a definitional evolution, both theoretically and in policy practice. What was previously state-centric—with emphasis on threat and the deployment of military might in the context of interstate relations, now emphasizes the broader conception of the human security paradigm (Buzan, Waever, & de Wilde, 1998). The emphasis on human security does not necessarily negate military strength and interstate conflict; it merely shifts the referent object in security analysis from the state to the individual. This is a particular response to changing trends in security. This paradigm, anchored by the liberal school of thought, emphasizes human rights and humanitarianism, and consequently emphasizes the need to protect refugees, as encapsulated within the broader human security framework. According to Adelman (2001), human security "encompass both the old notions of state security and the new non-state threats, thereby embracing the notions of protection and human rights" (p. 15). For refugees, these protections are not often accorded to them, neither are their human rights often respected.

As Yousaf (2017) notes, crime networks and other exploitative agents often prey on the vulnerabilities of refugees, particularly women and children. Refugees and IDPs are always at high risks of getting trafficked for example, and women and children, especially, after losing traditional channels of support, may be exploited as sex slaves, sold into slavery, or deployed as child soldiers (Brysk, 2009; Bales & Cornell, 2008). Furthermore, the process of transit to safer havens also poses danger for refugees and IDPs. For example, individuals fleeing conflict in the Middle East and are trying to get to Europe often travel through Turkey to Greece and across the Mediterranean, and they often use unseaworthy and overcrowded boats, and many of them have ended up sinking (Özdemir, 2018). Similarly, transit via land routes also poses a danger to refugees and IDPs, as do transit camps, which have been found at some times to be unsafe for refugees and IDPs. Refugees and IDPs who make it to safety often recount their ordeals, detailing how they witnessed others been abused and killed in transit, as well as witnessing the death of other migrants in camps due to conflict between camp mates or due to the breakout of a deadly disease, and also lack of adequate medical facilities (Özdemir, 2018).

Özdemir (2018) has argued that during the process of transit from a country of origin, up to getting to a camp in a host country, violence against refugees is often gendered. Indeed, the experiences of female refugees and IDPs regarding violence, their own perceptions of aggression toward them, as well as their vulnerabilities, are vital for human security analysis. Many women experience a plethora of traumatic incidents during displacement, and often face sexual and gender-based violence throughout the process of their migration (Özdemir, 2018). While on the move, migrants usually end up in very vulnerable conditions and have to deal with numerous social, political, economic, health, and environmental threats. Like women, refugee and IDPs children, smuggled or trafficked individuals, and disabled people, often end up in highly precarious conditions, either in transit or on arrival in a destination country. Given the marginalized status of refugees in their own countries of origin, they often face the prospects of further and heightened exploitation in a bid to get to safer regions. To tackle the migrant crisis, there is a need to engage the situation from a human security perspective.

The human security paradigm can provide a foundation for national and local authorities to wholly identify various levels and forms of vulnerabilities among domestic populations, with emphasis on those that may be the most vulnerable. This should help in the creation of tailored policies that mitigate against the hazardous human, economic, and social costs of migration and create holistic policies and collaborations that improve the protection of refugees and uphold their dignity. As Purkayastha (2017) asserts, there is a need to transcend the limited notion of security with the state as primary referent object of analysis. This is because, both nation-states and migrants' lives are now shaped by events globally and virtually, beyond traditional territorial boundaries; because migrants lives are now shaped by a plethora of actors beyond the state, and because the nation-state is not efficient on its own to deal with a crisis that has glocal (global and local) roots.

INTERNATIONAL LAW AND INVOLUNTARY MIGRATION

In this section, the chapter engages briefly with various legal instruments that have been designed to serve as a collective "guide" for how countries respond and cater for forced or involuntary migrants. It must be noted from the onset that these legal instruments are very political in nature, and sometimes highly idealistic and theoretical. We refer to them as guides in this chapter simply because they are not easily enforceable, and their interpretations often defer at national level as well as depending on the context. Nonetheless, their availability has ensured that various countries have a blueprint from which they can act and react to the ongoing refugee crisis, especially in such a manner that the human rights, security, and dignity of forced or involuntary migrants and IDPs are enforced and protected.

Broadly speaking, international human rights laws, such as the Universal Declaration of Human Rights (UDHR) (1948), the Convention on the Elimination of all forms of Discrimination against Women (CEDAW) (1979), and the Convention on the Rights of the Child (CRC) (1989), are all significant to forced or involuntary migrants. Nevertheless, there are international humanitarian law and refugee law which are more specific to forced or involuntary migration. Article 1 of the UDHR clearly states that "all human beings are born free and equal in dignity and rights" (United Nations, 1948). This statement primarily affirms that all individuals, irrespective of their status (refugee or not), are entitled to certain inalienable rights simply for the fact of being human. Thus, the legal outline provided as the universal framework of international human rights law, which applies to all humans without conditions, which are contained in the UDHR, the International Covenant on Economic, Social, and Cultural Rights, and the International Covenant on Civil and Political Rights (International Commission of Jurists, 2014). And as shall be explored in the subsequent section, these conventions and treaties are supplemented by regional human rights instruments of general breath. More specific treaties cater for specific groups of individuals, such as women and children. For example, the International Convention on the Protection of the Rights of All Migrant Workers and Members of Their Families (ICRMW) is the human rights document that seeks to deal with specific standards concerning migrant workers and their relatives. Unfortunately, this treaty is yet to be widely ratified, and no developed country is a party to the treaty (International Commission of Jurists, 2014).

Concerning involuntary migrants specifically, Betts (2011) and Blitz (2014) highlight that the governance of international migration and the importance of migration policy are particularly high on the agenda of developing countries. This is not to say that developed countries do not pay attention, especially since most countries today are either impacted as a source, a transit, or a destination for migrants (Zetter, 2014). Indeed, developed countries are the most attractive destinations for a large number of forced or involuntary migrants, thus these countries are under immense pressure as well. While voluntary migrants are protected by international conventions, norms, and standards, Zetter (2014) argues that for "forced migrants and for the countries they transit and for which they are destined" . . . "no similarly coherent paradigm either manages or protects this group of people on the move" (p. 24). The 1951 "Geneva Convention relating to the Status of Refugees" and the 1967 "Protocol" recognize one specific category of involuntary migrants as refugees. Under this convention, Article 1A (2) defines a refugee as an individual with a "well-founded fear of being persecuted" (Office of the United Nations High Commissioner for Refugees (UNHCR), 1951, 1967, p. 14); which unfortunately does not respond to the plethora of drivers of displacement characteristic of modern complex migration.

The convention defines the status of a refugee and outlines the rights of individuals who receive asylum in host countries, as well as the responsibilities of host countries. Following the provisions of Article 14 of the UDHR, which asserts the right of individuals to seek asylum in other countries in case of persecution, Article 5 of the convention highlights that a refugee may enjoy rights and benefits in a host country beyond those provided for in the convention. Within the broad principle of international law, conventions that have come into force are binding on its signatories, and enforcement must be carried out in good faith. Hence, those countries who have ratified the convention are expected to protect any refugee in their jurisdiction. The convention outlines a plethora of provisions that party-states which are signatories to it must adhere to. According to Article 2 of the convention, all refugees must conform to the laws and regulations of the territory in which they find themselves. On the part of party-states to the convention, they shall not expect reciprocity, because refugees are in their predicament because they also haven't been able to enjoy the protection of their home country (Article 7); in Article 12, a host country which is party to the convention shall ensure to uphold the personal status and accorded rights that come with it of a refugee, especially rights that involve marriage; party-states to the convention shall freely make courts accessible to refugees (Article 16), as well as provide administrative help to refugees (Article 25).

Significantly for the protection of the human rights of refugees, contracting parties to the convention shall not apply the provisions with any discrimination as a result of race, religion, or nationality (Article 3); parties shall not take exceptional measures against refugees for the sole reason of their nationality (Article 8); parties shall not prosecute refugees who enter their territories undocumented (Article 31); parties shall not expel refugees from their jurisdictions (Article 32); nor forcibly return or "refoul" refugees to their countries of origin (Article 33). Other numerous articles provide for situations where refugees must enjoy similar rights as nationals, as well as those situations where they shall enjoy certain benefits as nonnationals.

While the convention is technically "legally binding," there is no agency tasked with monitoring the compliance of parties to the document. The UNHCR serves a supervisory role, but this is undermined by its inability to enforce the provisions of the convention. Given these limitations, it is possible that regional, rather than international instruments are better equipped to protect refugees. In the following section, a brief comparative analysis of the ECOWAS and SADC frameworks may shed further light regarding the protection of the human rights of forced or involuntary refugees.

REGIONAL INFRASTRUCTURES: COMPARING ECOWAS AND SADC POLICY FRAMEWORKS

Regional and subregional bodies often adopt frameworks that are more suited to their specific challenges, thus, both the ECOWAS and SADC have developed their own frameworks for responding to the migrant crisis. In the sub-Saharan African region (SSA), ECOWAS citizens generally represent the largest proportion of first-time asylum applicants in the European Union (EU), with Nigerians representing about 23 percent of the general population of first-time asylum seekers between July 2016 and June 2017 (Dick & Schraven, 2018). Speaking at a meeting with the UNHCR in 2019, the ECOWAS Commission president (represented by Siga Fatima Jagne, the ECOWAS Commissioner for Social Affairs and Gender) argued for the "development of relevant regional and country specific legal frameworks, high level advocacy and sensitization for the implementation of existing protection frameworks and the improvement of the general protection environment in the ECOWAS space" (ECOWAS, 2019).

The ECOWAS, under its "Gender and Migration Framework and Plan of Action 2015–2020" broadly categorizes involuntary migrants to include all individuals who attempt to migrate away from their countries of origins through illicit channels, whether as a result of conflict or for socioeconomic reasons (ECOWAS Commission, 2014). The ECOWAS Treaty, the ECOWAS Common Approach on Migration, and the Treaty of the West African Economic and Monetary Union (UEMOA), all provide policy frameworks for the protection of forced migrants, refugees, and IDPs. The ECOWAS Treaty which was adopted in Lagos in 1975 provides for the free movement of people within the community of member-states, and Articles 2 (2d) and 27 (1, 2) basically encourages the need to facilitate migration within the region. The ECOWAS Agreement on the Free Movement of Persons between Member States (1979) and the Protocol on the Free Movement of Persons supplement these articles and grants migrants the Right of Residence and Establishment (ECOWAS Commission, 2014). The ECOWAS adopted a "Common Approach on Migration" in January 2008, which outlines the organization's policy toward migrants, asylum seekers, and refugees. The document provides a framework for addressing migration and development challenges in the subregion on six bases: the promotion of free movement within ECOWAS space; the promotion of the management of regular migration; policy harmonization; management of irregular migration and trafficking in humans; the promotion of the rights of migrants, asylum seekers, and refugees; and actions to ensure that the gender dimension of migration is accounted for always. Similarly, Article 91 of the UEMOA which was adopted in 1994 promotes the free mobility of individuals, services, and capital. However, the degree to which these treaties have had an impact on migratory flows in the subregion is quite scant. Nonetheless, they do provide a blueprint for responding to Africa's refugee crisis. Agyei and Clottey (2007), for example, highlight that the implementation of the Protocol on the Free Movement of Persons faces challenges that have to do with strict border checks, poor economic performances of member-states, delayed implementation of policies aimed at deepening integration, and a number of distractions and disruptions from member-states as a result of membership to a number of international organizations. How these impact on refugees and IDPs pose an interesting research problem.

In the southern African subregion, the diversity in history and development levels of SADC's fourteen member-states, which includes Angola and the Democratic Republic of Congo (DRC) from Central Africa and Tanzania from East Africa, often constrain their integration efforts, and have previously led to tensions in a bid to realize their goal of free movement within the subregion (Oucho, 2007). SADC came into existence in 1992, and despite Article 5 (2) (d) of the Treaty outlining the need to develop policies that will ensure the gradual elimination of all hindrances to the free movement of people within the subregional bloc, decades after these, aspirations remain largely unfulfilled. A SADC workshop on the free mobility of individuals was held in Zimbabwe in 1993, with a "Draft Protocol on the Free Movement of Persons," a product of this workshop (Dodson & Crush, 2015). As a result of objections from South Africa, Namibia, and Botswana, the protocol was unfortunately significantly revised, then suspended, then revived again, and finally formalized as the SADC "Protocol on the Facilitation of Movement of Persons" in August 2005. As Dodson and Crush (2015) argue, the alteration from "free" to "facilitation" in the wordings of the Protocol, "were more than merely semantic" (p. 6). Indeed, while the majority of SADC member-states have signed the protocol, only a handful have ratified it, including South Africa, Lesotho, Botswana, Zambia, Mozambique, and Swaziland, a minimal number still largely shy of the needed signatories to put the protocol into effect.

Significantly, this protocol has been categorized under SADC's Politics, Defence, and Security framework, rather than within the Economic Development, Social, and Human Development, or Poverty Eradication and Policy Dialogue framework. This implies that for the subregion, "migration is still viewed primarily as a security issue, rather than one of rights and protections for migrants themselves" (Dodson & Crush, 2015, p. 7). The "Strategic Indicative Plan for the Organ" on Politics, Defence, and Security Cooperation highlights strategies for the social reintegration of refugees. This is detailed under Objective 3 of the Strategic Indicative Plan for the Organ and recommends strategies that include the establishment of uniform understanding of the target groups for reintegration and the identification of donors; development of a handbook on social reintegration; exchange of experiences and practices in the region on social reintegration of demobilized combatants, refugees, and IDPs; and the organization of training seminars and workshops (SADC, 2010).

There is a sharp distinction between the ECOWAS and SADC frameworks, where the former treats migration as an essential ingredient for development, the latter considers it as a security matter. Furthermore, the ECOWAS seems to approach migration and the free movement of persons from a human development angle, while for SADC, migration is inextricably linked to regional security, and thus the subregional bloc merely approaches migration from the point of view of securing the region rather than the protection and promotion of the human rights of refugees and IDPs. Curiously, both subregional frameworks seem to emphasize general migration policies without any focus on refugees and IDPs and seem to largely depend on international frameworks for dealing with involuntary or forced migration. Given the poor implementation levels of international frameworks for the protection of the human rights of refugees and IDPs, as well as inadequate policy frameworks at subregional levels, there is a need for a fresh approach, one with a strong region-wide application.

CONCLUDING REMARKS: ADVOCATING FOR AN AU FRAMEWORK

Given the highly fragile state of many African countries and deepening socioeconomic inequalities, as well as a plethora of other natural disasters, the African refugee crisis might just get worse before it gets better. While there are international legal structures that aim to protect the rights of refugees and IDPs, the inability to ensure compliance remains problematic. This condition is worsened by weak legal structures at subregional levels, as has been demonstrated through a comparative analysis of the ECOWAS and SADC subregional blocs.

While these blocs have general migration policy frameworks, they all do not directly address the issue of the protection and promotion of the human rights and security of refugees, asylum seekers, and IDPs. They instead seem to depend largely on international frameworks, which have weakened implementation mechanisms. There is a need for a different approach.

The shift in the security paradigm from the state as a referent object to the individual as the primary object of analysis provides a fresh framework for tackling Africa's refugee crisis. However, this framework needs to be anchored to strong center—particularly, the AU. The AU remains one of the largest regional organization in the world, albeit with a weaker integration in comparison to the EU. Nonetheless, the consensual nature of decision-making within the regional body makes a prime candidate for the development and implementation of a migration crisis solution that emphasizes the human security of individual migrants. The AU can draw from the ECOWAS framework of connecting the free movement of people to development, while relying heavily on the recent shift to the human development paradigm. The AU is unique because its member-countries share similar national agendas and similarly face the same challenges. Environmental disasters, for example, will generally impact almost all SSA countries. As can be noted in the West African subregion, conflict in one country always has the potential of spilling into neighboring countries. Given the AU's continuing attempt to define itself as a unique regional bloc that stands out of the shadow of the EU, it has an opportunity to reorient the nature of the conversation around security in its member-states, and people the individual first in the heart of this conversation.

REFERENCES

Abdullahi, A. M. (1994, December 1). The Refugee Crisis in Africa as a Crisis of the Institution of the State. *International Journal of Refugee Law, 6*(4), 562–580. https://doi.org/10.1093/ijrl/6.4.562

Adelman, H. (2001). From Refugees to Forced Migration: The UNHCR and Human Security. *The International Migration Review, 35*(1), 7–32. Retrieved from https://www.jstor.org/stable/2676049

Anthony, C. G. (1991). Africa's Refugee Crisis: State Building in Historical Perspective. *The International Migration Review, 25*(3), 574–591. Retrieved from https://www.jstor.org/stable/2546761

Bales, K., & Cornell, R. (2008). *Slavery Today* (1st ed.). Toronto: Groundwood Books.

Banchio, P. R. (2021, March 17). *Refugee and Forced Migrant Crisis: A European Problem.* Retrieved April 2, 2021, from SSRN: https://papers.ssrn.com/sol3/papers.cfm?abstract_id=3782834

Betts, A. (2011). Introduction: Global Migration Governance. In A. Betts (Ed.), *Global Migration Governance* (1st ed., pp. 1–33). Oxford: Oxford University Press.

Blitz, B. (2014). *Migration and freedom: Mobility, Citizenship and Exclusion* (1st ed.). Cheltenham: Edward Elgar Publishing. https://doi.org/10.4337/9781781955840

Brysk, A. (2009). Beyond Framing and Shaming: Human Trafficking, Human Security and Human Rights. *Journal of Human Security, 5*(3), 8–21.

Buzan, B., Waever, O., & de Wilde, J. (1998). *Security: A New Framework for Analysis* (1st ed.). London: Lynne Rienner Publishers, Inc.

Clottey, J., & Aqyei, E. (2007). *Operationalizing ECOWAS Protocol on Free Movement of People among the Member States: Issues of Convergence, Divergence and Prospects for Sub-Regional Integration.* Amsterdam: International Migration Institute.

Dick, E., & Schraven, B. (2018). *Regional Migration Governance in Africa and Beyond: A Framework of Analysis.* Bonn: German Development Institute. http://dx.doi.org/10.23661/dp9.2018

Dodson, B., & Crush, J. (2015). *Migration Governance and Migrant Rights in the Southern African Development Community (SADC).* UN, Research Institute for Social Development. Geneva: United Nations Research Institute for Social Development.

ECOWAS. (2019, April 16). *Strengthening Protection and Solutions for Refugees and Asylum Seekers in West Africa Is Critical in Response to Mixed Population Flows, Say ECOWAS and UNHCR.* Retrieved April 12, 2021, from The Community Computer Centre (CCC) in collaboration with the Directorate of Communication: https://www.ecowas.int/strengthening-protection-and-solutions-for-refugees-and-asylum-seekers-in-west-africa-is-critical-in-response-to-mixed-population-flows-say-ecowas-and-unhcr/

ECOWAS Commission. (2008). *ECOWAS Common Approach on Migration.* ECOWAS, ECOWAS Commission. Abuja: ECOWAS Commission.

ECOWAS Commission. (2014). *ECOWAS Gender and Migration Framework and Plan of Action 2015-2020.* ECOWAS, ECOWAS Commission. Abuja: ECOWAS Commission.

Harrell-Bond, B. E. (1988, June 1). The Sociology of Involuntary Migration: An Introduction. *Current Sociology, 36*(2), 1–6. https://doi.org/10.1177/001139288036002003

International Commission of Jurists. (2014). *Migration and International Human Rights Law.* International Commission of Jurists. Geneva: International Commission of Jurists.

IOM. (2019). *Glossary on Migration.* United Nations (UN), UN Migration. Geneva: International Organization for Migration (IOM).

Knoll, A. (2016). *Africa's and Europe's Response to the Refugee Crisis.* Retrieved April 2, 2021, from European Centre for Development Policy Management (ECDPM): https://ecdpm.org/africa-europe-response-refugee-crisis/

Martin, M. (2020). *Migration and Human Security* (M. Babović, & I. Subotički, Editors). Retrieved April 5, 2021, from Human Security Course: http://

humansecuritycourse.info/module-4-human-security-in-diverse-contexts/issue-5-migration/

Migration Data Portal. (2021, March 30). *Forced Migration or Displacement.* Retrieved April 1, 2021, from https://migrationdataportal.org/themes/forced-migration-or-displacement

Mpedi, L. G. (2019). Africa and the Refugee Crisis: A Socio-Legal Inquiry. In E. Wacker, U. Becker, K. Crepaz, E. Wacker, U. Becker, & K. Crepaz (Eds.), *Refugees and Forced Migrants in Africa and the EU: Comparative and Multidisciplinary Perspectives on Challenges and Solutions* (1st ed., pp. 69–94). Springer Fachmedien Wiesbaden GmbH. https://doi.org/10.1007/978-3-658-24538-2

Nindi, B. (1986). Africa's Refugee Crisis in a Historical Perspective. *Transafrican Journal of History, 15*, 96–107. Retrieved from https://www.jstor.org/stable/24328609

Office of the United Nations High Commissioner for Refugees (UNHCR). (1951; 1967). *Convention and Protocol Relating to the Status of Refugees.* United Nations, Office of the United Nations High Commissioner for Refugees (UNHCR). Geneva: Office of the United Nations High Commissioner for Refugees (UNHCR). Retrieved from https://www.unhcr.org/3b66c2aa10

Oucho, J. O. (2007). *Migration in Southern Africa: Migration Management Initiatives for SADC Member States.* Pretoria: Institute for Security Studies.

Özdemir, Ö. (2018, September 1). *Forced Migration and Security Threats to Syrian Refugee Women.* Retrieved April 7, 2021, from e-International Relations: https://www.e-ir.info/2018/09/01/forced-migration-and-security-threats-to-syrian-refugee-women/

Purkayastha, B. (2017). Migration, Migrants, and Human Security. *Current Sociology Monograph, 00*(0), 1–25. https://doi.org/10.1177/0011392117736302

SADC. (2010). *Strategic Indicative Plan for the Organ on Politics, Defence and Security Cooperation.* Maputo: SADC.

SADC Secretariat. (2015). *Consolidated Text of the SADC Treaty.* SADC Secretariat, Legal Affairs Unit. Gaborone: SADC Secretariat.

United Nations. (1948). *Universal Declaration of Human Rights.* Geneva: United Nations.

Vietti, F., & Scribner, T. (2013). Human Insecurity: Understanding International Migration from a Human Security Perspective. *Journal on Migration and Human Security, 1*(1), 17–31.

Williams, W. (2019). *Shifting Borders: Africa's Displacement Crisis and Its Security Implications.* Washington, DC: Africa Center for Strategic Studies.

World Economic Forum. (2016). *The Global Risks Report 2016.* World Economic Forum, Global Risks Report. Geneva: World Economic Forum.

Yousaf, F. N. (2017). Forced migration, human trafficking, and human security. *Current Sociology, 00*(0), 1–17. https://doi.org/10.1177/0011392117736309

Zetter, R. (2014). *Protecting Forced Migrants: A State of the Art Report of Concepts, Challenges and Ways Forward.* Federal Commission on Migration FCM. Bern-Wabern: Federal Commission on Migration (FCM).

Chapter 11

ESTHER, Refugees, and Immigrants in the Fox Valley Region

Hannah P. Schmidt

INTRODUCTION

America is growing more diverse and requires our society to develop a deeper understanding of refugees and forced migration that begins with the desperate circumstances in their home country, their harrowing journeys, and the challenges they face when they arrive at a host country. This chapter explores the lived experiences of refugees and forced migrants in the Fox Valley area in Wisconsin. A region of sixty cities, villages, and towns located along the Fox River in the Northeastern part of Wisconsin, it is the fastest growing area in the state (Fox Cities Regional Partnership, 2019).

Specifically, the chapter shows the efforts put forth by ESTHER, an interfaith community organization located in the Fox Valley region whose mission is to empower all people and ensure they are treated fairly and equally. According to the United Nations High Commission for Refugees (UNHCR), a "refugee" is a person who has a well-founded fear of being persecuted for reasons of race, religion, nationality, membership of a particular social group or political opinion, is outside the country of his/her nationality and is unable, or owing to such fear, is unwilling to avail him, or herself of the protection of that country (UNHCR, 1951). "Asylum seekers" are people whose claim for refugee status has not been determined, and they have moved across international borders in search of protection under the 1951 Refugee Convention (UNHCR, 1951). In paragraph 5 of that Convention, the UNHCR, also defines "forced migration" as forced or involuntary displacement and is a distinction made between conflict-induced and disaster-induced displacement. It is a migratory movement involving force, compulsion, or coercion used to define the movements of refugees, displaced people, and victims of human trafficking.

Finally, this chapter highlights how ESTHER has influenced policy changes that empower people and seeks to understand the collective responsibility and commitment toward establishing a more empathetic society by understanding that with resources and support refugees and forced migrants would become contributing members of their new communities.

Geniesse (2010) describes his fellowship with ESTHER and acknowledges the impact of immigration on both the refugee and community. He understands that the transition is difficult and does not happen without incidents of racism and discrimination (Geniesse, 2010, xii). As Jacobson (2010) explains, tapping into the power of organizing communities allows people to work together to identify and remove systemic barriers. If people are aware of the casualties of an unjust system, their works of mercy are considerable (Jacobson, 2010, 19).

ESTHER AND FOUNDATIONS IN CATHOLIC SOCIAL JUSTICE TEACHINGS

ESTHER stands for empowerment, solidarity, truth, hope, equity, and reform. The nonprofit organization aims to unite different faith communities and is missioned to identify and act on issues of injustice. Located in the Fox Valley region of Wisconsin, it was founded by Reverend Maynard Beemer and began with efforts put forth by a group of interfaith religious leaders who recognized the need to improve the health of the Fox Valley community. Religious leaders started gatherings to collaborate to ensure that all members of the community are treated fairly and with dignity. Sister Selinsky (2019), member of ESTHER, explained that by considering all perspectives and belief systems and celebrating how God has revealed Himself in other traditions and in other cultures increases the power of the interfaith group. Sister M.J. Selinsky shared that her "involvement with ESTHER is about being a part of the larger beloved community, as they work together from differing traditions and then get to know each other, learn from each other, and bring about peace" (Selinsky, personal communication, 2019). In this way, she confirmed the words of Dom Helder, Brazilian Archbishop and champion of the poor, who said, "If I dream alone, it is only a dream. If we dream together, it is the beginning of reality" (Jacobson, 2001, 27).

ESTHER is an affiliate of WISDOM, the Wisconsin affiliate of GAMALIEL. On November 7, 2004, ESTHER hosted its founding covenanting event. It included six congregations committed to its grassroots efforts. Presently, ESTHER has grown to have fifteen member congregations and five project partners.

The people of ESTHER practice shared values of human dignity and equity and work to establish partnerships with public officials. They advocate that all people should have a voice and active role in developing just communities. ESTHER continues to strive toward strengthening communities by connecting people through strategic relationship building. ESTHER values and cherishes relationships and continually welcomes feedback from all people. ESTHER seeks to celebrate diversity and provide healing for suffering. Their work extends far beyond the segmentation of race, creed, and socioeconomic status. Dr. Van Lopik (2019), community organizer and director of ESTHER, affirmed that "One must take actionable steps toward creating policies which enfold migrants into the development of better communities." He explained further that, "people who are displaced are not moving by choice, they are struggling with circumstances beyond their scope of control."

Pope Paul IX, once said, "If you want peace, work for justice." As Sister Selinsky explained in 2019, the work of ESTHER follows the social justice teachings of the church and works on local, state, and national levels by responding to social justice concerns and vigilantly identifying causes of oppression, poverty, and injustice. The organization promotes the dignity of all people and works at building a power base of people so they can overcome their personal challenges of social injustice.

In a discussion on the work of ESTHER and the social justice perspective, Reverend Sister Barbieur described the importance of ESTHER in Northeast Wisconsin and related the work of ESTHER to the seven social teachings of the Catholic faith by explaining that one should respect life and human dignity. She noted in her social justice perspective that the social justice teachings revolve around the concept of human dignity. She said, "We are called to be members of family, community, and participation, and we are to participate in those communities to the best of our ability" (Barbieur, 2019). For her, "ESTHER is a family and a community, and one that is called to participate in bringing life to her community in the best way she can." She compares the work of ESTHER to rights and responsibilities that humans as spiritual people must have toward one another because we all deserve to be respected as persons.

Catholic social teachings practice preferential treatment for the poor. The difference between charity and justice is that we may be great with charity and doing charitable acts such as helping people out, but justice brings about systemic change. If charity is all we need and do, then that is where we will be. Society must move beyond charity and bring about systemic change by going deeper into social justice issues.

Another dimension of these teachings lies in the meaning of dignity of work and the rights of workers. Catholic social justice teaches that everyone has the right to a decent workplace, to an honest wage, and to organize and form unions. One should meet the challenge to see that change happens. The mission of ESTHER requires that we be in solidarity with others and recognize our diversity and work together regardless of religion, class, or race.

Yet another aspect of Catholic social teaching maintains that we must care for all God's creatures. We are called to be responsible. In the past, it was said that the Catholic social teachings were a best-kept secret in the Catholic church. But today, the ESTHER urges us to enact them daily and become involved politically to support social justice. In short, the work of ESTHER is not only humanistic but political, in that it involves creating systemic change through policy, laws, and involvement with law makers.

Collectively, the work of ESTHER is done by its members who actively accelerate policy changes by either supporting or opposing pieces of legislation. Members work diligently, to develop strategic plans to reduce and remove systemic barriers. Though the organization does not advocate for any political party or candidate, the members strongly promote voting and seek to cultivate strong relationships with elected officials to hold them accountable for promoting policy changes, empowering people, and creating equitable communities. As a member of ESTHER, one will appreciate the opportunity to be an agent of change. Unity and solidarity flow heavily among the people of ESTHER who bear the message of hope as they work diligently to achieve the goals of caring for refugees and migrants by organizing people and forming partnerships.

RELIGIOUS LEADERS CAUCUS

The Religious Leaders Caucus of ESTHER is a group comprised of religious leaders from the affiliated churches, who bind their philosophies in the mutual purpose that faith calls one to seek peace and justice for all God's children. Together, they identify community needs and seek to demonstrate unity in working toward improvement. ESTHER believes people should walk with each other in seeking justice for all. Clergy and professional staff bring forth the vision of ESTHER and create new objectives and initiatives that unify communities.

The Fox Valley local churches have historically been known for their charitable efforts in the community. However, the members of the Caucus feel that there is a need to provide support for individuals who struggle with social justice issues. The Caucus makes recommendations to the ESTHER Board, establishing new objectives which call for action. It is the social justice perspective that unifies the group of leaders who are committed to creating an equitable community with fair and just policies shaping the future.

The members of ESTHER recognize that refugees and migrants are here in search of stability and collectively feel that society has a responsibility to social justice issues. They actively engage with the community and gather stories about the importance of an individual's life experiences to enhance policy makers' understanding. Collectively, people within ESTHER advance change through advocacy, pushing for policy changes and creating progressive communities. Working through task forces, these efforts empower people by removing systemic barriers and by putting more equitable systems in place.

THE TASKFORCES OF ESTHER

Members of ESTHER advance positive change by forming taskforces. These action groups are comprised of interfaith communities committed to achieving policy changes. Each taskforce facilitates efforts which raise awareness and promote involvement from community members. The goal is to develop strategic plans focused on removing systemic barriers through advancing policy changes. The objectives are established by community members who have an interest in improving socioeconomic conditions and wish to voice their perspectives concerning ways to create a more equitable community. The congregations and members of ESTHER provide knowledge, support, and resources that support the uniqueness of each individual story. The taskforces of ESTHER affirm positive changes in the community by working with partners to advance policy changes on the local, state, and national levels.

ESTHER has several taskforces which are focused on specific areas of community health. The Oshkosh ESTHER Taskforce tackles social justice issues central to the Oshkosh community. The Transportation Taskforce works toward improving the Fox Valley transit system serving the Fox Valley area. The transit riders, local officials, and policy makers work toward improving the transportation network to provide better access and more reliability.

The Prison Reform and Restore Our Communities (ROC) Wisconsin Taskforce is relentlessly pursuing the goal to reduce the number of people in jails and prisons. The objective of this group promotes humane treatment of people who are incarcerated and advocates for more post-release programs. Safe community alternatives offer a proactive approach to reducing recidivism. The members of ESTHER demonstrate the shared belief that accountability through alternative treatment programs is more effective and less costly than prison. Prison does not create a healthy person or a healthy community. The incarceration rates in the United States have grown from 500,000 in 1980 to 2.3 million people in 2016 (Sawyer & Wagner, 2018). Statistics gathered from the Wisconsin Department of Corrections (DOC) Profile of Inmates in

Prison (2017) report that the incarceration rate in Wisconsin was 23,519. This number causes growing concern for ESTHER whose members are committed to putting the spotlight on prison practices.

The Immigration Taskforce strives toward improving policies to reduce systemic barriers related to immigration. The facilitators of this taskforce recognize the difficulties associated with assimilation and understand the need for support for migrants and refugees. Members of ESTHER recognize the value of migrant people and note the contributions they make to our community. ESTHER works on national comprehensive immigration reform as well as on a state level asking legislators to restore Wisconsin state drivers' licenses for resident undocumented workers. The Immigration Taskforce also supports instate tuition rates for all residents of Wisconsin meet the academic guidelines for acceptance into the Wisconsin public universities.

UNDERSTANDING IMMIGRATION IN AMERICA

During the Carter administration, the Refugee Act of 1980 was passed into law to align U.S. policy with international practice by defining "refugee" as anyone with well-founded fear of persecution or physical harm, regardless of the political regime of their country. This act stopped granting asylum to only those escaping communist nations and qualified more people for refugee status in order to allow them the privilege to work and seek welfare benefits. People who were denied refugee status were classified as "undocumented illegal aliens" and did not share the same advantages. It was difficult for people from Honduras, Guatemala, and El Salvador to legally enter the United States during the two Reagan administrations primarily because the U.S. government continued to grant asylum only to people fleeing communist countries and were mostly from Eastern Europe and South Asia (Portes & Rumbaut, 2006, 31).

During the Trump administration, there has been a strong effort to shut down the Mexican border and build a wall to stop the migrant flow with no consideration for the historical context of the problem. They did not acknowledge the political upheavals in countries such as Honduras, Mexico, and El Salvador from which refugees were fleeing. By exaggerating stories about gangs and drug cartels, they portrayed migrants as criminals and increased the public's fear of refugees. As a result, many communities did not welcome migrants.

Being a refugee is not a matter of individual choice but rather a government decision based on political and legal constraints (Portes & Rumbaut, 2006, 31). To understand the flow of refugees, Gordon (2017) explained that under current law state governments do not have the power to decide refugee resettlement. It is regulations and actions in the United Nations, the federal government, and a network of nonprofit agencies that determine immigrants' status. The Department of State recorded that resettlement programs brought 13,671 refugees to local communities in Wisconsin between 2002 and 2016. In that period, the Fox Valley has officially resettled approximately 1,100 refugees from 36 different countries. However, that data does not include undocumented migrants because they are either waiting for asylum or hiding in fear of deportation. People come into America for many different reasons and under different types of visas. Although not all migrants have visas or gain refugee status, each person has a story and should be treated fairly and with dignity.

America has always been a country of immigrants. There is a difference between "new" immigration and the "old" inflow of the early twentieth-century immigration (Portes & Rumbaut, 2006, 12). Portes and Rumbaut (2006), describe "old immigration" as primarily white Europeans, whereas the present-day flow is nonwhite and coming from third-world countries (2006, 12). Many Americans assume that people who migrate to the United States are poor and undereducated because their homeland is generally poor (Portes & Rumbaut, 2006, 13). By assuming that migration is associated with escaping hunger and persecution, Americans wrongly blame flaws of character for illegal and non-European migration (Portes & Rumbaut, 2006, 13).

When Americans ask why so many come and who they are Portes and Rumbaut suggest reversing the question to ask why so few have decided to endure the hardship of the journey (Portes & Rumbaut, 2006, 14). Of course, America receives migrants from various countries and different socioeconomic backgrounds. All don't come from the same circumstances. Though there are success stories, there are many who are not able to assimilate because of the insecurity associated with their legal status. They struggle to navigate the challenges associated with poverty and discrimination here (Portes & Rumbaut, 2006, 13). People who choose to migrate take immeasurable risks and must meet the challenges of learning a new culture and new language (Portes & Rumbaut, 2006, 14).

THE CONTEXT OF EXIT

The factors which drive people to migrate are often called the "push–pull" theory of migration. People who migrate involuntarily are perceived as unprepared and their move is typically a result of environmental disaster and government persecution (Portes & Rumbaut, 2006, 179). Within the Fox Valley area, migration has changed. In 2019, ESTHER member and Administrative

Assistant, Hiscocks explained that in the past people who migrated for jobs worked and then returned home. It was a routine way of life, and the government was prepared with a plan. Today, the reality is much different: more people are migrating out of well-founded fears for their very lives. They migrate to survive. Hiscocks (2019) further examined the struggles people experience during the process of seeking asylum. He said that asylum seekers live with uncertainty and are not able to look forward to returning home. They struggle to understand the long and difficult migration policies and that a government will determine their futures for them.

The factors which "pull" people into another country are generally employment or family reunification. Although both refugees and immigrants must deal with unforeseeable life changes, refugees have less control over the factors which determine the context of their exit (Portes & Rumbaut, 2006, 179). People who voluntarily move are assumed to be more prepared for the challenges that lie before them. Yet, Hiscocks (2019) explains that the struggles associated with the documentation process present challenges for people regardless of how prepared they are to leave their homes to improve their own lives and those of family members. Every migrant must cope with the daily challenges of staying in compliance with laws. For example, without driver's licenses or cars and the need to keep appointments at distant immigration offices in Milwaukee or Chicago is a big stressor (Hiscocks, 2019). Many live in the shadows of fear of deportation. Yet if they were treated with dignity and given the same benefits and rights as other Americans, they would be able to thrive and contribute to their new communities during the documentation process (Hiscocks, 2019). However, refugees and asylees are measured in terms of human capital: what they can contribute to the U.S. economy. Those who have entrepreneurial skills and are educated are valued more than those coming from Central America who are considered peasant farmers (Portes & Rumbaut, 2006, 33).

FORCED MIGRATION AND NAFTA REFUGEES

Geniesse explores the reality behind the North American Free Trade Agreement (NAFTA) and explains how the agreement was pivotal to the United States, Mexico, and Canada (Geniesse, 2010, 68). Put into effect on January 1, 1994, NAFTA made Mexico one of America's leading trade partners and promised to enrich their economy by reducing barriers to trade and increasing foreign investments (Geniesse, 2010, 66). However, the birth of NAFTA meant the loss of 1.3 million agriculture jobs in Mexico (Geniesse, 2010, 68). A study conducted by the Development Group for Alternative Policies found that governmental agencies caused the inevitable economic collapse in Mexico by causing the loss of livelihood among the small urban and rural farmers (Geniesse, 2010, 69) and fraying the nation's social fiber and economy.

This shift in policy resulted in an uprising in Chiapas, Mexico's most poor and indigenous state on the Guatemalan border. Sub-comandante Marcos, Leader of Ejercito Zapatista de Liberacion Nacional (EZLN) was the spokesperson for the protest, seeking to send the message that the NAFTA agreement would threaten their way of living. Local goods from poor peasant farmers were forced to compete at market with goods imported from the United States which were mechanically farmed, genetically modified, and grown using artificial fertilizer. The people of Chiapas feared that their culture and their way of life would be destroyed (Geniesse, 2010, 66, 67). As Marcos explained, "We didn't go to war to kill or to be killed, we went to war to be heard."

Mexican President Salinas promised his people that NAFTA would accelerate the economy and boost the country's development; however, Mexico's growth averaged only 3 percent a year under the NAFTA agreement. Pres. Salinas cut off crop subsidies and dissolved land programs. He sold off and rented *ejido* communal land. Small farmers lost access to credit and state support. The impact of NAFTA was much greater in rural communities yet statistics measured only urban unemployment to obscure the reality of the economic disaster. The downward spiral hit Mexico's economy overnight when the value of the peso fell from three Mexican pesos to ten U.S. dollars (10:1) to a low of 3:1. Wages declined by 21 percent. All parts of Mexico's population felt the impact of the meltdown. Investors pulled out of the country at the rate of 1.5 billion dollars per day. This started the northward flow of a half million people crossing into the United States in search of opportunities they would not find in Mexico. Approximately 3 million NAFTA refugees settled in the United States between 1995 and 1999 (Geniesse, 2010, 66–67, 69).

With the onset of NAFTA, came changes on the migrant trail. The flow of NAFTA refugees created a market for migrant trade. By the year 2000, 3,000 migrants traveling from Honduras, El Salvador, and Mexico, passed through the border town of Alta each day. Many undocumented people were smuggled in by "coyotes," profiteers baiting vulnerable migrants to work in the United States. For every 300 people intercepted by Border Patrol, 1,000 others successfully made it over the border into the perils of the Sonoran Desert. The Sonoran Desert claimed 5,000 lives in the past fifteen years. As Bishop Armando Ochoa of El Paso, Texas, preached, thousands of people who died along the 2,000-mile U.S.–Mexico border were poor people trying to provide for their families and achieve human dignity (Geniesse, 2010, 127–128).

DISPROVING THE THEORY THAT MIGRANTS COMMIT MORE CRIME

The present era of mass incarceration in the United States has coincided with the flow of mass migration (Portes & Rumbaut, 2006, 194). According to Portes and Rumbaut, a criminologist had predicted higher crime and incarceration rates among young adult males from minority groups who had lower levels of education (Portes & Rumbaut, 2006, 195). He had argued that the longer poor labor migrants and refugees lived in the United States, the higher the rate of incarceration because second-generation migrants were more susceptible to encounters with the criminal justice system. Although he argued that Americanization led to criminalization (Portes & Rumbaut, 2006, 194–195, 197), his theory was disproven by the Wisconsin Department of Corrections' (DOC) "Profile of Inmates in Prison" (2017) that reported that white and Black groups, not immigrants, comprised the most incarcerated groups (Wis. Dept. of Corrections, 2017, 2).

The reality is that our prisons are populated with more Black minorities. The DOC's "Profile of Inmates in Prison" (2017), data support Pettit and Western's theory that it is more likely for a Black male to have a criminal record than a military record or bachelor's degree (Portes & Rumbaut, 2006, 194–195, 197). Furthermore, statistics do not clearly indicate more incarcerated people from among minority groups which have migrated here from Asia, El Salvador, Honduras, and Mexico. Page two of the DOC's "Profile of Inmates in Prison" reports that the racial statistics of inmates is as follows: 9 percent male Hispanic and Latinos, and 3 percent female Hispanic and Latinos, 1 percent Asian males, 1 percent Asian females, 52 percent white males and 70 percent white females, 43 percent Black males, and 21 percent Black females, and American Indian/Alaskan Native 4 percent males and 8 percent females. The most recent data does not identify the Asian and Hispanic/Latino groups which migrate here nor does it show whether incarcerated Asians and Latinos are migrants or native-born. It does disprove the predictions of the criminologist who claimed that there would be more minorities incarcerated.

In fact, statistics from the past decade have shown that migrants do not commit more crime. In a 2018 study conducted by the Cato Institute, Nowrasteh (2018) collected data for sex crimes, homicide, larceny, and other criminal convictions and concluded that the rate of convictions of illegal immigrants in Texas was significantly less than that of native-born people.

In fact, in all criminal convictions in Texas in 2015, illegal immigrants had a rate of criminal convictions 50 percent lower than the native-born. Such data has confirmed that those who have migrated here have not become the criminals that media and some politicians have portrayed them to be.

EFFORTS TO IMPROVE MIGRANTS' SOCIOECONOMICS CONDITIONS

The Power of Congregation Community Organizing

ESTHER has effectively served the community through the power of congregations' community organizing. The interfaith harmony allows people of all religions to come together and contribute efforts which create more equitable communities. Jacobson explains that through collaboration and partnerships, community organizing by congregations encourages a "self-becoming process" that he describes as a journey of self-discovery which never arrives since it is always becoming (Jacobson, 2001, 57). Since individuals are obviously different, Jacobson says that one should respect the precise diversity of self-interest because it is critical to the deepening of growth and the continual unfolding of the self (Jacobson, 2001, 57). The vision must be realized through community organizing (Jacobson, 2001, 81). Using Milwaukee Intercity Congregations Allied for Hope (MICAH) as an example, he explains that their efforts established positive change within the Immigration and Naturalization Service (INS) offices in Milwaukee, Wisconsin. The success of community organizing prompted the INS to extend their business hours, hire bilingual staff, and establish a more efficient system to access information for immigrants seeking citizenship (Jacobson, 2001, 29).

Such community organizing has advanced progress to increase statewide funding for fifty-one additional SAGE schools in the Milwaukee Public School system (Jacobson, 2001, 30). The SAGE program reduces student teacher classroom ratio to 15:1 to allow more time for teachers to work independently with each student and diversify their instruction to deliver the appropriate level of challenge to the students (Jacobson, 2001, 30). This program is expected to help refugee students who have a language barrier and allow teachers to serve them more effectively in a diversified classroom.

ESTHER: Support for People Who Are Undocumented or Seeking Asylum

ESTHER demonstrates the shared value of commitment in providing support while assisting the needs of immigrants. ESTHER aims to identify what services are not being provided to migrants in the community. The members of ESTHER have worked with different departments within the Fox Valley community to advocate for fairness and equal access to resources within the community. They help navigate the systemic barriers that plague immigrants every day. They urge policy makers to maintain programs or create programs which serve people who are undocumented or seeking asylum. The members of ESTHER recognize the value of migrants in the Fox Valley community and advocate the importance of helping them cope during assimilation. For example, ESTHER also partners with World Relief in the Fox Valley area to help undocumented labor migrants and people fleeing the persecution of their governments. ESTHER also works with farmers in the community to urge them support policy changes to empower immigrants and improve working conditions.

A unique and special quality shared by the members of ESTHER is the mutual dedication to helping others. Although the organization does not provide translation and transportation services, the cohesive relationships weave a net of support that offers assistance within the community. Those who are not involved directly in policy change help with donations, they volunteer, and they organize events and provide empathy and support.

Migrant families experience continual challenges related to securing suitable housing within the Fox Valley area and understanding the terms of the rental agreement. Hiscocks (2019) shows that many people within the community experience problems with their housing contracts. She receives calls and provides support to individuals who are threatened with court action because, with limited language skills, they do not understand the renewal terms of the lease agreement and give verbal notice rather than a written notice as specified in the lease. Renters who do not understand the terms of the lease agreement are at risk of a lawsuit. Landlords often win large judgments in court for compensation for the time the unit was not occupied by the tenant. Such legal action puts people in poverty and makes it very difficult for them to find future housing. Some landlords may take advantage of people by demanding they pay money or go to court (Hiscocks, 2019). Some tenants have had their asylum status approved and are not afraid to go to court; however, many other people who do not have their status approved may pay the additional money while under duress and out of fear of deportation (Hiscocks, 2019).

Restoring Driver's Licenses to Residents Who Are Undocumented

Migrants and refugees in the Fox Valley are required to travel to appointments with immigration officials in Milwaukee or Chicago and must also attend local appointments. Yet public transportation in small cities and rural areas in Wisconsin is very limited. Before the events of 9/11 the undocumented could apply for driver's licenses. However, since Real ID went into effect in 2003, they no longer can legally acquire a driver's license. As a result, to help immigrants comply with state and federal regulations members of the Immigration Task Force volunteer to drive people to appointments. But this is no long-term solution to this problem. It also causes immigrants and asylum seekers to become marginalized and dependent on the good will of others rather than fostering the self-reliance so necessary for cultural assimilation. Furthermore, without drivers' licenses, their job opportunities are severely limited. In desperation, some people resort to driving without proper instruction and without a license. If they commit traffic violations, they may put their immigration status at risk and have to pay costly fines that further impoverish them. To improve their mobility, enable them to fulfill their obligations to keep appointments far from their homes, improve community health, and help to assure safe driving throughout the state, ESTHER is committed to working with state legislators to restore drivers' licenses and push for other policy changes. ESTHER argues that the state should acknowledge that by permitting immigrants to access drivers' licenses, more people will be certified to drive safely and then can contribute to the local economy by purchasing automobiles and paying the required taxes. More drivers would guarantee more revenue for insurance companies and local businesses. In fact, ESTHER has found that many representatives and sheriff's departments are in favor of restoring driver's cards to make roads safer and reduce number of uninsured drivers. Unfortunately, a recent resolution to license undocumented immigrants was dropped from the state budget. To benefit both individuals and communities, ESTHER will continue to push to restore drivers' licenses

Sanctuary Congregation

Sanctuary spaces are historically known as places established by moral duty to protect the vulnerable. Sanctuary offers protection from political reprisal and allows the individual time to seek alternatives. In addition, the Deferred Action for Childhood Arrivals program (DACA) allows undocumented individuals who came into the United States as children to apply for deferment of their immigration status if they were under the age of thirty-one on or before July 2015 when they arrived. Under this program, they may work for two years with the option to renew their status. About 700,000 people came to the United States undocumented and obtained temporary relief from deportation under DACA; however, such programs are subject to arbitrary change or elimination. For example, the Trump administration continually threatened to repeal DACA and again increased the need for sanctuary programs.

ESTHER has supported the initiative of the Fox Valley Unitarian Universalist Fellowship (FVUUF) in establishing themselves as a sanctuary congregation to better serve the refugee community in the Fox Valley area. After an advocate for local migrants explained the need for a sanctuary congregation in the community in the Spring of 2018, ESTHER and the FVUUF sanctuary congregation established the goal of providing sanctuary to individuals who are undocumented or seeking asylum.

The Fellowship began efforts to establish themselves as a sanctuary congregation. The FVUUF had previously engaged in immigration justice work as a sanctuary congregation by providing sanctuary to a Salvadoran couple seeking asylum in the late 1980s. The couple required assistance while waiting for asylum to be granted from either the United States or Canada. When Canada did grant the couple asylum status, the FVUUF assisted the couple with transportation to Canada. This kind of support during the immigration process is very critical to coping with the psychological stress of complying with federal expectations while lacking adequate transportation or money to finance transportation to avoid deportation. The church continues to offer this support and live the values of friendship and love within the church and across the community (Anonymous, personal communication, 2019).

The transition to becoming a sanctuary congregation requires a vote among the congregation. To understand how to provide effective support for immigrants and to educate the congregation, the sanctuary committee researched other sanctuary congregations to learn more about the process and possible implications. Legal representation during this process is critical but legal fees may be prohibitive. Through partnerships and collaborative efforts, ESTHER secured those very welcome services to begin to establish a sanctuary congregation. As part of the process, it was necessary to educate the members about the need for this program and the responsibilities of commitment. As a result of outreach efforts, hosting social events and engaging in many conversations, the members of the congregation become more aware of discrimination and the need to take a personal role to actively reverse it. In time, they voted nearly unanimously to become a sanctuary site.

There has been a great amount of member support to install the sanctuary space inside the church, donate needed items, and volunteer. The congregation sends the message that they welcome the stranger into the house of worship. The church recognizes that immigrants require support coping with the constraints of unjust policies as well as the challenges of getting to and from appointments, living on little income, and struggling with English. Furthermore, they understand that the people migrating here may also be coping with the trauma of their journey (Anonymous, personal communication, 2019). The people who seek asylum have had a dangerous and treacherous journey during which they were probably abused, abandoned, and deprived of food and water. Some lost shoes and were forced to walk barefoot the rest of the way across hot sand and stone. They grieve the families they have left behind and worry about uncertain futures. The reality is that thousands of people risk death crossing the Sonoran Desert in search of refuge. The sanctuary church welcomes the stranger and puts into practice the belief that all people should be cared for (Anonymous, personal communication, 2019).

The church can provide sanctuary for an individual at risk of deportation, and the congregation is also willing to provide volunteer support around the clock, every day. In the shelter, the immigrant has access to a kitchen, and volunteers will also provide food and prepare meals. There is a shower and bathroom as well as a recreational space with a fireplace and a sleeping area. Another welcoming touch is a beautiful, hand-crafted purple quilt donated by a local Quaker group (Anonymous, personal communication, 2019).

The fellowship recognizes the religious freedom of others and offers sanctuary without obligation to convert to another belief system. The sanctuary congregation encourages asylum seekers to worship and pray in their own religion. They encourage the immigrants' religious leaders to visit. It is the goal to create a space which allows them to live and thrive during a difficult time (Anonymous, personal communication, 2019).

WALK IN THEIR SHOES: UNDERSTANDING THE LATINO EXPERIENCE

An event sponsored by ESTHER is called "Walk in Their Shoes: Understanding the Latino Experience." This is very interactive, two-hour simulation to increase participants' awareness of the daily struggles of Latino migrants. Participants encounter the obstacles associated with school, employment, possible deportation, language, and prejudice. The experience allows participants to share their own personal reflections and communicate openly.

ESTHER's Board of Directors represents members of ESTHER who join as individuals rather than as congregations (Haas, 2019). Haas describes his experience participating and volunteering for "Walk in Their Shoes" as very eye-opening experience that deepens the understanding of real-life struggles associated with assimilation. The workshop simulates a four- day period in which each fifteen-minute session represents one day. The participants are assigned a life status and then must move through the given situations according to the imposed limitations found within the systemic barriers of U.S. policy. For example, as participants move through their assigned circumstances, they are presented with problems which bring uncertainty and frustration. For example, if their child must be enrolled in school, they must consider the obstacles such as transportation and not having a driver's license or access to public transportation. They must consider the challenges associated with language barriers and then find a translator to help them to understand the requirements of enrolling in school. Volunteers roleplay workers within community departments who act out the challenges related to each circumstance facing migrants including court hearings, medical appointments, employment, and housing. Once participants are aware of their circumstances and the limitations associated with their status, they must then solve the problems of providing for the basic needs for themselves and their families (D. Haas, personal communication, 2019).

VOICES OF HOPE

ESTHER also hosts events to educate communities and develop empathy by spreading awareness. "Voices of Hope" is a readers' theater program that uses music and stories to raise awareness about the struggles of migrants living in the Fox Valley. Three speakers share their stories about being smuggled into the United States.

One shows the historical moment and captures a point in time when people came to work in the fields and were sent back to their countries at the end of the season (Haas, 2019). "Deportees," the song by Woody Guthrie, is performed to capture what it was like to be a labor migrant (Haas, 2019). He sings,

> You won't have your names when you ride the big airplane. All they will call you will be deportees. The sky plane caught fire over Los Gatos Canyon, a fireball of lightning, and shook all our hills. Who are all these friends, all scattered like dry leaves? The radio says, they are just deportees.

Haas highlights the loss of those lives and emphasizes that all human life should be valued. Guthrie shows that the people who migrated here for employment were desperate and that society must start to wake up to their struggles. Through readers' theater, poetry, and song, events like "Voices of Hope" and "Walk in Their Shoes" reveal the realities immigrants face, they enhance understanding, generate empathy, and open debate about the consequences of government policies that affect immigrants and communities.

THE POWER OF PRAYER AND THE POWER OF CHOICE

During my experience with ESTHER, I have appreciated the interfaith quality of the organization which upholds human dignity and aims to ensure that all people have a voice. The welcoming and warm people confirm that all people have a place in our community. It is comforting to share prayer and celebrate diversity while recognizing that all people have their faith and should be free to choose their religious beliefs. In the Bible, Luke 6:31 says, "do unto others as you would want done to you," and Mathew 7:12 says, "in everything do unto others as you would have them do to you." In an ideal society living according to this philosophy, we would need no laws. The power of prayer would prepare us all to do God's will. We could live equitably and in harmony.

There is also a Cherokee Indian legend which illustrates the power of choice and describes the inner struggle between positive and negative thoughts, a battle believed to be inside of us all. The legend tells the story of a grandfather who sits silent on a hillside staring off into the horizon. His grandson comes to his side and asks him what he is doing. The grandfather explains to his grandson that he is watching the wolves. The grandson looks out across the landscape and sees no wolves and then asks the grandfather where he sees the wolves. The grandfather tells the boy the wolves are inside of him. The boy then asks what the wolves are doing, and the grandfather explains that they are fighting. The grandson wants to know why, and the grandfather tells him that there is a fight between two wolves inside us all. He continues to explain that one wolf represents evil, negativity, sorrow, resentment, self-pity, anger, arrogance, greed, regret, inferiority, lies, envy, superiority, hate, ego, guilt, and false pride. That wolf is mean and has no mercy. The other wolf is purity, honesty, positivity, generosity, serenity, peace, joy, humility, benevolence, compassion, hope, and faith. This wolf is loving, sensitive, and shows mercy. The boy sits with his grandfather and thinks about what he has heard and contemplates the fight between the wolves. Then he asks his grandfather, "Which one will win?" The grandfather looks to the boy and replies, "Whichever one you feed."

The future of our global health relies on each person shaping their desires to be like the pure and honest wolf who is full of joy and hope, the wolf who shows love and mercy. There is power in this choice. What we decide to do with that power is the true measure of a person's character. In the Cherokee legend as in the Bible, we recognize the power of individual choices to do to others as we would want them to do to us. As a collective behavior, each of us can choose to feed the pure and honest wolf. Then honesty and compassion survive throughout the community.

CONCLUSION

The members of ESTHER share the philosophy that all people should be treated fairly and with dignity. They believe that each person should treat others with equity and take responsibility for social justice. They identify injustice and speak out against oppression. They identify systemic barriers and help others to navigate them. They encourage everyone to be aware of actions, attitudes, and policies that discriminate and to actively work to reverse oppression. Working with ESTHER generates a positive flow of empathy and understanding because members naturally respond to challenges with optimism and a willingness to be readily available to act, or listen, and share insights. The members of ESTHER are not discouraged by struggle. They generate ideas and work together in solidarity with others. In this way, they identify ways to reverse oppression in everyone's personal lives, at workplaces, and within our communities. By modeling fairness and justice, they support immigrants and others who are seeking equity and inclusion while working for policy change. With knowledge based on facts, empathy based on understanding, and solidarity based on a shared purpose, they support refugees and asylees who have no time to wait for governments to decide their futures.

REFERENCES

Barbieur, Sister M. 2019. Personal communication. February 16, 2019.

Columbia University Mailman School of Public Health. 2019. "Forced Migration Learning Module." The Harriet and Robert Heilbrunn Department of Population and Family Health. May 11, 2019. Accessed April 20, 2019. http://www.columbia.edu/itc/hs/pubhealth/modules/forcedMigration/definitions.html

Fox Cities Regional Partnership. 2019. "Demographics of the Fox Cities Region – Power in Proximity." Accessed June 9, 2019. http://www.foxcitiesregion.com/demographics/

Geniesse, Peter A. 2010. *Illegal: NAFTA Refugees Forced to Flee.* Bloomington, IN: iUniverse.

Gordon, S. 2017. "Refugee Resettlement in Wisconsin by the Numbers: Where the States Refugees Come from and Where They Resettle." Accessed May 12, 2019. https://www.wiscontext.org/refugee-resettlement-wisconsin-numbers

Haas, D. 2019. Personal communication, June 20, 2019.

Hiscocks, F. 2019. Personal communication, June 19, 2019.

Jacobson, Dennis A. 2001. *Doing Justice: Congregations and Community Organizing.* Minneapolis, MN: Fortress Press.

Jerome, Harry. 2019. *Migration and business cycles.* SERBIULA (University of the Andes Library Service) (sistema Librum 2.0).

Migration Data Portal: The Bigger Picture. 2019. "Types of Migration, Forced Migration, or Displacement." Accessed May 12, 2019. https://migrationdataportal.org/theme/forced-migration-or-displacement

Nowraste, Alex. February 2018. "Criminal Immigrants in Texas: Illegal Immigrant Conviction and Arrest Rates for Homicide, Sex Crimes, Larceny, and Other Crimes." Cato Institute. Immigration and Research Policy Brief No. 4. Accessed May 12, 2019. https://www.cato.org/publications/immigration-research-policy-brief/criminal-immigrants-texas-illegal-immigrant

Performance Measurement Series. "Inmate Profile 2017." Wisconsin Department of Corrections. Accessed May 20, 2019. https://doc.wi.gov/DataResearch/DataAndReports/InmateProfile.pdf

Refugee Status Determination: Identifying Who Is a Refugee. Self-Study Module Two. United Nations High Commissioner for Refugees. Accessed May 12, 2019. https://www.unhcr.org/en-s/publications/legal/43144dc52/self-study-module-2-refugee-status-determination-identifying-refugee.html?query=refugee%20definition

Sawyer, S. and P. Wagner. 2018. Mass Incarceration: The Whole Pie. Accessed May 15, 2019. https:www.prisionpolicy.org

Selinsky, Sister M. 2019. Personal communication. February 16, 2019.

Van Lopik, W. 2019. Personal communication. May 23, 2019.

Wisconsin Department of Corrections. 2017. "Profile of Inmates in Prison."

Chapter 12

Migration and African Diasporic Living Conditions

Chibuzor Ayodele Nwaodike, Goodnews Osah, and Uduakobong Edy-Ewoh

INTRODUCTION

One of the most trending discourses in the social sciences in the contemporary era is the debate on African diaspora and the issue of migration which is complex and dynamic in nature. An average young person in Africa is frustrated due to bad governance and with the slightest opportunity would want to migrate to either Europe or America. In Nigeria, for instance, it is known as *japa* syndrome, meaning the exodus movement of Africans to Europe and America is believed to be influenced by many factors which include but are not limited to socioeconomic reasons and the quest for greener pastures. As of 2015, more than 16 million Africans had migrated to different countries (CSEA, 2022).

Historically, three notable epochs can be traced to African diasporic migration. The first was during the transatlantic slave trade between the sixteenth and nineteenth centuries. According to Segal (1995), Europeans captured about 12 million African slaves, mostly from West Africa, and transported them forcefully to Europe, South and North America. These Africans were captured from their native homes and subjected to inhuman treatments in plantations to boost economies of the metropole. As such, these Africans were dislodged from their place of birth and family members, as well as generational and symbolic ties. This era was considered the founding myth of African Diaspora in Europe and North America (Northwestern University Library, 2022). It is instructive to note that this era coincided with the period of colonization when the Industrial Revolution was also gaining momentum. The colonialists needed raw materials from Africa to sustain the industrialization.

The second phase of African Diaspora to Western Europe and America started from the 1950s, toward the end of colonization. The colonial masters and nationals of the colonies had strong economic, political, and social ties, which enabled Africans to willingly migrate to Europe and America in search of better working conditions and higher educational opportunities which were not readily available in African countries (Experience Africa, 2022).

The third and last phase of Africans in the diaspora started in the 1980s. At this time, the nature of migration of Africans to Europe and America changed in dimension. According to Omeje (2007), fleeing from broken and breakable states, wars, hopeless poverty, or political persecution became a major cause of emigration. It is worthy of note that this era constituted more of voluntary migration, however, involuntary migration including human trafficking constitutes a fraction but a significant trend in Africa's migration cannot be ruled out. The immigrants may relate and contribute to the well-being of their families in Africa most of them may tend not to have any plan to return home permanently, mostly because of the existing deplorable social and economic conditions. Basic infrastructures are not available which tend to make life hellish and using the worlds of Thomas Hobbes to be solitary, nasty, brutish, and short (Hobbes, 1668), which Donald Trump described as "shithole countries." The last two waves of migration mentioned above are known as contemporary diaspora (*Experience Africa*, 2022).

Africa is endowed with the richest concentration of resources such as natural gas, uranium, coal, gold, oil and gas, diamond, copper, bauxite, hardwood forests, lithium, and tropical fruits (Zahran, 2021). It is estimated that 30 percent of the earth's mineral resources are found in the African continent. Additionally, Africa has the world's biggest precious metal reserves on earth (WorldAtlast, 2022). There is hardly an African country without any deposit of natural resources. Paradoxically, the continent is rated as the poorest. In fact, in all definitions, Africa is poor, adrift, rural, and cannot compete with its counterparts in terms of human development index and human security (Ezebuilo, 2019).

Using the 2022 Human Development Index, thirty of the fifty-four countries in Africa were listed as least developed states. In these countries, infant mortality is high, life expectancy and education are low (UNDP, 2022). This situation has direct consequences on the living conditions of the people and may have necessitated voluntary migrations under discussion. It is upon this background that the chapter interrogated migration and African diasporic living conditions. The chapter is sub-grouped as follows: introduction, conceptualization of migration and diaspora, theoretical underpinnings using the push and pull theory, bases for African migration to the diaspora, living conditions of Africans in the diaspora, implications of African diasporic migration, and concluding remarks. The study leading to this chapter adopted the phenomenological design in qualitative studies to obtain the data on the lived experiences of African emigrants in the United Kingdom, United States, and Canada. Secondary sources of data were obtained from peer-reviewed articles, selected Immigration reports, government publications, newspapers, and the Internet. The data obtained were content analyzed and presented thematically.

CONCEPTUALIZING MIGRATION

Migration discourses have more than ever taken a center stage in policy circles not only in Africa but globally (Akokpari, 2000; Castles, 2011; McMahon and Sigona, 2021). Scholarly repertoires have been widely documented and analyzed about migration (Ahmed, Castañeda, Fortier and Sheller, 2020; Radel, Jokisch, Schmook, Carte, Aguilar-Støen, Hermans and Aldrich, 2019; Boyle and Keith, 2014; Gurak and Caces, 1992; Petersen, 1958) including Clements (2014) who queried if the development would reduce migration.

Contextualizing migration and expectations that have emerged throughout history, we trace the development to four models of migration that have been prevalent and which have been discussed extensively elsewhere (Cottier, Flahaux, Ribot, Seager and Sakdapolrak, 2022; Beyer, Schewe and Lotze-Campen, 2022; Freeman and Lewis, 2021; Adamson and Tsourapas, 2020). These models, according to Okolocha (2019), are the classical model (foreigners constitute the dominant population), colonial model (the former enclaves are favored immigrants policy of assimilation where Africans are assimilated as French citizens), the quest for workers model (foreign workers are freely admitted into a country on a temporary basis and may never become citizens in spite of the length of such stay), and illegal form of immigration (recent method as a result of migration into industrialized states). Accordingly, countries such as the United States, Canada, and Australia where foreigners constitute the dominant population are aptly referred to as nations of immigrants. In their contribution to migration discourse, Dun and Gemenne (2008) discussed the types of migration to include environmental migration, climate change-induced migration, ecological/environmental refugees, climate change migrants, and environmentally induced forced migrants.

Over generations, men have engaged in movements from one place to another in search of greener pastures. These movements are the courageous and prospective decisions by movers who take their destiny in their own hands to overcome poverty, disadvantage, and sundry adversities for a more fulfilling life, over long or short distances within or between countries, regions, or continents (Mou, Griffiths, Fong and Dawes, 2015). In this regard, Shaw (1975) averred that migration is "the relatively permanent movement of persons over a significant distance." But, migration nowadays is defined as involving a change in place of abode, which criterion has practically replaced the notion of "permanence."

For Africans, migration evokes the image of bolting away from one's own home. The Centre for the Study of the Economies of Africa (2022) noted that many Africans leave to go to other places within and outside the continent in what is seen as mass exodus. Of course, the slavery era witnessed a massive abduction of persons to other worlds for the main interest of developing the Western economies, which later metamorphosed to what Akinyemi (2022) calls the "diasporan syndrome" or what in Nigerian parlance is called "*Japa.*" This syndrome was predicted by the former president of Libya, Muammar Ghadaffi, who had warned Western leaders that he was the one who used Libya to keep refugees from flocking into Europe and that if he was overthrown, Europe would not be able to cope with the influx of refugees who would use Libya as the gateway into Europe. For various reasons, particularly but not exclusively economic, individuals, families, or other groups are involved in migration.

According to the 2020 UN International Migration Highlights, two-thirds of all international migrants live in twenty countries, of which the United States hosts the largest destination with over 51 million international migrants, followed by Germany with around 16 million and Saudi Arabia with 13 million, the Russian Federation records 12 million, and the United Kingdom 9 million. The report further revealed that growth in the number of international migrants has increased exponentially particularly after the opening of borders post-Covid-19 with the number reaching a record high of over 281 million people living outside their country of origin.

Migration of Africans to other regions has become not only dynamic but complex, mostly driven by economic and involuntary allusions (CSEA, 2022). The Africa Center for Strategic Studies (2021) reported that the push–pull forces driving African migration continue to intensify, portending expanding African migration within and off the continent, and that the number of documented migrants within and from the African region has nearly doubled since 2010 with Europe as the most pronounced destination. The CSEA Africa (2022) reports a similar figure. CSEA stated that increasingly, a large number of people leave sub-Saharan Africa (SSA) for economic reasons including a search for better jobs and opportunities. They migrate with the view that life is easier across the borders, which in reality is more demanding.

Available statistics provided by the Africa Center for Strategic Studies (2021) is that three North African countries namely Morocco, Algeria, and Tunisia accounted for between 5 and 11 million African migrants in Europe in 2021. Of course, the location of the three countries underscores the importance of proximity and the quest for diasporic economic opportunities. According to the UNDP (2010), migration may be the movement within or across borders, voluntary (e.g., for work, study, or family reasons) or forced (as a result of conflict or natural disasters), regular (with documentation) or irregular (without documentation), and temporary, seasonal or longer term (permanent).

PLACING EMPHASIS ON THE DIASPORA

One field of emphasis linked to the postcolonial studies since the 1970s and highly on the front burner is the diasporic discourse and particularly of the African diaspora (McLeod, 2020; Hall, 2015; Ashcroft, Griffiths and Tiffin, 2007; Chariandy, 2006). A plethora of definitions and explanations exist in the extant literature. Grossman (2019) posited that the deliberation includes dispersal or immigration, location outside a homeland, community, orientation to a homeland, transnationalism, and group identity.

Providing a definition, Falola (2018: 14) argued that diaspora refers to the movement of Africans to other continents beginning from the slave trade. He also noted that diaspora can also have many meanings as a historical event, a cultural idea, a metaphor, a pilgrimage, economic change, apolitical agenda, an intercultural concern, and a new identity.

Consequently, due to the extensive movement of Africans, a diaspora was formed which continued to view Africa as the homeland, allowing for a unity which allowed the construction of a Black identity. He enunciated that the politics of this diaspora is Pan-Africanism and centers on socialism with an emphasis on demanding political rights for Blacks. Of course, the notion of Pan-Africanism was historically expanded in several political and cultural movements across Africa (Sherwood, 2012; Katembo, 2008; Walters, 1997). Though without a uniform standard, diaspora is still united by blackness, historical experiences and turmoil, cultural remnants of Africa, and the incongruity of opinions about Africa from the European and African perspectives. Significantly, it highlights the importance of the movement of cultural ideas from Africans to other civilizations and vice versa. Braziel and Mannur (2003) challenged that by adding diaspora as specific subset of transnational movements between nation-state, that transnationalism should include the movement of information, goods, production, and capital across state borders.

Etymologically, Ashcroft, Griffiths, and Tiffin (2007) trace the diasporic concept to a Greek word *dia speiro*, rendered as "'to disperse,' the voluntary or forcible movement of peoples from their homelands into new regions" and originally concerned with "Jews living outside Israel" or what the Oxford Dictionary (2012) says is "the dispersion of the Jews beyond Israel." Tololyan (1991) explained that the concept of diaspora was provisionally used to indicate belief that described Jewish, Greek, and Armenian dispersion. Diaspora is also linked and shares meanings with a host of other words like immigrant, expatriate, refugee, guest-worker, exile community, overseas community, ethnic community. By linking the diaspora to Africa, Tavanti, Abdi and MacHarg (2016); Brubaker (2005) and Alpers (2001) noted that the African diaspora is the voluntary and involuntary movement of Africans and their descendants to various parts of the world during the modern and pre-modern periods.

REVISITING THE PUSH AND PULL THEORY OF MIGRATION

One of the major proponents of push and pull theory in migration studies was an American, researcher Everett S. Lee. He came up with a systematic theory of population migration known as push and pull theory in 1960s. Lee (1966) summarized the factors instigating migration into four. These are a place to move in, a place to move out, intermediate obstacles, and personal factors.

According to the theory, a combination of socioeconomic conditions necessitated the migration of people from one location to another. Therefore, the reasons that have led migrants to move is to improve their living conditions in the inflow areas have become the pull force of the floating populace, and the unfavorable socioeconomic conditions of the outflow areas have become the thrust of the floating migrants (Pan, 2019).

In relation to international migration as observed in the African diaspora, push factors are reasons that incite Africans to leave their home countries, while the pull factors are reasons that attract migrants to a particular country. The European University Institute (2022) observed that push factors include armed conflict, natural disaster, lack of job opportunities, the possession of economic and cultural capital, a fairly break up or dissatisfaction with an individual's life and surroundings. These are assumed to be prevalent in the case of African migration. On the other hand, pull factors are said to be determined by greater security, better job opportunities, or the prospect of a more exciting life. These are presumed to be prevalent in advanced countries notably Europe and America.

WHY AFRICANS ARE LEAVING

In recent years, tens of thousands of Africans continue to migrate to Europe and North America, and this seems only set to increase as current mobility trends emanating from national border posts demonstrate. From Nigeria, Senegal, Ghana, Egypt, Morocco, Mali, and other African countries, young people continue to migrate to other nations outside the continent. Some of these movements are most times undertaken in small boats in the case of Europe for weeks of which uncountable number have died in the process (Kuschminder, Bresser and Siegel, 2015).

While several reasons are advanced for the mass exodus including economic obstacles to reaching social adulthood, notions of masculinity, pride and honor, and religion (Hernández-Carretero and Carling, 2012), Achieng and El Fadil (2020) and (Fuankem, 2020) noted that the primarily precipitating factors are conflict, repressive governance, and limited economic opportunities. Unfortunately, nine of the top fifteen African countries of origin for migrants are in conflict (IOM, 2021).

Aside conflict, Connell, Zurn, Stilwell, Awases, and Braichet (2007) informed that one group that has significantly migrated are the skilled health workers, especially from the SSA, the inability to invest adequately in health systems and professional health education, the rising death toll from HIV/AIDS and international migration of health professionals are all major factors contributing to the ongoing health workforce crisis. Similarly, Luck, Fernandes and Ferrinho, 2000) also cited low wages, few incentives, or poor working conditions. Poor promotion possibilities, inadequate management support, heavy workloads, limited access to good technology and even to medicines have all been regularly cited as "push factors"—motivating health workers for example to leave their country of origin (Bach, 2003). These factors have accelerated recruitment from developed countries, where populations are aging, expectations of healthcare increasing, recruitment of health workers (especially nurses) is poor and attrition considerable, have intensified this crisis, raising complex ethical, financial and health questions (WHO, 2006). To corroborate the exodus of medical workers, statistics from Nigeria in October 2022 by the Nigeria Medical Association show that over 10,200 doctors abandoned Nigeria and are now practicing in the United Kingdom alone.

The African migration trends to watch in 2022 by the Africa Center for Strategic Studies (2021) revealed that African migrants in or heading toward Europe were previously either employed or in school at the time of their departure, but they left because they felt despair over their economic prospects. The report says that Tunisians fleeing economic pressures comprised more than a quarter of the irregular migrants intercepted crossing the Mediterranean to Italy in 2021.

LIVING CONDITIONS OF AFRICANS IN THE DIASPORA

It would appear that policy makers across the world are becoming increasingly interested in issues bordering on the living conditions of their citizens.

The concern is to address the fundamental needs of households that are critical to the safety and general well-being of citizens. Governments are concerned on programs, policies, and system changes that must be pursued and enacted to ensure quality of living, improved outcomes relative to households' health and well-being, and elimination of disparities in standards of living across different domestic populations. Good living circumstances are a must for a good existence.

The Handbook of Research on International Collaboration refers to living conditions as the availability of fundamental necessities such as food and water, as well as an establishment of objects of sociocultural value for a qualitative existence, independent of geographical affiliation (Erokhin and Gao, 2018). Living conditions, however, have also been described as the situations or factors that have an impact on how individuals live, particularly with regard to their well-being (Eurofound, 2022). Intuitively, living conditions include factors that influence people's daily lives, which frequently have an impact on their health, and a growing body of research supports this notion.

In assessing the living conditions of African migrants in the diaspora, consideration may also be given to their quality of live and their standard of living. While quality of life refers to an individual's experience of his or her own life as well as the living conditions in which people find themselves. It includes the way a person views their place in the world in respect to their objectives, standards, and concerns, as well as the culture and value systems they adhere to (WHO, 2012). On the other hand, standard of living refers to the degree of conveniences, facilities, and services that are available to a community or region as a whole, as opposed to simply one individual. The unifying force of the three concepts is the socioeconomic status of a people which is influenced by a variety of social and economic variables, including money, the level of education, the type and status of the job, the location of residence, and—in certain countries or portions of society—ethnic origin or religious background.

Dahlgren and Whitehead (1991) in their study identified and described the different factors which influence the health of the individuals. Although lifestyle decisions including diet, exercise, alcohol use, and smoking were thought to be the primary determinants of an individual's health, living conditions were also crucial. However, the primary distinction between a person's living conditions and lifestyle is which of these things they have influence over. Using a model, Dahlgren and Whitehead (1991) illustrated that most determinants of living conditions were circumstantial and often outside the influence of individuals. The determinants of living conditions included access to health care and education, quality housing, clean water, sanitation, and social protection. It is obvious from these factors that living conditions are premised on households' socioeconomic status. Public authorities have often been identified with the responsibility of improving living conditions for the disadvantaged population by providing easy access to affordable public services.

Africa is largely characterized by high emigration to developed Organization for Economic Cooperation and Development (OECD) countries. According to the OECD (2015), the highly skilled emigration rate from Africa—especially West and East Africa—is among the highest in the world. Considering the quest for better living conditions with emphasis on the determinants of living conditions proposed by Dahlgren and Whitehead (1991) we discuss the living conditions of Africans in the United Kingdom, United States, and Canada. While an important area of discourse, it would appear that very few studies have been conducted on living conditions of Africans in diaspora is adequately recognized and understood. Hence, all the determinants were not covered as literature was not readily available on education, health care, and, in some instances, housing.

The majority of Africans desire to emigrate to places with higher standards of living. This is often far from the reality as the Social Metrics Commission (2021) reported that almost half of people living in a family in the United Kingdom where the head of the household is Black are in poverty.

Considering housing, one of the basic determinants of living conditions, the households with the highest rates of overcrowding had Black African households (16 percent) at third position after Bangladeshi (24 percent) and Pakistani (18 percent) (GOV.UK, 2022). Overcrowded household have fewer bedrooms than it needs to avoid undesirable sharing, based on the age, sex, and relationship of household members.

Black and Minority Ethnic persons who seek mental health services are treated differently, and problems with access to care, coercive approaches, and poor experiences with care have all been well-documented (Browne, 2013). Corroborating this study, Watkinson, Sutton, and Turner (2021) found that compared to the white British group, ethnic minorities were found to have lower patient confidence in managing their own health, higher rates of long-term conditions or multimorbidity, poorer primary care experiences, inadequate support from local services, and higher levels of area social deprivation. It is however a myth to assume that all Africans in the United Kingdom are in penury.

With regard to the determinants of living conditions of Africans in the United States, Black immigrants stand out in terms of various socioeconomic indicators, such as household income and educational attainment. For instance, Black immigrants who are twenty-five years of age and older have a higher percentage of college degrees. According to a previous study by the U.S. Census Bureau (2014), the high levels of educational attainment among Africans were in part caused by the big number of educated Africans who made the decision to emigrate, as well as by the significant number who came to the country to pursue academic courses. The chapter went on to explain how educational achievement differed among Africans depending on where they were born. For instance, 64 percent of Egyptian-born people, 61 percent of Nigerians, 57 percent of South Africans, 47 percent of Kenyans, and 35 percent of Ghanaians were graduates.

Comparatively, African immigrants have been the main engine for most of the general recent expansion in the Black immigrant population, contributing to a significant percentage to national output. Families headed by Black migrants were also noted as having a high median houschold income in 2019 ($57,200). In terms of population growth, Black African immigrants increased in number by 246 percent between 2000 and 2019, going from 600,000 to 2.0 million. As a result, the percentage of Black individuals who were born abroad has increased significantly from 2000, when it was just 23 percent, to 42 percent as noted by Tamir and Anderson (2022). According to Echeverria-Estrada and Batalova (2019), in 2017, Africans and sub-Saharan Africans in particular were far more likely to work in management, business, science, and the arts than in the natural resources, construction, and maintenance industries.

An article by the New American Economy (2018) however presented a divergent view by noting that compared to the general U.S. population, Africans have greater levels of education and are more likely to have degrees in STEM fields (Science, Technology, Engineering, and Math).

Though current socioeconomic factors appear to indicate that Africans are doing well comparatively in the United States, the AAQL (2008) report had noted that African Americans trailed other ethnic groups in many socioeconomic areas. In 2012, Matthews et al. (2012) reported key racial differences in access to health care between white Americans and the Black immigrants. The Affordable Care Act however provided opportunity for millions of people, particularly African Americans specifically to have access to health insurance coverage. In 2017, sub-Saharan Africans were about as likely to be covered by private health insurance as the overall foreign-born population, and slightly less likely to be uninsured. More recently however, President Biden has also made Americans' access to health care a priority for his administration. On January 27, 2022, statement, he stated that "Health care should be a right, not a privilege, for all Americans (both black and white. . . . " Biden's focus on racial equity in health, and specifically Black health and wellness, was highlighted in the Foreign Press Center briefings of April 08, 2022 (US Departments of States, 2022).

According to a 2012 US Census Bureau analysis, the home value disparity between Blacks and whites has grown over time. Tesfai (2016) noted that Black home ownership rates in the United States have remained 25 percent lower than those of whites since the 1990s while examining whether Black immigrants are disadvantaged due to racial stratification or are able to leverage human or ethnic capital into favorable housing market outcomes.

The Canadian Encyclopedia noted that numerous Black individuals departed Canada, in part due to the unfavorable living circumstances. Those who remained encountered challenges due to weak agricultural prospects and harsh winters which worsened their enslaving poverty. In addition, fierce competition from a large white labor pool ensured that Black people stayed in low-paying occupations. However, with the help of the church-groomy distinctive character and a strong sense of group identification, Black Canadians were able to create a close-knit community that served as a haven from white prejudice.

Though the education of Africans in Canada suffered from unequal access to resources during the nineteenth century, the tide has changed as Africans in Canada have a somewhat higher percentage of university graduates than the general population. In 2001, 19 percent of African adults (fifteen and older) had graduated from college, compared to 15 percent of the adult population. In 2016, there were 27.5 percent of women and 27.7 percent of males in Africa who had a bachelor's degree or higher from a university (Statistics Canada, 2007, 2016).

According to Statistics Canada (2007), Canadians of African heritage are more likely to be jobless. Africans made up 13.1 percent of the labor force in 2001, compared to the overall labor force of 7.4 percent unemployment rate. In 2001, there were 21 percent more male African labor market participants aged fifteen to twenty-four who were jobless than there were male Canadians in this age group (14 percent) overall. At the same time, 13 percent of all females in this age group were jobless, compared to 20 percent of African women in the labor market who were between the ages of fifteen and twenty-four. This pattern continued through 2016, when Africans aged twenty-five to fifty-nine had a lower employment rate than the general population. In 2016, Black men and women had employment rates of 78.1 percent and 71.0 percent, respectively, compared to 82.6 percent and 75.5 percent for the rest of the population (Oreopoulous, 2011, Census of Population, 2016; Houle, 2020). Additionally, according to statistics from the 2016 General Social Survey, African workers aged fifteen or older reported experiencing unfair treatment or discrimination at work more frequently than their peers in the rest of the population did. At the same time, 85 percent of Black women and 90 percent of Black males in the population said they were very satisfied with their jobs.

From further data, African Canadians are more than twice as likely to have poor salaries as the general population as compared to their white counterparts. Additionally, the salaries of Africans in Canada are often lower than those of the overall population. People who identified as being of African ethnic origins aged fifteen and over had an average annual income from all sources of just under $24,000 in 2000, which was about $6,000 less than the national average. Black males continue to earn less than their peers in the rest of the population on average, according to Statistics Canada (2021). Compared to other ethnic groups in Canada, more Africans live in poverty. Compared to 12 percent of their counterparts in the rest of the population, 21 percent of Black people aged twenty-five to fifty-nine in 2016 lived in a low-income scenario. Living in a couple with children (34 percent) was the most prevalent condition for the Black population in terms of household living arrangements, a finding that is comparable to what is seen in the rest of the population. But compared to the general population, the percentage of Black people who lived in lone-parent families was at least twice as high (19 percent vs. 8 percent). Nearly 70 percent of these lone parents in the Black community were female (Statistics Canada, 2019, 2020).

In relation to housing, most Africans in Canada reside in subpar housing. African renters also frequently face landlord prejudice, which makes finding a sufficient home difficult. Additionally, African tenants may be discouraged from renting by being refused a rental or facing financial hardship in Canada (Government of Canada, 2020).

IMPLICATIONS OF AFRICAN DIASPORIC MIGRATION

Europe is a top destination for African diasporic migration. For instance, IOM (2020) noted that in 2019, 26.9 percent (i.e., 10.6 million) of the total 39.4 million African migrants worldwide lived in Europe, followed by Asia (4.6 million) and North America (3.2 million) (IOM, 2020). It must be stated that in spite of the exodus movement of Africans in diaspora, there are costs and benefits derivable in the migration. In some instances, it has been a blessing in disguise for those seeking greener pastures and economic stability, and they have been able to sustain their immediate and extended families and by extension African states. While, on the other hand, the reverse is the case and Africa has been on the receiving end.

One of the benefits of diasporic migration is remittances which have contributed to marginal development of African states. Remittances to the developing states, particularly in Africa were reported to be more than foreign aid in 2003 to the sum of $100 billion (Wucker, 2004). Oxford University (2022) defined remittances as transfers of money from residents of one country to residents of another country and are often associated with migrants sending money to families and communities. While Bank for International Settlements and World Bank (2007) revealed that remittances are cross-border person-to-person payments of relatively low value. For a sender, the average amount of their earnings that are remitted is around 15 percent, which implies that most of their funds remain in the host country (Ponsot et al., 2017). Though remittances take many forms, including social and political, undoubtedly, financial remittances have the most important role to play in helping reduce poverty (Adams and Page, 2005). It must be noted that most African migrants in the diaspora have consistently sent money to their families, friends, local community, personal investment for savings, and different requests for daily expenditures.

They bring longer term benefits for the recipients and their communities which are used for medical bills and tuition fees (Amega, 2018). In other instances, such remittances as well are used in setting up business investments and building houses. Migrants in the United Kingdom for instance send money home using several channels. These channels include family and friends returning home, money transfers operators such as Western Union and MoneyGram, banks, and informal hawala brokers (House of Commons, 2004).

These aforementioned channels were used in 2018 for financial inflows to Africa to a sum of USD 81 billion and the main remittance recipient countries in Africa are Nigeria and Egypt that accounted for over 50 percent of the total cash inflow. Other significant receivers include Algeria, Ghana, Morocco, and Senegal (World Bank, 2018). The majority of funds that are sent to Africa originate from migrants in France, Germany, Italy, Spain, the United Kingdom, and North America (Natali and Isaacs, 2020).

It is also instructive to note that certain developmental gains are achieved when some of the migrants return to Africa, either permanently or on a temporary bases; there is every indication that they bring with them new technologies, skills, trade, investment, and social norms (European Commission, 2011). Though it has also been observed that the rates of return of migrants are however low, as Ratha et al. (2011) observed out of the total number of international migrants, only 3 percent in Nigeria, 9 percent in Senegal, and 25 percent in Burkina Faso returned to their country of origin in the fifteen-year period after migration. The reason for not returning for the longer period is that for the most part of these years they have not found their feet and in some instances gotten their residency permit or green cards. As low as the returns may be, we cannot underestimate the value of the remittances in driving developmental gains. It is on record that remittances account for more than donor aids flow to Africa, and the migrants constitute the biggest group of foreign investors in Africa (Khan, 2003). In Eritrea, remittances account for 83 percent of exports, in Mali, payments from migrants account for 20 percent of gross national product, in Somalia, remittances were $500 million annually, in 1999, remittances from Egyptians abroad were estimated at

$2.959 billion, $1.772 billion for Moroccans, $1.198 billion for Nigerians, $696 million for Tunisians, and $607 million for Sudanese (Khan, 2003; Wucker, 2004; Adams, 2003). Most of the funds remitted through migrants in Europe and America were targeted for investment and business purposes; the adverse effect is the promotion of job creation and advancement of economic growth in Africa.

However, there are areas of concern which have not benefitted Africa in the migration to the diaspora. The evidence is the negative implications of the brain drain syndrome and diasporic migration of high-skilled talents. For example, Versi (2003) noted that an estimated 5 million African entrepreneurs and professionals are living in the diaspora; 40 percent of African professionals and higher level managers reside outside African states. While the United States Census Bureau (2000) noted that there were an estimated 881,300 African immigrants in the United States. The worst hit in African diasporic migration is health and medical sciences. For instance, Tankwanchi et al. (2013) observed that the number of sub-Saharan African physicians in the United States of America had increased by 38 percent between 2002 and 2011 and that more than half of this increase was accounted for by Nigerian doctors, although Liberia was the most affected as 77 percent of its estimated 226 physicians migrated to the United States.

In Nigeria, 10,296 medical doctors migrated to the United Kingdom from 2015 to 2021. Dispersion of the emigration data for Nigerian-trained doctors to the United Kingdom is as follows: 233 in 2015, 279 in 2016, 475 in 2017, 852 in 2018, 1,347 in 2019, 833 in 2020, and 932 in 2021(Hassan-Wuyo, 2022). According to statistics obtained from the United Kingdom Council's website, Nigeria has the highest number of African doctors in the United Kingdom, Egypt came second with 7,034 registered doctors, while South Africa has the third highest African representation with 5,166 registered medical doctors (Akinkuotu, Olokor, Adepegba and Ojerinde, 2022). In some instances, these medical practitioners from Africa are being exploited, used as slave labor, subjected to excessive working hours, and left vulnerable to a range of salary deductions (Adejoro, 2022). It is, therefore, important to note that the migration of high-trained individuals, especially in health sciences and other fields has affected African states with fiscal burdens in economic productivity and shortage of manpower in public service delivery.

CONCLUDING REMARKS

We have indicated in this chapter that the migration of Africans to the diaspora started in the era of transatlantic slave trade when Europeans captured

Africans from their native homes and transported them to the New World to work in plantations in an inhuman manner. The second phase was during colonization when colonial masters created strong political, economic, and social ties which enabled Africans to willingly migrate to Europe and America for education and better living conditions. The last phase was a result of political instability and bad governance that created unfavorable economic environment which led young people to voluntarily migrate for greener pastures. Regrettably, migration has subjected many African immigrants to unfavorable living conditions. This situation has also affected Africa's socioeconomic and political development, while Africa is at the receiving end, Europe and America are the major beneficiaries of diasporic migration.

REFERENCES

Adams, R. and Page, J. (2005). Do International Migration and Remittances Reduce Poverty in Developing Countries? *World Development*, 33(10), 1645–1669.

Adams, Jr., Richard, H. (2003). International Migration, Remittance and Brain Drain: A Study of 24 Labor-Exporting Countries. World Bank Policy Research Working Paper 3069, World Bank, Washington, DC, pp. 1–29.

Adamson, F. B. and Tsourapas, G. (2020). The Migration State in the Global South: Nationalizing, Developmental, and Neoliberal Models of Migration Management. *International Migration Review*, 54(3), 853–882.

Adejoro, L. (2022, October 12). Nigerian Doctors in UK Lament Exploitation, Slave Labour. Retrieved from https://punchng.com/Nigerian-doctors-in-uk-lament-exploitation-slave-labour

Ahmed, S., Castañeda, C., Fortier, A. M. and Sheller, M. (2020). Introduction: Uprootings/Regroundings: Questions of Home and Migration. In *Uprootings/Regroundings Questions of Home and Migration*. Routledge.

Akinkuotu, E., Olokor, F., Adepegba, A. and Ojerinde, D. (2022, July 24). Number of Nigerian Doctors in United Kingdom Rises to 7,875. Retrieved from https://punchng.com/number-of-nigerian-doctors-in-united-kingdom-rises-to-7875

Akinyemi, A. B. (2022). *Towards a New World Order*. Lagos: Nigeria Institute of International Affairs.

Akiwumi, P. and Chiumya, C. C. (2020). Migration and Trade in Africa. In International Organization for Migration (IOM). (2020). Africa Migration Report: Challenging the Narrative. Kirkos Sub-City, Wereda 8 Yemez Building (Near UNECA) Addis Ababa Ethiopia.

Akokpari, J. K. (2000). Globalisation and Migration in Africa. *African Sociological Review/Revue Africaine de Sociologie*, 4(2), 72–92.

Alpers, E. A. (2001, October 25). Defining the African Diaspora. In Center for Comparative Social Analysis Workshop. Retrieved from https://www.ces.uc.pt/formacao/materiais_racismo_pos_racismo/alpers.pdf

Amega, K. (2018). Remittances, Education and Health in Sub-Saharan Africa. *Cogent Economics and Finance*, 6(1). https://doi.org.10.1080/23322039.2018.1516488.

American Quality of Life Final Report. (2008, April). Addressing Community Needs Together. https://www.austintexas.gov/edims/document.cfm?id=125797

Ashcroft, B., Griffiths, G. and Tiffin, H. (2007). *Post-Colonial Studies: The Key Concepts* (2nd ed.). New York: Routledge.

Beyer, R. M., Schewe, J. and Lotze-Campen, H. (2022). Gravity Models Do Not Explain, and Cannot Predict, International Migration Dynamics. *Humanities and Social Sciences Communications*, 9(1), 1–10.

Boyle, P. and Keith, H. (2014). *Exploring Contemporary Migration*. Routledge.

Browne, D. (2013, October 1). The Mental and Emotional Wellbeing of Africans in the UK. *African Health Policy Network*. Research and Discussion Paper. Retrieved from https://moderngov.lambeth.gov.uk/documents/s64820/22MentalandEmotionalWellbeingofAfricansintheUKAHPN2013139.pdf

Brubaker, R. (2005). The 'Diaspora' diaspora. *Ethnic and Racial Studies*, 28(1), 1–19.

Castles, S. (2011). Migration, Crisis, and the Global Labour Market. *Globalizations*, 8(3), 311–324.

Centre for the Study of the Economies of Africa (CSEA). (2022). Africa's Migration-Trends, Drivers and Policy Implementations. Retrieved from https://cseaafrica.org/africas-migration-trends-drivers-and-policy-implications

Chariandy, D. (2006). Postcolonial Diasporas. *Postcolonial Text*, 2(1). Retrieved from https://www.postcolonial.org/index.php/pct/article/view/440/839

Clemens, M. A. (2014). Does Development Reduce Migration? *International Handbook on Migration and Economic Development*. Retrieved from https://scholar.google.com/scholar?q=Clemens,+M.+A.+(2014).+Does+development+reduce+migration%3F.+International+handbook+on+migration+and+economic+development.&hl=en&as_sdt=0&as_vis=1&oi=scholart

Connell, J., Zurn, P., Stilwell, B., Awases, M. and Braichet, J. M. (2007). Sub-Saharan Africa: Beyond the Health Worker Migration Crisis? *Social Science & Medicine*, 64(9), 1876–1891.

Cottier, F., Flahaux, M. L., Ribot, J., Seager, R. and Ssekajja, G. (2022). Framing the Frame: Cause and Effect in Climate-Related Migration. *World Development*, 158, 106016.

Dahlgren, G., & Whitehead, M. (1991). *Policies and Strategies to Promote Social Equity in Health*. Stockholm: Institute for Future Studies, 1–69. Retrieved from https://core.ac.uk/download/pdf/6472456.pdf

Dun, O. V. and Gemenne, F. (2008). Defining 'Environmental Migration'. *Forced Migration Review*, 31, 10–11.

Echeverria-Estrada, C. and Batalova, J. (2019, October 23). Sub-Saharan African Immigrants in the United States. *Migration Information Source*. Retrieved October 23, 2022, from https://www.migrationpolicy.org/article/sub-saharan-african-immigrants-unitedstates-2018

Erokhin, V. and Gao, T. (2018). Handbook of Research on International Collaboration, Economic Development, and Sustainability in the Arctic. IGI Global

Publishers. Retrieved from https://www.igi-global.com/book/handbook-research internationalcollaboration-economic/201490#table-of-contents

Eurofound. (2022, October 20). Living Conditions. Retrieved from https://www.eurofound.europa.eu/topic/living-conditions

European Commission. (2011, November 18). Commission Staff Working Paper: Migration and Development. Brussels. Retrieved from https://op.europa.eu/en/publication-detail/-/publication/b0dbfb9f-58a8-4f32-a0df-8ca0b9dc30c6/language-en.

European University Institute. (2022). An Introduction to Push and Pull Factors. Retrieved from https://www.futurelearn.com/info/courses/migration-theories/0/steps/35073

Experience Africa. (2022). Introduction to the African Diaspora across the World. Institute for Cultural Diplomacy Inc. Retrieved from https://www.experience-africa.de/index.php?en_the-african-diaspora

Ezebuike, H. C. (2019). African Diaspora and the Problems of Poverty and Development in Africa. *Interdisciplinary Journal of African and Asian Studies*, 5(2), 312–327.

Falola, T. (2018). *The Toyin Falola Reader on African Culture, Nationalism, Development and Epistemologies*. Austin, TX: Pan-African University Press.

Freeman, R. and Lewis, J. (2021). Gravity Model Estimates of the Spatial Determinants of Trade, Migration, and Trade-and-Migration Policies. *Economics Letters*, 204, 109873.

Fuankem, A. (2020). The Refugee and Migrant Crisis: Human Tragedies as an Extension of Colonialism. *The Round Table*, 109(1), 52–70.

Government of Canada. (2020, September 8). Social Determinants and Inequities in Health for Black Canadians: A Snapshot. Retrieved from https://www.canada.ca/content/dam/phacaspc/documents/services/African

GOV.UK (2020) Ethnicity Facts and Figures. Retrieved from https://www.ethnicity-facts-figures.service.gov.uk/housing/housing-conditions/overcrowded-households/latest

Grillo, R. and Mazzucato, V. (2008). Africa<> Europe: A Double Engagement. *Journal of Ethnic and Migration Studies*, 34(2), 175–198.

Grossman, J. (2019). Toward a Definition of Diaspora. *Ethnic and Racial Studies*, 42(8), 1263–1282.

Gurak, D. T. and Caces, F. (1992). Migration Networks and the Shaping of Migration Systems. *International Migration Systems: A Global Approach*, 150–176.

Hall, S. (2015). Cultural Identity and Diaspora. In Laura Chrisman and Patrick Williams (Eds.), *Colonial Discourse and Post-Colonial Theory* (pp. 392–403). Routledge.

Hassan-Wuyo, I. (2022, October 25). Over 10,000 Doctors Left Nigeria for UK in Last 7 Years-NMA. Retrieved from https://www.vanguardgr.com/2022/10/over-10000-doctors-left-nigeria-for-uk-in-last-7years-nma

Hernández-Carretero, M. and Carling, J. (2012). Beyond Kamikaze Migrants: Risk Taking in West African Boat Migration to Europe. *Human Organization*, 71(4), 407–416.

Hobbes, T. (1668). *Leviathan*. Hackett Publishing Company.

Houle, R. (2020, August 13). Changes in the Socioeconomic Situation of Canada's Black Population, 2001 to 2016. Retrieved from https://www150.statcan.gc.ca/n1/pub/89-657-x/89-657x2020001-eng.htm

House of Commons International Development Committee. (2004). *Migration and Development: How to Make Migration Work for Poverty Reduction*. London: House of Commons.

United Nations. (2021, January 15). International Migration 2020 Highlights. Retrieved from https://www.un.org/en/desa/international-migration-2020-highlights

International Organization for Migration (IOM). (2020). *Africa Migration Report: Challenging the Narrative*. Kirkos Sub-city, Wereda 8 Yemez Building: Addis Ababa Ethiopia.

Katembo, B. (2008). Pan Africanism and Development: The East African Community Model. *Journal of Pan African Studies*, *2*(4), 107–116.

Khan, F. (2003, July 14). Population: African Union courts Africans in the diaspora, Global Information Network, p. 1. Retrieved from https://digitalcommons.kennesaw.edu/cgi/viewcontent.cgi?article=1103&context=jgi

Kuschminder, K., Bresser, J. D. and Siegel, M. (2015). Irregular Migration Routes to Europe and Factors Influencing Migrants' Destination Choices. *Maastricht University*. Retrieved from https://www.merit.unu.edu/publications/uploads/1436958842.pdf

Lie, J. (1995). From International Migration to Transnational Diaspora. *Contemporary Sociology,* 24(4), 303–306.

Matthews, A. K., Tejeda, S., Johnson, T. P., Berbaum M. L. and Manfredi, C. (2012). Correlates of Quality of Life Among African American and White Cancer Survivors. *Cancer Nursing Journal,* 35(5), 355–364.

McLeod, J. (2020). Beginning Postcolonialism. In *Beginning Postcolonialism (Second Edition)*. Manchester University Press.

McMahon, S. and Sigona, N. (2021). Death and Migration: Migrant Journeys and the Governance of Migration during Europe's "Migration Crisis". *International Migration Review*, 55(2), 605–628.

Mou, J., Griffiths, S. M., Fong, H. F. and Dawes, M. G. (2015). Defining Migration and Its Health Impact in China. *Public Health*, 129(10), 1326–1334.

Natali, C. and Isaacs, L. (2020).Remittances to and from Africa. In International Organization for Migration (IOM) (2020). *Africa Migration Report: Challenging the Narrative*. Wereda 8 Yemez Building, Addis Ababa Ethiopia.

New American Economy (2018, October 23). Power of the Purse: How Sub-Saharan Africans Contribute to the U.S. Economy. Retrieved from https://research.newamericaneconomy.org/wp

Northwestern University Library. (2022). African Diaspora in the Americas and the Caribbean: Resistance, Culture and Survival. Retrieved from https://libguides.northwestern.edu/AfricanDiaspora

Omeje, K. (2007). The Diaspora and Domestic Insurgencies in Africa. *African Sociological Review*, 11(2), 94–107.

Oreopoulos, P. (2011). Why Do Skilled Immigrants Struggle in the Labor Market? A Field Experiment with Thirteen Thousand Resumes." *American Economic Journal: Economic Policy*, 3(4), 148–171.

Pan, G. (2019). The Push-Pull Theory and Motivations of Jewish Refugees. A Study of Jewish Refugees in China (1933–1945), 123–131. https://link.springer.com/chapter/10.1007/978-981-13-9483-6_9

Petersen, W. (1958). A general typology of migration. *American Sociological Review*, 23(3), 256–266.

Ponsot, F., Terry, D., Vasquez, B. and de Vasconcelos, P. (2017) *Sending Money Home: Contributing to the SDGs, One Family at a Time*. Rome: International Fund for Agricultural Development. Retrieved from www.ifad.org/en/web/knowledge/publication/asset/39407416.

Radel, C., Jokisch, B. D., Schmook, B., Carte, L., Aguilar-Støen, M., Hermans, K. and Aldrich, S. (2019). Migration as a feature of land system transitions. *Current Opinion in Environmental Sustainability*, 38, 103–110.

Ratha, D., Mohapatra, S., Ozden, C., Plaza, S., Shaw, W. and Shimeles, A. (2011) *Leveraging Migration for Africa: Remittances, Skills, and Investments*. Washington, DC: World Bank. Retrieved from https://openknowledge.worldbank.org/handle/10986/2300.

Ravenstein, E. G. (1885). The Laws of Migration. *Journal of the Statistical Society of London*, 48(2), 167–235.

Sawahel, W. (2014, October 23). US-Based African Immigrants More Educated. University World New. Retrieved from https://www.universityworldnews.com/post.php?story=20141015211150498

Segal, R. (1995). *The Black Diaspora: Five Centuries of the Black Experience Outside Africa*. New York: Farrar, Straus and Giroux.

Sherwood, M. (2012). *Origins of Pan-Africanism: Henry Sylvester Williams, Africa, and the African Diaspora*. Routledge.

Southwood, T. R. E. (1962). Migration of Terrestrial Arthropods in Relation to Habitat. *Biological Reviews*, 37(2), 171–211.

Social Metrics Commission. (2021, October 22). Measuring Poverty Before the Covid-19 Pandemic A Report of the Social Metrics Commission. Retrieved from https://socialmetricscommission.org.uk/measuring-poverty-before-the-covid-19-pandemic/

Statistics Canada. (2020, October 23) Canada's Black Population: Education, Labour, and Resilience. Retrieved from https://www150.statcan.gc.ca/n1/pub/89-657x/89-657-x2020002-eng.htm

Tamir, C. and Anderson, M. (2022). One-in-Ten Black People Living in the U.S. Are Immigrants. *Pew Research Center*. Retrieved from https://www.pewresearch.org/race-ethnicity/2022/01/20/one-in-ten-black-peopleliving-in-the-u-s-are-immigrants/

Tankwanchi, A. B., Ozden, C., Vermund, S. H. (2013). Physician Emigration from Sub-Saharan Africa to the United States: Analysis of the 2011 AMA Physician Masterfile. *PLOS Medicine*, 10(12). doi:10.1371/annotation/64ffd514-00bb-4a5e-9e2e-584763637d14

Tavanti, M., Abdi, C. and MacHarg, B. (2016). Gender Democracy and Women's Self Empowerment: A Case of Somali Diaspora Civil Society. In *Women's Emancipation and Civil Society Organisations* (pp. 209–234). Policy Press.

Tölölyan, K. (1991). The Nation-State and Its Others: In Lieu of a Preface. *Diaspora* 1(1), 3–7.

UNDP. (2022). Human Development Report 2021–2022: Uncertain Time, Unsettled Lines; Shaping our Future in a Transforming World. https://hrd.undp.org/content/human-development-report-2021-22

United States Census Bureau. (2000). Summary File 3, Matrix PCT19. Washington, DC: Government Printing Office.

US Departments of States. (2022). Racial Equity in Health Series: Efforts to Expand Access to Healthcare in the United States. Retrieved from https://www.state.gov/briefingsforeign-press-centers/efforts-to expand-access-to-healthcare-in-the-united-states

Versi, A. (2003). Bring Home the Best and Brightest. *African Business*, Issue 286, 11.

Walters, R. W. (1997). *Pan Africanism in the African Diaspora: An Analysis of Modern Afrocentric Political Movements*. Wayne State University Press.

Watkinson, R. E., Sutton, M. and Turner, A. J. (2021). Ethnic Inequalities in Health-Related Quality of Life Among Older Adults in England: Secondary Analysis of a National Cross-Sectional Survey. *The Lancet Public Health,* 43(8), e145–e154.

Williams, D. W. and Walker, J. W. (2021, March 15). Black History in Canada Until 1900. The Canadian Encyclopedia. Retrieved from https://www.thecanadianencyclopedia.ca/en/article/black-history-until-1900

WHO. (2012, March 1). The World Health Organization Quality of Life (WHO-QOL). Retrieved from https://www.who.int/publications/i/item/WHO-HIS-HSI-Rev.2012.03

WorldAtlas. (2022). Which Continent Is The Richest In Natural Resources? https://www.worldatlas.com/articles/which-continent-is-the-richest-in-natural-resources.html

World Bank. (2018). Migration and Remittances: Recent Developments and Outlook. Migration and Development Brief 30, December 2018.

World Bank. (2017). Migration and Remittances: Recent Developments and Outlook. Special Topic: Global Compact on Migration. Migration and Development Brief 27, April 2017.

Wucker, M. (2004). Remittances: The Perpetual Migration Machine. *World Policy Journal,* 21(2), 37–46.

Zahran, S. (2021). Africa: Challenges and Opportunities. *Article 10,* 1(1), 1–5. https://journals.ekb.eg/article_138232.html

Chapter 13

Complexities of Boko Haram-Induced Displacement in Nigeria

Michael Ihuoma Ogu and Olajumoke Yacob-Haliso

INTRODUCTION

On Tuesday, January 17, 2017, a Nigerian Airforce Fighter Jet dropped a bomb on an internally displaced persons (IDP) camp in Rana, in Kale Balge local government area in Borno state. Initial figures announced by Medecins sans Frontieres (MSF, or Doctors without Borders), indicated that 52 persons were killed immediately and more than 120 wounded as a result of the bomb (Haruna and Owoseye, 2017). Unfortunately, staff of the MSF, the ICRC, and the Nigerian Red Cross working in the camp were among the victims. Although the Nigerian Air Force apologized and called the incident a mistake (Erunke, 2017), if there was one event that demonstrated the gross insecurity of life and living as an IDP induced by the Boko Haram conflict, and the arguable negligence and carelessness on the part of the military in responding to insecurity in Nigeria, this one demonstrated it best. How could it be that the very armed forces of the Nigerian state, mandated to provide protection to these vulnerable persons, had turned out to become their attacker and a threat to their safety and security? The basic principles of humanitarian involvement in protection were also violated when aid workers were also hit by the bombs.

In the period around 2009, when the Boko Haram insurgency became a national emergency, massive displacement has accompanied the rampage of the terrorist group (Mbiyozo, 2017; Olanrewaju, Omotoso and Alabi, 2018). The problems encountered have ranged from such state-induced catastrophes as the "accidental" bombing reported above to embezzlement of funds for IDP relief, and to personal abuse experienced by IDPs. While many authors have identified the human dimensions of this disaster, in this chapter we analyze the dimensions of terrorism-induced displacement as a function of state dysfunction and (mis)management and adopt a human security critique of the consequences of these failures.

While a definition of human security has remained a subject of debate over the years, there have remained certain shared characteristics emphasized in the various understandings of the concept, Heinbecker (2000) identified some of these as: starts from individual citizens and communities in which they live, rather than from states; recognizes that the security of state is essential but not sufficient to guarantee person-centered security; and focuses on threat to persons, whether or not the origin of such threats are military. Homan (2008) further argued that the priority placed on human rights is the distinguishing factor of human from traditional military security and that in human security operations, the protection of civilians, not defeating the enemy, is an end in itself. Following the many debates and literature on the dimensions of human security—economic security, food security, health security, environmental security, community security, political security, and personal security—since the 1994 United Nations Development Programme Report, the human security discourse has been categorized into freedom from fear, freedom from want, and freedom from indignity. In this chapter, we focus on all three categories, emphasizing the implications of Boko Haram terrorism on various aspects of security in Nigeria, particularly those of IDP.

In four sections, with the exception of the introductory and concluding sections, the chapter addresses conflict and displacement from a wider African perspective, paying close attention to the magnitude of the displaced population; x-rays Boko Haram terrorism in Nigeria with particular focus on the nature of internal displacement attendant to the terrorist activities; interrogates the challenges that have further complicated the internal displacement induced by Boko Haram terrorist activities in Nigeria; and analyzes the various efforts by the government of Nigeria and other local and foreign groups and organizations to manage the many aspects of the crisis of terrorism-induced internal displacement in Nigeria.

BOKO HARAM AND DISPLACEMENT IN NIGERIA

Ferris (2012), reviewing the challenge of internal displacement in Africa, reported that there were much more IDPs in Africa—about five times more—than there were refugees. She observed further that almost a decade ago, there were around 2 million refugees in Sub-Saharan Africa, as opposed to the corresponding figure of around 11 million IDPs. In her words, "Africa is, and has long been, the region with the largest number of IDPs in the world" (p. 1).

The definition of "internally displaced persons" has continued to undergo a series of arguments and varied perspectives, as a result of issues relating to the scope of the definition and the reach of protection provided to those captured within the existing definitions. The United Nations Guiding Principles on Internal Displacement provides an apt definition of the concept as

> people or groups of people who have been forced or obliged to flee their homes or places of habitual residence, in particular as a result of or in order to avoid the effects of armed conflict, situations of generalized violence, violations of human rights or natural or human-made disasters and who have not crossed an internationally recognized state border. (p. 6)

Displacement is not uniquely a Nigerian problem, neither is it confined to the borders of any other state or region of the world. The menace of displacement arising from violent conflicts and acts of terror continues to constitute a challenge for several regions of the world, although the nature, devastation, and complications of this challenge, as well as management process may vary from one state to the other. The IDMC (2019) reported that by the end of 2018, 16.5 million people in Sub-Saharan Africa were internally displaced as a result of conflict. In 2018 alone, the number of new displacements in Sub-Saharan Africa accounted for 36 percent of all new displacements worldwide. 7.4 million persons were newly displaced following conflict in the region, and 2.6 million new displacement were associated with disasters. Ethiopia, being the country with the highest new displacements globally, recorded 2.9 million new displacements associated with conflict and four times more than the numbers in 2017. The Democratic Republic of Congo recorded more than 1.8 million new displacements that were influenced by continued conflict and insecurity in North and South Kivu, Tanganyika, and Kasai Central provinces. In Nigeria, the more than 541,000 new displacements in 2018 were associated with the endemic violent attacks by the Boko Haram terrorist group and growing conflict between herders and farmers, which accounted for 341,000 and 200,000 new displacements, respectively, bringing the total number of displaced persons in Nigeria to 2.2 million by the end of 2018 (IDMC, 2019).

The Boko Haram sect has arguably attracted more attention in Nigeria over the last few years. This status, Abdulazeez observes, arises from the following realities: it is the longest insurgency Nigeria has had to battle with, beginning significantly in the year 2002 since the period of the Kanama disturbance; it has caused the highest wave of displacement (refugees and IDPs) in the country, outnumbering the 1967–1970 civil war; it triggered the highest rise in Nigeria's defense spending, rising up to about 6 billion dollars in the year 2015 and about 9 billion dollars by 2018 (Munshi, 2018), and it has put Nigeria on the list of countries that have to cope with terrorism.

The United Nations (2015) observed that millions of people have fled territories controlled by terrorist and violent extremist groups, leading to increased migratory flows away from and toward the conflict zones and involving those seeking safety as well as those lured into the conflict as foreign terrorist fighters, further destabilizing the regions concerned. This assertion further confirms the ubiquity and perennial nature of displacement caused by terrorist and other extremist groups across the globe. Schmid reported that "many of the countries suffering from terrorism were Muslim countries, and the perpetrators as well as the victims of the terrorist activities were also Muslims" (Schmid, 2016: 5). Nigeria was also reported as the country with the second highest number of terrorist fatalities from a total of 32,685 in 2014. The World Bank further confirms that Nigeria recorded the highest number of victims of terrorism in the last seven years, where Boko Haram killed some 20,000 people in Borno state alone (World News Ghana, 2016).

The United Nations Office for the Coordination of Humanitarian Affairs (UNOCHA) reported that internal displacement in Nigeria, particularly in Borno, Yobe, and Adamawa states, has continued on a steady upward trend. The report observed that between 2010 and 2011, IDPs in these states rose from 100,000 to 130,000; by 2012, the number rose to 200,000; and 290,000 in 2013. Although the number slightly reduced to 250,000 between May 2013 and March 2014, it almost doubled to about 436,608 between May and June 2014 and drastically increased to 600,000 between August and December same year (United Nations, 2014). In addition to this seeming geometric progression of IDPs, the Boko Haram activities further increased the influx of Nigerian refugees into neighboring nations; there are over 30,000 Nigerian refugees in Northern Cameroun, 1,000 in Chad (on Lake Chads Choua Island) and more than 50,000 in the Diffa region of South East Niger. Although the attacks and activities of the sect, arguably, began to decline in the aftermath of the 2015 general elections in Nigeria, the challenge of internal displacement would remain evident and obvious in Nigeria for a long time. In fact, the 2019 Global Terrorism Index reported that "ten countries accounted for 87 per cent of deaths from terrorism in 2018." Of these ten countries, Nigeria ranks second with 508 deaths from terrorists attacks in 2018 alone. Others are Afghanistan, Mali, Mozambique, Burkina Faso, Indonesia, Colombia, Chad, Tajikistan, and Venezuela in descending order, accounting for 2,726, 208, 110, 40, 39, 37, 34, 32, and 24 deaths, respectively.

Turning to management of displaced persons in Nigeria, there appears to be a lot of issues needing interrogation. The few IDP camps in Nigeria are sited in schools, palaces of traditional rulers, churches and mosques, Youth Orientation Camps, tertiary institutions, government buildings among others, and managed by the National Emergency Management Agency (NEMA), with the support of international organizations like the United Nations

High Commissioner for Refugees (UNHCR), International Organization for Migration (IOM), the Red Cross, United Nations Children's Fund (UNICEF), among others. The living conditions in most of these camps have become a source of concern to researchers and humanitarian institutions alike. Most of the camps are overcrowded with little access to living space, government-employed cooks are available in some of the camps, while displaced women are organized into cooks, cooking virtually the same meals every day and having to feed the camp only once a day, as opposed to government claims that displaced persons are fed thrice daily with assorted nutritional meals. Health care in the camps is almost absent, except for the presence of buildings and some immunization kits for children, education has become more or less impossible, except for the UNICEF shared school initiative providing educational materials and books to displaced persons, but the learning conditions remain grossly inadequate (Abdulazeez, 2016).

Other challenges associated with the management of displacement in Nigeria include lack of access to relief materials; embezzlement of funds for the camps by state governments and camp officials, who swell the number of displaced persons to get even more funding; trafficking of women, young girls, and children from the camps; and the presence of armed guards at the camp entrance who would not allow access to researchers and investigators, for obvious reasons (Abdulazeez, 2016). In addition, a Human Rights Watch (HRW) 2016 report observed that among the challenges in IDP camps in Nigeria is a sharp rise in the number of persons suffering from and requiring treatment for HIV and other sexually transmitted diseases. The report noted that, in one of these camps hosting 10,000 displaced persons, the number of persons requiring treatment had risen from 200 cases in 2014 to more than 500 as at July 2016, also that 66 percent of 400 displaced persons in Adamawa, Borno, and Yobe states insisted that camp officials sexually abused displaced women and girls.

CHALLENGES OF BOKO-HARAM-INDUCED DISPLACEMENT IN NIGERIA

The IOM, in its 2016 Displacement Tracking Matrix Report on Nigeria, estimated that there were a total number of 1,822,541 IDPs from 321,514 households in Adamawa, Bauchi, Borno, Gombe, Taraba, and Yobe states, as of October 31, 2016. This figure represents a decline from the 2,152,000 reported at the end of 2015 by the Internal Displacement Monitoring Centre (IDMC). Children below eighteen years of age accounted for 55 percent of the IDP population and 48 percent of these children below eighteen years of age were actually under five years old; 9 percent of displaced persons in the 161 displacement sites were lactating mothers, 5 percent elderly persons, 2.5 percent pregnant women, 2 percent single-women-headed households, 1 percent single-male-headed households, and 1.5 percent orphaned children (International Organization for Migration, 2016).

Majority of displaced persons in Nigeria live with relatives and friends: 87 percent live with host communities and 13 percent live in camps or camp-like settings, and as a matter of fact this has some impact on the accuracy of the statistics provided on the number of displaced persons in Nigeria, as well as provides opportunities for mismanaging relief materials, increased sexual assaults, theft and human rights abuses from within and outside the camp resulting from inefficient security and accountability, among others challenges, which influence the care provided for displaced persons by government and its agencies. Reporting the vulnerability of displaced persons in Nigeria, Alobo and Obaji (2016: 26) asserted that a total of 43 displacement sites have been identified in Adamawa, Borno, and Taraba states, comprising 154,008 individuals within 19,348 households. They further observed that:

> 62% of the IDPs in these sites are female while 38% are male. Half of the total numbers of individuals residing in sites are children under 17 years old . . . 3.33% are single headed-households, 2.26% are breastfeeding mothers while 1.22% are pregnant women. In addition, 1.61% of the IDPs have been identified as unaccompanied and separated children.

From the various preceding arguments, it can be argued that violent conflicts are the primary cause of displacement globally. However, there are other issues that result in internal displacement, especially in the Nigerian state, in addition to violent conflicts, although those are not treated in this study. Another cause, however, of internal displacement in Nigeria, are endemic clashes between Fulani herdsmen and farmers; which seem to be assuming a terrorist dimension, as sources have alleged that suspects are non-Nigerians and some even confessing to be members of the Boko Haram sect. Violence resulting from the arguably endemic competition between groups of local farming communities and nomadic herders continues to plague Nigeria and seems to have escalated to arguably every geopolitical zone of the country, while leaving in its tracks, tolls of human and material casualties, as well as forcing people to leave their homes. Clashes between farmers and Fulani herdsmen in states of Benue, Taraba, Zamfara, and Kaduna displaced 100,000 persons in 2014 (Itumo and Nwobashi, 2016). Raising fears of links with Boko Haram, Nigeria's former Minister of State for Agriculture, Senator Heineken Lokpobiri reported that: "We have discovered that the herdsmen, attacking Nigerians across the country, are not Fulani but another gang of Boko Haram insurgents from other countries" (Aborishade, 2016: 1). He further expressed this possibility by confirming that some of the suspected herdsmen arrested by law enforcement could not speak Fulani or any other Nigerian language. Ogu (2016) also observed that these clashes between groups of farmers and "killer" herders is further complicated, in the recent past, by the increasing use of sophisticated weapons used in these conflicts, which has increased the casualties from the conflict.

Human Rights Watch (2016) has observed that: Nigerian politics has always revolved around an obsession with the difficult task of forging a nation out of Nigeria's complex diversity while ensuring that no ethnic group, religion, or geographical region could ever come to dominate the rest of the country. Boko Haram insurgency is also arguably linked to the many tensions and controversies surrounding balance in the allocation of political power and government resources in Nigeria, leading a few to resorting to terrorism to protest their exclusion. Extreme poverty and the high rate of unemployment in the Nigerian state, particularly in the northern region of the country, are other possible causes of the Boko Haram terrorism. Nwagwu (2014) observed that poverty is a product of unemployment, inequality, economic marginalization, illiteracy, and more importantly, many of the survivors of terrorist activities continue to struggle with displacement that is complicated by poverty and very low standards of living. Again, unemployment and illiteracy constitute a veritable recruitment tool for the Boko Haram, as it has been argued that many of the members of Islamic fundamentalist sect; including Boko Haram, are neither very knowledgeable of the Quran nor have any form of formal education and are basically lured into such acts. Also, members of the Boko Haram sect are mostly jobless youths who are frustrated due to inequality and economic deprivation that have kept them unemployed (Onuoha, 2014).

Several efforts have been made by government and agencies in Nigeria to manage the challenge of displacement and contain the various circumstances or events that result in and from displacement. Several agencies have been established, such as the NEMA, to respond to emergencies. Some other committees have been set up, policies formulated, and strategies adopted to curtail the menace of displacement in Nigeria, but all these efforts have proven little success. The National Commission for Refugees (2012: 1) asserted that:

> undue emphasis on disaster-induced displacement led to government prioritizing disaster risk reduction and narrowing its focus to responding to disaster-induced displacement. This approach has largely ignored non-disaster-induced internal displacement and lack of strategic framework to address the plight of such displaced populations and to provide durable solutions to all types of displacement.

The nature of displacement in Nigeria has resulted in several other complications which have left the Nigeria state, especially those who have been displaced wondering if they could ever have a normal life, and if their communities could be healed from the varied consequences of this humanitarian challenge. Aside the predominant vulnerability of women and children, sexual abuse and other gender-based violence seem to be another complication from displacement in Nigeria. Incidents of rape, sexual harassment, forced marriage, infant marriage, sexual diseases, and uncontrolled birth have been reported especially inside the displacement camps, leading to increasing infant and maternal mortality in Nigeria. Children, on the other hand, are being exposed to forceful conscription and indoctrination by insurgents as child soldiers, suicide bombers, and sex slaves, leading to abrupt discontinuation with their education as among the least consequences. Alobo and Obaji (2016) observed that so far, at least 196 teachers and 314 school children have been killed by insurgents, and at least 338 schools have been destroyed by attacks.

Increasingly, malnutrition and several other health-related challenges have continued to heighten, as amenities and access to food and other welfare needs become more and more extinct in these communities. It may be posited that the most accommodations for displaced persons in Nigeria, and in fact other parts of the world are tents, while many others live in churches, schools, uncompleted buildings, and other public places—under the bridges and even on the streets. These kinds of conditions would most likely expose these individuals to various epidemics and diseases resulting from poor hygiene. Alobo and Obaji (2016) further observed that the condition of displaced people is complicated by the fact that:

> access to health care in Nigeria generally and the North East in particular is severely constrained for both the IDPs and host communities as a result of the destruction of health care facilities and health care workers. Outbreak of disease has increased in areas affected by dislocation. There is also the case of lack of access to vaccinations. The number of cholera cases among IDPs is seriously on the increase.

In addition to these health implications, displaced people have been forced to engage in some vices such as theft, prostitution, trafficking, ritual killings, among others, while other criminal elements have taken advantage of this unfortunate humanitarian crisis to perpetrate various kinds of criminal activities, which also have implications for the safety of individuals and the progress of the society both in and out of the various IDP camps.

MANAGEMENT OF TERRORISM-INDUCED DISPLACEMENT IN NIGERIA

The Boko Haram insurgency has obviously complicated the nature of internal displacement in Nigeria, creating complexities that required a multiplicity of actors and approaches to help manage this apparent humanitarian challenge, as well as a need to coordinate the activities and programs of these actors for maximum effectiveness. The management of IDPs is guided by international and national instruments and policies, and the process is overseen by a range of actors whose responsibilities it is to implement these guidelines and provide physical, psychosocial, socioeconomic, and legal protection to the displaced victims of the Boko Haram insurgency.

The only international instrument recognizing the status of, and protecting, IDPs was the UN Guiding Principles on Internal Displacement. When, in 2009, the African Union adopted the Kampala Convention; otherwise known as the African Union Convention for the Protection and Assistance of Internally Displaced Persons in Africa, and after it came into force on December 12, 2012, this novel regional instrument was hailed as containing "important and progressive" provisions that would "advance the normative standard on internal displacement in a number of important areas" (Asplet and Bradley, 2013). Together these two instruments, in agreement and without prejudice to national protections and international human rights and humanitarian laws, provide the framework by which states, including Nigeria, and various other agencies; the United Nations, relief organizations, community based and international governmental and nongovernmental agencies work to assist and protect IDPs. The legal instruments contain provisions that address the protection needs of IDPs from before displacement, prohibiting arbitrary displacement by governments and other actors, through displacement, whether in camps or elsewhere, and to the experience of solutions including return, integration, and relocation. In the Nigerian case under study, displacement has not been properly managed to avert many of the violations anticipated by these instruments.

On September 12, 2005, the UN Inter-Agency Standing Committee, comprising the heads of the major relief and development organizations in the world; governmental and nongovernmental, assigned the UNHCR the primary responsibility of protecting, managing, and coordinating humanitarian response to IDPs in the absence of a dedicated UN agency. At the global level, perhaps no other agency had the preparation and experience to assume this role than the UNHCR (Cohen, 2005). The efforts of the UNHCR in managing the displacement induced by Boko Haram's attacks are complemented by various humanitarian organizations including the Nigerian Red Cross Society, International Committee of the Red Cross, MSF, and others. On the national level, the body with the lead responsibility for IDPs is the NEMA. All these relief agencies are being supported by the Nigerian government and a host of other security and social services agencies and departments.

One of the most vital duties embarked upon by the humanitarian agencies in managing the Boko Haram crisis is the provision of vital statistics about the population, locations, locale, and conditions of displaced people in the war-ravaged northeast. The IOM's works with NEMA, State Emergency Management Agencies (SEMA), the Nigerian Red Cross Societies, and other humanitarian partners to produce the important figures that map displacement and make it possible to plan for its remedies and support for IDPs, particularly those displaced by Boko Haram insurgency. These statistics are hosted and disseminated on the website of these agencies, as well as of the UN-accredited IDMC (IDMC, 2016). Beyond these, these agencies also help to track and report the various violations of protection and rights of IDPs that occur in the areas and camps housing the displaced persons. For instance, the bombing of the IDP camp in Rana in January 2017 was first reported by the MSF staff that witnessed it happen and immediately provided the initial figures of dead and wounded (France-Presse, 2017). The presence of international organizations such as MSF and their statistical inclination in the management of displaced persons no less prevents cover-ups for such tactical mistakes by the Nigerian security forces and forestalls any attempt to cover-up current or future event. In addition, these agencies issue press releases condemning such events, thereby maintaining a normative environment that limits and constrains the activities of various actors to the expected humanitarian principles and standards.

The various agencies involved in managing the IDP usually provide an assessment of ongoing humanitarian efforts, in order to call attention to lapses and thereby maintaining pressure on the Nigerian government and other governments, donors, and the UN to step up their efforts in attenuating the vast humanitarian tragedy that affects over 2 million people. For example: UN Office for the Coordination of Humanitarian Affairs estimates that in the three states most affected, almost 7 million people are in need of humanitarian assistance, more than 50 percent of which are children. More than 4.8 million people are in urgent need of food assistance and 5.1 million were predicted to be food insecurity in 2017 if not supported by the international community with funds and aid. Furthermore, up to 450,000 children in the three states will suffer from severe acute malnutrition in 2017 if not urgently assisted. Security remains extremely fragile in up to 80 percent of the area, severely limiting access for humanitarian actors (United Nations, 2017; World Food Programme, 2017). Toward the end of 2016, corroborating the UN estimates and predictions above, several Nigerian media reports called attention to the overcrowding of camps, the deep hunger, the inadequacy of aid and small food rations, lack of medicines for treatment, and the high mortality of children below five years of age.

The reality of the forecast by the international organizations and news reported by various media in Nigeria were confirmed by the various protests by IDPs. It was reported on the August 25, 2016, that over 500 IDPs took to the streets of Maiduguri, the Borno state capital to protest what they termed as neglect by the federal government (Shaban, 2016). A few days later, on August 30, the *Vanguard Nigeria* reported that hundreds of IDPs from Bakassi camp took to the streets in protest of the poor feeding and barricaded the Maiduguri-Biu road within the city (Marama, 2016). Also, on September 6, around 6,500 IDPs blocked the Maiduguri-Jos road, protesting hunger, the grossly inadequate food they had been receiving and the subsequent loss of lives of mostly children and some adults from hunger-related illnesses (Olatunji, 2016). Confronted by the outcry, the Borno SEMA claimed that "the major challenges of hunger, diseases and deaths were not evident in government-controlled camps, but in IDP camps in host communities" (Umokoro, 2016).

The Punch (2016) reported that photos had appeared online and in social media showing food aid with the donor logos that had been displayed for sale in shops causing huge public outcry at the time. The arguable explanation was that the officials who were in charge of the food meant for the IDPs were diverting it and selling for personal profit. While the Nigerian Senate launched an investigation into the allegations in September when the IDP protests broke out, the Nigerian President Muhammadu Buhari had mandated the inspector-general of police to arrest and "make an example" of any government officials suspected of stealing and selling food aid meant for victims of the Boko Haram crisis, or any other for that matter. Compounding the public outrage at this time was an allegation that the Presidential Initiative for the North-East (PINE), a committee created by President Muhammadu Buhari to ensure that relief efforts met the needs of the region could not account for a sum of N2.5 billion earmarked for rebuilding the ruined region. Furthermore, a total sum of N270 million was fraudulently diverted and embezzled under the guise of "clearing invasive plant species" that never existed (Agency Report, 2016).

Some of the egregious crimes committed against the IDPs by care and security officials were cases of sexual abuse and exploitation, which became rampant and remained unchecked until a Human Rights Watch report systematically documented and exposed it. Interviews of forty-three women and girls in seven IDP camps revealed that government officials and other authorities in Nigeria raped and sexually exploited women and girls displaced by Boko Haram insurgency and that the government was not doing enough to protect displaced women and girls and ensure their access to basic rights and services or sanction the abusers, who include camp leaders, vigilante groups, policemen, and soldiers (Human Rights Watch, 2016). In response to this report, the federal government, within a week, ensured the deployment of a hundred female police officers to the IDP camps to provide female law enforcement presence as well as to investigate and arrest culprits (News24, 2016).

Although the Nigerian government continues to advance efforts in managing displacement and has promptly responded to most of the protests and allegations of abuse and dissatisfaction on humanitarian assistance by IDPs and other international organizations, more people continue to be displaced by pockets of violence in Nigeria, many of them linked to the seeming never-ending clashes between Boko Haram terrorist and Nigerian military, and also the health and humanitarian conditions in the existing IDP camps and the north-eastern region, in general, continue to demand attention.

CONCLUSION

Without a doubt, Nigeria's northeast may be aptly dubbed the biggest humanitarian crisis in the world outside Iraq and Syria. The dimensions of the emergency are staggering, and the dynamics are increasingly complex. Over 2 million people are arguably destitute, displaced, and maybe without much remedies in sight. The socioeconomic consequences of the conflict include the developmental challenge of critical infrastructure, farmlands, houses, and productive capacities being arguably destroyed by the protracted Boko Haram insurgency. Despite the many efforts by the government and relief agencies in the state, the management of the Boko Haram-induced displacement in Nigeria remains largely unsatisfactory, partly due to the endemic nature of the Boko Haram insurgency and resultant increasing displacement, but more importantly, due to neglect, corruption and maladministration, lack of will to implement the safeguards promised in the various international and national laws, among other reasons.

It is firmly believed that for IDPs in the northeast to experience the reliefs and remedies promised in the relevant legal instruments nationally and internationally, the Nigerian government must provide the moral, political, and strategic leadership necessary. The government must "stand up, show up and stay up." Principle 3 (1) of the Guiding Principles state explicitly that "National authorities have the primary duty and responsibility to provide protection and humanitarian assistance to internally displaced persons within their jurisdiction" (United Nations, 2004). The Kampala Convention, which Nigeria has ratified, reiterates the same call to duty in Article 5 (1): "States Parties shall bear the primary duty and responsibility for providing protection of and humanitarian assistance to internally displaced persons within their territory or jurisdiction without discrimination of any kind" (African Commission on Human and Peoples' Rights, 2015: 1). When the Nigerian state lives up to its responsibility, in cooperation with other humanitarian actors, the plights of internally displacement persons will be largely reduced and development and growth may return to Nigeria's northeast zone, which appears the most affected by the Boko Haram-induced internal displacement.

REFERENCES

Abdulazeez, Medinat. 2016. "The Boko Haram Insurgency and Internal Displacement". In *State Secretariat for Migration SEM, Section Analyses*. Berne-Wabern: Federal Department of Justice and Police, 2016, 3–12.

Aborishade, Sunday. 2016. "Herdsmen Attacking Farmers are Foreign Terrorists –FG". *Punch Newspaper*, May 11, https://punchng.com/herdsmen-attacking-farmers-foreign-terrorists-fg/, accessed September 2018.

African Commission on Human and Peoples' Rights. 2015. "Press Release on the Ratification of the African Union Convention for the Protection and Assistance of Internally Displaced Persons in Africa (Kampala Convention) by the Republic of Congo", January 21, 2015. http://www.achpr.org/press/2015/01/d247/, accessed February 21, 2017.

African Union and Norwegian Refugee Council, "Africa Report on Internal Displacement". *Internal Displacement Monitoring Centre (IDMC)*, Geneva, Switzerland, 2016, 5, http://www.internal-displacement.org/sites/default/files/inline-files/20161209-IDMC-Africa-report-web-en.pdf, accessed September 6, 2017.

Agency Report. 2016. "SGF Frustrating Probe of Billions Spent on Internally Displaced Persons – Reps", *Premium Times*, October 7, http://www.premiumtimesng.com/news/top-news/212236-sgf-frustrating-probe-billions-spent-internally-displaced-persons-reps.html, accessed February 20, 2017.

Alobo, Eni and Synda Obaji. 2016. "Internal Displacement in Nigeria and the Case for Human Rights Protection of Displaced Persons". *Journal of Law, Policy and Globalization*, 51: 26.

Asplet, Mike and Megan Bradley. 2013. "Introductory Note to the African Union Convention for the Protection and Assistance of Internally Displaced Persons in Africa (Kampala Convention)". *International Legal Materials* 52(1): 397–410.

Cohen, Roberta. 2005. "UNHCR: Expanding its Role with IDPs". *Brookings Institute*, October 1, 2005, 9–11. https://www.brookings.edu/wp-content/uploads/2016/06/20050923_rc_idp_supplement.pdf, accessed February 20, 2017.

Erunke, Joseph. 2017. "Nigeria: Accidental Bombing of IDPs Camp - Nigerian Airforce Apologise". *Vanguard*, January 18, https://www.vanguardngr.com/2017/01/accidental-bombing-of-idps-campnigerian-airforce-apologizes-over-action/, accessed September 2018.

Ferris, Elizabeth. 2012. "Internal Displacement in Africa: An Overview of Trends and Opportunities". *Brookings*, May 3, 2012, https://www.brookings.edu/research/internal-displacement-in-africa-an-overview-of-trends-and-opportunities/, accessed November 2, 2017.

France-Presse, Agence. 2017. "Updated: Military Airstrike Kills Dozens in IDPs Camp". *Punch Newspapers*, January 17, http://punchng.com/military-bombs-idps-camp-borno-50-feared-dead/, accessed February 20, 2017.

Haruna, Abdulkareem and Ayodamola Owoseye. 2017. "UPDATE: 52 Dead, 120 Injured After Nigerian Jet Accidentally Bombed IDP Camp." *Premium Times*, January 17, https://www.premiumtimesng.com/news/headlines/220797-update-52-dead-120-injured-nigerian-jet-accidentally-bombed-idp-camp.html, accessed February 20, 2017.

Heinbecker, Paul. 2000. "The Concept of Human Security". *RUSI Journal*, 145(6): 27–32.

Homan, Kees. 2008. "The Military and Human Security". *Security and Human Rights*, 19(1): 73–81. https://doi.org.10.1163/187502308784048582

Human Rights Watch. 2016. "Nigeria: Officials Abusing Displaced Women, Girls: Displaced by Boko Haram and Victims Twice Over." *Channels Television*, October 31, https://www.hrw.org/news/2016/10/31/nigeria-officials-abusing-displaced-women-girls, accessed February 20, 2017.

Institute of Economics and Peace. 2019. Global Terrorism Index 2019: Measuring the Impact of Terrorism, page 16, http://visionofhumanity.org/app/uploads/2019/11/GTI-2019web.pdf

Internal Displacement Monitoring Centre (IDMC), *Global Report on Internal Displacement*, 9, (IDMC, 2019), https://www.internal-displacement.org/sites/default/files/publications/documents/2019-IDMC-GRID.pdf, accessed March 20, 2020.

Internal Displacement Monitoring Centre (IDMC), *Global Report on Internal Displacement*, 9, (IDMC, 2016), http://www.internal-displacement.org/globalreport2016/, accessed February 20, 2017.

International Organization for Migration. 2016. "Nigeria", *Round 12, Displacement Tracking Matrix (DTM)*, October 2016), https://reliefweb.int/sites/reliefweb.int/files/resources/01_dtm_nigeria_round_xii_report_october_2016.pdf, accessed January 12, 2017.

International Organization for Migration, "Response to the IDP Crisis in Iraq", (Round 64, Displacement Tracking Matrix Dtm, 2017), http://iraqdtm.iom.int/downloads/DTM%202017/February%202017/Round%2064%20-%2002%20February%202017/Round64_Report_English_2017_February_02_IOM_DTM.pdf, accessed June 4, 2017.

Itumo, Anthony and Humphrey Nwobashi. 2016. "Nigerian State and Responses to Plights of Persons Internally Displaced by Boko Haram Insurgents: Implications for Socio-Economic and Political Development", *Research on Humanities and Social Sciences*, 6(15): 25.

J. 'Bayo Adekanye, *Linking Conflict Diagnosis, Conflict Prevention, and Conflict Management in Contemporary Africa: Selected Essays*. Lagos & Ibadan: Ababa Press & Centre for Gender, Governance and Development [CEGGAD], 2007, 213.

Marama, Ndahi. 2016. "Again, Borno IDPs Protest Poor Method of Feeding in Camps", *Vanguard*, August 30, http://www.vanguardngr.com/2016/08/borno-idps-protest-poor-method-feeding-camps/, accessed February 20, 2017.

Mbiyozo, Aimée-Noël. 2017. "How Boko Haram Specifically Targets Displaced People", *Institute for Security Studies*, https://reliefweb.int/sites/reliefweb.int/files/resources/policybrief109.pdf, accessed April 4, 2020.

Munshi, Neil. 2018. Under fire: why Nigeria is struggling to defeat Boko Haram. *Financial Times*, December 5, https://www.ft.com/content/62928c8e-f7b8-11e8-8b7c-6fa24bd5409c

National Bureau of Statistics. "Unemployment/ Under-Employment Watch" (Quarter 1, 2016), www.nigerianstat.gov.ng/download/397, accessed March 4, 2017.

National Commission for Refugees. 2012. "National Policy on Internally Displaced Persons (IDPs) in Nigeria", Abuja, http://infopointmigration.org.ng/wp-content/uploads/national-idp-policy.pdf, accessed February 15, 2017.

News24. 2016. "Sexual Abuse: Nigeria Deploys 100 Female to IDP Camps", November 8, 2016, http://www.news24.com/Africa/News/sexual-abuse-nigeria-deploys-100-female-to-idp-camps-20161108, accessed February 20, 2017.

Nwagwu, Ejikeme J. 2014. "Unemployment and Poverty in Nigeria: A Link to National Insecurity", *Global Research Journal of Politics and Law*, 2(1): 19–35.

Office of the United Nations High Commissioner for Human Rights. Human Rights, "Terrorism and Counter-terrorism Fact Sheet No. 32", 1, http://www.ohchr.org/Documents/Publications/Factsheet32EN.pdf, accessed September 8, 2017.

Ogu, Michael I. 2016. "Pastoral/Agricultural Conflicts, Small Arms Proliferation, and Insecurity in Nigeria". Doctoral Dissertation, Ogun State: Babcock University, 135.

Olanrewaju, Faith O., Femi Omotoso, and Joshua O. Alabi. 2018. Datasets on the Challenges of Forced Displacement and Coping Strategies Among Displaced Women in Selected Internally Displaced Persons' (IDPs) Camps in Nigeria. *Data in Brief*, 20: 152–158. https://doi.org/10.1016/j.dib.2018.07.042

Olatunji, Omirin. 2016. "Nigeria: More IDPSs Protest in Maiduguri", *Daily Trust*, September 7, 2016. http://allafrica.com/stories/201609070425.html, accessed February 20, 2017.

Onuoha, Freedom C. 2014. "Why Do Youth Join Boko Haram?", *United States Institute of Peace Special Report*, 2014, https://www.usip.org/sites/default/files/SR348-Why_do_Youth_Join_Boko_Haram.pdf, accessed September 2018.

Punch. 2016. "Buhari Orders Arrest of Officials Diverting IDPs' Food", *Punch Newspaper,* September 2, 2016. http://www.dailytrust.com.ng/news/general/buhari-orders-arrest-of-officials-diverting-idps-food/161131.html, accessed February 20, 2017.

Schmid, Alex. 2016. "Terrorism and Migration: An Exploration", *Research Paper, International Centre for Counter Terrorism (ICCT) – The Hague*, 7(4): 3–63.

Shaban, Abdurahman A. 2016. "Displaced People in Nigeria's Borno State Protest Over Neglect", *Africa News*, August 25, 2016. http://www.africanews.com/2016/08/25/displaced-people-in-nigeria-s-borno-state-protest-over-neglect//, accessed February 20, 2017.

Umokoro, Arukaino. 2016. "Time Bomb: Borno IDP Camps of Hunger, Malnourishment and Death… 120,000 Children May Die of Hunger in IDP Camps Next Year – UN", *Punch Newspapers*, December 25, http://punchng.com/time-bomb-borno-idp-camps-hunger-malnourishment-death-120000-children-may-die-hunger-idp-camps-next-year-un/, accessed February 20, 2017.

United Nations, Guiding Principles on Internally Displacement, 2nd (ed.), *Brookings,* (New York, 2004), 6, https://www.brookings.edu/wp-content/uploads/2016/07/GPEnglish.pdf, accessed June 3, 2017.

United Nations. 2017. "UNHCR's Grandi: Failures Behind Nigeria's IDP Camp Tragedy Must be Identified", *High Commission for Refugees, 2017*, http://www.unhcr.org/news/press/2017/1/587f6a734/unhcrs-grandi-failures-behind-nigeria-idp-camp-tragedy-must-identified.html?query=idps, accessed February 20, 2017.

United Nations, *Humanitarian Needs Overview 2016* (Office for the Coordination of Humanitarian Affairs (OCHA), November 2015, 8, http://goo.gl/4pLzx3, accessed February 4, 2017.

United Nations. 2017. "Nigeria: About the Crisis", *Office for the Coordination of Humanitarian Affairs (UNOCHA)*, 2017. http://www.unocha.org/nigeria/about-ocha-nigeria/about-crisis, accessed February 20, 2017.

United Nations. 2014. "An Overview and Response to Humanitarian Crises in Northern Nigeria", *Situation Report No.1, Office for the Coordination of Humanitarian Affairs (OCHA)*, March 2014, 8, http://www.reliefweb.int/rwarchive/rwb.nsf/db900sid/392052515502b13b256ea00067634c?OpenDocument&Click-, accessed November 5, 2017.

United Nations. 2015. *Plan of Action to Prevent Violent Extrimism*, 70th Session of the General Assembly, New York, United Nations, December 24, 2015, p. 1. (A/70/674), https://www.un.org/counterterrorism/ctitf/plan-action-prevent-violent-extremism, accessed June 4, 2017.

World Food Programme. 2017. "Nigeria Emergency", https://www.wfp.org/emergencies/nigeria, accessed February 20, 2017.

World News Ghana Web, "Nigeria's Borno State Lost $9.5bn to Boko Haram – World Bank", March 21, 2016.

http://www.ghanaweb.com/GhanaHomePage/NewsArchive/Nigeria-s-Borno-state-lost-9-5bn-to-Boko-Haram-World-Bank-424798, accessed June 4, 2017.

Chapter 14

Public Art, Public Voices

Changing the Narrative on Borders and Belonging

Shane Boeder

FORCED DISPLACEMENT

Escaping violence in search of sanctuary and hope takes courage. As a Guatemalan refugee said, "Every two blocks sometimes you'd find a body" (Int. Rescue Committee). Persevering in the face of kidnapping, extortion, and rape on the journey takes courage. Using art to share the intimacy of those stories takes courage. Together, refugees and artists use their creativity in public spaces as art activism, as "a form of social action, . . . a very mighty tool of the political imagination" (Maria R. 2016) and for human rights.

In his work *Hoping to Survive,* Afghan artist Razieh Gholami reveals the shattered hopes of migrants forcibly displaced by violence at home that is made more tragic by the violence of rejection at the border of a nation where they had expected to find sanctuary. In Gholami's 2019 canvas, massive, white hands with fingernails painted the colors of flags of many nations form an impenetrable barricade on the beach where tiny dinghies and row boats try to land. With endless precision, the manicured white fingers flick the tiny, dark-skinned refugees back into the sea. Savagely indifferent to the tragic plight of desperate migrants, their actions compound the trauma already suffered by the beleaguered travelers. The politics of exclusion, racism, xenophobia, and a militant citizenry forbid entry to the shore and safety. As a refugee himself, Gholami uses a canvas to compel even the casual onlooker to look again in order to make sense of this visual re-enactment of power relationships. With each public showing, his work of activist art arouses some empathy for the tiny figures and suggests a compelling counter-narrative about forced displacement. Gholami paints his testimony as a form of visual activism. His work shames the ultra-nationalist politicians and their media supporters who stoke public hostility toward immigrants and the rise of what sociologist Rene Flores calls "social illegality" (Gale, 2018).

According to the UN Refugee Agency (UNHCR), Latin American migrants from the Northern Triangle Countries (NTC) of El Salvador, Guatemala, and Honduras leave one of the most dangerous places on earth. Gang violence, threats, extortion, persecution, and sexual violence have forced hundreds of thousands of people to flee their homes in search of safety and a better life. Approximately 500,000 people have sought refuge in neighboring countries and more than 250,000 have been internally displaced inside the region (Central America Refugee Crisis, UN Refugee Agency).

United Nations' statistics show that forced displacement from Central America has increased 33 percent since 2018 (Displacement, UN). The impact of government corruption; political persecution; drug cartels; gang recruitment; gender violence toward women and the LGBTI community; and the Covid-19 pandemic have all increased the vulnerability of marginalized people in the three NTC nations and in Nicaragua and Mexico. "Overall, more than 890,000 people from the NCA [North of Central America] and Nicaragua have been uprooted from their homes" (UN, Displacement). These crises have fueled a massive exodus to other nations in addition to a growing number of internally displaced people. The failure of governments to protect their own citizens results in neighborhoods abandoned to poverty and local power brokers like gangs and drug cartels. For example, with an estimated poverty rate of 48 percent (Call) "Honduras is one of the poorest countries in the Western hemisphere. It has experienced one of the world's highest homicide rates, with multiple forms of violence linked to drug trafficking groups and gangs" (Bermeo 2021). Rampant political corruption at the highest levels empties the national coffers and offers impunity to these groups. For such reasons, Honduran President Juan O. Hernández is known there as the "narco-president." "[F]ederal prosecutors in the United States have sought to show that the president [Hernández] built a symbiotic relationship with drug traffickers who provided financial support for his political ascent in return for protection from prosecution" (Porter 2021). Honduras is a nearly lawless nation where "corruption riddles the political system" (Porter 2021). A Honduran refugee told Doctors Without Borders that "Gang-related murders, kidnappings, extortion, and sexual violence are daily facts of life." He continued, "In my country, killing is ordinary—it is as easy as killing an insect with your shoe" (Migration Crisis-Doctors). As a result, the most vulnerable Hondurans who are further impoverished by increased food insecurity caused by droughts and back-to-back hurricanes in November 2020, trek northward in search of work and protection.

With a similarly tragic story from El Salvador, twenty-three-year-old Valentina fled to the United States after her family was threatened by gangs. She said to the International Rescue Committee that "The hardest part about living in El Salvador is the violence, . . . This is what makes life hard, because you leave your house and you don't know if you'll return. So, yes, this is a war" (What is happening? 2021).

Yet as Cheatham at the Council on Economic Relations explains it has been interventions by the U.S. government, especially since the Cold War "including support for a coup in Guatemala, brutal government forces in El Salvador, and right-wing rebels based in Honduras known as the Contras—[that] helped destabilize the region" (Cheatham 2019). Such politically expedient U.S. policies have resulted in political instability and "planted the seeds for the complex criminal ecosystem that plagues the region today, which includes transnational gangs such as Mara Salvatrucha (MS-13) and the Eighteenth Street Gang (M-18)" (Cheatham 2019). United States' political interference; economic and military assistance to groups trying to topple democratically elected regimes; aid to U.S. corporations doing business in Central America; deportations of gang members; the War on Terror; and the War on Drugs have resulted in some of the world's highest homicide and femicide rates in the world in the Northern Triangle nations in Central America.

Desperate to survive, people walk northward to the nation born of immigrants: the United States. "No más muertes"/No more deaths plead desperate parents forced to flee their homes. "No más muertes," they whisper as they gather a few items to squeeze into their bulging backpacks. "Ni una más/Not one more." "Not my son. Not my daughter. Not my husband, my brother, my sister, my mother, my grandchild," they intone to themselves as they sew some bills into the lining of their clothes. "No más muertes," they pray as they slip out of their tiny homes to rendezvous with the coyote/smuggler who has promised to guide them on the trek north. They have sold their worldly good as well as their honor and their souls to raise the $5,000–$10,000 necessary to pay the guide they must trust. Yet, he is the same guide who may abandon them at any time. These desperate migrants are now homeless and soon stateless.

"No más muertes" they breathe as they grasp their children's hands and take another step toward hope. They walk with blisters bursting. They hide when uniforms or people whose curious eyes will sell them to the authorities for a few dollars are nearby. They join others as their ragtag caravan fords a river or challenges border guards armed to shoot border crossers. They hush a baby as they tremble and cower in the mesquite of the desert. Too tired to whisper their hope, they lift an exhausted child and settle him on their shoulders, atop their shrinking backpack and continue. On the trail, they leave behind the party shoes, the extra sweater, the empty water bottle. Sometimes they glimpse "No más muertes" scrawled in paint on a wall as a warning, a reminder, a goal. Barely thinking, they just plod on as the realities of crossing borders burrows deep inside them. Soldiers with assault weapons from the

United States confront them. Police roust them from uneasy sleep and drive them away. Gangs rape grandmothers, mothers, and daughters then slash everyone's clothes searching for money. Police watch. Every new horizon has bigger barriers, more barbed wire, more drones, more steel-toed boots, and weapons at the ready. The consequences of United States' border imperialism assail them at every crossing and infest every cell of their own bodies.

The sheer number of these stories reveals the magnitude of the human rights crisis of forced migration from the Americas. In 2017, Francisca Vigaud-Walsh of Refugees International underlined the central question about the United States' responses to the scale of this displacement of Central Americans fleeing nations plagued by political corruption. She said, "The obvious question is whether . . . the United States is meeting its humanitarian, legal, and ethical obligations surrounding protection when it deports people to such conditions" (Vigaud-Walsh 2017).

In the United States, politicians have distorted the human cost of this violence that denies families the most basic of protections. Instead, they question "Who belongs?" Who belongs in our neighborhood? In our nation? In the story of our shared identity? The media are overflowing with epithets disparaging refugees, separated families, people seeking asylum, immigrants, dreamers, hardworking but undocumented farmworkers, laborers, factory workers, and so many others who live in the shadows. Although they are essential to our economy and the diversity that strengthens our nation, immigrants are often assailed with open hostility, hate speech, slurs, discrimination, and tacit endorsements of violence.

Made invisible in the United States through a politics of denial, this crisis has become a crisis of understanding that has, in turn, generated a crisis of empathy. Misguided, ill-informed, and complacent U.S. Americans vociferously defend their "American way of life" against "invaders." Driven by ignorance, self-serving politicians, and social media, they deem the arrival of refugees a social and economic crisis. They don't agree with Doctors Without Borders that as "a humanitarian crisis, it demands a humanitarian response" (Desperate Journey 2018).

Yet the economic, social, and cultural reality is that nearly one in every four U.S. Americans is an immigrant or the son or daughter or grandson or grand-daughter of an immigrant (Pew 2015 and National Academy of Sciences 2017). In 1938, Pres. Franklin Delano Roosevelt counseled, "Remember, remember always that all of us, and you and I especially, are descended from immigrants and revolutionists" (Ratcliff 2016). In fact, this historic diversity has proven to be an economic stimulant, not a crisis, for the United States. Nevertheless, although these creative and hardworking immigrants have always contributed to the economy and cultural richness, they are increasingly vilified as a threat to our security and national identity.

Scandalously, more politicians today, than in the past, have openly used their platforms to arouse more hostility, fuel xenophobia, and impose drastic sanctions on the non-native-born. Their hate speech increasingly fosters racial slurs and violent actions against immigrants and others identified as "different" and not worthy of belonging.

Since the 1960s, the United States has increasingly militarized the U.S. border in reaction to this perceived threat from "alien hordes." Through punitive polices that defy international human rights accords protecting refugees seeking asylum, the United States has imposed a new form of border imperialism on the land route used by desperate immigrants from the Americas, Asia, and Africa. With threats to stifle trade, promises of funding to fight the drug war, and enticements of providing more military weapons and counter-terrorism training, the federal government has coerced the governments of Honduras, El Salvador, Guatemala, and Mexico to accede to its demands to make each of their borders impenetrable and to repatriate anyone who evades checkpoints or even those who present themselves as refugees in search of asylum. Within the United States and at the U.S.–Mexico border, congress and executive actions have further denied undocumented immigrants their basic human rights by limiting health care, social services, education, access to social service agencies, etc. They have denied refugees and asylees due process, forced their repatriation, separated children from parents, and ended Temporary Protective Status (TPS) programs. On media platforms, in melodramatic speeches and with skewed statistics, these political tactics have intentionally fomented fear of "invasion," job loss, rape, murder in the United States, and justified further measures to exclude immigrants.

ART AS ACTIVISM

The statistics about the global displacement of some 71 million people (UN Refugee Agency) are overridden by all the negative hype about hordes of migrants breaching the border, destroying culture, and stealing jobs. In response, activist artists like Chilean-American Alfredo Jaar accept the challenge to "get people to really see each other" (Rushe 2019). Their art compels viewers to examine the narratives of loss, hope, fear, doubt, and rugged determination that drive the migrants themselves. He, like other activist artists, finds innovative ways to use public spaces to "address issues of sociopolitical and cultural significance, and to encourage community or public participation as a means of effecting social change" (Felshin 1995, 10).

For example, Adrian Paci's 2007 video, *Centro di permanenza temporanea* (Temporary Detention Center), was part of a larger exhibition called *Warmth of Other Suns: Stories of Global Displacement* at the Phillips Museum in

Washington D.C. in 2019. One provocative still from the film shows men and women crowded onto a moveable stairway that is alone on the tarmac at an airport. They are waiting to board a plane. But there is no plane. In the distance, the viewer glimpses another plane taking off, but their plane never arrives (Lefrak 2019). They have been abandoned in a state of perpetual waiting, much like the current wave of migrants seeking refuge in the United States. Perhaps a more literal, but oxymoronic, translation, of the film's title "Center for Temporary Permanence" better evokes the perplexity of those waiting and the limbo of their status. Through art, images like this snapshot draw immediate reactions of incomprehension, concern, and, eventually, outrage from viewers as they begin to really see and feel the inhumane treatment of migrants seeking sanctuary.

With works such as these, activist artists are using public spaces to counter the vitriol and misinformation in prevailing narratives that demonize migrants. They invite viewers and participants to examine the human plight of migrants. In this way, activist art intentionally interrogates the politics of exclusion, arouses empathy, and acts as catalysts for change. Through what Bell Hooks calls "visual politics" (Hooks 1995), they assert the dignity and humanity of those fleeing political and economic violence and reveal the injustice of the United States' anti-immigration policies. Since politics "is a struggle for power" (Bonikowski 2016) over resources, status, and "the ability to define legitimate categories of thought" (Bonikowski 2016), activist artists also use canvasses, murals, performances, installations, photography, music, and multimedia to legitimize and empower the immigrants themselves (Hooks 1995, 3). Their work confirms that "[r]epresentation is a crucial location of struggle for any exploited and oppressed people asserting subjectivity and decolonization of the mind" (Hooks 1995, 3). In addition, activist arts democratize public spaces by revealing the presence of immigrants as part of the fabric of community in our neighborhoods. By asserting the presence of people intentionally excluded from the social imaginary, they contest prevailing discourses and political actions that distort perceptions about immigrants, their journeys, and their contributions to communities and the nation. By inviting viewers and audiences to participate as co-creators of meaning, activist art works, installations, and events change the public discourse on belonging.

For example, in 2017 cartoonist Mike Lukevich used sardonic humor to reveal how the Trump administration's acts of exclusion impact the nation's identity and foster erroneous perceptions about refugees. He drew a passenger ship carrying hopeful immigrants arriving in the New York harbor that is dwarfed by the pedestal of the Statue of Liberty seen in the foreground. But in this cartoon Lady Liberty, who has been a beacon of hope, freedom, justice, and enlightenment since 1886, has abandoned her pedestal. The statue itself is gone. A voice from the ship explains, "She resigned." Circulating widely in print and online, Lukevich's sketch of absence critiques the Trump administration's brutal policies of exclusion. The "Mother of Exiles," and "New Colossus" (Statue of Liberty), as poet Emma Lazrus called her, has fled. She no longer welcomes the "huddled masses yearning to breathe free" (Statue of Liberty). In despair, Lady Liberty herself has succumbed to the prevailing narrative that immigrants "don't belong here."

To restore Lady Liberty to her pedestal and relight her beacon of hope, activist artists like Lukevich use a variety of media and platforms to invite viewers to question "dominant cultural representations and . . . the configuration of power" (Felshin 1995, 25–6). On canvas, on walls, inside museums, on streets, in social media, in installations in unlikely places, and in art actions, activist artists let the immigrants speak for themselves. They reveal the campaigns of disinformation and the political tactics used both inside the United States and in the nation's imperialist policies in Latin America and other nations. With clear political intent, activist artists use various modes of storytelling to lay bare the violence of prevailing narratives that dehumanize immigrants and to critique the United States' role in fostering state violence in Latin American nations in order to assure its own political and economic hegemony. "Not content to simply ask the questions, these artists engage in an active process of representation, attempting at the very least to 'change the conversation,' to empower individuals and communities, and ultimately, to stimulate social change" (Felshin 1995, 26).

VIOLENCE OF U.S. ECONOMIC POLICIES AND BORDER IMPERIALISM

Political corruption, climate change, natural disasters, and the Covid-19 pandemic have worsened the basic structural inequalities in education, health care, and jobs in Central America. According to the Council on Foreign Relations, five of the six poorest countries in the Americas are in the Northern Triangle (Honduras, El Salvador, Guatemala). Yet many of the root causes of migration lie in the United States' own economic, political, and legal polices. The United States has supported corrupt regimes that have enriched themselves at the expense of the welfare of their own citizens. Trade agreements such as NAFTA (1994) CAFTA (2005) and the United States–Mexico–Canada Agreement (USMCA) (2020) have favored big business in the United States while impoverishing subsistence farmers in Central America. In the 1960s–1970s and 1980s and still today, the United States has financed the overthrow of legitimately elected governments. More recently, the U.S. War on Drugs and the War on Terror have militarized regimes that maintain power by force. The United States has deported gang members bred in the streets of Los Angeles from U.S. prisons to their home countries where they have established brutal networks of trafficking of drugs, weapons, and persons. In short, through its imperialistic interventions, the United States has created the conditions in failing states that compel people to seek refuge in the United States.

Meanwhile, successive administration in the United States have more aggressively militarized the border with Mexico and implemented more draconian policies that drastically restrict immigration, limit legal bids for asylum, refuse to extend Temporary Protective Status (TPS) and protections for the Dreamers and millions of undocumented immigrants already in the United States. In 2019, the Trump administration enacted the Remain in Mexico policy ironically called the Migrant Protection Protocols (2019) that protects no migrants, especially those with a credible fear of persecution if they return to their home countries. Blatantly abrogating international accords and its own policies about refugees seeking asylum, this policy has kept "more than 65,000 asylum seekers stuck in Mexican border towns" (Echavarri 2020). Furthermore, since "March [2020], the Trump administration has used the pandemic to seal shut an already virtually closed U.S–Mexico border to migrants who turn themselves in to border agents and to asylum seekers" (Echavarri 2020).

Using language that intentionally distorts the national narratives of home and belonging Donald Trump, as presidential candidate, as president (2016–2020), and as ex-president overtly engaged in what some human rights activists have called "moral terrorism." By manipulating language in public addresses, interviews, and social media and advocating violence to justify their policies of Zero Tolerance, Trump and other white supremacists and xenophobic ultra-nationalists have shattered the promises of our immigrant heritage.

Activist artists have responded by creating "art that is a form of political or social currency, actively addressing cultural power structures rather than representing them or simply describing them" (Activist Art Tate). They use found items, unexpected spaces, and the border wall itself as a canvas to counter negative stereotypes of migrants and to reveal the grim realities they flee at home. Using experiential and visual forms of art as a "catalyst for transformation" (Hooks 1995, 6), they reveal the human consequences of U.S. border imperialism such as Prevention Through Deterrence (since 1994–) that drive the very migration they propose to deter. In a variety of media, activist artists reveal the horrors that refugees face on their journey and at the border where they seek asylum.

WE ARE HUMAN BEINGS

Many activist artists draw on their own experiences as refugees or undocumented immigrants or, as artist Michelle Angela Ortiz explains, by "interviewing and collecting stories from local undocumented families" (Tokaver 2019). They use texts, images, and direct experience to foster dialogue about the deportation of undocumented migrants. In 2015, Ortiz created a series of five art installations called *Familias Separadas/Separated Families* in Philadelphia. Arresting because of its monumental size and location, one installation appeared outside City Hall. Eighteen feet tall, it was a portrait of Maria, an undocumented immigrant detained nearby whose story should arouse pathos and empathy, not retribution. In another bold commentary on policies of exclusion, Ortiz and thirty volunteers, community members, and undocumented families used stencils to paint the words of Ana, an undocumented mother detained by ICE. Her canvas? A hyper-politicized space: the street outside the ICE building in Philadelphia. On the pavement, they painted a message of defiance: "We Are human Beings, Risking Our Lives for Our Families and Our Future." For Ortiz, the word "we" in the title includes the community of volunteers who painted and the immigrants themselves. Furthermore, its very public location broadens its meaning to include members of the community and the very state and federal apparatus that carries out policies. To raise awareness that both victims and perpetrators are bound by this humanitarian crisis, Ortiz surprises and unsettles the complacent.

In 2018, in the second phase of the *Familias separadas* project, Ortiz used murals and billboards to draw attention to the glaring human rights abuses committed at the Berks County Family Detention Center in Harrisburg, Pennsylvania. Ortiz installed an 88-foot-long image of Salvadoran refugee Karen and her 5-year-old son who had been detained in that facility for 651 days. Offering an enormous visual testimony of a harmless refugee mother and child, Ortiz forced viewers to confront the impact of the politics of separation, detention, and deportation ironically purported to keep U.S. citizens safe from migrants who Trump characterized as "stone cold criminals" (Edwards 2019). Ortiz highlighted the tragic irony that United States' policies have criminalized and incarcerated mothers and children whose only crime has been to walk across the U.S. border without permission. The artist explained, "I'm not giving the mothers a voice. They already have a voice. I'm not giving them power. I'm helping energize that existing individual and collective power that they have" (Tokaver 2019).

VIOLENCE ON THE JOURNEY AND THE LOSS OF HOME

During the journey, migrating "foot people" suffer even more violence. Waiting in make-shift tents or huddled on the ground in Mexico or Guatemala or even in the United States, they live with the constant threat of further separation from their families, hunger, dehydration, rape, extortion, and death. Assuming a sociopolitical role, activist artists work to "give voice to the disenfranchised and to connect art to a wider audience" (Felshin 10) because, as Chinese dissident and activist artist Ai Weiwei has said, "If anything, art is . . . about morals, about our belief in humanity. Without that, there simply is no art" (Tate, Activist Art n.d.).

For example, Salvadoran activist Salomón painted *Los nuevos refugiados/ The new refugees* for the 2020–2021 exhibit *Refugiarte/Refugee Art* sponsored by the United Nations. In the center of his canvas, a group of tiny people carrying boxes, bundles, suitcases, and children are walking toward the foreground. They are dwarfed by the word "VIOLENCIA"/Violence that forms a wall corralling them on all other sides. Inscribed on each letter of "VIOLENCIA" are symbols and words that name some of the threats in their homeland that they are escaping: pandilla/gang, extorción/extortion, etc. With their return blocked, they must move forward into the unknown and undefined space before them.

In this way, artists like Salmón restore both agency and dignity to those suffering from "invisible wars." Their art offers testimony of the complex narratives of refugees' lives and urges viewers to embrace, not revile, migrants. Using a variety of media to dramatize the migrants' desperation, they assert that public spaces are effective sites for a democratizing people's theater to address power structures and to feel the shared humanity that binds us. They reconstruct symbols, images, and fragmented narratives to replace the prevailing, distorted public perceptions about immigrants, their homeland, their journeys, and their hope with true stories.

SHOES AND THE LOSS OF HOME

The "Migrant Trail" from Honduras to the United States' border is a harrowing journey of 2,550 miles long by car (Travel Math.com) and further on foot. It may take a month or more during which migrants risk kidnapping, extortion, rape, murder, and certain violence from the two drug cartels that control trains, buses, and all roads small and large in Mexico. The Sinaloa Cartel controls the west coast of Mexico from Guatemala to the U.S. border at California, Arizona, and New Mex. The Zetas control the east coast from Belize and Guatemala to the Texas border. As Crow explains, "The migrant experience includes a great deal of corporeal suffering through harsh environmental conditions, profound physical stress, psychological terror, dehydration and malnutrition, and the specter of maltreatment at the hands of others"(Crow 2013).

To create *Caminando/Walking* Argentinean artist Javier Garrido interviewed Honduran refugees about their experiences on the journey. His work appeared in the traveling exhibit Refugiarte: 2020–2021/Refugee Art sponsored by the United Nations Refugee Agency (UNHCR) to raise awareness about forced displacement and the refugee crisis. Comprising works by more than fifty Latin American artists, the exhibit was designed as a "cultural action" to "reduce intolerance . . . [and] to promote positive attitudes towards this population" (RefugiArte).

In *Caminando/Walking,* Garrido paints a figure bent double under the weight of bulging sacks on his back. Walking in a desert landscape, the man carries remnants of his home with him. These are the memories that will sustain him on his journey and when he finds the protection he seeks. Weighing him down are a mango tree alongside a guitar, a cemetery headstone, a chicken, a small image of the Virgin María, a water bottle, a radio, a cat peeking out of a jug, a radio, and more. Plodding toward asylum, this solitary figure embodies endurance, resilience, and determination in every step. This portrait humanizes the loss of home and intensifies the hardships of the journey itself. As Garrido's painting moves from one venue to another as part of the United Nation's traveling exhibit, its audience grows and viewers begin to question what they have accepted as truth. Like so many others, this canvas "reinterprets 'what previously was seen and known' so that alternative understandings may emerge. These reinterpretations help reveal existing power relations within society" (Moller 2016).

As alarm in the United States about the arrival of migrant caravans or unaccompanied children crescendos in social media and news outlets alike, the physical suffering of migrants remains largely invisible beyond a few sporadic reports. Consider, for example, the magnitude of the exodus of foot people from Venezuela. Their own government denies that the economy has collapsed and refuses to keep records of displaced emigrants and those who have died as foot people seeking refuge. Yet bodies line the backroads and others vanish without a trace on the treacherous journey over mountains to Colombia toward promises of safety and security. In spite of the cold and hunger and their growing desperation, the migrants have no alternative but to keep going. Like the Honduran migrant in *Caminando*, Angelis, a severely malnourished ten-year-old Venezuelan migrant girl said to her mother, "Let's go, mamá. I'll walk in my broken shoes" (Armario 2018). Wearing only her leggings and a light jacket, she and her mother began to walk the 2,700 miles from home to Peru in 2018. At first, they slept huddled together beside the road in a mountain pass. With only six dollars tucked beneath her clothes, her mother urged her daughter forward in a trek nearly equivalent to the distance from New York City to Los Angeles (Armario 2018). Nearby they saw another migrant with feet so blistered that he had made sandals from a broken water bottle and strips torn from his own shirt (Armario 2016).

In another arresting image of the misery of the foot people, immigrant artist Javad Karimi, of Afghanistan, painted *Poverty* in 2019. He drew shoes, the shoes of a migrant not unlike those described by the Venezuelan child Angelis or shoes abandoned in the Sonoran Desert by the delirious foot people whose water has run out and whose energy has vanished. The work is simple: just two shoes, cracked, patched, and worn through. Both big toes protrude. The viewer sees the shoes from above just as the migrant must see them as he looks down when he pauses before a swath of blue in the foreground that is apparently a body of water. The water suggests a barrier to the walker, another dilemma without an apparent solution. As a work of activist art, Karimi's canvas complicates the narrative of refugee's search for sanctuary and pleads for the viewer to really see and really care. Furthermore, by painting his own struggle Karimi confirms his own agency. He is the narrator of his own story, not the object of others' derision or misunderstanding. He becomes empowered, as, by extension, do other migrants whose stories mirror his.

Another work prominent in *Refugiarte 2020–2021* is *El corazón en la mochila* (My heart in my backpack) by Mexican artist Ana Espriella. Inspired by testimonies of Honduran refugees she met, Espriella uses deft but subtle lines, to trace the nearly translucent image of a young woman. Dressed in black and slightly bent by the weight of a backpack, she is an anonymous figure carrying a valuable cargo. With just her head and torso visible, and a red heart painted on her cheek, she projects a steadfast determination to continue walking into the ill-defined space around her. Although she herself is colorless, the viewer first registers her black sweater that is prominent before an amorphous sky of pale blue and white. She is alone amid the clouds except for her backpack in the shape of a human heart. She may be anonymous, nearly invisible, and bereft of other possessions, but her heart carries memories of home and beats out the cadence of hope as she walks on. Espriella has captured the essence of her resilience and invites the viewer to urge her onward.

Commenting on these powerful evocations of the refugees' plight and efforts to make their circumstances more visible, some art critics, like Jason Farago of the *New York Times*, say that the museum is the only refuge for honest yet provocative portraits of these desperate migrants (Farrago 2019) because the "[c]atastrophes that once elicited horror, charity and promises of change now go nearly unnoticed" (Farago 2019). He asserts that museum exhibits are safe venues to counter political hysteria and awaken compassion among those ready to really see and feel the trauma of statelessness and the search for sanctuary. To this end, he describes *The Warmth of Other Suns,* the 2019 exhibit at Phillips Museum in Washington, D.C. In that exhibit canvasses, installations, videos, photos and the texts of intellectuals like Hannah Arendt re-historicized the role of art in humanizing the losses felt by migrants and revealed the true global scope of forced migration.

Yet even stately museums in the heart of the capital city may not offer sanctuary for art or migrants. In Washington D.C., the city transit authority refused to let buses carry advertisements for the exhibit. Their rationale? They prohibited advertisements "intended to influence public policy" (Lefrak 2019) and "influence members of the public regarding an issue on which there are varying opinions" (Lefrak 2019). In short, the art in the exhibit was deemed too political. The resulting publicity about censorship soon piqued heightened public interest. Public outrage at the attempt at censorship soon caused the authorities to reverse their decision. As a result, 100 works of art from throughout the world were shown on three floors of the museum. The exhibit was celebrated as public and art activisms that had defied multiple layers of censorship: the refugees' stories of anguish and rejection, the effectiveness of the art works in arousing awareness and empathy toward the migrants, and publicity inviting the community in the nation's capital to participate in a shared experience at the exhibit.

DRAWING STRENGTH FROM TELLING THEIR OWN STORIES

However, many activist artists eschew curated exhibits, even those that travel throughout the United States and the Americas. They prefer to take their struggle for power over prevailing discourse to the streets themselves. They want everyone to hear the voices of the displaced lamenting, "You can't live in my country anymore. It's too dangerous." Some works of refugee art in Mexico are enshrined on walls near points of entry where migrants arrive. "Migrant murals . . . act as a meeting point where human stories converge. They are like mirror reflections in which each migrant passing through can recognize themselves" (Nat'l Human Rights Commission 2020, 130). Because it is so difficult to understand migrants' experiences and "the intermediary space between the place of origin and the desired endpoint" (Nat'l Human Rights Commission 2020, 133–4), displaying the voices and art of migrants themselves offers testimony to their presence at one point on their journey.

Some shelters and other transit points in Mexico invite refugees to contribute to collective murals painted on their walls. For example, one refugee from Guatemala cried, "You can't live in my country anymore, . . . I'm scared" (Verza 2017) when she arrived at a migrant shelter in the central state of San

Luis Potosi. Both she and her daughter had been raped and her husband was attacked and nearly murdered as they fled Guatemala. Although she had never before held a paintbrush, for her the act of painting was "an act of empowerment, and solidarity" (Verza 2017). In her art, she was the subject of her own narrative, not an object of political manipulation or sexual violence. By revealing her story on the mural, she validated her experiences as a woman and as a refugee. By painting her visual testimony on the exterior wall of the shelter, she became a co-creator of public art and helped to "break down stereotypes, leave accounts of the passage of migrants and pull them out of invisibility" (Verza 2017) as Luis Nava, of the Tres Gatos collective and an organizer of the program sponsored by the United Nations and Mexican National Commission on Human Rights said.

Valuing true narratives and authentic voices in 2018, activist artists Marion Coleman and Ramon Carrillo of the nonprofit Oakland Workers Collective in Oakland, California, worked with thirteen-day laborers for a year to elicit their stories of migration and survival in the hostile climate during the Trump administration. They guided the undocumented immigrants in using "paint, textile art, and oral storytelling" (Rasilla 2018) to express the traumas they had suffered at home, as migrants, and living in the shadows without papers in the United States. Their exhibit called *Undocumented Heart: Oakland Day Laborers Tell Their Stories* was held both indoors and outdoors in a public park in Oakland. Conquering their fears about revealing their identities in such a public event, the immigrants felt empowered to tell their stories of migration and loss as a legitimate part of the narrative of diversity enriching the national identity in the United States. By locating their stories on a timeline of historical and cultural events in both Central America and the United States, the exhibit clearly linked the stories of displacement of Central Americans to the United States' political and economic imperialism in Latin America. By enticing passersby to participate, this multimedia art action became "a catalyst for transformation" (Hooks 1995, 6) for both the storytellers and the viewers. Both shared a bond as they became more aware of the human consequences of the machinations of power in the United States.

ARTISTS RESPOND TO THE WALL AS SYMBOL AND POLICY

The U.S.–Mexico border is 1,952 miles long, much of it desert and mountains. In campaign slogans and during his administration, Donald Trump's divisive and bombastic rhetoric to "make America great again" promised that he would construct a "big, beautiful wall" to establish absolute hegemony by barricading the United States from undesirable immigrants who would sully the purity of his nation. As *New York Times* columnist Shae Bauer says, "If anything, Trump's wall is the embodiment of a longstanding illusion of American permanence and superiority. Its bold symbolism inspires [the] 'Conservatives, Patriots & Freedom Fighters'" (Rodriguez 2021) that the Republican party has courted. Before Trump's presidency, "various types of fencing totaling 654 miles (just over 1,000 km) were already in place" (Giles 2021). His administration spent $15 billion to complete merely 452 miles of wall and only 40 of those miles were new construction. The rest was spent on strengthening or rebuilding existing barriers near urban areas.

As a trope for power, the wall is a disaster. It "has become a monument to failure, xenophobia, human rights abuse, and environmental damage" (Isacson 2020). It has irreparably damaged relations with Latin American nations by making them handmaidens of United States' policies of border imperialism. To further extend the southwestern border of the United States, in 2019, Trump coerced Guatemala into accepting the Asylum Cooperation Agreement (ACA) under which Honduran and Salvadoran refugees requesting asylum at the U.S. border would be immediately deported to Guatemala where they could petition for asylum in that nation. In flagrant denial of their rights to due process and a court hearing in the United States, migrants have been abandoned in another nation that is incapable of offering them the services and protections that international law requires. In response, Eric Schwartz, President of Refugees International called Trump's plan an "astonishing distortion of U.S. asylum law. . . . It is unconscionable and inhumane for the United States of America to force Guatemala to agree to being a safe third country, and, thus, a haven for Central American asylum seekers when, in truth, it is nothing of the sort" (Refugees 2019).

Activist artists responded quickly and publicly. On the day that Donald Trump was named the Republican Party's candidate for president, guerrilla artist Plastic Jesus created a tiny art installation in a public venue highly prized by Trump. On July 20, 2016, amid constant foot traffic in Los Angeles, he built a concrete wall around Trump's star on the Walk of Fame. The artist outfitted the miniature wall with tiny "Keep Out" signs and barbed wire. Inside he planted tiny American flags at the corners. It was a short-lived but searing critique of Trump's violent and racist anti-immigrant rhetoric. In this highly visible and highly symbolic public spot that is a favorite tourist destination, Plastic Jesus made Trump's plans an object of derision because, as he explained "art encourages dialogue and debate like no other media" (Cascone 2018).

In a later guerrilla art installation in 2017, Plastic Jesus used another public place to provoke a reaction about Trump's policy of interning undocumented immigrants and refugees. In an abandoned lot, he hung "signs on padlocked fences declaring 'Lot reserved for: Future Internment Camp by order: Donald J. Trump. President United States of America. Executive order 9066'" (Cascone 2018). Since many spaces were being commandeered by Homeland Security to house increasing numbers of immigrants apprehended at the border or undocumented immigrants picked up in their homes or at work, these signs were credible. They recalled actions of the Third Reich or Argentina or Chile in the 1970s and 1980s to detain and disappear a class of undesirables. But with a closer look, the QR code on the corner showed that the signs were not authentic but part of an art installation to denounce Trump's "racism, bigotry, homophobia, and sexism" (Cascone 2018).

"ART AT AN INTERNATIONAL BORDER IS INHERENTLY POLITICAL" (MORLAN 2017)

During a carefully curated media event at which Pres. Trump was inspecting prototypes for "his" border wall, a young mother was watching from her home made of scrap wood in Mexico (Bauer 2020). In simple phrases filled with tragic irony, she wondered why Trump needed another wall. Herself a victim of anti-immigration policies, she explained that she was born in the United States but raised in Mexico and couldn't get the documents to prove her citizenship. "Between her house and the United States there is already a nine-foot barrier of corrugated metal, and behind that there is another that is twice as tall. Then there is the impossible-to-navigate bureaucracy that keeps people like her out . . . " (Bauer 2020). For her, as for other refugees and undocumented immigrants, the most profound barriers to freedom from persecution and violence are the xenophobic policies and virulent hate speech in the United States.

The wall itself, as a contested space that bisects nations and communities and prevents cultural exchange, is a perfect site for art projects that critique its very existence. Media events, visual installations, and performance art arouse curiosity, provoke emotional responses, and foster dialogue about the human consequences of the restrictive politics of exclusion.

LaTorre explains that

> Border art can be defined as forms of creative expression that focus on the social, political, and cultural realities of life in regions like the U.S.–Mexico border, but can also speak to the broader experience of marginalization and oppression due to the imposition of invisible yet socially-restricting borders. (LaTorre 2012)

An early installation that mocked the myth of the United States as a nation of immigrants is performance artist Richard Lou's installation called *Border*

Door. Built in 1988 in the desert near the Tijuana International Airport, it predates the current vitriol about belonging. It is a solitary, half-open wooden door near some decrepit barbed wire fence that then served as the barrier between the two nations. Provocative, it seems like an illusion that suggests an invitation to enter this bleak, undeveloped area but with caution. "Row upon row of keys, 134 in all, hung from nails hammered into the door on the Mexican side. The door opened only one way—into the United States" (Knight 2018).

> As a performative extension to The Border Door, Lou visited local colonias [working class neighborhoods] and a shelter house for the poor called Casa de los Pobres [Home of the Poor] in Tijuana to hand out additional keys, thus encouraging people to pass through his door (Border Arts Workshop 46). Lou then documented the reaction of the various individuals who received keys, encountering everything from confusion to knowing recognition of Lou's intentions as a community-driven artist. (La Torre)

Too visible, too bold, this critique of border imperialism was removed by the Border Patrol just two days later. Nevertheless, it has endured as a multidimensional artistic spoof examining the politics of welcome and was recently displayed in the museum of East Los Angeles College in 2018.

In 1997, Tijuana artist Marcos Ramirez Erre tried to breach the fence with humor. He and other artists built a "33-foot tall, two-headed wooden horse sculpture" (Morlan 2017). With playful satire, they called it *Toy an Horse* to recall the Greek myth of the Trojan Horse in which Greek soldiers hid inside a similar, hollow wooden horse to breach the gates of Troy during the siege of that city. "Trojan Horse" has become a metaphor for a subversive maneuver to defeat a competitor. At the border checkpoint of San Ysidro, California, *Toy an Horse* was an art installation visible to about 50,000 people who crossed there every day. But with two heads, one facing toward Mexico and the other toward the United States, this wheeled horse could move in either direction to suggest that man-made barriers are subject to "invasions" from the north and the south. In this case, a military strategy had become a temporary art installation. Paying homage to artistic ingenuity, the *Troy an Horse* raises questions about physical, political, and imagined barriers and how to breach them. It boldly confirms that the interdependence of nations and mutual cultural exchange enrich both nations while mocking the increasingly militarized space that links them.

In many ways, the border itself serves as a gallery for art activists. As part of his world-wide tour called *Inside Out* French installation artist JR takes photos of people, enlarges the images, and pastes them on walls as a participatory social art project. In his outsize satire of anti-immigration policies, in 2017, he pasted a seventy-foot-tall portrait of the Mexican child Kikito who is peering over the border wall into California from the Mexican town of Tecate. The image of this curious, innocent baby challenges the power of walls to deter migrants. Kikito lives with his sister and mother in Mexico, not far from this site. When his mother consented to using her son's photo she said, "I hope this will help people see us differently than what they hear in the media, that they will stop taking us like criminals or rapists" (A. Schwartz 2017). To involve more people in conversation about border politics, JR posted this image and its location on social media. As expected, people made pilgrimages to the site and began a "human conversation" not a "hate debate" (A. Schwartz 2017) both in-person and online. Further underscoring the absurdity of $15 billion spent on wall construction during the Trump era and the venomous rhetoric was the fact that thirty minutes to the east of this site, there was no border wall at all (A. Schwartz).

Art on the border wall itself extends the exhibition space and enlarges the public imaginary to include new spaces, new narratives, and new modes of political activism. For example, while politicians talk of building more impenetrable walls, performance, and installation artist Ana Teresa Fernández works to erase them. Holslin explains that for "Fernández 'the border is a site of utopian possibility. Yet, at the same time the border wall is an aggressive reminder of the violent subjugation of Mexico through the instruments of NAFTA and the Merida Initiative and resulting drug war'" (Holslin). In 2011, and again in 2016, Fernández painted the metal slats of the wall between Tijuana and San Diego where the wall itself extends into the Pacific Ocean. She used an azure blue paint by Behr called "Seashore Dreams" on the Mexican side as a means of "Borrando la frontera"/Erasing the border. Now the color of the sky and the sea, the metal slats that resemble the bars of a jail cell seem to disappear. By 2016, 70 feet of the border fence between the so-called Friendship Park on the U.S. side and the park attracting locals to picnic and play on the Mexican side had been made invisible with blue paint.

PERFORMANCE ART: INTERACTIVE, PARTICIPATORY ART

In 2018, Mexican American artist Felipe Baeza asserted the need to humanize the issue of migration by "transforming, redefining, and re-imagining the global phenomenon of migration" (M Fernandez 2018). In the same year, Mexican artist Bosco Sodi constructed a facsimile of the border wall in Washington Park in New York City and invited local residents to literally dismantle it. To create this installation, he and Mexican craftsmen first molded and fired 1,600 clay bricks by hand in his studio in southern Mexico and then carried them "to New York along the same route an illegal immigrant might take" (M. Fernandez 2016). Later that same afternoon in New York, each participant in the park took home a remnant of the wall that had metaphorically bisected their own community and separated the intertwined stories of neighbors. Empowered as art activists or "artivists," they deconstructed both the tangible and symbolic barrier between people. In doing so, their actions were integral to other performance art that the Tate Museum describes as "an event scripted, or not, as well as film, video, photographic and installation-based artworks through which the actions of artists, performers or the audience are conveyed" (Tate Perform Art).

Since the 1970s, works of performance art have engaged sometimes unsuspecting members of the audience as co-creators. Together they collaborate publicly to create art that critiques or deconstructs generally accepted narratives. Moller calls them "artivists" and asserts that "such image-makers are political agents" (Moller 2016). Through direct experience, they interact with a shared sense of understanding and agency to assert their right to reframe the prevailing narrative about belonging and exclusion. At the same time, by collaborating in a local event, they defy racial and ethnic barriers in order to reclaim shared spaces to strengthen their own community.

MAPPING MIGRANT DEATHS IN THE U.S. DESERT

By December, the year 2020 was the deadliest for migrant foot people crossing the desert. 225 Mexican and Central American migrants had died in the jurisdiction of just one coroner in Arizona (Caetano 2021). In medical terms, they died of dehydration, hypothermia, and hyperthermia. Rugged terrain, record temperatures soaring to 120° in the summer of 2020, and no access to safe water were often fatal.

But data and reports from the morgue don't tell the whole story. A militarized border, political decisions that brand migrants as expendable people and language that fuels intolerance do. Consider the words of Pres. Trump who wanted to erect an electrified wall topped with spikes and a "water-filled trench, stocked with snakes or alligators" (Scott 2019) to stop the invasion of "murders and rapists." If those measures failed, he suggested that Border Patrol agents shoot refugees in the knee because they have "violently overrun our country" (Scott, 2019). In contrast, Santa Cruz County [Arizona] Sheriff Estrada explained that "Desperation and hope drive them. . . . These have got to be a real special kind of people that are willing to do just about anything if you give them a chance" (Hunter 2020).

The human cost of increased border "security" has increased dramatically since the Clinton administration launched the policy of Prevention through Deterrence in 1994. By increasing the authority and range of the Border Patrol to 100 miles inland, militarizing the border itself, and constructing larger and multiple physical barriers, they intentionally funneled migrants into the more treacherous and inhospitable terrain of mountains and deserts. As a result, far from policy makers in Washington, D.C. and beyond the imagination of people throughout the nation, the epicenter of migration deaths became the Sonora Desert. In 2014, the Pima County Morgue in Tucson, Arizona, was the busiest morgue in the world. Between 1998 and 2020, nearly 7,000 migrants' remains had been recovered by the Border Patrol along the Southwestern border (Humane Borders). Surely an under-count of actual deaths of migrants abandoned by smugglers when too sick or injured to travel, some human rights groups estimate that more than 10,000 migrants have died in the desert where remains disappear quickly in the heat.

3,200 TOE TAGS. 3,200 LIVES. *HOSTILE TERRAIN 94*

Humane Borders/Fronteras Compasivas actively maps the deaths of migrants in the Sonoran Desert in Arizona. In 2020, geographer Sam Chambers used the "geographical information system (GIS) modeling" (Cataneo 2021) to map the number of migrants crossing the Sonoran Desert that covers "100,000 square miles in Arizona, California, and Mexico" (Cataneo 2021). Raising awareness of border deaths as a political and human rights issue, anthropologist Jason de León used Chambers' map as an integral part of an installation and performance art project in Santa Fe, New Mexico.

In the summer of 2020, The School of Advanced Research and others sponsored "*Beyond Borders*. It was a powerful series of art installations and events that used the lens of art and social sciences to examine the global refugee crisis and realities of migration and border policy in the Northern hemisphere" (Beyond). It included *Hostile Terrain 94* by anthropologist Jason de León as a participatory art project sponsored and organized by the Undocumented Migration Project, a nonprofit research-and art-education media collective (de León 2020). As a participatory experience linking art/politics/identity, the title *Hostile Terrain 94* clearly links the 1994 Prevention Through Deterrence policy that initiated policies militarizing the U.S.–Mexico border to their human consequence. As an art performance "engaging directly with social reality, the specifics of space and the politics of identity" (Tate, Performance Art), it "simultaneously will take place at a large number of institutions, both nationally and globally in 2021 and throughout 2022"

(Hostile). By eliciting public participation, it jars people from their ignorance or complacency to critique policies that dehumanize refugees and weaponize border control.

Duplicating the gruesome work of morgue attendants who struggle to piece together the identities of migrants from remnants of belongings found in the desert, participants fill out 3,200 toe tags, one for each victim from 2000 to 2019. Each tag "includes the name, age, sex, cause of death, condition of body, and location of recovery for each person" (Beyond) to document the presence of formerly invisible victims of U.S. immigration policies. Participants then locate each tag on a map to further defy the migrants' erasure from the history of their home nation and the United States as well as from public conscience. With increasing horror, each participant engages in what artist Jeff Kelly calls "a dialogical process that changes both the participant and the artist" Felshin 1995, 233) because it is "politically viable, publicly visible and . . . aesthetically meaningful" (Felshin 1995, 233). Traveling throughout the United States and other nations, De León's performance art stimulates a growing awareness of migrants' stories as human stories. Furthermore, while participants at each site engage in a dialogue about migrants' rights and political dynamics, they too become empowered as art activists.

PORTRAIT OF AMERICA

Other tactics of activist artists may be more subtle, yet equally effective, as political statements in changing the narrative about inclusion. Skilled in using socially engaged art that "can include any artform which involves people and communities in debate, collaboration or social interaction" (Tate, Socially Engaged Art), they may include viewers who become unwitting participants in an art performance to create a more inclusive "Portrait of America."

For example in 2012, the *Undocubus* campaign traveled from Phoenix, Arizona, to the Democratic National Convention in North Carolina. Recalling the Freedom Riders of the Civil Rights Movement who faced grave risks at each stop, the bus boldly carried undocumented residents through communities that had enacted policies hostile to immigrants and Dreamers. To "challenge racist, anti-immigrant attacks through strength in numbers" (Chen 2012), they demanded "racial and economic justice." One rider, Daniela Cruz, explained the irony of moving a bus full of undocumented immigrants across the nation as a mode of political activism. She said, "Normally buses separate families and deport them. This bus is strengthening our community" (Saavedra 2012) by letting the victims of U.S. policies share their stories. It is public art action as an act of civil disobedience.

47 Stories: We Are All Migrating Together is another public art installation that demonstrates that we are all migrants or people intermingling in shared spaces to enrich neighborhoods as culturally inclusive communities. Together they "contribute their knowledge, networks, and skills to build stronger, more resilient communities" (International Migrants Day 2020). In 2016, Philadelphia artists Laura Deutch and Shira Walinsky interviewed riders and people along the route of city bus #47 to elicit both individual and collective stories of the community. Then they decorated the bus both inside and out as a moving installation. On its 10-mile-long bus route, bus # 47 carries 17,000 daily passengers through "more than a dozen immigrant ethnic communities" (Dolen). "Riders include people born in the U.S., Korea, Russia, Brazil, Indonesia, Haiti, Cambodia, China, Laos, Burma, Thailand, Mexico, and Vietnam" (Dolen). Inside the bus are "quotes from riders and images of landmarks and businesses along the route, including a Cambodian restaurant, a Mexican bakery, and an African hair-braiding salon" (Dolen). As they commute, the passengers form a changing community of migrants that is bound to each other and to the places they traverse. As publicity about the bus grew, it attracted riders from outside the community to appreciate the diversity of languages, histories, shops, and services that immigrants contribute. As artist Walinsky explained, "The bus is a great metaphor for migration and journey, and a great space to contemplate and reflect [while challenging] … "many types of barriers: physical, psychological, and emotional" (Rapaport-Stein 2016).

CONCLUSION: ACTIVIST PUBLIC ART ADDRESSES STATELESSNESS, SAFE SPACES, AND SANCTUARY

The violence of forced migration has been compounded by U.S. policies of border imperialism that have extended the U.S. border to southern Mexico, Guatemala, and beyond. At the same border checkpoints where hundreds of semi-trailer trucks carrying goods from Central American maquiladoras to feed consumer desire in the U.S. pass easily each day, desperate refugees are refused entry. Their pleas for protection are rejected out of hand or they are told to wait in Mexico or Guatemala, indefinitely.

By June 2018, fewer than 15 percent of people applying for asylum were allowed to proceed through the process, down from nearly 33 percent a year earlier. And as of December 2020, the United States agreed to accept fewer refugees than it had in more than forty years (Edwards 2019). By doing so, the United States abrogates accords that delineate our legal responsibility to refugees that were again clarified on the 50th anniversary of the 1967 U.N. Protocol that in 1979 became U.S. Refugee Law. Robert Barsky of Vanderbilt University explained:

> We are bound to refugees and asylum seekers by our collective humanity, and, through this treaty [1967 Protocol], by our adherence to the rule of law. The current rhetoric and treatment of asylum seekers who have reached our borders or are on the way, is not just immoral; it is illegal as well. (Barsky 2018)

Yet as xenophobic rhetoric dominates social media, everyday language and political campaigns, public activist art offers a form of enlightened political discourse. It counters portrayals of refugees, asylum seekers, and undocumented immigrants as criminals, economic sycophants, and threats to national security and cultural identity. As Cuban artist Tanya Bruguera says, "Art and ethics cannot be separated. . . . They are interdependent, they define each other" (Solomon 2020). As Leonard Bernstein, composer and conductor said, "art never stopped a war . . . That was never its function. Art cannot change events. But it can change people. It can affect people so that they are changed—they then act in a way that may affect the course of events . . . by the way they behave, the way they think" (Breen 2019).

Bold or subtle, impudent or satirical, art in public spaces reveals, questions, alerts, cautions, and critiques. As Colombian street artist DjLu, says, it sends "out a message using situations we are all part of but often prefer to ignore" (Ruíz 2011, 79). It examines power relations. It resists discourse that dehumanizes refugees and their human rights. It resists marginalizing. It resists forgetting. It resists erasing people. Instead, activist art reasserts narratives of belonging through art actions, installations, public storytelling, painted walls, posters, canvasses, and more.

Public art is participatory by intent, by message, and by process. It draws the viewer in to wonder, to question, to reflect. No longer passive observers, but as witnesses to the stories of marginalized people "politically engaged citizens can become *artivists* too" (Moller 2016) by engaging in dialogue about critical issues. It invites collaboration among the migrants who are victims of misrepresentation, the artists, the viewers, and even neighbors. Young and old volunteers may pick up paintbrushes to work on a collective mural project to celebrate the achievements of immigrants or local diversity. They may map border deaths. They may paint border barriers the color of the sky so that they disappear. They may mimic crossing the border in a tank or a Trojan Horse. They may fly kites across the border wall or picnic together on both sides. As co-creators, their work is therapeutic for each of them and creates a community of resistance to militarized borders and dehumanizing rhetoric. Together, artists and *artivists* insist on a richer, more inclusive narrative that honors our traditions of sanctuary and justice for victims of violence and persecution and integrates undocumented immigrants who have already proven themselves integral to our Portrait of America.

REFERENCES

Am, K. and Cerasi, J. 2020. *Who's Afraid of Contemporary Art?* Thames & Hudson.

Armario, C. 2018. "I'll walk in my broken shoes: Mom, daughter flee Venezuela." *Associated Press News*, October 18, 2018. https://apnews.com/article/immigration-caribbean-venezuela-international-news-venezuela-exodus-43ef9f6848c14041aeb0876ec4a864d8.

Balmy Alley Murals. *Atlas Obscura.*

Barsky, R. 2018. "Legal responsibilities of the United States towards asylum seeker." Center for Migration Studies, December 4, 2018. https://cmsny.org/publications/barsky-us-legal-responsibilities-asylum-seekers/.

Batz, G. 2021. "U.S. policy toward Central America continues legacy of displacement." North American Congress on Latin America, April 2, 2021. https://nacla.org/news/2021/04/28/us-policy-central- america-migration-displacement?eType=EmailBlastContent&eId=212d29b2-9c37-4c79-b436-1d8825aed95d.

Bauer, S. 2020. "What is the status of Trump's 'big, beautiful wall'?" *New York Times,* September 25, 2020. https://www.nytimes.com/2020/07/02/books/review/14-miles-dw-gibson.html.

Bermeo, S. and Leblang, D. 2020. "Climate, violence, and Honduran migration to the United States." Brookings Institute, April 1, 2020. https://www.brookings.edu/blog/future-development/2021/04/01/climate-violence-and-honduran-migration-to-the-united-states/.

Bishari, N. S. 2018. "Behind Clarion Alley hides the lesser-known Balmy Alley." *San Francisco Weekly*, July 5, 2018. https://www.sfweekly.com/topstories/behind-clarion-alley-hides-the-lesser-known-balmy-alley/.

Bonikowski, B. 2016. "Introduction to political sociology." [Course description] Harvard University. https://scholar.harvard.edu/bonikowski/classes/introduction-political-sociology.

Bristol, M. 2020. "Political art at the U.S.-Mexico border." *Panoramas*, February 18, 2020.

Center for Latin American Studies at the University of Pittsburgh. https://www.panoramas.pitt.edu/art-and-culture/political-art-us-mexico-border.

Call, Charles T. 2021. "The imperative to address the root causes of migration from Central America." Brookings, January 29, 2021. https://www.brookings.edu/blog/order-from-chaos/2021/01/29/the-imperative-to-address-the-root-causes-of-migration-from-central-america/.

Cascone, S. 2018. "Walk of shame? A Guerrilla Artist Put Donald Trump's Hollywood Star Behind Bars—Literally." ArtNet, September 19, 2018. https://news.artnet.com/art-world/plastic-jesus-donald-trump-hollywood-1351822.

Cataneo, E. 2021. "Mapping migrant deaths in the desert." *High Country News-Colorado*, April 2, 2021. https://www.hcn.org/articles/immigration-mapping-migrant-deaths-in-the-desert.

Cheatham, A. 2019. "Central America's turbulent northern triangle." Council on Foreign Relations, October 1, 2019. https://www.cfr.org/backgrounder/central-americas-turbulent-northern-triangle.

Chen, M. 2012. "Get on the Undocubus." Common Dreams, July, 25, 2012. https://www.commondreams.org/views/2012/07/25/get-undocubus.

Chomsky, A. 2014. *Undocumented: How immigration became Illegal.* Beacon Press.

Corchado, A. "Central American migrants face grueling journey North." Mexico Bureau of Dallas Morning News. http://res.dallasnews.com/interactives/migrantroute/.

Crow, C. H. C. 2013. "The material culture of migrant life at the U.S. México border." Masters thesis. University of Arkansas. Scholarworks. http://scholarworks.uark.edu/etd/826.

Cuffe, S. 2021. "Fleeing the pandemic and two hurricanes, thousands of migrants walk toward the U.S." *Los Angeles Times,* January 16, 2021. https://www.latimes.com/world-nation/story/2021-01-16/fleeing-the-pandemic-and-two-hurricanes-thousands-of -migrants-walk-toward-the-united-states.

De León, J. 2020. *Beyond borders: Hostile terrain 94.* [Video]. Accessed July 21, 2020. https://www.youtube.com/watch?v=4-pE_y8YiA0.

Delgado, R. 2020. "Conversations with the wall." Trans. Samantha Schnee. In *Let's talk about your wall: Mexican writers: Respond to the immigration crisis.* C. Boullosa and A. Quintero (eds.), The New Press. Accessed at Google Books. https://books.google.com/books?id=55_LDwAAQBAJ&pg=PA140&lpg=PA140&dq=Tres+Gatos+collective+Mexico&source=bl&ots=kBfj5aNqEy&sig=ACfU3U3LcFc3yY39RRuMzypajwTnoI46rQ&hl=en&sa=X&ved=2ahUKEwipsK7m6NPwAhUPQ80KHT3-A0iQ6AEwDnoECBEQAw#v=onepage&q=Tres%20Gatos%20collective%20Mexico&f=false.

Displaced: Contemporary artists confront the global refugee crisis: March 21–September 6, 2020. [Exhibit's Gallery Guide] Site Santa Fe. Org. https://sitesantafe.org/wp-content/uploads/2020/03/GallerGuide_Displaced_v.3_pages-compressed.pdf

Doctors Without Borders/Médecins Sans Frontières. 2018. "Desperate journey: Fleeing invisible wars in Central America." *Alert* 19:3 (Fall 2018). https://www.doctorswithoutborders.org/what-we-do/news-stories/story/desperate-journey-fleeing-invisible-wars-central-america.

Donohue, C. 2021. 'Caravana': A flourishing of Central American art, both political and inventive. 48 Hills, March 2021. https://48hills.org/2021/03/in-caravana-a-flourishing-of-central-american-art-both-political-and-inventive.

Drescher, T. "Balmy Alley: A historical approach: Historical essay." San Francisco Digital Archive. https://www.foundsf.org/index.php?title=Balmy_Alley:_a_Modernist_Approach

Duperesep, K. 2016. "15 public art projects that boldly advocate for social justice." *Mashable*, September 24, 2016. https://mashable.com/2016/09/24/public-art-social-good/.

Echavarri, F. 2020. "2020 was the deadliest year on record for migrants crossing the Arizona Desert." *Mother Jones,* December 2020. https://www.motherjones.com/politics/2020/12/record-deaths-migrants-arizona-desert/.

Edwards, H. S. 2019. "The stories of migrants risking everything for a better life." *Time,* January 24, 2019. https://time.com/longform/migrants/.

Espriella, A. *El corazón en la mochila*. Painting. In *RefugiArte: The refugee crisis illustrated by Latin American artists*. UN Refugee Agency. https://www.unhcr.org/refugiarte/.

Facts about the humanitarian crisis in Mexico and Central America. 2019. Doctors Without Borders, February 5, 2019. https://www.doctorswithoutborders.org/what-we-do/news-stories/news/facts-about-humanitarian-crisis-mexico-and-central-america.

Familias separadas. https://www.familiasseparadas.com/phaseshome/phaseone.

Farago, J. 2019. "The museum is the refugees' home." *New York Times*, August 13, 2019. https://www.nytimes.com/2019/08/13/arts/design/the-museum-is-the-refugees-home.htm.

Felshin, N. ed., 1995. *But Is It Art?: The spirit of art as activism*. Seattle: Bay Press.

Fernández, A. T. *Borrando la frontera/Erasing the border* [Art Installation]. https://anateresafernandez.com/borrando-la-barda-tijuana-mexico/.

Fernandez, M. 2018. "The Latin American artists challenging trump's narrative on immigration". i D Vice, June 22, 2018. https://i-d.vice.com/en_us/article/gykej7/the-latin-american-artists-challenging-trumps-narrative-on-immigration.

Fishman, Elliot. 2019. "Moral terrorism." *The Nation* (September 9, 2019):10.

"Fleeing the Gangs in El Salvador: Carlos's story." New American Story Project. https://newamericanstoryproject.org/story/fleeing-the-gangs-in-el-salvador.

Gale, S. F. 2018. "Cultural stereotypes drive negative perceptions of undocumented immigrants." University of Chicago News, October 23, 2018. https://news.uchicago.edu/story/cultural-stereotypes-drive-negative-perceptions-undocumented-immigrants.

García-Navarro, L. [Host]. 2021. "Behind asylum seekers' experiences at the U.S.-Mexico Border [Radio Interview]." Weekend Edition Sunday. *National Public Radio*, March 21, 2021. https://www.npr.org/2021/03/21/979683437/behind-asylum-seekers-experiences-at-the-u-s-mexico-border.

Garrido, J. (2020). *Caminando* [Painting]. "RefugiArte 2020–2021: The Refugee crisis illustrated by Latin American artists." United Nations Refugee Agency. https://www.unhcr.org/refugiarte/.

Gholami, R. 2019. *Hoping to survive* [Painting] "We never chose this: Refugees use art to imagine a better world—in pictures." *The Guardian*, December 25, 2019. https://www.theguardian.com/global-development/gallery/2019/dec/25/we-never-chose-this-refugees-use-art-to-imagine-a-better-world-in-pictures.

Giles, C. 2021. "Trump's wall: How much has been built during his term?" *BBC*, January 12, 2021. https://www.bbc.com/news/world-us-canada-46748492.

"Guatemala resists border imperialism." 2019. Network in Solidarity with the People of Guatemala (NISGUA), September 2019. https://nisgua.org/wp-content/uploads/R101-final-and-updated-. ACAs.pdf.

Heneage, G. 2020. "Statelessness and safe spaces: how can the arts help refugees?" June 26, 2020. https://georgiaheneage.journoportfolio.com/articles/statelessness-and-safe-spaces-how-can-the-arts-help-refugees/.

Hilden, N. "Activist Art: The Power of Art to Change the World." *Artzine*. https://artzine.com/articles/activist-art-the-power-of-art-to-change-the-world.

Holslin, J. 2011. *Borrando la frontera/Erasing the border.* https://anateresafernandez.com/borrando-la-barda-tijuana-mexico/.

Hooks, B. 1995. *Art on My Mind: Visual Politics.* New York: New York Press.

Hostile Terrain 94. Undocumented Migration Project. https://www.undocumentedmigrationproject.org/hostileterrain94.

Hughes, S. A. 2018. "A mural on the capitol steps decries the detention of immigrant families." *Billy Penn Newsletter*, October 25, 2018 WHYY Radio Station in Philadelphia, PA. https://billypenn.com/2018/10/25/a-mural-on-the-capitol-steps-decries-the-detention-of-immigrant-families/.

Human Borders. 2020. "2020 was deadliest year for migrants crossing unlawfully into US via Arizona." Humane Borders, February 12, 2020. https://humaneborders.org/2020-was-deadliest-year-for-migrants-crossing-unlawfully-into-us-via-arizona/.

Hunter, C. 2021. "Report: Migrant deaths in Arizona desert have reached seven-year high." *Arizona Daily Star*, January 5, 2021. https://tucson.com/news/state-and-regional/report-migrant-deaths-in-arizona-desert-have-reached-seven-year-high/article_636fd548-d8ff-5906-9fbc-917dabc478b6.html.

International Crisis Group. 2017. "El Salvador's Politics of Perpetual Violence." Report 64: Latin America and Caribbean, December 19, 2017. https//www.crisisgroup.org/latin-america-caribbean/central-america/el-salvador/64-el-salvadors-politics-perpetual-violence.

"International migrants day 2020." 2020. United Nations December 18, 2020. https://www.un.org/en/observances/migrants-day.

International Rescue Committee. 2021. "What is happening at the U.S. southern border?" *Rescue Organization*, March 24, 2021. https://www.rescue.org/article/what-happening-us-southern-border

Isacson, A. 2020. "400 miles of harm: There is nothing to celebrate about border wall construction." Washington Office on Latin America (WOLA), October 29, 2020. https://www.wola.org/analysis/400-miles-of-harm-nothing-to-celebrate-about-border-wall-construction/

Kaplan, E. 2020. "What isolation does to undocumented immigrants." *The Atlantic,* May 27, 2020. https://www.theatlantic.com/family/archive/2020/05/isolated-undocumented-immigrant/612130/.

Karimi, J. 2019. *Poverty* [Photograph of Painting]. In 'We never chose this: refugees use art to imagine a better world – in pictures'. *The Guardian*, December 25, 2019. https://www.theguardian.com/global-development/gallery/2019/dec/25/we-never-chose-this-refugees-use-art-to-imagine-a-better-world-in-pictures.

Khan, K. 2020. "Latino artist uses paintings to counter anti-Immigrant attitudes." *Voice of America News*, February 6. https://www.voanews.com/usa/immigration/latino-artist-uses-paintings-counter-anti-immig2020/ rant-attitudes.

Knight, C. 2018. "'Border door' provided a poetic welcome to immigrants 30 years ago: An art show brings back its message." Art review. *Los Angeles Times*, May 4, 2018. https://www.latimes.com/entertainment/arts/la-et-cm-soul-mining-vpam-20180504-htmlstory.html.

Labossiere, P., Hahshahani, A. and González, D. R. 2021. "Root causes of forced migration: Neoliberalism, imperialism, and militarization [Webinar]." National Lawyers' Guild-San Francisco Bay Area Chapter, May 4, 2021. https://nlgsf.org/event/root-causes-of-forced-migration-neoliberalism-imperialism-and-militarization-part-1/.

Latorre, G. 2012. "Border consciousness and artivist aesthetics: Richard Lou's performance and multimedia artwork." *American Studies Journal* 57. https://doi.org.10.18422/57-05.

Lefrak, M. 2019. "Metro banned ads for this art exhibition on the immigration crisis, then changed its mind." American University Radio, August 7, 2019. https://wamu.org/story/19/08/07/metro-banned-ads-for-this-art-exhibition-on-the-immigration-crisis-then-changed-its-mind/.

Lescaze, Z. 2018. "13 artists on: Immigration." *New York Times Magazine*, June 19, 2017. https://www.nytimes.com/2018/06/19/t-magazine/immigration-art.htm.l.

Lou, R. 2017. *Border Door* (1988) [Art installation]. In K. Morlan "The most memorable acts of protest art at the border." *The Voice of San Diego*, February 27, 2017. https://www.voiceofsandiego.org/topics/arts/the-most-memorable-acts-of-protest-art-at-the-border.

Lukevich, Mike. 2017. *She resigned* (Image 162556). [Cartoon]. The Cartoonist Group, September 6, 2017. https://www.cartoonistgroup.com/store/add.php?iid=162556.

Maria, R. 2016. "15 influential political art pieces: Artwork(s) in focus." WideWalls, November 26, 2016. https://www.widewalls.ch/magazine/political-art.

Martinez, D. and Escalón, C. 2021. "Hundreds of migrants set out from Honduras, dreaming of U.S." *Associated Press News*, March 30, 2021. https://apnews.com/article/guatemala-honduras-latin-america-united-states-1dd5b1c6f4b75f0c3eb5ffcef024f70a.

Martinez, O. "A brief history of El Salvador, gangs, the U.S., and the difficulties of empathy." [Interview]. New American Story Project. https://newamericanstoryproject.org/context/brief-history-of-el-salvador.

Maslin, S. E. 2016. "Life and death among the gangs of Central America." [Review of the book *Violence: A history of living and dying in Central America.* by E. Martínez]. *New Republic*, April 11, 2016. https://newrepublic.com/article/132156/life-death-among-gangs-central-america.

McNulty, J. 2017. "Murals tell a story of pan-Latino solidarity in San Francisco's Mission district." *News* of University of California Santa Cruz, August 21, 2017. https://news.ucsc.edu/2017/08/ramirez-murals.html.

Meyerson, J. A. 2012. "Riders of the 'UndocuBus' have 'no papers', no fear." *In These Times*, September 5, 2012. https://inthesetimes.com/article/riders-of-the-undocubus-have-no-papers-no-fear.

"Migration crisis in the Americas." Doctors without borders. https://www.doctorswithoutborders.org/migration-crisis-americas

Moller, F. 2016. "Politics and art." *Oxford Handbook Online*. https://doi.org.10.1093/oxfordhb/9780199935307.013.13. https://www.oxfordhandbooks.com/view/10

.1093/oxfordhb/9780199935307.001.0001/oxfordhb-9780199935307-e-13?rskey=AinGby&result=3.

Morlan, K. 2017. "The most memorable acts of protest art at the border." *The Voice of San Diego,* February 2017. https://www.voiceofsandiego.org/topics/arts/the-most-memorable-acts-of-protest-art-at-the-border.

Morlan, K. 2017. *Toy an Horse* [Art Installation 1997] "The most memorable acts of protest art at the border." *The Voice of San Diego,* February 27, 2017. https://www.voiceofsandiego.org/topics/arts/the-most-memorable-acts-of-protest-art-at-the-border.

National Academy of Sciences, Engineering, Medicine. 2017. "Economic and Fiscal Consequences of Immigration." https://www.nap.edu/read/23550/chapter/5.

National Human Rights Commission of Mexico. 2020. "Make art, not walls" (Ellen Jones trans.) in *Let's Talk About Your Wall: Mexican Writers: Respond to the Immigration Crisis* by C. Boullosa and A. Quintero (Eds.), The New Press. 2020. https://books.google.com/books?id=55_LDwAAQBAJ&pg=PA140&lpg=PA140&dq=Tres+Gatos+collective+Mexico&source=bl&ots=kBfj5aNqEy&sig=ACfU3U3LcFc3yY39RRuMzypajwTnoI46rQ&hl=en&sa=X&ved=2ahUKEwipsK7m6NPwAhUPQ80KHT3-A0IQ6AEwDnoECBEQAw#v=onepage&q=Tres%20Gatos%20collective%20Mexico&f=false.

National Park Service. "The new colossus: Statue of liberty." Statue of Liberty National Monument. https://www.nps.gov/stli/learn/historyculture/colossus.htm.

Office of High Commissioner for Human Rights of United Nations. "Human Rights and Refugees: Fact Sheet No. 20." https://www.ohchr.org/Documents/Publications/FactSheet20en.pdf.

Open Society Foundation. 2019. "Why does the U.S. need immigration reform?" The Open Society Foundation, May 2019. https://www.opensocietyfoundations.org/explainers/why-does-us-need-immigration-reform.

Ortiz, M. A. 2016. "Familias Separadas." [Blog post]. Americans for the arts, August 19, 2016. https://blog.americansforthearts.org/2019/05/15/%E2%80%9Cfamilias-separadas%E2%80%9D.

Ortiz, M. A. 2019. "We are human beings Familias Separadas." *The Justice*, November, 2016. https://www.thejustice.org/article/2019/11/activist-discusses-her-new-art-installations-on-immigration-brandeis.

Peters, J. F. 2017. *Kikito* [Photo of art installation]. In A. Schwartz. "The artist JR lifts a Mexican child over the border wall." *The New Yorker*, September 11, 2017. https://www.newyorker.com/news/as-told-to/the-artist-jr-lifts-a-mexican-child-over-the-border-wall.

Plastic Jesus. 2016. *Trump's Walled Star* [Art installation]. Photo by David Livingston in S. Cascone, "Walk of shame? A guerrilla artist put Donald Trump's Hollywood star behind bars—Literally." *News at* ArtNet. https://news.artnet.com/art-world/plastic-jesus-donald-trump-hollywood-1351822 .

Porter, E. and Senple, K. 2021. "A damning portrait of presidential corruption, but Hondurans sound resigned." *New York Times*, March 23, 2021. https://www.nytimes.com/2021/03/23/world/americas/honduras-juan-orlando-hernandez-drug-trial.html.

"Prevention through deterrence." Undocumented Migrant Project. https://www.undocumentedmigrationproject.org/background.

Quade, K. V. 2017. "The other side of the wall: A new generation of Latino art." *New York Times*, August 17, 2017. https://www.nytimes.com/2017/08/17/t-magazine/art/contemporary-latino-art.html.

Raja, P. and Peterhans, L. 2020. "How arts and culture can serve as a force for social change." World Economic Forum, October 29, 2020. https://www.weforum.org/agenda/2020/10/how-arts-and-culture-can-serve-as-a-force-for-social-change/.

Rapaport-Stein, C. 2016. "We are all migrating together: Laura Deutch and Shira Walinsky talk about *47 Stories*." [Blog]. Mural Arts Philadelphia, December 13, 2016 https://www.muralarts.org/blog/migrating-together-laura-deutch-shira-walinsky-talk-47-stories/.

Rasilla, A. 2018. "In 'Undocumented heart,' day laborers turn their migration stories into art." KQED/ Public Radio. October 1, 2018. https://www.kqed.org/arts/13842864/in-undocumented-heart-day-laborers-turn-their-migration-stories-into-art.

Refugees International. 2019. "Trump's Guatemala plan 'An astonishing distortion of U.S. asylum law'." *Refugees International*, June 18, 2019. https://www.refugeesinternational.org/reports/2019/6/18/refugees-international-president-trumps-guatemala-plan-an-astonishing-distortion-of-us-asylum-law.

Rodriguez, S. 2021. "Trump's partially built 'big, beautiful wall'." *Politico*, January 12, 2021. https://www.politico.com/news/2021/01/12/trump-border-wall-partially-built-458255.

Ruiz, M. 2011. *Nuevo mundo: Latin American streetaArt*. Gestalten.

Rushe, D. 2019. "Art provocateur Alfredo Jaar: 'I want to change the world; I fail all the time'." *The Guardian*, August 1, 2011. https://www.theguardian.com/artanddesign/2019/aug/01/alfredo-jaar-artist-interview-change-the-world-pinochet-chile-edinburgh.

Saavedra, M. 2012. "Undocubus tour: No papers, no fear." *America's Voice*, July 30, 2012. https://americasvoice.org/blog/undocubus-tour-no-papers-no-fear/.

Salomón. 2020. *Los nuevos refugiados* [Painting]. RefugiArte 2020–21: RefugiArte: The refugee crisis illustrated by Latin American artists. United Nations Refugee Agency. https://www.unhcr.org/refugiarte/.

Schmidtke, R. 2020. "Critical policy advice for president-elect Biden: Protecting the forcibly displaced in Central America" [Issue brief]. Refugees International, December 3, 2020. refugeesinternational.org/reports/2020/11/30/critical-policy-advice-for-president-elect-biden-protecting-the-forcibly-displaced-in-central-america.

School of Advanced Research. 2020. "Beyond borders and hostile terrain 94." https://sarweb.org/beyond-borders-2020/t.

Schwartz, A. 2017. "The artist JR lifts a Mexican child over the border wall." *New Yorker*, September 11, 2017. https://www.newyorker.com/news/as-told-to/the-artist-jr-lifts-a-mexican-child-over-the-border-wall.

Schwartz, E. 2019. "Forced migration and the U.S. southern border." [Speech] Refugees International, May 8, 2019. https://www.refugeesinternational.org/reports/2019/5/8/forced-migration-and-the-us-southern-border.

Scott, E. 2019. "Trump's most insulting—and violent—language is often reserved for immigrants." *Washington Post*, October 2, 2019. https://www.washingtonpost.com/politics/2019/10/02/trumps-most-insulting-violent-language-is-often-reserved-immigrants/.

Solomon, T. 2020. "Tania Bruguera's most famous works: How the artist has challenged oppressive forces with incisive performances." *ArtNews*, July 16, 2020. https://www.artnews.com/feature/tania-bruguera-most-famous-works-performances-1202694439/.

Taggart, E. 2021. "Ai Weiwei artworks that bravely call attention to social issues in China." *My Modern Met,* April 12, 2021. https://mymodernmet.com/ai-weiwei-art/.

Téllez, J. *One flew over the void/ Bala perdida* [Art installation]. Guggenheim Museum. https://www.guggenheim.org/artwork/33126.

The Drug Policy Alliance. "The international drug war." https://drugpolicy.org/issues/international-drug-war.

The Tate Museum. "Activist art." https://www.tate.org.uk/art/art-terms/a/activist-art.

The Tate Museum. "Performance art." https://www.tate.org.uk/art/art-terms/p/performance-art.

The Tate Museum. "Socially engaged practice." https://www.tate.org.uk/art/art-terms/s/socially-engaged-Practice.

Tokaver, J. 2019. "Activist discusses her art installations on immigration." *The Justice of Brandeis University*, November 26, 2019. https://www.thejustice.org/article/2019/11/activist-discusses-her-new-art-installations-on-immigration-brandeis.

Toy an Horse [Installation]. 1997 In Site Archive in Special Collections and Archives of the library at University of California at San Diego. https://calisphere.org/item/ark:/20775/bb7033772w/.

Travel Math. "The driving distance from Honduras to United States." https://www.travelmath.com/drive-distance/from/Honduras/to/United+States.

Trimble, L. 2018. "How 10 Artists Tackle Immigration." *Phoenix New Times*, June 22, 2018. https://www.phoenixnewtimes.com/arts/how-10-artists-tackle-immigration-issues-10537598.

United Nations Refugee Agency. "Central America Refugee Crisis." https://www.unrefugees.org/emergencies/central-america/.

United Nations Refugee Agency. "RefugiArte: The refugee crisis illustrated by Latin American Artists." https://www.unhcr.org/refugiarte/.

United Nations Refugee Agency. 2021. "Central America Displacement Crisis Explained." UN Refugees, January 6, 2021. https://www.unrefugees.org/news/central-america-displacement-crisis-explained/.

Vargas, S. 2015. "Seizing public space." Development and Cooperation (EU), October 30, 2015. https://www.dandc.eu/en/article/politically-relevant-street-art-has-long-tradition-latin-america.

Verza, M. 2017. "Migrants from Central America paint hopes and dreams as murals in Mexico City." *Orange County Register,* August 18, 2017. https://

www.ocregister.com/2017/08/18/migrants-from-central-america-paint-hopes-and-dreams-as-murals-in-mexico-city/.

Vigaud-Walsh, F. 2017. "Displacement and violence in the northern triangle." *Refugees International*, November 21, 2017. https://www.refugeesinternational.org/reports/2017/11/27/displacement-and-violence-in-the-northern-triangle.

Weinik, S. 2015. *We are human beings* [Photo of art installation]. Familias Separadas. https://www.familiasseparadas.com/phaseshome/phaseone.

Weinik, S. 2016. *We are all migrating together* [Photo of art installation]. *47 stories we are all migrating together: Laura Deutch and Shira Walinsky talk about 47 Stories* by C. Rapaport-Stein .Mural Arts.org. December 13, 2016. https://www.muralarts.org/blog/migrating-together-laura-deutch-shira-walinsky-talk-47-stories/.

"We never chose this: Refugees use art to imagine a better world—in pictures." 2019. *The Guardian*, December 25, 2019. https://www.theguardian.com/global-development/gallery/2019/dec/25/we-never-chose-this-refugees-use-art-to-imagine-a-better-world-in-pictures.

Woodhouse, M. J. 2014. "Inside the Arizona morgue at the epicenter of the migration crisis." [Film Review]. *Aljazeera* America.com March 7, 2014. http://america.aljazeera.com/watch/shows/al-jazeera-america-presents-borderland/multimedia/2014/3/identifying-unknownbodiesinthepimacountrymorgue.html

Chapter 15

Border Crosser

Donald F. Hones

On a hot, dusty hillside trail in the Sonoran desert
Mid-August, midday
Alfred, three steps ahead
Turned to me and said
"¡Cuidado! Amigo.
Watch out for the snake."
Cuidado
His first word in Spanish
The title of one of his poems
About the human snakes
That prey upon refugees crossing borders
Amigo
his name for me since our journey to the frontier

"I have walked these trails before" he said
"A trail like this took me to Kenya."
He was a border crosser
Fleeing violence and war in Uganda
Running for his life, for his freedom
He crossed the ocean to Kansas City
And later, came north to
Oshkosh, Wisconsin
He brought his warmth to our winter
His laughter melted the icy distance between us

He was a poet who crossed frontiers
Of the heart, of the spirit
Who spoke truth to power
Who fought oppression with

Words of unity
and community
He was a sociologist who understood
The boundaries of human interaction
A counselor who recognized our weaknesses
Did not judge
Reached out a hand
He taught—he lived—human service

Alfred celebrated life and honored
Those who have passed on
One time
We set a car on fire on the way to my aunt's funeral in Texas
Shocked, I watched flames and black smoke billow in the sky
Alfred said, "Look, amigo.
Your Auntie is speaking to us."

Now ndugu, my brother
You have crossed the last border
And I ask myself
How will Alfred speak to me now?
His eyes look back from a photo in challenge:
"I have done my part. What will you do, amigo?"
And I understand:
When a beam of light breaks through the
Dark clouds on the horizon
Alfred is speaking to us
When people stand up to bullies in the
School yards or in the White House
Alfred is speaking to us
When we tear down the walls that divide us from
Our neighbors, our families, ourselves,
Alfred is speaking to us
When we drop what we are doing to play with a child
Alfred is speaking to us
When we look into the eyes of another with love
Alfred is speaking to us
When the hungry are fed, the thirsty get a drink,
And the homeless find shelter
Alfred is speaking to us
When the prisoner finds freedom
Alfred is speaking to us
When, after a long journey
We find a true friend
Alfred is speaking to us

Asante rafiki
You have shown us the way
To cross borders with respect, dignity and love
May we have the courage to follow

Dedicated to the memory of
Alfred Kisubi, 1949–2018

A Refugee

Jodi Meyer

Head down
Eyes dull
Shoulders dropped
Belly groan—ing
Knees shaking
Feet blistered
Arms—out-stretched with sacrifice of life . . .
        "My life, for my daughter's?"
Escaped, yet caged
Starved, but no longer hungry
Angry, but broken
Heartsick, helpless, homeless
Humbled—Head bowed down
Horrified—Eyes left dull
Hopeless—Shoulders dropped in agony
Hungry—Belly aching, groan—ing
Afraid—Knees weak and shaking
Afflicted—Feet battered and blistered
Abandoned—Arms—out-stretched with sacrifice of life . . .
        "My life, for my daughter's?"
Escaped, but trapped within inhumanity
Starved, but no longer hungry for "The American Dream"
Heartsick, helpless, homeless and humiliated
Pleading, begging, begging God, . . . Please help my daughter, my baby

Appendix

Questionnaires for Mayra Pasayes and Txerthoj Vang

For Mayra Pasayes:

What are some of your earliest memories of growing up in El Salvador? What was the name of your town? How big was it? Is that the only town you lived in in El Salvador?

Tell me about your family: Your mom, dad, brother, extended family. What are some memories of family that you have from growing up?

When did you first become aware of the civil war in El Salvador? How did it affect your family and community?

Why did you decide to leave El Salvador? Can you explain?

How did you leave El Salvador? Can you explain?

What was your status when you arrived in the United States (visa?)? What was it like for you when you first came? What surprised you the most? What was most difficult for you? Did you come directly to Wisconsin?

What was the process for you to become a citizen in the United States? How long did it take?

Can you describe your work in the public schools and at Fox Valley Tech? What draws you to this work with immigrant young people? How has this work impacted your life?

In thinking about having official status in a country: How has the lack of documentation (e.g., legal residency) shaped the lives of the students and community members that you have known?

What changes would you recommend for U.S. immigration policy, especially for people coming from Latin America?

For Txerthoj Vang:

What are some of your earliest memories of growing up in Laos? What was the name of your village? How big was it? Is that the only place you lived in in Laos?

Tell me about your family: Your mom, dad, brothers, sisters, extended family. What are some memories of family that you have from growing up?

When did you first become aware of the "secret" war inside Laos? How did it affect your family and community?

How did you first become a soldier in the secret army? How old were you? How were you trained? What were your duties?

What were the most difficult moments for you as a soldier?

What happened in Laos after the Americans left the war (after 1975)? Why did you continue to fight? Can you tell something of your time with the resistance (Chao Fa?)?

Why did you decide to leave Laos? Can you explain?

How did you leave Laos? Can you explain?

Can you describe your time in the refugee camp? Why did you stay there so long? At what point did you decide to go to the United States?

What was your status when you arrived in the United States (visa?)? What support did you receive as a refugee? What was it like for you when you first came? What surprised you the most? What was most difficult for you?

What was the process for you to become a citizen in the United States? How long did it take?

Can you describe your work in the public schools of Oshkosh? What draws you to this work with immigrant young people? How has this work impacted your life?

In thinking about having official status in a country: How have refugee status and U.S. residency shaped the lives of the students and community members that you have known?

What changes would you recommend for U.S. immigration policy, especially for all people who are fleeing war and persecution? Should the United States accept more refugees?

Index

About the Contributors

Fonkem Achankeng, PhD, Hubert H. Humphrey International Fellow, and a conflict scientist, is a professor at the University of Wisconsin Oshkosh. Prior to joining the faculty at the University of Wisconsin Oshkosh, Dr. Fonkem taught at Marian University (2002–2006), University of Wisconsin Parkside (2005–2006), and the University of Wisconsin Fox Valley (1999–2004). He also served for a decade and a half as a senior official in the Ministry of Foreign Affairs of Cameroon and was the founder and executive director of the Association for Nonviolence in Cameroon (1993–1998). Dr. Fonkem also earned his B.A. (summa cum laude) from the University of Benin, Benin City Nigeria, a master's degree from the University of Buea and his second master's from Antioch University, Yellow Springs, Ohio. His research interests encompass peace and conflict studies; postcolonial nationalism and conflict; nonviolence; identity, culture, and conflict; human and people's rights; international mediation; and crisis intervention. In addition to over twenty-seven peer-reviewed articles and book chapters, Dr. Fonkem's recent books include *Porcupine in a Python's Throat: The Ambazonia Story in West Central Africa*, Lexington Books, 2023; *After the Rain Began*, Babcock University Press, 2023; *Crime, Second Chances & Human Services: Creating a Pathway to Ordinary Life for the Convicted*, Lexington Books, 2019; *Nationalism & Intra-State Conflicts in the Postcolonial World*, Lexington Books, 2015; *British Southern Cameroons: Nationalism & Conflict in Postcolonial Africa*, BC, Canada: FriesenPress, 2014; *Lefua in Lebialem: Decline or Transformation*, Nkemnji Global Tech, 2006. Dr. Fonkem is currently a member of the Executive Council of the Wisconsin Institute for Peace & Conflict Studies (WIPCS) as the representative of the University of Wisconsin Oshkosh. He also serves on the Global Education & Research Team of the Dignity &

Humiliation Studies (DHS) and on the Leadership & Scientific Committee of the Transnational Education & Learning Society (TELS).

Ali R. Abootelabi is a professor of Middle Eastern and Global Politics at the University of Wisconsin, Eau Claire (UWEC). He is the author of *Islam and Democracy: State-Society Relations in Developing Countries, 1980–1994* (Garland, 2000) and coauthor, with Stephen Hill, of *Introduction to World Politics: Prospects and Challenges for the United States* (Kendall Hunt, 2013), as well as numerous articles on Iran, Arab Politics, Civil Society and Democracy, and U.S. foreign policy. He is an executive council member of the Wisconsin Institute for Peace and Conflict Studies and is a research committee member of the Center for Global Nonkilling (CGNK). He can be reached at abootaar@uwec.edu.

Osita Adah is a legal practitioner based in Asaba, Delta State, Nigeria. He holds a PhD in political science with specialization in law and diplomacy. His research interests are in public international law, international politics, Human Rights Law, Internal Displacement, and Forced Migration Studies. He is the author of *Law of Defamation in Nigeria* (2010) and *Nigeria Bail Application Report* (2011). He has also contributed to reputable journals across the globe.

Shane Boeder is a professor of Spanish at Marian University in Fond du Lac, Wisconsin, USA. Her research interest is in the lived experiences of Latin American migrant populations.

Uduakobong Edy-Ewoh is a lecturer in the Department of Economics, Veronica Adeleke School of Social Sciences, Babcock University, Ilishan-Remo, Nigeria.

Patience E. Fonkem, PhD, is adjunct professor of special education at the University of Wisconsin Oshkosh. Prior to coming to the University of Wisconsin, Dr. Fonkem studied education at universities in Cameroon, Canada, Israel, and the United States. She also taught in K-12 for several years.

Donald F. Hones has been a professor in the College of Education and Human Services at the University of Wisconsin Oshkosh since 1997. He has published two books and many articles concerning immigration and education and currently chairs the Department of Teaching and Learning.

Uzzibi Methuselah Irmiya has an academic background in International Relations. Her areas of interest concern the structural causes of exclusion and vulnerability in various segments of society. With specialization in defense and strategic studies, her current research examines the intersection between human security and youth vulnerability, with a focus on rural populations in Northern Nigeria.

Abiola Abayomi Isikalu has a specialized academic background in International Law and Diplomacy, as well as Defense and Strategic Studies. He has a core research focus on Human Security in Nigeria, specifically the key dynamics revolving around youth capacity and vulnerability. His research explores the intersection between education and skills reproduction security. Other key areas of interest are strategic autonomy and military operations.

Eric Kraemer received his PhD in Philosophy from Brown University. He served as a professor of Philosophy at the University of Wisconsin–La Crosse from 1991 to 2019. Long interested in ethical issues related to migration and immigration, Kraemer has also published articles and book chapters on ethics, political philosophy, metaphysics, and epistemology. Kraemer's recent research has focused on the relation between the intellectual and moral virtues.

Pao Lor is a professor in the Professional Program in Education in the College of Health, Education, and Social Welfare at the University of Wisconsin–Green Bay. Pao has widely published and presented on the Hmong American experience.

Tatah Mentan is a prolific Theodore Lentz Scholar in Peace and Security Studies and professor of Political Science. He is currently teaching Research Methods and Practice online at the Bamenda University of Science and Technology, Cameroon.

Jodi Meyer, a poet, lives in Appleton with her family. She takes pleasure in working with newly arrived immigrant families in the Fox Valley area of Wisconsin.

Nwadiuto Franca Nwakanma specializes in international relations, with a key focus on issues revolving around migration and its impact on vulnerable populations. Her research tackles issues relating to youth and demographic vulnerabilities, inter-tribal and/or communal clashes as a result of forced migration. She also has key interests in military operations and peacekeeping.

Chibuzor Ayodele Nwaodike, PhD, is a senior lecturer in the Department of Political Science and Public Administration, Babcock University, Nigeria. He is currently the postgraduate coordinator in the Department of Political

Science and Public Administration, Babcock University and has supervised numerous undergraduate and postgraduatc students. His areas of research interests span comparative politics, governance and development administration. His latest publications are "Ethnicity and Electoral Contest: Presidential Elections in Nigeria," 1999–2003, in John Ayotunde Isola Bewaji and Rotimi Omosulu (Eds.) *Fragmented Identities of Nigeria: Sociopolitical and Economic Crises,* Roman and Littlefield (2022); and "Women and Colonialism in West Africa," in Olajumoke Yacob-Haliso and Toyin Falola (Eds.) *Palgrave Handbook of African Women's Studies*, 2021.

Michael Ihuoma Ogu is a faculty and researcher with the Department of Political Science and Public Administration at Babcock University in Nigeria. He has authored several peer-reviewed articles in scholarly journals. He is also a recipient of the William J. Fulbright Scholarship, with over a decade of university teaching experience in Nigeria and the United States of America, and his areas of core research interest are in governance, international relations, and development studies.

Goodnews Osah lectures in the Department of Political Science, Babcock University, Ilishan-Remo, Ogun State, Nigeria. He holds a PhD in Political Science. His teaching and research interests are conflict prevention, management, and resolution; demilitarization of ethnic militias; post-conflict peacebuilding; defense and security studies He holds membership with several academic and professional bodies including the Nigerian Political Science Association (NPSA), Society for Peace Studies and Practice (SPSP). He is a fellow of the Institute of Policy Management Development and The Institute of Management Consultants. He has published in many journals globally.

Mayra Pasayes fled the war and violence in El Salvador and arrived in the United States at age fifteen. She has worked for the Appleton Area School District and Fox Valley Technical College as a liaison with Latinx and Native American students and currently works full-time for Fox Valley Tech as a multicultural advisor. She is also pursuing a master's degree in counseling.

Hannah P. Schmidt is currently a member of the ESTHER Fox Valley Organization, where she serves the communities of Wisconsin at the Department of State Health Services, in the Bureau of Community Health Promotion Family Health Section, in the Maternal and Infant Mortality Prevention Unit. She is a first descendent of the Lake Superior Band Keweenaw Bay Indian Community, a wife, a mother, and an alumnus of the College of the Menominee Nation. She earned a Master of Science, Education Policy and Leadership degree from the University of Wisconsin Oshkosh, achieved Sigma Alpha Pi leadership status through the National Society of Leadership and Success, and received International Honors granted through the Golden Key Foundation. Hannah's leadership philosophy resides on the foundation of ethics, and she strives to achieve equitable communities. She values diversity, is compassionate and understanding toward community needs, sensitive to social justice issues, and is engaged locally as well as internationally. She believes that through continuous learning, and active participation in communities, we may establish health equity. Hannah believes in providing a platform to all people, allowing their voices to be heard and their stories to be told. It is her life goal to contribute to stewardship between nations and pave our path towards global health ensuring a sustainable future for all of humanity.

Philip Sutherland S. J. earned a degree in religious studies and chemistry from Gonzaga University in Spokane, Washington. While attending college he served as an ongoing intern with the Washington State Division of Developmental Disabilities and served as an assistant to the L'Arche community. He completed his First Studies at Loyola University Chicago and performed his regency at St. Andrew Nativity School in Portland, Oregon, and Gonzaga University in Spokane. He completed his Theology studies at Boston College School of Theology and Ministry. He was ordained in 2017 and then returned to student life. Currently, he is a doctoral student in philosophy at Marquette University in Milwaukee, Wisconsin.

Txerthoj Vang was a soldier in the "secret war" in Laos before becoming a refugee and relocating to the United States. He has worked for over twenty years as a bilingual assistant with the Oshkosh Area School District. He also teaches courses at the University of Wisconsin Oshkosh, including Hmong Language, Culture and Learning, and Hmong Literacy.

Olajumoke Yacob-Haliso is professor of Political Science at Babcock University in Nigeria. Her research focuses on women in conflict and peace, gender and politics, and the comparative politics of African states. Olajumoke is co-editor of the *Journal of Contemporary African Studies*, co-editor of the new Rowman and Littlefield book series, "Africa: Past, Present and Prospects," and lead editor of the forthcoming *Palgrave Handbook of African Women's Studies*. She is the recipient of numerous research grants and several fellowships including from the Harry Frank Guggenheim Foundation, the American Council of Learned Societies (ACLS), the Graduate Institute of International and Development Studies, Geneva, Switzerland, Council for the Development of Social Science Research in Africa (CODESRIA), African Studies Association, African Association of Political Science (AAPS), University for Peace Africa Program, among others.

www.ingramcontent.com/pod-product-compliance
Lightning Source LLC
LaVergne TN
LVHW091524200926
848483LV00002B/300
* 9 7 8 1 7 9 3 6 2 1 6 5 8 *